*The Sacred Dramas of J.S. Bach*

# The Sacred Dramas of J.S. Bach

## A Reference and Textual Interpretation

### W. Murray Young

McFarland & Company, Inc., Publishers
*Jefferson, North Carolina, and London*

British Library Cataloguing-in-Publication data are available


Library of Congress Cataloguing-in-Publication Data

Young, W. Murray, 1920–
    The sacred dramas of J.S. Bach : a reference and textual
interpretation / by W. Murray Young.
        p.   cm.
    Includes bibliographical references and index.
    ISBN 0-89950-812-X (lib. bdg. / 50# alk. paper) ∞
    1. Bach, Johann Sebastian, 1685–1750. Vocal music.   2. Sacred
vocal music—History and criticism.   I. Title.   II. Title: Sacred
dramas of JS Bach.
    ML410.B13Y8   1993
    782.2'2'092—dc20                                    92-51104
                                                          CIP
                                                          MN

Manufactured in the United States of America

*McFarland & Company, Inc., Publishers*
  *Box 611, Jefferson, North Carolina 28640*

To the memory of Albert Martin and Leonard Rush
—like J.S. Bach, devoted to God

# Table of Contents

# Table of Contents

# Introduction

The libretti upon which Johann Sebastian Bach composed his cantatas and oratorios gave him scope to display his dramatic gifts, even though he composed no operas and had no inclination to do so. His oratorios, especially, are certainly dramatic works; to them must be added the *Magnificat*, the passions and the masses, which were all dramatic.

I have tried to trace such drama in my recent book, *The Cantatas of J.S. Bach: An Analytical Guide* (McFarland, 1989). A similar examination of the texts of Bach's other major vocal works seems necessary, because the passions, the *Magnificat* and the masses were written at the same time as the cantatas and often contained movements borrowed from them.

In the sacred dramas Bach derives his musical imagery from the libretto, bringing the words to life through sung dramatic declamation. Perhaps this was his closest approach to opera. The soprano expresses radiant joy or deep sorrow and plays the part of a Christian who comments upon the action in her song. The tenor is the Evangelist who mostly narrates the events as the drama develops, but who sings some arias also. The bass represents Christ in the passions, but he may also frequently take the role of commentator on the unfolding drama by his solo arias, especially in Bach's cantatas.

Representation of the Passion was well known in sixteenth and seventeenth century Italy and Germany, and survives in the modern Oberammergau play, but Bach brought it to its highest achievement. Bach took the secco (plain-chant) narrative and the chorale parts from these earlier passions, adding to the old format the modern (eighteenth century) da capo arias and choruses and the accompanied recitatives. In the passions, the Evangelist recites the Biblical narrative, while the actors (singers) represent Jesus, the Apostles, Herod, Pilate and others present at the time of the Crucifixion. Their singing roles dramatize the action; their individual arias comment emotionally on it. For the masses, of course, Bach had to adhere to the regular liturgy, but this did not prevent him from perceiving the drama in the text. Surely a sense of the dramatic was innate to him. Bach termed some of his secular cantatas of the 1730s *dramma per musica* (drama in music), all truly theatrical but without costumes.

At the beginning and the end, as well as within the dramatic development, the choruses and the chorales perform in ways similar to those of ancient Greek tragedy—to introduce and to end the play, and to express feelings on the events as they occur. Bach uses the melody of the chorales to bring out their meaning, not only from their given text, but also from those texts adjacent to it. No other composer of his time relied so much on the chorale for its musical and dramatical effects. Throughout all of Bach's religious compositions for voices and or instruments, the chorale was the basis on which he built. His use of the traditional

1

hymn in German made his own settings appealing to Lutheran congregations; they might even "sing along" with the choir as they listened to the well-known melody. Thus Bach's "staging" of the chorale gave support for the drama, because it involved the audience vocally and emotionally in the scene being presented or suggested as part of the main plot. And this enhanced drama, produced by the use of choruses and chorales, is not limited only to the passions, but is demonstrated in the *Magnificat* as well.

For the masses, the drama is less apparent, but the words still motivated Bach to give them his own musical interpretation, which has dramatic impact on the listener through the pictorial themes evoked.

Bach seized upon individual words in his libretti that showed such motifs as fear, anger, calm, rising, falling, steps, joy, grief, tumult and movement, just as he had done with the libretti for his cantatas (see Schweitzer 1955, II, ch. 23). These motifs recur in his other vocal works, especially in the passions.

For the Lutheran church services of the sixteenth to the eighteenth centuries, Latin as well as German was used. Spitta (1884-5, II, 263-78) discusses the use of both languages in the order of the service. The length of the morning service was from 7 to about 10:30. When the *Hauptmusik* (chief music) was a long cantata, it was divided before and after the sermon, but the usual short cantata (30 minutes or less) was sung before the sermon. This division may have been done in the case of the passions, omitting many parts of the ritual in order to fit into the time allotted.

The significant sections (the musical of which are denoted *) of the morning service were:

* 1. Organ prelude
* 2. Latin motet—sung by the choir
* 3. Missa (Kyrie and Gloria—in Latin)—sung by the choir
  4. Epistle—intoned in German by the pastor
* 5. Hymn—sung in German by the congregation
  6. Gospel—intoned in German by the pastor
  7. Credo—intoned in Latin by the pastor
* 8. Cantata, short mass, passion (or motet?)—sung by the choir in German or Latin according to how it was written as the *Hauptmusik* (chief musical piece)
* 9. Hymn—Luther's German version of the Creed sung by the congregation
  10. Sermon—in German—given by the pastor
*11. Hymn—related to the Gospel and sung in German by the choir and congregation
  12. The Lord's Prayer—intoned in German by all
*13. Communion—during which hymns in German or a motet in Latin might be sung by the choir
  14. Blessing—intoned in German by the pastor

Texts for each extant work will, in the case of the *Magnificat*, the passions and the masses, be taken in chronological order. Section IV, Motets, and Section V, Sacred Songs, are treated according to the BWV order.

# I. The *Magnificat* in D Major

## (c. 1728–1731 in Leipzig; BWV 243)

This great work, one of Bach's masterpieces, began as *The Magnificat in E♭ Major*, BWV 243a, which was first performed in St. Thomas's Church, Leipzig, during the Vespers service on Christmas Day, 1723. It was presented right after the sermon in a much curtailed service (but one which included a cantata) as was customary for Vespers, beginning about 1:45 P.M. and lasting until dusk. As the singing of a cantata opened this particular evening service, one may conclude that only the last half of the morning service was used. This earlier version included four Christmas chorales (two in German and two in Latin) interpolated into the Latin text. It was scored from a five part chorus with five soloists and a large orchestra of recorders, oboes, trumpets, timpani, strings and organ continuo.

Bach transposed this score subsequently to D major, leaving out the Christmas chorales, because he wished to use the work for the other chief festivals: Easter and Whitsuntide. For this later version in D major, he substituted flutes for the original recorders. This is the version which is usually heard today. I have, however, included the four Christmas chorales, so that the libretto would be complete. Nor did Bach forget them, as he borrowed the melody of the fourth chorale, *Virga Jesse floruit* (The Branch of Jesse Hath Flowered), for

the soprano/tenor duet of his later Christmas cantata, BWV 110 "Unser Mund sei voll Lachens" (May Our Mouths Be Full of Laughter), 1734.

It seems surprising that the Bach-gesellschaft (Bach Society) did not include a *Magnificat* for solo soprano in its original listing of Bach's works, and Spitta (II, 374) states that such a work by Bach is unknown. Whittaker, however, in our own century, discovered that a solo *Magnificat* did and does still exist. He quotes the German text and discusses the movements (Whittaker I, 22–32). This he was able to do from a photostat copy sent to him from Moscow, where the manuscript had ended up after it had been presented by the Royal Library of Berlin in 1857.

Thus Whittaker concludes that his solo *Magnificat* is genuine, having Bach's usual initials J.J. (Jesus, Help Me) at the beginning and "Soli Dei Gloria" (To God Alone the Glory) at the end, and thinks that it was composed in Arnstadt before Bach went to Mülhausen. Yet he states that the light scoring for solo soprano, one flute, one violin and continuo would indicate that it was only performed as chamber music with a female singer, and not for a church service in which women were not allowed to be vocalists at that time.

Bach took as his libretto the Biblical text of Luke I: 46–55, and added the

3

Doxology for the final chorus of BWV 243. The score shows a five part chorus, two sopranos, an alto, a tenor, and a bass, with two flutes, two oboes, three trumpets, strings and continuo. The chorus with all instruments appears in the first, ninth and the final numbers.

1. *Chorus.* A brilliant, concerto-like overture introduces the play, which may be interpreted as a depiction of the manger scene in Bethlehem. Then the choir enters, like a chorus of angels, to sing in canon with many repeats on "Magnificat": Magnificat anima mea Dominum, (My soul doth magnify the Lord). The Protestant emphasis on the individual's faith in God can be detected in the joy motif, in which the words *anima mea* (my soul) represent Mary's happiness alone and, at the same time, the joy felt by the shepherds and all mankind at this miraculous Birth. The scene comes to life through the music.

2. *Aria (Soprano two) — da capo with strings and continuo*: Et exultavit spiritus meus in Deo salutari meo. (And my spirit hath rejoiced in God my Savior.) Runs on *exultavit* and *salutari* enhance the joy motif of this aria. There is a feeling of thankfulness and humility before God mixed with Mary's joy, which is very impressive. The audience would have no difficulty in identifying Mary as the actress for the solo soprano and alto roles in this drama, remembering, however, that these parts were sung by boys or men in Bach's time.

3. *Chorus — a cappella with continuo.* This is the first inserted chorale, sung in German, as translated and set originally by Martin Luther. The congregation sang it usually before the sermon at Christmas; they must have been impressed now when the choir sang it within an otherwise Latin libretto. Rather than

being one angel's song to the shepherds, it represents a group of angels dramatically announcing Christ's birth in a motif of joy. "Vom Himmel hoch da komm' ich her, / ich bring' euch gute neue Mär. / Der guten Mär bring' ich so viel, / davon ich singen und sagen will." (From heaven above to earth I come, / I bring you good news. / I bring you so much good news, / About which I wish to sing and tell.)

4. *Aria (Soprano two) — accompanied by oboe d'amore and continuo*: "Quia respexit humilitatem ancillae suae"; (For He hath regarded the low estate of His handmaiden;). Bach seizes upon the word *humilitatem* to tonally paint a portrait of the Madonna, with the descending tone of *ancillae suae* to reinforce her bowing in humility before God. "[E]cce enim ex hoc beatam me dicent" (for behold, from henceforth shall call me blessed). The rising melody of this incomplete verse contrasts with the first part of the aria. The joy motif now bursts forth to be heightened by the subject, which alone is reserved for the following chorus.

5. *Chorus — two flutes, two oboi d'amore, strings and continuo*: "Omnes generationes." (All generations.) From these two words Bach is inspired to write a mighty fugue, symbolic of the piling up of generation upon generation. Repetition of the word *Omnes* gives a dramatic touch to the sweeping panorama of his music, which seems to embrace all Christendom forever in respect for the Virgin. It resembles one of the turba (crowd) choruses of his passions in the tumult motif of voices and instruments.

6. *Aria (Bass) — da capo with continuo*: "Quia fecit mihi magna qui potens est, / et sanctum nomen ejus." (For He who is powerful hath made me great, and holy is His name.)

Whether Bach felt that he must use the bass voice to express the motif of solemnity heard in the rhythm of the first line, or whether he wished to contrast it with the motif of beatific peace in the last line, his overall effect merits his choice. The bass might well represent a shepherd, speaking (singing) Mary's thoughts.

7. *Quartet — SATB with continuo*: This second chorale in German could be a continuation of the angels' song (three). The joy motif is repeated. Freut euch und jubiliert. / zu Bethlehem geboren wird / das herzeliebe Jesulein, / das soll euer Freud' und Wonne sein. (Rejoice and be glad; / in Bethlehem has been born / dear little Jesus, / Who shall be your joy and gladness.)

8. *Duet — (Alto, Tenor) — two flutes, strings and continuo, da capo*: Et misericordia a progenie in progenies timentibus eum. (And his mercy is from generation to generation on those who fear Him.) This is the most awesome number in the work, where Bach reveals his inmost mystical feeling. Schweitzer describes it thus: "the muted strings and the flutes give out ritornelli that seem to come from a superterrestrial world" (Schweitzer, II, 169). Bach must have been aware of the dramatic effect of his music for this incomparable scene. Repeats and runs occur on the last two words, *timentibus eum*.

9. *Chorus — two flutes, two oboes, three trumpets, timpani, strings and continuo*: The inexorable power of God for crushing the pride of man, which results from his worldly wealth and self-esteem, is the theme of this chorus. In the adagio close, Bach's pompous musical setting of the separate words illustrates such self-importance. Fecit potentiam in brachio suo; / dispersit superbos / [Adagio] mente cordis sui. (He hath showed strength with His arm; / He hath scattered the proud / [Adagio] in the imagination of their hearts.)

10. *Chorus — two oboes, strings, continuo*: This is the third interpolated chorale — this time in Latin. We see a scenario of a choir of angels praising God, and complementing the previous chorus (nine). Note the repetition of the first line three times for symbolic significance. Gloria in excelsis Deo! / Et in terra pax hominibus bona voluntatis! (Glory to God on high! / And on earth peace, good will to men!)

11. *Aria (Tenor) — unison violines, continuo — da capo*: Deposuit potentes de sede / et exultavit humiles. (He hath put down the mighty from their position / and hath exalted the humble.) Bach uses three motifs for this aria: that of falling, that of the step to portray a downward motion of the powerful, and the rising tone of the last three words to illustrate the text. The change of melody gives the listener a visual as well as musical picture from Bach's admirable interpretation of his text.

12. *Aria (Alto) — two flutes and continuo — da capo*: Contrast reappears here between the motif of calm joy in the first line and that of a step motion in the halting tempo of the second line, as each word is emphasized. Esurientes implevit bonis, / et divites demisit inanes. (He hath filled the hungry with good things, / and the rich He hath sent empty away.)

13. *Duet (Soprano, Bass) with organ continuo*: This is the fourth and final chorale verse interpolated into the Biblical text. Bach must have thought highly of this number, because he used its melody again in 1734 for cantata BWV 110. Long runs occur on *hominibus* and *Alleluja*. Virga Jesse floruit, / Emanuel noster apparuit; / induit carnem hominis, / fit

puer delectabilis. / Alleluja. (The branch of Jesse hath flowered; / Our Emmanuel hath appeared. / He hath taken on the flesh of man; / He hath made Himself a charming youth. / Halleluja. Schweitzer thinks that the four interpolated hymns were sung by a small choir in a gallery apart from the main choir, and that these hymns were included in the evening services at Leipzig (cf. Schweitzer II, 166–67).

14. *Trio (Sopranos one and two, and Alto — two unison oboes, violoncellos and continuo*: Suscepit Israel puerum suum / recordatus misericordiae suae, (He hath holpen His servant Israel, / in remembrance of His mercy). It seems that a trio of angels has reappeared on the stage. They sing in canon to an accompaniment of a quiet, melancholy theme, expressing a pathetic longing. This mystical emotion is typical of Bach's style when he reveals his personal thoughts on a deeply felt religious concept.

15. *Chorus — continuo*: Continuing the text of the preceding trio, this chorus bursts forth in a five part fugue with another joy motif of reassurance. Sicut locutus est ad patres nostros, / Abraham et semini eius in saecula. (As he spake to our fathers, Abraham and his seed forever.)

16. *Chorus — two flutes, two oboes, three trumpets, timpani, strings and continuo*: To close his drama Bach adheres to church tradition and quotes the Doxology, beginning with a thrice repeated *Gloria*, symbolic of the Trinity. He creates a movement of monumental grandeur by building up a crescendo repetition at the beginning, and then ending with an accelerated diminuendo tempo. Gloria Patri, Gloria Filio, / Gloria et Spiritui sancto. / Sicut erat in principio, et nunc, et semper, / et in saecula saeculorum. / Amen. (Glory to the Father, Glory to the Son, / And Glory to the Holy Ghost. / As it was in the beginning, is now, and ever, / World without end. / Amen.) This final number, which uses the same joy motif as the opening chorus, leaves little doubt that Bach has achieved the drama of classical plays in his own musical format. Other composers before and after him have set the *Magnificat* to music, but none has ever surpassed his setting. A contemporary composer in Dresden, Jan Dismas Zelenka, set a version of it with a beautiful double fugue in the "Amen" at the end, on 26 November 1725, for soprano, alto and chorus with orchestra. This is almost two years after Bach's original *Magnificat in E♭ Major* and is only about one quarter of the length of Bach's work. Moreover, Zelenka's work seems hurried in comparison. It would be interesting to discover whether Bach had encouraged Zelenka to imitate him, since they were well acquainted with each other!

# II. The Passions

Why did Bach begin to compose passions for the Lutheran Church, and why did he suddenly cease to do so? His early efforts led to his greatest achievement in the *St. Matthew Passion* with which no other work in this genre can compare. After such success, why would a composer turn his efforts to create other vocal works in which he might even surpass the expertise that he had demonstrated in his passions?

During the seventeenth and the beginning of the eighteenth century, the passion had progressed from its medieval format of Latin plain-chant, originating in the mystery plays, and replaced it by the new recitative, invented about 1600, and by the da capo aria which was developed from about 1670. Da capo choruses and the well-established Lutheran Church chorales, which were both in German, were added to create this newer type of libretto, that had evolved from seventeenth century Italian oratorio and opera.

However, in Leipzig the change to the new style of passion was not as rapid as in some other German cities. Terry notes in his book, *Bach: The Passions* (8) that "Uninterrupted by the Reformation, the Passion Story had been sung in Holy Week at Leipzig since the fifteenth century, a plainsong Recit, with simple faux bourdon chorus passages. The continuity of the tradition was not broken until 1721, two years before Bach's ap-

pointment." He goes on to say that Bach's predecessor, Johann Kuhnau's *St. Mark Passion* was the first passion to be sung to concerted music in the new style on Good Friday of that year in St. Thomas's Church. No other passion was performed until Bach's *St. John Passion* of 1723, also in St. Thomas's Church, and repeated the next year in St. Nicholas's Church.

There was a trend in Northern Germany towards the end of the seventeenth century to produce annual passion plays in the vernacular and new style at Easter. These plays were very popular when presented during Lutheran Church services at the turn of the seventeenth and eighteenth century. That Bach should be attracted to try his hand at composing in this genre is not at all surprising, since his cantatas (Hauptmusik — chief music) had been accepted in the church services, and they were similar to the passions in their format: chorus, aria, recitative, chorale, even though shorter in length.

The question of for how many passions did Bach compose music has led to controversy from the time of his first biographer, Nikolaus Forkel in 1802. Then it was thought that Bach wrote music for five passions to correspond with his five annual cycles of cantatas, yet like these latter, some have been lost.

According to Spitta later in the century, Bach did compose five passions in the order: one in St. Luke, two St.

7

John, and one St. Matthew—a total of four, one St. John, the second version, being lost. Subsequent research in the twentieth century has brought the fifth passion, St. Mark, to light by identifying its music from the *Trauerode* BWV 198, which was performed at the memorial service for Queen Christiane Eberhardine in 1727.

Thus there would appear to be actually four of Bach's passions extant, although many musicologists have doubted the authenticity of the St. Luke. Mendelssohn denied that it was Bach's work, as did Schweitzer (II, 171–72). Yet Spitta is just as firm in his belief that it is genuine, because Bach inscribed on the title page J.J. (Jesus, help me), which he never wrote on copies he made of works by other composers. Moreover, Spitta maintains that Bach's style in the *St. Luke Passion* resembles that of his Weimar composing period, even though the manuscript was written on three different kinds of watermarked paper at intervals from 1732 to 1734. Spitta asserts, also, that Bach's lavish use of chorales in this work would show that he was following the older passion format of Central Germany, but adding the new Italian-style arias and recitatives to it. Therefore, he concludes that the text had been written about 1710 in Weimar by an unknown librettist or by Bach himself.

Bach possibly did compose the *St. Luke* in Weimar, whether it was performed there or not, and later revised and recopied his original text in Leipzig, intending to present it there. He must have had great self-confidence to have undertaken this new type of musical endeavor when he was Kapellmeister to the irascible Duke Wilhelm in Weimar and later to the benevolent Prince Leopold in Cöthen, because the demands of this position were great—in Weimar for weekly cantatas for the royal chapel in the Himmelsburg, and in Cöthen for instrumental music for the royal court. But Bach was quick to realize that passion music had found favor with the public in Hamburg and was spreading quickly throughout Protestant Germany in his time. Therefore Bach composed music for the four works that have been ascribed to him by many musicologists, and treated in their presumed chronological order. Whether he wished to supplement his cantata composition for the church calendar cycles, or whether he simply wanted to impress the public as other composers of passions had done before him, is open to conjecture.

However, unlike some passion composers of his time, such as Telemann and Keiser, Bach retained the traditional chorales of the original German passions in order to help advance the action, for which recitatives alone were for him insufficient. In fact, referring to the *St. Luke Passion*, and what he takes as proof that it dates from the Weimar period, Spitta writes: "We get an impression that it is the work of a composer who has had but little practice in writing recitatives; and this agrees with the facts of the case, for in the earlier church cantatas to which Bach had hitherto devoted himself there is, as we know, no recitative" (Spitta, II, 512).

As the passions and the cantatas prove, Bach made the chorale an effective vehicle to convey both music and drama in these works. Where did he find so large a supply of hymn texts? Terry notes that the only hymn book found among Bach's possessions after his death was Paul Wagner's, published in 1697 under the title "Andächtiger Seelen geistliches Branch- und Gantz-Opfer. Das ist: vollständiges Gesangbuch in acht unterschiedlichen Theilen" (Spiritual Burnt and Full Offering of Devout Souls. That is: Complete Hymnal in Eight Various Parts). Of the 154 hymns that Bach used in his cantatas, passions, oratorios and motets, all but 11 are found in Wagner. The result seems to have been that Bach had little research to do to find which hymn text he needed to fit into a particular place in a work (cf. *Bach's Chorals,* Part II, 47).

Bach collected all the hymn tunes that he used in his passions and cantatas. In collaboration with Georg Christian Schemelli, who was Cantor at Naumburg-Zeitz near Leipzig, Bach had published 954 hymns with only 69 melodies, of which about a quarter were Bach's settings. Breitkopf, Leipzig published this work in 1736, and after Bach's death, his son Carl Philipp Emmanuel edited and published the 100 hymn tunes that it now contained in 1765.

In the *St. John* and the *St. Matthew* passions, recitative writing comes to the assistance of the dramatic development in the form of dialogues, melismas and ariosos. With the last work, the *St. Mark Passion,* recitative becomes simply the quoting of the Biblical text without any musical embellishment, according to Terry. Probably the reason for this was Bach's dissatisfaction with his employers, the Leipzig Town Council, who were withholding the financial support he needed to produce effectively the choral music that he had labored so long to achieve. Hence in October 1730, Bach was looking for other employment and did not have his heart in his last passion, the *St. Mark.*

So both the first passion, the *St. Luke* and the last, the *St. Mark,* stress the chorale by the frequency of its use — in the former work, because it was traditional when Bach began to write passion music, and in the latter, because Lutheran chorales were readily available to Bach who, it appears, had been losing interest in this genre and by their help would not have to compose much new material for his last effort in this genre of musical composition.

Yet by 1731 Bach had reached his peak in passion writing with his two masterpieces—the *St. John* and the *St. Matthew.* Nothing he could do after 1729 would improve on them. The intense drama of the former and the monumental length of the latter with its reflective lyricism testify to the ultimate aim to which Bach had brought perfection, i.e. external realism, internal reflection.

The importance of drama in all of Bach's passions is often overlooked by the audience because Bach's melodies and sound motifs are not heard as illustrations of the text, but rather for their intrinsic beauty alone. This drama comes to life in the turba (crowd) choruses, in the chorales reinforcing the action described in the recitatives, and in the arias where the individual "actor" expresses in song his or her emotions after any event. By its very nature, a passion performance depended on a visual scenario or spectacle with spoken words upon which the musical theme could be built.

As Eva and Sydney Grew observed regarding the *St. John Passion* in their book *Bach*: "the theme was real for Bach in a human way. It was drama. As drama, it was something of which he was a part. ... Expression of his theme was therefore expression of himself, sublimated, transfigured and glorified, yet still himself. Emotion consequently dominated him" (94).

Similarly, they note of the *St. Matthew Passion* that the chorales (hymns) are dramatic and at the same time spiritual (174).

The stage representation of Biblical events began with the miracle plays in Latin of the Middle Ages, which featured the Birth, Crucifixion and Resurrection of Christ. This changed to the semi-dramatic musical style of the seventeenth century Italian composer Carissimi, whose oratorios were still in Latin with an Evangelist. But as Spitta points out (II, 500), "Long before any Italian oratorio existed at all, performances of the Passion had been customary in the churches of Germany." So in Italy and in Germany the passion apparently developed independently by language; in the Catholic parts of Germany and Italy, Latin was the language heard, while German was used for religious plays in the Protestant churches. As modern seventeenth/eighteenth century music added the sacred aria, choruses and the chorale to the Gospel narrative, the German passion with Bach reached its peak of achievement.

During this transition, the tendency had been to eliminate the costumes worn by the actors (singers) for performances of passions within the church, although they were worn by the actors for other sacred plays outside the church (e.g. the Oberammergau passion play, done with lavish décor and costumes).

Without costumes, it seems that the drama would be more difficult to present, since it would depend on the clarity of the declamation of the singers to reveal the role that each was playing. Rather than impose the dramatic development, Bach's treatment of his libretto identifies each character by his speech or actions without the need to specifically name them or identify them by their costumes. Yet in the early mystery plays and their development into the Latin passions, Latin was the language, and

as the audience knew little Latin, costumes and gestures would be indispensable to comprehend the action.

It must have been evident to Bach that each of the passions he composed was theatrical: each has an opening and a closing chorus, just as a play begins and ends with the opening and the closing of the curtains. These choruses introduce the action and finally bring it to an end, yet within the play there are arias and chorales to supplement the continuing narrative of the recitatives. By careful choice of musical pitch, Bach painted the words of the text he was setting in sound.

Bach could paint such dramatic scenes by contrasting the group effect of the choral singing with that of the solo arias and ariosos. Sometimes the chorus would represent a single person, as in the *Magnificat*, or sometimes it might portray the emotions of each member of the congregation.

Dramatic emphasis may also be found in Bach's recitatives, ariosos (part aria and part recitative in style) and arias (including duets and trios) in which the players (singers) portray their emotions in their given texts. By highlighting certain words as they are declaimed with whatever instrumental accompaniment he prescribes for them, Bach brings these connecting movements to life in support of the preceding or following arias and choruses. Although these movements may be narrative, they reveal the thoughts or the personality of the actor who declaims or sings their words. With Bach, the recitative is more than "dry narrative" (secco — recitative).

It is generally thought that the chorales were sung only by the choir during a performance of one of Bach's passions, even though these hymns were familiar to the congregation (who often sang chorales with the choir in Bach's cantatas). But the purpose of the chorale in Bach's passion plays was to comment on the immediate past action as narrated in the previous recitative; therefore the congregation should not become actively involved with the choir, especially since the choir often assumed the role of an actor or of actors.

Why did Bach cease his composing of passions after 1731? It is well known that he was discontented with his position as cantor in St. Thomas's Church and had complained to the Leipzig Town Council (his employers) about his own high expenses in that city, and that he was not receiving from them sufficient funds to enable him to carry out the training of singers and musicians in the churches for which he was responsible. No doubt he was thinking of the support given to his contemporary composers, Zelenka and Hasse, in the Dresden Royal Chapel and in the Dresden Opera, and automatically contrasted the Royal favor that they received in the capital with the lack of any help for him in Leipzig. Moreover, since these Dresden composers were Bach's acquaintances and friends and both Roman Catholic, Bach as a Lutheran would feel his inferiority even more.

Accordingly, what better way could he find of showing his disapproval of the Leipzig Lutheran Town Council than to seek employment elsewhere? This he tried by writing to his former school friend in Lüneburg, Georg Erdmann, now Imperial Russian Agent in Danzig. Nothing came of this, however, so Bach remained in Leipzig. To add to his personal income in Leipzig, Bach took over the direction of the weekly concerts of the Collegium Musicum—a group of university musicians offering public concerts and instituted about 20 years before by Telemann in Leipzig.

Thus Bach had neither the time nor the desire to compose further passions after the *St. Mark*, first performed on Good Friday 1731, and subsequently neglected until its reconstruction in the twentieth century.

Accordingly, in order to further improve his lot in Leipzig and to signal his merit to the Elector in Dresden, Bach turned to the composition of masses to emulate the royal composers there, his friends Zelenka and Hasse. These Lutheran masses were in Latin; the language continued to be used in Lutheran churches for the Hauptgottesdienst (main service) on Sundays and on festivals. The Leipzig Prayer Book of 1694, used by Bach, lists those parts of the liturgy retained by Luther: Kyrie, Gloria, Credo and Sanctus.

Bach's first offering to the Elector, Augustus II (The Strong) at Dresden, was the Kyrie and the Gloria of his *Mass in B minor*, 1733. He sent this to support his application for the position of Composer to the Electoral Court, but did not receive this title until 1736 under the new ruler, Augustus III.

Bach would not use the chorale again for any of the masses that he would set, because it did not conform with the liturgy of the mass. But he would return to the chorale when he composed his motets in German. Therefore, except for the interlude of composing masses, Bach remained faithful to the Lutheran chorale for all his vocal works. Indeed, one might say that it was the foundation upon which his sung music was built.

# The St. Luke Passion

## (Weimar c. 1710 and or Leipzig 1732–34; BWV 246)

As this passion would appear to be either the first or the last of Bach's settings of this genre, I would prefer to take it as his first for its early style with frequent chorales shows that Bach was following the seventeenth century tradition for such writing.

Schweitzer's comment (II, 172), "To the practical musician it is a matter of pure indifference whether the *St. Luke Passion* is proved to be authentic or not, since he will hardly ever be tempted to perform it" may be true, but I have attended a very moving performance at a Lutheran church in Hamilton, Ontario, on Good Friday 1985, and felt that I was listening to genuine Bach. Perhaps its performance has not been so rare as Schweitzer thought, especially since George Barati with the Vienna State Opera Orchestra and Chorus made the first recording (Lyrichord, LL 110) about 20 years ago.

The score calls for four voices (SATB) with a choir for the choruses and the chorales; the instrumental accompaniment consists of two transverse flutes, two oboes, a bassoon, two violins, a viola and organ. The use of a bassoon may point to Bach's known favoring of this instrument while he was composing cantatas in Weimar, thus identifying this passion with that city.

The Gospel narrative, related by the tenor, is taken from Luke 22 and 23 to verse 53, with 31 chorales, sung a cappella with organ continuo, inserted into the libretto. Choruses and arias are sung in the new da capo style.

The actors in this religious drama are: Evangelist—tenor; Jesus—bass; Two Maids—soprano and alto; Man Servant—tenor; Unrepentant Thief— tenor; Repentant Thief—bass; Joseph of Arimathea—tenor, and women (boys) for the soprano and alto arias.

## PART I

1. *Chorus.* "Furcht und Zittern, Scham und Schmerzen, / Herr, zerknirschen unsre Herzen / beim Gedächtnis deiner Not. / Wir sind Sklavenknecht und Sünder, / du bist Herrscher und Entbinder, / und erwählst für uns den Tod." (Fear and trembling, shame and pain, / Lord, crush our hearts / At the memory of Thy distress. / We are slaves and sinners, / Thou art Master and Redeemer, / And choosest death for our sake.)

This opening da capo chorus with its motif of grief sets the stage for the portrayal of the coming tragedy and its effect on the audience. Repetition of the nouns in the first line and the contrasting rallentandi in lines three to six with emphasis on the words *Not* and *Tod* reinforce this tone of sadness.

2. *Recitative—Evangelist.* The Biblical narrative begins now: Es war aber das Fest des süssen Brot, das da Ostern heisset. Und die Hohenpriester und Schriftgelehrten trachteten, wie sie ihn töteten, und fürchten sich vor dem Volke. Es war aber der Satanas gefahren in den Judas, genannt Ischariot; der war aus der Zahl der Zwölfen. Und er ging hin und redete mit den Hohenpriestern und mit den Hauptleuten, wie er ihn wollte überantworten. (It was near the feast of unleavened bread, which is called Passover. And the chief priests and scribes conspired how they might kill Him and feared the people. However, Satan had entered into Judas, called

Iscariot; he was of the number of the Twelve. And he went away and spoke with the chief priests and officials how he wanted to betray Him.)

3. *Chorale.* This is the first of the 31 a cappella chorale interjections sung by the choir to comment on the preceding number in the manner of ancient Greek tragedy. These chorale verses seem also to reflect the religious feelings of the audience or congregation at that particular moment of the drama. Bach (or the unknown librettist) must have chosen them with care. Verruchter Knecht, wo denkst du hin, / wie denkst du nur an Goldgewinn / und fürchtest nicht die Hölle? / Willst du um schnödes Geld und Gut / verraten deines Meisters Blut, / als Satanasgeselle? / Denk an die lange Ewigkeit, / kehr um, kehr um, noch ist es Zeit! (Wicked servant, of what are you thinking; / How do you think only about gain of gold / And do not fear Hell? / Do you wish, as Satan's companion, / To betray your Master's blood / For worthless money and goods? / Think about long eternity; / Turn back, turn back, there is still time!)

4. *Recitative—Evangelist.* Und sie wurden froh, und gelobten ihm Geld zu geben. (And they became glad and promised to give him money.)

5. *Chorale.* For the choral reaction to this recitative, Bach chooses the melody of Hans Leo Hassler's "Herzlich tut mich verlangen" (Heartily I long for), which has become known as the "Passion Chorale"—"O Haupt voll Blut und Wunden" (O Sacred Head now wounded) and which he will repeat in the later *St. Matthew Passion.* Die Seel' weiss hochzuschätzen, / was Hand und Kasten füllt, / was Augen kann ergötzen / und Lust der Sinne stillt. / Sie ringt nach eitlen Dingen / und bleibt der ew'gen bar; / wer reisst sie aus den Schlingen / der tödlichen

Gefahr? (The soul knows what to esteem, / What fills our hands and coffers, / What can delight our eyes / And calms the joy of our senses. / It struggles for vain things / And remains destitute of the eternal; / Who will tear it out of the snares / Of deadly danger?)

6. *Recitative—Evangelist.* Und er versprach sich, und suchte Gelegenheit, dass er ihn überantwortete ohne Rumor. (And he promised, and sought opportunity to betray Him without commotion.)

7. *Chorale—accompanied by strings and the organ.* Stille, stille! ist die Losung / der Gottlosen in der Welt; / traue ja nicht der Liebkosung, / wenn sie sich zu dir gestellt. / Spricht der Mund ein gutes Wort, / hegt das Herze Trug und Mord, / und dass es die List erfülle, / ist die Losung: Stille, stille! (Silence, silence is the answer / To the godless in the world; / Do not trust their flattery, / When they associate with you. / If their mouth speaks a good word, / Their heart holds deceit and murder. / And so that cunning may fill it, / The answer is: Silence, silence!)

It is to be noted that the soprano alone sings the words *Stille, stille,* as though Bach wanted to impress the lesson of silence before evil as stated in the text.

8. *Recitative—Dialogue with Chorus—strings and continuo.* Bach creates a very interesting number here. He adds a chorus of the Apostles to the dialogue between the Evangelist and Jesus, thus bringing out the realism of this scene. Most of the following recitatives are also in dialogue, according to the libretto.

EVANGELIST: Es kam nun der Tag des süssen Brot, / auf welchem man musste opfern das Osterlamm. / Und er sandte Petrum und Johannem, und sprach: JESUS: Gehet hin, bereitet uns das Osterlamm, / auf dass wir's essen. EVANGELIST: Sie aber sprachen zu ihm: APOSTLES (CHORUS): Wo willst du, dass wir's bereiten? / EVANGELIST: Er sprach zu ihnen: JESUS: Siehe, wenn ihr hinein kommt in die / Stadt, wird euch ein Mensch begegnen, der trägt / einen Wasserkrug. Folget ihm nach in das Haus, / da er hineingehet, und saget zu dem Hausherrn: / Der Meister lässt dir sagen: "Wo ist die Herberge, / darinnen ich das Osterlamm essen möge mit meinen / Jüngern? (The day of the unleavened bread came, / when the Passover must be sacrificed. / And He sent Peter and John, saying: / Go and prepare for us the Passover, / so that we may eat. / But they spoke to Him: / Where wilt Thou that we prepare? / He spoke to them: / Behold, when you come into the city, / a man will meet you, carrying a jug / of water. Follow him into the house / where he goes and tell the owner: / The Master asks: "Where is the guest- / chamber, in which I may eat at the / Passover with my Disciples?)

9. *Chorale — continuo.* Feasting at the Passover brings in this well chosen third verse of the prayer-like hymn by Johann Flittner (1661), which will recur as a leitmotif for three subsequent chorales in this passion.

Weide mich und mach mich satt, Himmelsspeise! / Tränke mich, mein Herz ist matt, Seelenweide! / Sei du meine Ruhestatt, Jesu, Ruh der Seelen! (Pasture me and make me full, Heaven food! / Give me drink, my heart is weary, Soul pasture! / Be Thou my resting place, Jesus, repose of souls!

10. *Recitative — Dialogue.* The narrative resumes, but somewhat less dramatic than before. JESUS: Und er wird euch einen grossen / gepflasterten Saal zeigen, daselbst bereitet es. EVANGELIST: Sie gingen hin, und funden, wie er ihnen gesagt hatte,

und bereiteten das Osterlamm. / Und da die Stunde kam, setzte er sich nieder / und die zwölf Apostel mit ihm; und er sprach / zu ihnen: JESUS: Mich hat herzlich verlanget, das Osterlamm / mit euch zu essen, ehe denn ich leide. (And he will show you a big furnished hall; / make the same ready. / They went there, and found as He / had told them, and prepared the Passover. / And when the hour came, He sat down / and the twelve Apostles with Him; and / He spoke to them: / I have heartily longed to eat at the Passover with you, before I suffer.)

11. *Chorale — continuo.* For the second time, Johann Flittner's hymn recurs with its fourth verse here: Nichts ist lieblicher als du, liebster Liebe; / Nichts ist freundlicher als du, milde Liebe; / Auch nichts süsser ist als du, Jesu, süsse Liebe. (Nothing is lovelier than Thou, dearest Love; / Nothing is friendlier than Thou, gentle Love. / Also nothing is sweeter than Thou, Jesus, sweet love.)

12. *Recitative — Dialogue.* JESUS: Denn ich sage euch, dass ich hinfort / nicht mehr davon essen werde, bis das erfüllt / werde im Reich Gottes. EVANGELIST: Und er nahm den Kelch, dankte / und sprach: JESUS: Nehmet denselben, und teilet ihn / unter euch; denn ich sage euch: Ich werde / nicht trinken von dem Gewächse des Weinstocks, / bis das Reich Gottes komme. EVANGELIST: Und er nahm das Brot, dankte / und brach's, und gab's ihnen, und sprach: JESUS: Das ist mein Leib, der für euch / gegeben wird; das tut zu meinem Gedächtnis. (For I say to you, that furthermore / I shall not eat thereof, until that / will be fulfilled in God's Kingdom. / And he took the cup, gave thanks, and spoke: / Take the same, and share it among you; / for I say to you: I shall not drink / of the growth of the vine, until / the King-

dom of God comes. / And He took
the bread, gave thanks / and broke it,
and gave it to them, saying: / That is
my Body, which is given for you; / do
that for my remembrance.

13. *Aria — Soprano — oboes and
strings.* This is the first of the six arias
in the work, all of which are supercharged with emotion. Even though
the voice is a soprano, the listener
might believe that one of the Apostles
is singing the very thoughts that occur
to him as he sits listening. Dein Leib,
das Manna meiner Seele, / erquickt
und stärkt die matte Brust. / Es
schmecket, wenn ich es geniesse, /
dem Geist so wunderbarlich süsse /
und schafft ihm lauter Himmelslust.
(Thy Body, the manna of my soul, /
Refreshes and strengthens my weary
breast. / It tastes, when I enjoy it, / So
wonderfully sweet to my spirit / And
creates for it pure joy of heaven.)

14. *Recitative — Dialogue.* EVAN-
GELIST: Desselbigen gleichen auch
den Kelch / nach dem Abendmahl,
und sprach: JESUS: Das ist der Kelch,
das neue Testament / in meinem
Blut, das für euch ergossen wird.
(Likewise also the cup / after supper,
and spoke: / That is the cup, the new
testament / in my blood, which is
shed for you.)

15. *Aria — Alto — flutes, strings and
continuo.* As in the previous soprano
aria, the alto seems to personify one of
the Disciples on the stage, but certainly expresses the emotions felt by
all the audience. Bach's use of pizzicato strings highlights the grief and
the tear motifs of his text. Du gibst
mir Blut, ich schenk' dir Tränen; /
nur ist mein Tausch gar schlecht am
Wert. / Du triefst, und ich wein' um
die Wette. / Ach! dass ich so was
Kostbar's hätte, / als mir dein Kraft-
kelch hier gewährt! (Thou givest me
blood; I give Thee tears; / Only my
exchange is quite worthless. / Thou

dost drip, and I weep in emulation. /
O, had I such a thing as precious / As
Thy cup, which here gives me
strength!)

16. *Recitative — Dialogue.* JESUS:
Doch siehe, die Hand meines Ver-
räters / ist mit mir über Tische, und
zwar, des Menschen / Sohn gehet hin,
wie es beschlossen ist; doch / wehe
demselbigen Menschen, durch welchem / er verraten wird. EVANGELIST:
Und sie fingen an zu fragen unter /
sich selbst, welcher es doch wäre unter
ihnen, / der das tun würde? (But
behold, the hand of my betrayer / is
with me at the table, and truly / the
Son of man goeth forth, as it is /
determined; yet woe to this same
man, / by whom He is betrayed.)
(And they began to ask among themselves / who it was among them, who
would do that?)

17. *Chorale — continuo.* This appears to be one of the usual Passion-
tide hymns, perhaps reflecting each
Apostle's conscience and definitely
that of each member of the congregation. Ich und meine Sünden, / die
sich wie Körnlein finden / des Sandes
an dem Meer, / die haben dir erreget
/ das Elend, das dich schläget, / und
das betrübte Marterherz. (I and my
sins, / Which are found like little
grains / Of sand at the sea, / They
have caused for Thee / The misery
which smites Thee, / And Thy sad
martyr's heart.)

18. *Recitative — Dialogue.* EVAN-
GELIST: Es erhub sich auch ein Zank /
unter ihnen, welcher unter ihnen solle
/ für den Grössten gehalten werde. /
Er aber sprach zu ihnen: JESUS: Die
weltlichen Könige herrschen, / und
die Gewaltigen heisset man gnädige /
Herren. Ihr aber nicht also; sondern /
der Grösseste unter euch soll sein wie
/ der Jüngste, und der Fürnehmste
wie / ein Diener. Denn welcher ist der
Grösseste? / Der zu Tische sitzet, oder

der da dienet? / Ist's nicht also, dass der zu Tische sitzet? / Ich aber bin unter euch wie ein Diener. / Ihr aber seid's, die ihr beharret habet / bei mir in meinen Anfechtungen. (There arose a quarrel among them / as to who of them should be / accounted the greatest. / But he spoke to them: The worldly kings rule / and the powerful are called noble lords. / But you are not so but / the greatest among you shall be as / the youngest, and the foremost as / a servant. For who is the greatest? / He who sits at the table, or he who serves there? / Is it not so; it is he who sits at the table? / But I am among you as a servant. / You are those, who waited / with me in my temptations.)

19. *Chorale.* This number might be intended to show the avowal of fidelity on behalf of both Peter and individuals in the congregation, here represented by the choir. Ich werde dir zu Ehren alles wagen, / kein Kreuz nicht achten, / keine Schmach noch Plagen, / nichts von Verfolgung, / nichts von Todesschmerzen / nehmen zu Herzen. (I will risk everything to honor Thee, / Not heed any cross, / Nor disgrace, nor torments. / Nothing from persecution / Nor pain of death / Will I take to heart.)

20. *Recitative.* JESUS: Und ich will euch das Reich bescheiden, / wie mir's mein Vater beschieden hat, dass ihr / essen und trinken soll über meinem Tisch in / meinem Reich, und sitzen auf Stühlen, und / richten die zwölf Geschlechte Israel. (And I will allot to you the Kingdom, / as my Father has assigned it to Me, / so that you shall eat and drink at my / table in my Kingdom, and sit on seats, / and judge the twelve tribes of Israel.)

21. *Chorale — continuo.* Referring to the preceding number, the choir sings this short psalm of praise. Der

heiligen zwölf Boten Zahl / und die lieben Propheten all, / die teuren Märt'rer allzumal / loben dich, Herr, mit grossem Schall. (The number of twelve holy Disciples / And all the dear prophets, / Together with the dear martyrs / Praise Thee, Lord, with mighty sound.)

22. *Recitative — Dialogue.* EVANGELIST: Der Herr aber sprach: JESUS: Simon, siehe, der Satanas hat euch / begehrt, dass er euch möchte sichten wie / den Weizen; aber ich habe für dich / gebeten, dass dein Glaube nicht aufhöre; / und wenn du dermaleinst dich bekehrest, / so stärke deine Brüder. EVANGELIST: Er aber sprach zu ihm: PETRUS: Herr, ich bin bereit, mit dir / in's Gefängnis und in den Tod zu gehen. EVANGELIST: Er aber sprach: JESUS: Petre, ich sage dir: der Hahn / wird heute nicht krähen, ehe denn du / dreimal verleugnet hast, dass du mich kennest. EVANGELIST: Und er sprach zu ihnen: JESUS: So oft ich euch gesandt habe / ohne Beutel, ohne Tasche und ohne Schuhe, / habet ihr auch je Mangel gehabt? EVANGELIST: Sie sprachen: (The Lord spoke: / Simon, behold, Satan has desired thee / that he might sift thee like wheat; / but I have prayed for thee / that thy faith do not cease; / and when thou returnest once more, / strengthen thy brethren. / And he said to him: / Lord, I am ready to go with Thee / into prison and into death. / He replied: / Peter, I say to thee: the cock / will not crow today, before thou hast / thrice denied that thou knowest Me. / And He said to them: / As often as I have sent you / without a purse, without a wallet and shoes, / have you ever been lacking? / They said:)

23. *Chorus — Apostles.* Nie keinen, nie keinen. (Never anything, never anything.) This repeated reply of the twelve Apostles in a turba (crowd)

motif gives a very realistic and dramatic touch to the end of the above recitative. Bach will use this motif again in his other passions for its spectacular value.

24. *Recitative — Dialogue.* EVANGELIST: Da sprach er zu ihnen: JESUS: Aber nun, wer einen Beutel hat, der / nehme ihn, desselbigen gleichen auch die Tasche; / wer aber nicht hat, verkaufe sein Kleid, und / kaufe ein Schwert. Denn ich sage euch: / es muss noch das auch vollendet werden an mir, / das geschrieben stehet: "Er ist unter die / Übeltäter gerechnet." Denn was von mir / geschrieben stehet, das hat eine Ende. EVANGELIST: Sie sprachen aber: (Then He said to them: / But now, whoever has a purse, let him / take it, and likewise with his wallet; / but whoever does not, sell his garment / and buy a sword. For I tell you: / this must be finished in Me, / which stands written: "He has been / reckoned among the evildoers." For what / stands written about Me, that has an end. / But they said:)

25. *Chorus — Apostles.* Herr, siehe, hier sind zwei Schwert. (Lord, behold, here are two swords.)

26. *Recitative — Dialogue.* EVANGELIST: Er aber sprach zu ihnen: JESUS: Es ist genug. EVANGELIST: Und er ging hinaus nach / seiner Gewohnheit an den Ölberg. / Es folgeten ihm aber seine Jünger nach / an denselbigen Ort. Und als er dahin kam, / sprach er zu ihnen: JESUS: Betet, auf dass ihr nicht in Anfechtung fallet. (And He spoke to them: / It is enough. / And he went out as He usually did to / the Mount of Olives. / His Disciples followed Him / to the same place. And when He came there, / He spoke to them: / Pray, so that ye do not fall into temptation.)

27. *Chorale.* The choir sings this short prayer, which is aptly chosen to fit the last words of Jesus in the previous recitative. Wir armen Sünder bitten, / du wollest uns erhören, / lieber Herre Gott! (We poor sinners ask / That Thou wilt hear us, / Dear Lord God!)

28. *Recitative — Dialogue.* EVANGELIST: Und er riss sich von ihnen / bei einem Steinwurf, und kniete nieder, / betete, und sprach: JESUS: Vater, willt du, so nimm diesen Kelch / von mir; doch nicht mein, sondern dein Wille / geschehe! (And He moved from them / about a stone's cast away, knelt down, / prayed, and said: / Father, if Thou wilt, take this cup / from Me; yet not Mine but Thy will be done!)

29. *Chorale.* The melody for this chorale is the same as that used in Martin Rinckart's hymn "Nun danket alle Gott" (Now all thank God) (1644). Again, it refers to the words that Jesus has just uttered in submission to His Father's will. Mein Vater, wie du willt, so bin ich auch zufrieden, / was du mir auf der Welt zu meinem Teil beschieden. / Ich nehm' es auf dein Wort, dein Wille werd' erfüllt, / und sage allezeit: Mein Vater, wie du willt! (My Father, as Thou wishest, so I am content too / With what Thou hast allotted to me in the world. / I take it as Thy word that Thy will be done, / And always I say: My Father, as Thou willest!)

30. *Recitative.* EVANGELIST: Es erschien ihm aber ein Engel / vom Himmel, und stärkete ihn. Und es kam, dass / er mit dem Tode rang, und betete heftiger, / es war aber sein Schweiss wie Blutstropfen, / die fielen auf die Erde. (There appeared to Him an angel / from heaven, and strengthened Him. / And it happened, as He struggled with / death and prayed more earnestly, / His sweat was like drops of blood, / which fell to the earth.)

31. *Chorale.* This interjection by the choir is a prayer, again resulting from the recitative. Durch deines Todes Kampf und blutigen Schweiss hilf uns, lieber Herre Gott! (Through Thy struggle with death and bloody sweat, help us, dear Lord God!)

32. *Recitative — Dialogue.* EVAN-GELIST: Und er stund auf von dem Gebet, / und kam zu seinen Jüngern, und fand sie / schlafend vor Traurigkeit, und sprach zu ihnen: JESUS: Was schlafet ihr? Stehet auf und betet, / auf dass ihr nicht in Anfechtung fallet. (And He stood up from prayer, / and came to His Disciples, and found them / sleeping because of grief, and spoke to them: / Why do ye sleep? Stand up and pray, / lest ye fall into temptation.)

33. *Chorale.* We hear the contrite reply of the Apostles for having fallen asleep while Jesus was praying. But it is also a prayer to Christ from each person in the congregation that He help him to overcome his own weakness and to bolster up his faith. Lass mich Gnade für dir finden, / der ich bin voll Traurigkeit. / Hilf du mir selbst überwinden, / so oft ich muss in den Streit. / Meinen Glauben täglich mehr, / deines Geistes Schwert verehr', / damit ich den Feind kann schlagen, / alle Pfeile von mir jagen. (Let me find mercy before Thee, / I who am full of sadness. / Help me to overcome myself, / As often as I must fight. / Make my faith daily more; / May I honor the sword of Thy Spirit, / So that I can strike the enemy, / And deflect from me all his arrows.)

34. *Recitative — Dialogue.* EVAN-GELIST: Da er aber noch redet, siehe, / die Schar und einer von den Zwölfen, / genannt Judas, ging für ihnen her, und / nahete sich zu Jesu, ihn zu küssen. / Jesus aber sprach zu ihm: JESUS: Juda, verrätest du des

Menschen / Sohn mit einem Kuss? (As He was still speaking, behold, the crowd and one of the Twelve, / called Judas, went before them, and / he drew near Jesus to kiss Him. / But Jesus said to him: / Judas, dost thou betray the Son of man / with a kiss?)

35. *Chorale.* The choir deplores this treacherous action of Judas by a little sung sermon on the hypocrisy of many people: Von aussen sich gut stellen, / im Herze böse sein, / zu Judas sich gesellen, / trägt nur Verdammnis ein. / Wenn du mit Judasküssen / verrätest des Menschen Sohn, / du wirst es büssen müssen / einst vor des Richters Thron. (To show oneself outwardly as good, / To be evil at heart, / To join with Judas, / Brings only damnation. / When you, with Judas's kisses, / Betray the Son of man, / You will have to atone for it / Sometime before the Judge's throne.)

36. *Recitative.* EVANGELIST: Da aber sahen, die um ihn waren, / was da werden wollte, sprachen sie zu ihm: (When they who were about Him saw / what would happen there, they said to Him:

37. *Chorus — Apostles (turba motif).* Herr, sollen wir mit dem Schwert drein schlagen? (Lord, should we strike into them with the sword?)

38. *Recitative — Dialogue.* EVAN-GELIST: Und einer aus ihnen schlug / des Hohenpriesters Knecht, und hieb ihm / ein Ohr ab. Jesus aber antwortete und sprach: JESUS: Lasset sie doch so ferne machen! EVANGELIST: Und er rührete sein Ohr an, / und heilete ihn. (And one of them struck / the high priest's servant, and / cut off one of his ears. But Jesus / answered and said: / Let them do thus far! / And he touched his ear and healed him.)

39. *Chorale.* The compassion which Jesus has just shown brings to mind His teaching on loving our enemies:

Ich will daraus studieren, / wie ich mein Herz soll zieren / mit stillem sanftem Mut, / Und wie ich die soll lieben, / die mich so sehr betrüben / mit Werken, so die Bosheit tut. (I want to study from that / How I should embellish my heart / With quiet gentle courage, / And how I should love those, / Who grieve me so much / With deeds done by wickedness.)

40. *Recitative—Dialogue.* EVANGELIST: Jesus aber sprach zu den Hohenpriestern / und Hauptleuten des Tempels und den Ältesten, die / über ihn kommen waren: JESUS: Ihr seid, als zu einem Mörder, mit / Schwertern und mit Stangen ausgegangen. Ich bin / täglich bei euch im Tempel gewesen, und ihr habt / keine Hand an mich gelegt; aber dies ist eure / Stunde und die Macht der Finsternis. EVANGELIST: Sie griffen ihn aber, und führten ihn, / und brachten ihn in des Hohenpriesters Haus. / Petrus aber folgete von ferne. (Then Jesus spoke to the high priests / and captains of the temple and to / the elders, who had come upon Him: / Ye have come out, as against a murderer, / with swords and with staves. I have / been daily with ye in the Temple, and / ye have laid no hand on Me. But this / is thy hour and the power of darkness. / Then they seized Him, and led Him, / and brought Him into the high priest's house. / However, Peter followed from afar.

41. *Chorale.* The choir gives a short comment on the above account by quoting these words from the Lord's Prayer: Und führe uns nicht in Versuchung, sondern erlöse uns von dem Übel. (And lead us not into temptation, but deliver us from evil.)

42. *Recitative.* The librettist brings the dramatic action to life in this unique scene by having five actors on the stage. EVANGELIST: Da zündeten sie ein Feuer an / mitten im Palast, und setzten sich zusammen. / Und Petrus setzte sich unter sie. Da sahe ihn / eine Magd sitzen bei dem Lichte, und sahe eben / auf ihn, und sprach zu ihm: MAGD (MAID): Dieser war auch mit ihm. EVANGELIST: Er aber verleugnete ihn, und sprach: PETRUS (PETER): Weib, ich kenne sein nicht. EVANGELIST: Und über eine kleine Weile sahe ihn / eine andre, und sprach: 2TE MAGD (2ND MAID): Du bist auch der einer. EVANGELIST: Petrus aber sprach: PETRUS (PETER) Mensch, ich bin's nicht. EVANGELIST: Und über eine Weile, bei einer Stunde, / bekräftigt' es ein Andrer, und sprach: SERVUS (SERVANT): Wahrlich, dieser war auch / mit ihm, denn er ist ein Galiläer. EVANGELIST: Petrus aber sprach: PETRUS (PETER): Mensch, ich weiss nicht, was du sagest. EVANGELIST: Und alsbald, da er noch redete, / krähete der Hahn. Und der Herr wandte sich / und sahe Petrum an. (Then they lit a fire / in the middle of the palace, and sat together. / And Peter sat among them. / A maid saw him sitting by the light, and / just looked at him and said: / This man was also with Him. / But he denied Him and said: / Woman, I do not know Him. / And after a little while, another / saw him and said: / You are also one of them. / But Peter said: / Man, I am not. And after a while, about / an hour, another confirmed it, saying: / Truly, this one was with Him, for / he is a Galilean. / Peter said: / Man, I do not know what you say. / And immediately, while he was speaking, / the cock crew. And the Lord turned and / looked at Peter.)

43. *Chorale.* This is a choral lament over Peter's denial of Jesus. Kein Hirt so fleissig gehen / nach dem Schaf, das sich verläuft. / Sollt'st du Gottes Herze sehen, / wie sich da der Kummer häuft, / wie es dürstet, jächt und

brennt / nach dem, was sich abgetrennt / von ihm und auch von den Seinen, würdest du für Liebe weinen. (No shepherd goes so diligently / After the sheep that has run away. / Should you see God's heart, / How worry increases in it, / How it thirsts, aches and burns / For that from which it is separated, / From Him and also from His, / You would weep from love.)

44. *Recitative.* EVANGELIST: Und Petrus gedachte an des Herren Wort, als er zu ihm gesagt hatte: "Ehe denn der Hahn krähet, wirst du mich dreimal verleugnen," und Petrus ging hinaus und weinet bitterlich. (And Peter remembered the Lord's words, when He had said to him: "Before the cock crows, thou wilt deny Me thrice," and Peter went out and wept bitterly.)

45. *Aria—Tenor.* The mention of tears leads naturally into this third da capo aria. The imagery of a torrent overwhelming the sinner is well expressed by Bach's motif of motion in the first four lines. Peter is the actor in this number. Den Fels hat Moses' Stab geschlagen, / drum quillt aus ihm ein starker Fluss. / Gesetz und Fluch schreckt den Verbrecher; / er fürchtet einen harten Rächer; / selbst sein Gewissen wird ihm sagen, / dass er des Todes sterben muss. (Moses's staff has struck the rock. / Therefore a mighty river poured from it. / Judgment and curse terrifies the sinner. / He fears a hard avenger. / Even his conscience will tell him / That he must die his death.)

46. *Chorale—Tenor.* This is the only chorale sung solo by one actor, who can be identified as Peter, because the same tenor had just sung the previous aria.

Bach had composed his first extant cantata, BWV 131, on this complete Psalm 130 while in Mühlhausen, and the chorale tune for it was well known to all Lutherans. Here we hear only the first line of the hymn, but the sentiment accurately portrays Peter's remorse. PETRUS (PETER): Aus der Tiefe rufe ich; / Jesu Gnade tröste mich. / ich hab' Unrecht zwar getan, / aber Jesus nimmt mich an. (Out of the depths I call. / Merciful Jesus, comfort me. / I have surely done wrong, / But Jesus accepts me.)

## PART II

Only the two oboes and the bassoon are heard playing a grief motif in the chorale "Ich habe mein Sach' Gott heimgesellt" (I have left my affairs to God), which serves as a fitting overture for the sad events about to take place.

47. *Recitative.* EVANGELIST: Die Männer aber, die Jesum hielten, verspotteten ihn, und schlugen ihn, verdeckten ihn, und schlugen ihn in's Angesicht, und fragten ihn, und sprachen: (And the men, who held Jesus, mocked Him, and struck Him, covered Him, and struck Him in the face and asked Him saying:)

48. *Chorus (Men).* Weissage, wer ist's, der dich schlug? (Prophecy, who is it who struck Thee?)

49. *Chorale.* Dass du nicht ewig Schande mögest tragen, / lässt er sich schimpflich ins Gesichte schlagen; / weil dich zum öfters eitler Ruhm erfreuet, / wird er verspeiet. (So that you do not bear eternal shame, / He lets Himself be beaten in the face disgracefully. / Because your vanity often makes you glad, / He is being spat upon.)

50. *Recitative.* EVANGELIST: Und viel andre Lästerungen sagten sie wider ihn. Und als es Tag ward, sammelten sich die Ältesten des Volks, die Hohenpriester und Schriftgelehrten, und führten ihn hinauf vor ihren Rath, und sprachen: (And they said many other blasphemous things against Him. And when it became

day, the elders of the people, the high priests and the scribes gathered together and led Him up before their council, saying:)

51. *Chorus (The Elders)*. Bist du Christus? Sage es uns! (Art Thou Christ? Tell us!)

52. *Recitative — Dialogue*. EVANGELIST: Er aber sprach zu ihnen: JESUS: Sag' ich's euch, so glaubet ihr's nicht; / frage ich aber, so antwortet ihr nicht, und / lasset mich doch nicht los. Darum von nun an / wird des Menschen Sohn sitzen zur rechten / Hand der Kraft Gottes. EVANGELIST: Sie sprachen aber: (He spoke to them: / If I tell you, you will not believe it; / if I ask you, you will not answer, and / not let me go free. Therefore, from / now on the Son of man will sit at the / right hand of the power of God. / But they said:)

53. *Chorus (The Elders)*. Bist du denn Gottes Sohn? (Art Thou then God's Son?)

54. *Chorale*. Du König der Ehren, Jesu Christ, / Gott Vaters ew'ger Sohn du bist. (Thou, King of honor, Jesus Christ, / Thou art the eternal Son of the Father.)

55. *Recitative — Dialogue*. EVANGELIST: Er sprach zu ihnen: JESUS: Ihr sagt's, denn ich bin's. EVANGELIST: Sie sprachen aber: (He spoke to them: / You said it, for I am. / But they said:)

56. *Chorus (The Elders) — turba (crowd) motif*. Was, was dürfen wir weiter Zeugnis? Wir haben's selbst gehört, wir haben's selbst gehört aus seinem Munde. (Why, why do we need further witness? We have heard it ourselves, heard it out of His mouth.)

57. *Recitative*. EVANGELIST: Und der ganze Haufe stund auf, und führete ihn vor Pilatum, und fingen an ihn zu verklagen, und sprachen: (And the whole crowd stood up, and led Him before Pilate, and began to accuse Him saying:)

58. *Chorus (The Elders)*. Diesen finden wir, dass er das Volk abwendet, und verbeut, den Schoss dem Kaiser zu geben, und spricht, er sei Christus, ein König. (We find this Man perverting the people, and He forbids giving tribute to Caesar, saying He is Christ, a King.)

59. *Recitative — Dialogue*. EVANGELIST: Pilatus aber fragte ihn, und sprach: PILATE: Bist du der Jüden König? EVANGELIST: Er antwortete ihm: JESUS: Du sagest's. (And Pilate asked Him, saying: / Art Thou the King of the Jews? / He answered him: / Thou sayest so.)

60. *Chorale*. Dein göttlich Macht und Herrlichkeit / geht üb'r Himmel und Erden weit. (Thy divine might and majesty / Goes far over heaven and earth.)

61. *Recitative — Dialogue*. EVANGELIST: Pilatus sprach zu den Hohenpriestern / und zu dem volk: PILATE: Ich finde Keine Ursach' an diesem menschen. (Pilate spoke to the high priests / and to the people: I find no fault in this man.)

62. *Chorale*. Bach will set this same verse in his later *St. Matthew Passion* (number 16). Ich bin's, ich soll büssen, / an Händen und an Füssen / gebunden in der Höll. / Die Geisseln und die Banden, / und was du ausgestanden, / das hat verdienet meine Seel'. (It is I who should do penance, / Bound on hand and foot / In hell. / The lashes and the fetters / And what Thou hast endured / My soul has deserved that.)

63. *Recitative*. EVANGELIST: Sie aber hielten an, und sprachen: (But they persisted, saying:)

64. *Chorus — (The People): turba (crowd) motif*. Er hat das Volk erreget damit, dass er gelehrt hat hin und her im ganzen jüdischen Lande, und hat in Galiläa angefangen bisher. (He has aroused the people, teaching through-

out all Jewry, beginning in Galilee to here.)

65. *Recitative.* EVANGELIST: Da aber Pilatus "Galiläa" hörte, fragte er, ob er aus Galiläa wäre. Und als er vernahm, dass er unter Herodis Obrigkeit gehörte, übersandte er ihn zu Herodes, welcher auch an demselbigen Tage zu Jerusalem war. Da aber Herodes Jesum sahe, war er sehr froh, denn er hätte ihn längst gerne gesehen, und hoffete, er würde ein Zeichen von ihm sehen, und fragte ihn mancherlei, und er antwortete ihm nichts. (When Pilate heard "Galilee," he asked whether He was from Galilee. And when he understood that He belonged to Herod's jurisdiction, he sent Him to Herod, who was also on the same day in Jerusalem. When Herod saw Jesus, he was very glad, because, for a long time, he would have liked to see Him, and hoped he would see a proof from Him, and asked Him many times, but He answered nothing.)

66. *Aria—Tenor—oboes and the bassoon with continuo.* The prominent tone of the bassoon obbligato in this fourth da capo aria produces an atmosphere of sadness in keeping with what the Evangelist has just related and the grief motif that Bach draws out of the text. The tenor's coloratura runs on the word *leidet* (suffers) seem to reveal an insight into Bach's philosophy of life—Christian acceptance of evil, to be overcome by good. Das Lamm verstummt vor seinem Scherer / und leidet alles mit Geduld. / Wenn man bei Rach' und Bosheit schweiget, / gelassen ist und Grossmut zeiget / verwandelt sich oft Wut in Huld. (The Lamb remains silent before His shearer / And suffers all with patience. / If one keeps quiet before revenge and evil, / Is calm and shows magnanimity / Rage is often changed to clemency.)

67. *Recitative.* EVANGELIST: Die Hohenpriester aber und Schriftgelehrten stunden und verklagten ihn hart. Aber Herodes mit seinem Hofgesinde verachtete und verspottete ihn, legte ihm ein weiss Kleid an, und sandte ihn wieder zu Pilato. (And the high priests and scribes stood and accused Him harshly. But Herod with his court followers despised and mocked Him, put a white robe on Him and sent Him again to Pilate.

68. *Chorale.* The mention of the white robe worn by Jesus leads again into a very apt hymn. Was kann die Unschuld besser kleiden, / als des Herodes weisses Kleid. / Ob auch die Juden wie die Heiden, / entbrennen voller Hass und Neid, / sie zeugen trotz der Spötterei, / dass Jesus Christ unschuldig sei. (What can clothe innocence better / Than Herod's white robe? / Whether the Jews as well as the heathens / Burn up with hate and envy, / They give evidence despite their mockery / That Jesus Christ is innocent.)

69. *Recitative—Dialogue.* EVANGELIST: Auf den Tag wurden Pilatus und Herodes Freunde miteinander, denn zuvor waren sie einander Feind. Pilatus aber rief die Hohenpriester und die Obersten das Volk zusammen, und sprach zu ihnen: (On that day Pilate and Herod became friends with each other, for before they were enemies. Pilate called the high priests and the leaders of the people together, and said to them:) PILATUS: Ihr habt diesen Menschen zu mir gebracht, als der das Volk abwende, und siehe! ich habe ihn vor euch verhöret, und finde an dem Menschen der Sachen keine, der ihr ihn beschuldiget. Herodes auch nicht. Denn ich habe euch zu ihm gesandt, und siehe! man hat nichts auf ihn gebracht, das des Todes wert sei. Darum will ich ihn züchtigen und loslassen. (You have brought this Man to me, as one who

perverts the people, and behold! I have heard Him before you, and find nothing in the Man of which you accuse Him. Nor does Herod. For I have sent you to Him, and see, nothing has been brought against Him worthy of death. Therefore I will chastise and release Him.)

70. *Chorale.* Such a self-explanatory hymn is again suitable for this moment in the tragedy. Ei, was hat er denn getan, / Was sind seine Schulden, / dass er da vor jedermann / solche Schmach muss dulden? / Hat er etwa Gott getrübt / bei gesunden Tagen, / dass er ihm anitzo gibt / seinen Lohn mit Plagen? / Nein, fürwahr, wahrhaftig nein! / er ist ohne Sünden; / sondern was der Mensch für Pein / billig sollt empfinden, / was für Krankheit, Angst und Weh / uns von Recht gebühret, / das ist's, so ihn in die Höh' / an das Kreuz geführet? (O, just what has He done; / What are His faults, / That He before everyone / Must endure such disgrace? / Has He perhaps offended God / In His days of health / That He gives Him now / His reward with miseries? / No, certainly, truly no! / He is without sin. / But only that kind of pain / That man should justly feel, / Sickness, worry and sorrow / Which rightly pertain to us. / Is that what leads Him / Up high to the Cross?)

71. *Recitative.* EVANGELIST: Denn er musste ihnen einen nach Gewohnheit des Festes losgeben. Da schrie der ganze Haufe, und sprach: (For he had to release one to them according to the custom of the feast. Then the whole crowd cried out, saying:)

72. *Chorus (The People) — turba motif.* Hinweg, hinweg mit diesem, und gieb uns Barrabas los! (Away, away with this Man, and give us Barabbas free!)

73. *Recitative.* EVANGELIST: Welcher war um eines Aufruhrs, so in der Stadt geschah, und um eines Mord's willen in's Gefängnis geworfen, Da rief Pilatus abermals zu ihnen, und wollte Jesum loslassen. Sie riefen aber, und sprachen: (Which man had been thrown into prison, because of a revolt in the city and because of a murder. Then Pilate called again to them and wanted to release Jesus. But they cried out, saying:)

74. *Chorus (The People) — turba motif.* Kreuzige ihn! (Crucify Him!)

75. *Recitative — Dialogue.* EVANGELIST: Er aber sprach zum dritten Mal zu ihnen: (He spoke for the third time to them:) PILATUS: Was hat er denn Übels getan? Ich finde keine Ursache des Todes an ihm, darum will ich ihn züchtigen und loslassen. (What evil has He done? I find no cause for death in Him. Therefore I will chastise Him and let Him go.) EVANGELIST: Aber sie lagen ihm an mit starken Geschrei und forderten, dass er gekreuziget würde. Und ihr und der Hohenpriester Geschrei nahm überhand. Pilatus aber urteilte, dass ihre Bitte geschähe, und liess den los, der um Aufruhr's und Mord's willen war in's Gefängnis geworfen, um welchen sie baten. Aber Jesum übergab er ihrem Willen. (But they objected with loud shouting, and demanded that He be crucified. And their and the high priests' shouting prevailed. Pilate judged that their request should happen, and released him for whom they asked, who because of revolt and murder had been thrown into prison. But he gave Jesus over to their will.)

76. *Chorale.* Es wird in der Sünder Hände / überliefert Gottes Lamm, / dass sich dein Verderben wende; / Jud' und Heiden sind ihm gram / und verwerfen diesen Stein, / der ihr Eckstein sollte sein. / Ach, dies leidet der Gerechte / für die bösen Sündenknechte! (God's Lamb was delivered /

Into the hands of sinners, / So that your destruction be averted. / Jews and heathens dislike Him / And throw this stone away / Which should be their cornerstone. / Ah, the righteous One suffers this / For wicked sinners!)

77. *Recitative.* EVANGELIST: Und als sie Jesum hinführeten, ergriffen sie einen, Simon von Cyrenne, der kam von Felde; und legten das Kreuz auf ihn, dass er's Jesu nachtrüge. Es folgte ihm aber ein grosser Haufe Volks und Weiber, die klagten und beweineten ihn. (And when they led Jesus away, they seized one Simon of Cyrene coming from the field, and placed the cross upon him, so that he might carry it after Jesus. There followed Him a large crowd of people and women, who lamented and wept for Him.)

78. *Trio — Two Sopranos and the Alto — only two obbligato flutes to accompany them.* This number may be considered the fifth aria in this passion. The three women soloists, bewailing the sad scene that they witness, combine their grief motif with a motif of felicity in the melody of the flutes to produce a very dramatic effect. This magnificent setting of the text alleviates the monotony of the Biblical narrative and of the frequent chorale comments heard since the last aria. Weh und Schmerz in dem Gebären / heisst nichts gegen deine Not. / Ach, wir armen Sünderinnen / werden itzt den Fluch recht innen, / und wir trügen mit Geduld / unsrer ersten Mutter Schuld, / retteten dich uns're Zähren / nur von deinem bittern Tod! (Woe and pain in childbirth / Are as nothing to Thy agony. / Ah, we poor sinners / Become now really aware of the curse, / And we would bear with patience / The guilt of our first mother, / If only our tears would save Thee / From Thy bitter death!)

79. *Recitative — Dialogue.* EVANGELIST: Jesus aber wandte sich um zu ihnen, und sprach: (But Jesus turned around to them and said:) JESUS: Ihr Töchter von Jerusalem, weinet nicht über mich, sondern weinet über euch selbst und über eure Kinder. Denn siehe! es wird die Zeit kommen, in welcher man sagen wird: Selig sind die Unfruchtbaren und die Leiber, die nicht geboren haben, und die Brüste, die nicht gesäuget haben. Dann werden sie anfangen zu sagen zu den Bergen: Fallet über uns! und zu den Hügeln: Decket uns!; denn so man das tut am grünen Holz, was will am dürren werden?) (Ye daughters of Jerusalem, do not weep over Me, but weep over yourselves and over your children. For behold!, the time will come, in which it will be said: "Blessed are the barren, the wombs which have not born, and the breasts which have not given suck." Then they will begin to say to the mountains: "Fall upon us," and to the hills: "Cover us." For if they do that to a green tree, what will be done to a dry one?) EVANGELIST: Es wurden aber auch hingeführet zween andre Übeltäter, dass sie mit ihm abgetan würden. Und als sie kamen an die Stätte, die da heisset Schädelstätte, kreuzigten sie ihn daselbst und die Übeltäter mit ihm, einen zur Rechten und einen zur Linken. Jesus aber sprach: (And also two other evildoers were led to be executed with Him. And when they came to the place, which there was called Place of the Skull, they crucified Him and the two evildoers with Him, one at the right hand, and one on the left. Jesus then said:) JESUS: Vater, vergieb ihnen, denn sie wissen nicht was sie tun. (Father, forgive them, for they do not know what they are doing.)

80. *Chorale.* Sein' allererste Sorge war, / zu schützen die ihn hassen; / bat, dass sein Gott der bösen Schar / wollt ihre Sünd' erlassen. / Vergieb!

sprach er aus Lieb', / o Vater, ihnen allen; / ihr'r keiner ist, der säh und wüsst's, / in was für Tat sie fallen. (His very first concern was / To protect those who hate Him. / He asked that God / would remit the sins of the wicked crowd. / Forgive!, He spoke from love, / Them all, O Father. / There is none of them, / who sees and knows / Into what a deed they fall.) 81. *Recitative.* EVANGELIST: Und sie teileten seine Kleider, und wurfen das Los drum, und das Volk stund, und sahe zu. Und die Obersten samt ihnen spotteten sein, und sprachen: (And they divided His clothing, and cast lots for it, and the people stood looking on. And the rulers with them derided Him saying:) 82. *Chorus — (The People) — turba (tumult) motif.* Er hat andern geholfen; er helfe ihm selber, ist er Christ, er helfe ihm selber, der Auserwählte Gottes. (He has helped others. Let him help himself, if He is Christ, the chosen of God.) 83. *Recitative.* EVANGELIST: Es verspotteten ihn auch die Kriegsknechte, traten zu ihm, und brachten ihm Essig, und sprachen: (The soldiers also mocked Him, came to Him bringing Him vinegar, and said:) 84. *Chorus — tumult motif.* Bist du der Jüdenkönig, so hilf dir selber! (If Thou art the King of the Jews, help Thyself!) 85. *Chorale.* This is the fifth verse of Johann Flittner's hymn, used for the fourth time in this passion. Ich bin krank, komm, stärke mich, meine Stärke! / Ich bin matt, erquicke mich, süsser Jesu! / Wenn ich sterbe, tröste mich, Jesu du mein Tröster! (I am sick come strengthen me, my Strength! / I am weary, refresh me, sweet Jesus! / When I die, comfort me, Jesus Thou my Comforter!) 86. *Recitative.* EVANGELIST: Es war auch oben über ihn geschrieben die

Überschrift, mit griechischen und lateinischen und ebräischen Buchstaben: "Dies ist der Jüden König." (There was written over Him the superscription in letters of Greek, Latin and Hebrew: "This is the King of the Jews.") 87. *Chorale.* Das Kreuz ist der Königstron, / drauf man dich wird setzen. / dein Haupt mit der Dornenkron' / bis in Tod verletzen; / Jesu, dein Reich auf der Welt / ist in lauter Leiden, / so ist es von dir bestellt / bis zum letzten Scheiden. (The Cross is Thy kingly throne, / On which they will set Thee. / Thy head with the crown of thorns / Hurting until death; / Jesus, Thy kingdom in this world / Is nothing but suffering. / So has it been ordained by Thee / Until our last parting.) 88. *Recitative.* This number is another very dramatic scene, presenting the two criminals as the actors who speak the Biblical words in dialogue as the Evangelist announces their entry on stage. EVANGELIST: Aber der Übeltäter einer, die da gehenket waren, lästerte ihn und sprach: (But one of the malefactors, who were hanged there, reviled Him and said:) IMPIOUS CRIMINAL: Bist du Christus, so hilf dir selbst und uns. (If Thou be Christ, help Thyself and us.) EVANGELIST: Da antwortete der andre, strafte ihn, und sprach: (Then the other answered, blamed him, and said:) PENITENT CRIMINAL: Und du fürchtest dich auch nicht vor Gott, der du doch in gleicher Verdammnis bist? Und zwar, wir sind billig drinnen, denn wir empfangen, was unsre Taten wert sind. Dieser aber hat nichts Ungeschicktes gehandelt. (And do you not even fear God, you who are in the same condemnation? And truly, we are justly in it, for we receive what our deeds merit. But this Man has done nothing amiss.) EVANGELIST: Und sprach zu Jesu: (And he spoke to Jesus:) PENITENT CRIMINAL: Herr, gedenke an mich, wenn du in dein Reich kommest. (Lord, think of me, when Thou comest into Thy Kingdom.)

89. *Chorale.* The second verse of Johann Flittner's hymn appears here for the fourth and last time. It is quite evident that this verse befits the end of the previous recitative. Tausend mal gedenk ich dein, mein Erlöser, / und begehre dich allein, mein Erlöser, / sehne mich bei dir zu sein, mein Erlöser, / Jesu, mein Erlöser! (A thousand times I think of Thee, my Redeemer, / And desire only Thee, my Redeemer. / I long to be near Thee, my Redeemer. / Jesus, my Redeemer!)

90. *Recitative.* EVANGELIST: Und Jesus sprach zu ihm: (And Jesus spoke to him:) JESUS: Wahrlich, ich sage dir: heute wirst du mit mir im Paradies sein. (Truly I say to thee, "Today shalt thou be with me in Paradise.")

91. *Chorale.* Freu' dich sehr, o meine Seele, / und vergiss all Not und Qual, / weil dich nun Christus, dein Herre, / ruft aus diesem Jammertal; / aus Trübsal und grossem Leid / sollst du fahren in die Freud', / die kein Ohr hat gehöret / und in Ewigkeit auch währet. (Rejoice greatly, O my soul, / And forget all trouble and torment, / Because Christ, your Master, / Calls you now out of this vale of tears. / From grief and great sorrow / You shall travel to that joy / Of which no ear has heard / And lasts even into eternity.)

92. *Recitative.* EVANGELIST: Und es war um die sechste Stunde, und es ward eine Finsternis über das ganze Land bis an die neunte Stunde; und die Sonne verlor ihren Schein, und der Vorhang des Tempels zerriss mitten entzwei. (And it was about the sixth hour, and there was a darkness over the whole country until the ninth hour. And the sun lost its shine, and the veil of the Temple was torn apart in the middle.)

93. *Aria — Soprano — strings and organ continuo.* This is definitely the fifth solo aria in the work, not counting the Trio (number 78). Spitta (II, 512) finds this aria to be "meagre and insignificant" whereas he has only praise for the others, saying (II, 512–13): "The rest of the arias, on the other hand, are so full of power and individuality that no one but Bach can be named who could have written them."

Yet this aria is also not lacking in force, because of the terror motif given to the accompanying melody in the strings. Bach's word painting of his text makes the listener visualize the trembling scene in the first three lines. Selbst der Bau der Welt erschüttert / über frecher Menschen Wut. / Er erkennt was ihr gemacht; / sie vergiessen unbedacht / ihres eignen Schöpfers Blut. (Even the structure of the world shakes / Over the rage of insolent men. / It sees what you have done; / They thoughtlessly shed / Their own Creator's blood.)

94. *Recitative — Dialogue.* EVANGELIST: Und Jesus rief laut, und sprach: (And Jesus cried aloud and said:) JESUS: Vater, ich befehle meinen Geist in deine Hände. (Father, I commend my Spirit into Thy hands.) EVANGELIST: Und als er das gesagt, verschied er. (And when He had said that, He departed.)

95. *Sinfonia.* The two oboes and the bassoon play a funeral lament which suits the atmosphere at this moment of the drama.

96. *Chorale.* Derselbe mein Herr Jesus Christ / vor all mein' Sünd gestorben ist / und auferstanden mir zu gut; / der Höllen Glut gelöscht / mit seinem teuren Blut. (The same my Lord Jesus Christ / Has died for all my sins / And has arisen for my benefit. / He has extinguished hell's fire / With His precious blood.)

97. *Recitative — Dialogue.* EVANGELIST: Da aber der Hauptmann sahe,

was da geschah, preisete er Gott und sprach: (When the centurion saw what had happened, he praised God saying:) CENTURION: Fürwahr, dieser ist ein frommer Mensch gewesen. (Certainly, this was a righteous Man.) EVANGELIST: Und alles Volk, das dabei war und zusahe, was da geschah, schlugen sie an ihre Brust, und wandten wiederum um. (And all the people, who were present and saw what had happened there, smote their breasts and turned around again.)

98. *Chorale.* Straf mich nicht in deinem Zorn, / grosser Gott, verschone, / ach, lass mich nicht sein verlo'n, / nach Verdienst nicht lohne. / Hat die Sünd / dich entzünd't, / lösch ab in dem Lamme / deines Grimmes Flamme. (Do not punish me in Thy anger, / Mighty God, spare me. / Ah, let me not be lost; / Do not reward me as I deserve. / If my sin / Has kindled Thy wrath, / Extinguish in the Lamb / The flame of Thy fury.)

99. *Recitative.* EVANGELIST: Es stunden aber alle seine Verwandten von ferne, und die Weiber, die ihm aus Galiläa waren nachgefolget, und sahen das alles. Und siehe, ein Mann, mit Namen Joseph, ein Ratsherr, der war ein guter frommer Mann, der hatte nicht gewilliget in ihren Rat und Handel; der war von Arimathia, der Stadt der Jüden, der auch auf das Reich Gottes wartete; der ging zu Pilato, und bat um den Leib Jesu. (And all His kinfolk and the women who had followed after Him out of Galilee stood afar off and saw all that. And behold, there was a man, named Joseph, a counsellor, a good pious man who had not consented to their counsel and action. He was of Arimathea, the city of the Jews, and who was also waiting for the Kingdom of God. This man went to Pilate and asked for the body of Jesus.)

100. *Aria — Tenor — strings and organ, with solo organ in the ritornelli.* This is the sixth and last aria in this passion, and it is a miracle in music! The personal grief that the tenor (Joseph) expresses in this da capo aria is beyond description. We feel that Bach includes all his own emotions with this beautiful interpretation of his libretto. There is scarcely any other Bach aria which moves the listener as much as this one, nor which lasts so long in his memory. The deeply felt grief motif which permeates the entire number is enhanced by the tenor's coloratura runs on *Wangen* and *Verlangen,* so that a visual picture of the burial of Jesus is evoked as are the emotions every human experiences at the death of a loved one. Lass mich ihn nur noch einmal küssen, / Lass mich ihn nur noch einmal küssen, / und legt denn meinen Freund in's Grab. / Geliebter, deine blassen Wangen / erwecken mir die Verlangen, / denn meine Liebe stirbt nicht ab. (Let me only kiss Him once more; / Let me only kiss Him once more, / And lay my Friend into His grave. / Beloved, Thy pale cheeks / Awaken longing in me, / For my love does not die.)

101. *Recitative.* EVANGELIST. Und nahm ihn ab, wickelte ihn in Leinwand, und legte ihn in ein gehauen Grab, darinnen niemand je gelegen war. (And he took Him down, wrapped Him in linen, and laid Him in a hewn sepulchre, in which nobody had ever been placed.)

102. *Chorale.* This final hymn seems to point to the chorale conclusions that Bach will use in his subsequent passions. Nun ruh', Erlöser in der Gruft, / bis dich des Vaters Stimme ruft. / Wir müssen die Verwesung seh'n, / wenn wir dereinst zu Grabe geh'n; / dein heil'ger Leib wird aufersteh'n / und nimmer die Verwesung seh'n. Gott lob, dass unser

treuer Hirt, der für uns starb, uns wecken wird. (Now rest, Redeemer, in Thy tomb, / Until Thy Father's voice calls Thee. / We must see decay, / When we once go to the grave. / Thy holy body will arise / And never see corruption. / Praise God that our faithful Shepherd, / Who died for us, will waken us.)

From the internal evidence seen in the *St. Luke Passion,* there appears to be little doubt of Bach's authorship, despite the problems of the manuscript's dating and other subsequent judgments passed on it during the twentieth century. Nobody can deny that it is a masterpiece — whether or not it represents Bach's first attempt at the passion genre. It is all too easy to say that it is spurious once Mendelssohn had decided it was!

# The St. John Passion
## Leipzig 1723; BWV 245

Bach composed his first setting of this passion during the winter of 1722–23 while he was in Cöthen. Terry (*The Passions,* I, 11–12) says that it was first performed in St. Thomas's Church on Good Friday 1723, more than three months before he was appointed cantor of that Church (May 31, 1723). However, subsequent research proved that the first performance was given in St. Nikolaus's Church, April 7, 1724.

The second version, based on Picander's libretto and amended by Bach, was performed in St. Thomas's Church, March 30, 1725. Nothing is certain about another presentation of the *St. John Passion* after this date, but possibly again in 1727 (cf. Table given by Boyd, *Bach,* 141–42). Yet Bach did transfer movements from this original work, substituting others to replace them, so that the version we hear today would appear to be that of 1736 (date of the third performance?), less the chorus "O Mensch, bewein' dein' Sünde gross" (O Man, weep for thy great sin), which was transferred to the end of Part I of the *St. Matthew Passion* at that time.

Even before the first performance in the Nikolaikirche (St. Nikolaus's Church), Bach took out the chorale "Christe, du Lamm Gottes" (Christ, Thou Lamb of God) for the last movement of his cantata BWV 23 (1724) "Du wahrer Gott und Davids Sohn" (Thou true God and David's Son). This he replaced by the chorus (number 67) "Ruht wohl, ihr heiligen Gebeine" (Rest well, ye holy limbs).

The dramatic tendency is more pronounced in the *St. John Passion* than it was in the *St. Luke* or will be in the coming *St. Matthew.* As the probable librettist of the first version, Bach places less emphasis on the da capo arias and choruses, and concentrates more on the spectacle presented by the text (John: 18, 19).

Both Bach and Picander drew on the passion texts of two contemporary Hamburg librettists, Barthold Heinrich Brockes and Christian Friedrich Postel, whose texts for the *St. John Passion* were used by Handel for his work of the same title. Their texts were published in 1712 and in 1704 respectively, both being very popular for musical productions of the passion in and around Hamburg at that time. Therefore Bach and Picander could not be blamed for imitating and borrowing from them as they composed their own free texts for this passion. These free numbers are: 1, 11, 13, 19, 31, 32, 48, 58, 60, 62, 63 and 67.

Of the twelve chorales in this work, Paul Stockmann's "Jesu Leiden, Pein und Tod" (Jesus's suffering, pain and death) occurs three times, almost as a leitmotif. For Bach the chorale was of prime importance, whether he was composing a cantata or a more lengthy vocal work.

The names and dates of the librettists and the composers of the melodies, and the musical form of each chorale of *The St. John Passion* are as follows:

*Number 7.* Words—Johann Heermann (1585–1647); Melody—Johann Crüger (1598–1662); Form—two flutes, two oboes, strings, organ, continuo (called "simple" by Terry)

*Number 9.* Words—Martin Luther (1483–1546); Melody—unknown composer; Form—as for No. 7

*Number 15.* Words: Paul Gerhardt (1607–76); Melody—Heinrich Isaak (b. circa 1440); Form—as for No. 7

*Number 20.* Words: Paul Stockmann (1602?–36); Melody—Melchior Vulpius (1560?–1615); Form—as for No. 7

*Number 21.* Words—Michael Weisse (1480?–1534); Melody—Seth Calvisius (1556–1615); Form—as for No. 7

*Number 27.* Words—Johann Heermann (see No. 7); Melody—Johann Crüger (see No. 7); Form—as for No. 7

*Number 40.* Words: unknown author; Melody—Johann Hermann Schein (1586–1630); Form—as for No. 7

*Number 52.* Words: Valerius Herberger (1562–1627); Melody—Melchior Teschner (fl. 1613); Form—as for No. 7

*Number 56.* Words: Paul Stockman (see No. 20); Melody—Melchior Teschner (fl. 1613); Form—as for No. 7

*Number 60.* Words—Paul Stockmann (see No. 20); Melody—Melchior Vulpius (see No. 20); Form—The Chorale is sung by soprano, alto, tenor, and bass in eight detached phrases inserted into the bass aria (organ and continuo)

*Number 65.* Words—Michael Weisse (see No. 21); Melody—Seth Calvisius (see No. 21); Form—"simple" as for No. 7

*Number 68.* Words—Martin Schalling (1532–1608); Melody—anonymous, but published by Bernhard Schmidt in 1577; Form—"simple" as for No. 7

The cast for this drama includes the four soloists: soprano, alto, tenor, bass, who may be identified, like the choruses, to represent characters. By tradition, the role of the Evangelist is sung by a tenor, and that of Jesus by a bass. Pilate is a bass, Peter a tenor. A Servant is also a tenor, and a Maid a soprano.

Bach employs the usual four part chorus with a full orchestra: two flutes, two oboes, two oboi da caccia, a bassoon, two viola d'amore, two viola da gamba, a lute, strings, and organ.

## PART I

1. *Chorus (free text).* This is a large scale tutti number for all voices and all instruments. It is a stunning opening, beginning with an instrumental prelude to give the melody, and a ritornello before the da capo repeat. Herr, unser Herrscher, dessen Ruhm / in allen Landen herrlich ist! / Zeig' uns durch deine Passion, / dass du, der wahre Gottessohn, / Zu aller Zeit, / Auch in der grössten Niedrigkeit, /

Verherrlicht worden bist. (Lord, our Ruler, whose glory / Is magnificent in all countries! / Show us through Thy Passion / That Thou, the true Son of God, / At all times, / Even in the greatest humiliation, / Hast become glorified.)

Note the three repeats of *Herr*— Bach's symbolic way of calling on the Lord — and the lowering tone on *Niedrigkeit* (humiliation) to illustrate this word. There is a peculiar throbbing in the rhythm — perhaps to suggest the mystery of the heartbeat of Jesus influencing the whole world? This powerful chorus is sung in canon; its prayer-like motif after the invocation is very impressive. Then a motif of joy seems to assert Christ's triumph over death and our confidence in Him.

This chorus contrasts with the opening choruses of the *St. Luke* and the *St. Matthew* passions, where the grief motif predominates.

2. *Recitative — continuo.* Following the Gospel text, the action begins *in medias res.* EVANGELIST (TENOR): Jesus ging mit seinen Jüngern über den Bach Kidron; da war ein Garten, darein / ging Jesus und seine Jünger. Judas aber, der ihn verriet, wusste den Ort auch, / denn Jesus versammelte sich oft daselbst mit seinen Jüngern. / Da nun Judas zu sich hatte genommen die Schar, und der Hohenpriester und Pharisäer / Diener, kommt er dahin mit Fackeln, Lampen und mit Waffen. / Als nun Jesus wusste alles, was ihm begegnen sollte, ging er hinaus und sprach zu / ihnen: (Jesus went with His disciples over the Brook Cedron; there was a garden into / which Jesus and His disciples entered. And Judas, who betrayed Him, knew the / place also, for Jesus often resorted there with His disciples. / Now when Judas had gathered the band of servants of the chief priests and Pharisees, / he comes there with torches, lanterns and with weapons. / Now when Jesus knew everything that should happen to Him, He went out and spoke / to them:) JESUS: Wen suchet ihr? (Whom seek ye?) EVANGELIST: Sie antworteten ihm: (They answered Him:)

3. *Chorus — This is the first turba (crowd) motif — a short tutti (all voices and instruments).* Jesum von Nazareth. (Jesus of Nazareth.) Note again the repetition of *Jesum* three times.

4. *Recitative — continuo.* EVANGELIST: Jesus spricht zu ihnen: (Jesus speaks to them:) JESUS: Ich bin's! (I am He!) EVANGELIST: Judas aber, der ihn verriet, stund auch bei ihnen. Als nun Jesus zu ihnen sprach: Ich bin's! wichen sie zurücke und fielen zu Boden. Da fragte er sie abermals: (But Judas, who betrayed Him, stood also with them. Now when Jesus spoke to them: I am He! they went backward, and fell to the ground. Then He asked them again:) JESUS: Wen suchet ihr? (Whom seek ye?) EVANGELIST: Sie aber sprachen: (But they said:)

5. *Chorus — A short triple repeat in turba style.* Jesum, Jesum, Jesum von Nazareth. (Jesus, Jesus, Jesus of Nazareth.)

6. *Recitative — continuo.* EVANGELIST: Jesus antwortete: (Jesus answered:) JESUS: Ich hab's euch gesagt, dass ich's sei. Suchet ihr denn mich, so lasse diese gehen. (I have told you that I am He. Therefore if ye seek Me, let these go.)

7. *Chorale — tutti.* This is verse 7 of "Herzliebster Jesu" (Dearest heart, Jesus) by Johann Heermann (1630), set to Johann Crüger's melody (1640). The same chorale will be heard again in number 27. In the *St. Matthew Passion,* too, the first chorale is a stanza of this hymn with the same melody.

As noted in the *St. Luke Passion,*

the chorale verses are always well chosen for commenting on the preceding number, and in this instance on Jesus's plea not to arrest His disciples with Him. Being sung in the first person, the text probably refers to the emotions of one of the disciples or of one of the congregation. O gross Lieb', o Lieb' ohn' alle Masse, / Die dich gebracht auf diese Marterstrasse! / Ich lebte mit der Welt in Lust und Freuden, / Und du musst leiden! (O great love, o limitless love, / Which has brought Thee on this torture-way! / I have lived with the world in pleasure and joy, / And Thou must suffer!)

8. *Recitative — continuo.* EVANGELIST: Auf dass das Wort erfüllet würde, welches er sagte: Ich habe keine verloren, die du mir gegeben hast. Da hatte Simon Petrus ein Schwert und zog es aus und schlug nach des Hohenpriesters Knecht und hieb ihm sein recht' Ohr ab und der Knecht hiess Malchus. Da sprach Jesus zu Petro: (So that the word might be fulfilled, which He spake: I have lost none of those which Thou gavest Me. Then Simon Peter, having a sword, drew it out and smote at the high priest's servant and cut off his right ear. The servant's name was Malchus. Then Jesus said to Peter:) JESUS: Stecke dein Schwert in die Scheide. Soll ich den Kelch nicht trinken, den mir mein Vater gegeben hat? (Put thy sword into its sheath. Am I not to drink the cup which My Father hath given Me?)

9. *Chorale — tutti.* This is verse 4 of Martin Luther's German version of the Lord's Prayer: "Vater unser in Himmelreich" (Our Father Who art in Heaven), set by himself or by an anonymous composer. How well it echoes Jesus's words to Peter or the prayer of any Christian expressing submission to God's will! Dein Will' gescheh', Herr Gott, zugleich / Auf Erden wie im Himmelreich; / Gib uns Geduld in Leidenszeit, / Gehorsamsein in Lieb' und Leid, / Wehr' und steur' allem Fleisch und Blut, / Das wider deinen Willen tut. (May Thy will be done, Lord God, both / On earth as in the Kingdom of Heaven. / Give us patience in time of sorrow, / Obedience in love and in suffering. / Defend and guide against all flesh and blood, / That works against Thy will.)

10. *Recitative — continuo.* EVANGELIST: Die Schar aber und der Oberhauptmann und die Diener der Juden nahmen Jesum und bunden ihn, und führeten ihn aufs erste zu Hannas, der war Kaiphas' Schwäher, welcher des Jahres Hohenpriester war. Es war aber Kaiphas, der den Juden riet: Es wäre gut, dass ein Mensch würde umbracht für das Volk. (Then the crowd, the captain and the servants of the Jews took Jesus and bound Him, and led Him first to Annas, who was Caiaphas's father-in-law and high priest of that year. Now Caiaphas was he who advised the Jews: It would be well that one man would be put to death for the people.)

11. *Aria — Alto — two oboes, a bassoon and continuo.* Based on a free text, this da capo aria has repeats of each half before the final da capo. A grief motif is very prominent throughout. Although she might represent any woman in the congregation, she could well be Mary Magdalene (cf. number 58, also an aria for alto in this work). Von den Stricken / Meiner Sünden / Mich zu entbinden, / Wird mein Heil gebunden; / Mich von allen / Lasterbeulen / Völlig zu heilen / Lässt er sich verwunden. (From the bonds / Of my sins / To release me / My Redeemer is bound. / Me from all / Infection of vice / Fully to heal / He lets Himself be wounded.)

12. *Recitative — continuo.* Simon

Petrus aber folgete Jesu nach und ein andrer Jünger. (Simon Peter followed after Jesus, and so did another disciple.)

13. *Aria — Soprano — two flutes and continuo.* Obviously, the soprano is intended to represent one of the disciples, as the following recitative will indicate. Perhaps Bach chose the light tone of the soprano voice to emphasize the tripping step motif in the words of this free text, while it is dramatically realistic in depicting a hastening to Jesus, which Bach will use again in the duet for soprano and alto (number 2) of BWV 78, "Jesu, der du meine Seele" (Jesus, Thou Who My Soul), a chorale cantata composed over ten years after this work. Ich folge dir gleichfalls mit freudigen / Schritten, und lasse dich nicht, / Mein Leben, / Mein Licht. / Befördre den Lauf und höre nicht auf, / Selbst an mir zu ziehen, / Zu schieben, zu bitten. (I follow Thee likewise with joyful / Steps, and do not leave Thee, / My Life, / My Light. / Further my way and do not stop / Drawing Thyself to me, / Pushing and imploring.)

14. *Recitative — continuo.* The speaking roles of five actors now focus our attention on the action, which they develop in sung narrative and dialogue. EVANGELIST: Derselbige Jünger war dem Hohenpriester bekannt und ging mit Jesu hinein in des Hohenpriesters Palast. Petrus aber stund draussen vor der Tür. Da ging der andere Jünger, der dem Hohenpriester bekannt war, hinaus, und redete mit der Türhüterin und führete Petrum hinein. Da sprach die Magd, die Türhüterin zu Petro: (The same disciple was known to the high priest and he went with Jesus into the high priest's palace. But Peter stood outside before the door. Then the other disciple, who was known to the high priest, went out and spoke with the girl who kept the door and brought in Peter. Then the maid, the door-keeper, spoke to Peter:) MAID: Bist du nicht dieses Menschen Jünger einer? (Art thou not one of this Man's disciples?) EVANGELIST: Er sprach: (He said:) PETER: Ich bin's nicht. (I am not.) EVANGELIST: Es stunden aber die Knechte und Diener und hatten ein Kohlfeu'r gemacht, denn es war kalt, und wärmeten sich. Petrus aber stund bei ihnen und wärmete sich. Aber der Hohenpriester fragte Jesum um seine Jünger und um seine Lehre. Jesus antwortete ihm: (The officers and the servants stood, and had made a coal fire, for it was cold, and warmed themselves. Peter stood beside them and warmed himself. But the high priest asked Jesus about His disciples and about His teaching. Jesus answered him:) JESUS: Ich habe frei, öffentlich geredet vor der Welt. Ich habe allezeit gelehret in der Schule und in dem Tempel, da alle Juden zusammenkommen, und habe nichts im Verborg'nen gered't. Was fragest du mich darum? Frage die darum, die gehöret haben, was ich zu ihnen geredet habe; siehe, dieselbigen wissen, was ich gesaget habe! (I have spoken freely and openly before the world. I have always taught in the synagogue and in the Temple, where all Jews gather, and have spoken nothing in secret. Why dost thou ask Me? Ask those who have heard what I have said to them; behold, they know what I have said!) EVANGELIST: Als er aber solches redete, gab der Diener einer, die dabei stunden, Jesus einen Backenstreich, und sprach: (When He spoke thus, one of the servants who stood by gave Jesus a slap on the cheek, saying:) SERVANT: Solltest du dem Hohenpriester also antworten? (Shouldst Thou answer the high priest so?) EVANGELIST: Jesus aber antwortete: (But Jesus answered:) JESUS:

Hab' ich übel gered't. so beweise es, dass es böse sei; hab' ich aber recht gered't, was schlägest du mich? (If I have spoken evil, then show that it is bad; if I have spoken rightly, why smitest thou Me?)

15. *Chorale—tutti.* Verses 3 and 4 of Paul Gerhardt's hymn "O Welt, sieh' hier dein Leben" (O World, see here thy life) are fittingly inserted here to the well-known secular melody "O Welt [Innsbruck] ich muss dich lassen" (O World [Innsbruck], I must leave thee) by Heinrich Isaak. Wer hat dich so geschlagen, / mein Heil, und dich mit Plagen, / so übel zugerich't? / Du bist ja nicht ein Sünder, / wie wir und unsre Kinder, / von Missetaten weisst du nicht. / Ich, ich und meine Sünden, / die sich wie Körnlein finden / des Sandes an dem Meer, / die haben dir erreget / das Elend, das dich schläget, / und das betrübte Marterheer. (Who has struck Thee so, / My Redeemer, and with torment / so badly judged Thee? / Thou art certainly not a sinner / Like we and our children; / Of wrong-doing Thou knowest not. / I, I and my sins, / Which are found like little grains / Of sand at the seaside, / They have caused Thee / The misery that strikes Thee / And the sad army of tortures.)

16. *Recitative.* EVANGELIST: Und Hannas sandte ihn gebunden zu dem Hohenpriester Kaiphas. Simon Peter stund und wärmete sich; da sprachen sie zu ihm: (And Annas sent Him bound to the high priest Caiaphas. Simon Peter stood and warmed himself. Then they said to him:)

17. *Chorus—turba motif—tutti with continuo.* Bist du nicht seiner Jünger einer? (Art thou not one of His disciples?)

18. *Recitative—continuo.* The drama continues here following numbers 14 and 16. EVANGELIST: Er leugnete aber und sprach: (But he lied

and said:) PETER: Ich bin's nicht! (I am not!) EVANGELIST: Spricht des Hohenpriesters Knecht einer, ein Gefreund'ter des, dem Petrus das Ohr abgehauen hatte: (One of the high priest's servants, a friend of him whose ear Peter had cut off said:) SERVANT: Sahe ich dich nicht im Garten bei ihm? (Did I not see thee in the garden beside Him?) EVANGELIST: Da verleugnete Petrus abermal und alsobald krähete der Hahn. Da gedachte Petrus an die Worte Jesu, und ging hinaus und weinete bitterlich. (Then Peter denied again and immediately the cock crew. Thereupon Peter thought about the words of Jesus, and went out and wept bitterly.)

Note the melisma on the last two words, *weinete* and *bitterlich,* which give an arioso.

19. *Aria—Tenor—strings, bassoon, and continuo.* This free text aria reveals Peter's overflowing guilt at denying his Master. He expresses his sorrow in a profound grief motif. His guilty conscience, from which he can find no escape, finds lyrical relief in this monologue, which is really an elegaic tone poem in itself. Ach, mein Sinn, / Wo willst du endlich hin, / Wo soll ich mich erquicken? / Bleib' ich hier, / Oder wünsch' ich mir / Berg und Hügel auf den Rücken? / Bei der Welt ist gar kein Rat, / Und im Herzen / Steh'n die Schmerzen / Meiner Missetat, / Weil der Knecht den Herrn verleugnet hat. (Ah, my mind, / Whither wilt thou finally go, / Where shall I be refreshed? / Do I stay here, / Or do I wish / Mountains and hills far behind me? / In the world there is no advice at all, / And in my heart / Stand the pains / Of my misdeeds, / Because the servant has denied his Lord.)

20. *Chorale—tutti.* This is verse 10 of Paul Stockmann's Passion hymn, "Jesu Leiden, Pein und Tod" (Jesus's

Suffering, Pain and Death), which is set to the melody of Melchior Vulpius's "Jesu Kreuz, Leiden und Pein" (Jesus's Cross, Suffering and Pain). Both of these works were composed in the 17th century. Bach will use this chorale again in numbers 56 and 60 of this passion.

This verse is a prayer to God to move us to repent when we know that we have, like Peter, done wrong. Petrus, der nicht denkt zurück, / Seinen Gott verneinet, / Der doch auf ein'n ernsten Blick / Bitterlichen weinet; / Jesu, blicke mich auch an, / Wenn ich nicht will büssen; / Wenn ich Böses hab' getan, / Rühre mein Gewissen. (Peter, not thinking back / Denies his God; / Yet, who at a serious glance / Weeps bitterly. / Jesus, look at me, too, / When I do not want to repent; / When I have done wrong, / Touch my conscience.)

## PART II

21. *Chorale.* Bach uses the melody by Seth Calvisius for Michael Weisse's translation of the Latin hymn "Patris sapientia, veritas divina" (Wisdom of the Father, Divine Truth) dating from the 16th century. Its rhythm of solemnity is well suited to the tragedy which will be enacted in Part II. Christus, der uns selig macht, / Kein Bös's hat begangen; / der ward für uns in der Nacht / als ein Dieb gefangen, / geführt vor gottlose Leut' / und fälschlich verklaget, / verlacht, verhöhnt und verspeit, / wie denn die Schrift saget. (Christ, who makes us blessed, / Has committed no evil. / He was for us at night / Taken as a thief, / Led before godless people / And falsely accused, / Jeered at, mocked and spat upon / As Holy Writ saith.)

22. *Recitative.* The narrative resumes now with interpolated questions and answers by the principal protagonists. EVANGELIST: Da führeten sie Jesum von Kaiphas vor das Richthaus, und es war frühe. Und sie gingen nicht in das Richthaus, auf dass sie nicht unrein würden, sondern Ostern essen möchten. Da ging Pilatus zu ihnen hinaus und sprach: (Then they led Jesus from Caiaphas to before the judgment hall, and it was early. And they did not go into the judgment hall, lest they should become unclean, but that they might eat at the Passover. Then Pilate went out to them and said:) PILATE: Was bringet ihr für Klage wider diesen Menschen? (What kind of accusation do you bring against this Man?) EVANGELIST: Sie antworteten und sprachen zu ihm: (They answered, saying to him:)

23. *Chorus — turba motif.* Wäre dieser nicht ein Übeltäter, wir hätten dir ihn nicht überantwortet. (If this Man were not an evil-doer, we would not have delivered Him to you.)

24. *Recitative.* EVANGELIST: Da sprach Pilatus zu ihnen; (Then Pilate said to them:) PILATE: So nehmet ihr ihn hin, und richtet ihn nach eurem Gesetze. (Then take Him away, and judge Him according to your Law.) EVANGELIST: Da sprachen die Juden zu ihm: (Then the Jews said to him:)

25. *Chorus — turba motif.* Wir dürfen niemand, niemand töten. (We may not kill anyone, anyone.)

26. *Recitative.* EVANGELIST: Auf dass erfüllet würde das Wort Jesu, welches er sagte, da er deutete, welches Todes er sterben würde. Da ging Pilatus wieder hinein in das Richthaus und rief Jesu und sprach zu ihm. (So that the word of Jesus would be fulfilled, which He said, when He indicated what death He would die. Then Pilate went again into the judgment hall, calling to Jesus and speaking to Him:) PILATE: Bist du der Juden König? (Art Thou the King of

the Jews?) EVANGELIST: Jesus antwortete; (Jesus answered:) JESUS: Redest du das von dir selbst oder haben's dir andere von mir gesagt? (Sayest thou that of thyself or did others tell it to thee of Me?) EVANGELIST: Pilatus antwortete: (Pilate answered:) PILATE: Bin ich ein Jude? Dein Volk und die Hohenpriester haben dich mir überantwortet; was hast du getan? (Am I a Jew? Thy people and the high priests have delivered Thee to me; what has Thou done?) EVANGELIST: Jesus antwortete: (Jesus answered:) JESUS: Mein Reich ist nicht von dieser Welt. Wäre mein Reich von dieser Welt, meine Diener würden darob kämpfen, dass ich den Juden nicht überantwortet würde! Aber, nun ist mein Reich nicht von dannen. (My kingdom is not of this world. If My kingdom were of this world, my servants would fight so that I would not be delivered to the Jews! But now My kingdom is not from there.)

27. *Chorale.* This comprises verses 8 and 9 of "Herzliebster Jesu" (Dearest heart, Jesus) which was the first chorale, number 7, in this work. Ach grosser König, gross zu allen / Zeiten, wie kann ich g'nugsam / diese Treu' ausbreiten? Kein's / Menschen Herze mag indes ausdenken, / was dir zu schenken. Ich kann's / mit meinen Sinnen nicht erreichen, / womit doch dein Erbarmen zu vergleichen. / Wie kann ich dir deine Liebestaten / im Werk erstatten? (Ah, great King, great at all / Times, how can I sufficiently / Proclaim this fidelity? / No human heart may think / Of what to give Thee. I cannot / With my mind grasp / What to compare with Thy compassion. / How can I repay Thy loving deeds / In my own doings?)

28. *Recitative.* The dramatic narrative continues. EVANGELIST: Da sprach Pilatus zu ihm: (Then Pilate

said to Him:) PILATE: So bist du dennoch ein König? (So Thou art a King then?) EVANGELIST: Jesus antwortete: (Jesus answered:) JESUS: Du sagt's, ich bin ein König. Ich bin dazu geboren und in die Welt kommen, dass ich die Wahrheit zeugen soll. Wer aus der Wahrheit ist, der höret meine Stimme. (Thou sayest I am a king. I was born to that end and have come into the world so that I should bear witness of the truth. Whoever is of the truth heareth My voice.) EVANGELIST: Spricht Pilatus zu ihm: (Pilate says to Him:) PILATE: Was ist Wahrheit? (What is truth?) EVANGELIST: Und da er das gesaget, ging er wieder hinaus zu den Juden und spricht zu ihnen: (And when he said that, he went out again to the Jews, saying to them:) PILATE: Ich finde keine Schuld an ihm. Ihr habt aber eine Gewohnheit, dass ich euch einen losgebe: wollt ihr nun, dass ich euch den Juden König losgebe? (I find no fault in Him. But you have a custom, that I should release one to you. Do you now want me to release the King of the Jews to you?) EVANGELIST: Da schrieen sie wieder allesamt und sprachen: (Then they all cried out again, saying:)

29. *Chorus — turba, in unison.* Nicht diesen sondern Barrabas! (Not this Man, but Barrabas!)

30. *Recitative.* EVANGELIST: Barrabas aber war ein Mörder. (But Barrabas was a murderer.) Da nahm Pilatus Jesum und geisselte ihn. (Then Pilate took Jesus and scourged Him.)

31. *Arioso — Bass, free text: two violas d'amore, lute, bassoon and continuo.* Apparently this reflection on Jesus's agony is sung by a disciple who witnessed the lashing. Betrachte, meine Seel', mit / ängstlichem Vergnügen, mit bittern / Lasten und hart beklemmt von Herzen, / dein höchstes Gut in Jesu Schmerzen. /

Wie dir auf Dornen, so ihn stechen, / die Himmelsschlüsselblume blüht. / Du kannst viel süsse Frucht von / seiner Wermut brechen. / Drum sieh ohn' Unterlass auf ihn. (Consider, my soul, with / Anxious joy, with bitter / Burdens and hard oppressed at heart, / Thy highest good in Jesus's pains. / [Consider] how for thee, on thorns which stab Him, / The primrose flower blooms. / Thou canst gather much sweet fruit / From His bitterness. / Therefore look to Him incessantly.)

32. *Aria—Tenor, free text: two violas d'amore and continuo.* The grief motif at the beginning of the preceding arioso, changing to a bright motif of hope in the last part, is imitated exactly by Bach in this number. The actor is Peter, reflecting on the sad sight of his scourged Master whom he denied. The da capo of this aria really brings out his regrets, which he vocalizes with repeats and runs on *erwäge* (consider). His very long melisma on the word *Regenbogen* (rainbow) demonstrates Bach's skill in giving pictorial color to his text— Christ's bloodstained back representing a heavenly rainbow, symbolic of God's forgiveness to sinners. Erwäge, wie sein blutgefärbter Rücken in allen Stücken, / Dem Himmel gleiche geht! / Daran, nachdem die Wasserwogen / Von uns'rer Sündflut sich verzogen, / Der allerschönste Regenbogen / Als Gottes Gnadenzeichen steht. (Consider, how His bloodstained back in all its parts / Is like the sky! / In it, after the waves / Of the tide of our sins has gone, / The most beautiful rainbow appears / As a sign of God's pardon.)

33. *Recitative.* EVANGELIST: Und die Kriegsknechte flochten eine Krone von Dornen und setzten sie auf sein Haupt, und legten ihm ein Purpurkleid an, und sprachen: (And the soldiers plaited a crown of thorns and put it on His head, and placed a purple robe on Him, saying:)

34. *Chorus—turba.* Here again is a crowd scene, which gives life-like action to the continuing recitatives. Sei gegrüsset, lieber Judenkönig! (Greetings, dear King of the Jews!)

35. *Recitative.* EVANGELIST: Und gaben ihm Backenstreiche. Da ging Pilatus wieder heraus und sprach zu ihnen: (And they gave Him slaps on the cheeks. Then Pilate went out again and spoke to them:) PILATE: Sehet, ich führe ihn heraus zu euch, dass ihr erkennet, dass ich keine Schuld an ihm finde. (Behold, I bring Him out to you, so that ye may know that I find no blame in Him.) EVANGELIST: Also ging Jesus heraus, und trug eine Dornenkrone und Purpurkleid. Und er sprach zu ihnen: (So Jesus went out, wearing a crown of thorns and a purple robe. And he [Pilate] said to them:) PILATE: Sehet, welch ein Mann! (Behold, what a Man!) EVANGELIST: Da ihn die Hohenpriester und die Diener sahen, schrieen sie und sprachen: (When the high priests and officers saw Him, they cried out saying:)

36. *Chorus—turba motif, tutti.* Kreuzige, kreuzige! (Crucify, crucify!)

37. *Recitative.* EVANGELIST: Pilatus sprach zu ihnen: (Pilate spoke to them:) PILATE: Nehmet ihr ihn hin und kreuziget ihn, denn ich finde keine Schuld an ihm! (Take Him away and crucify Him, for I find no fault in Him!) EVANGELIST: Die Juden antworteten ihm: (The Jews answered him:)

38. *Chorus—turba motif, tutti.* Wir haben ein Gesetz, und nach dem Gesetz soll er sterben, denn er hat sich selbst zu Gottes Sohn gemacht. (We have a law, and according to that law He should die, for He hath made Himself the Son of God.)

39. *Recitative.* EVANGELIST: Da

Pilatus das Wort hörete, fürchtet'er sich noch mehr, und ging wieder hinein in das Richthaus, und sprach zu Jesu: (When Pilate heard that word, he was even more afraid, and went again into the judgment hall and spoke to Jesus:) PILATE: Von wannen bist du? (Whence comest Thou?) EVANGELIST: Aber Jesus gab ihm keine Antwort. Da sprach Pilatus zu ihm: (But Jesus gave no answer to him. Then Pilate said to Him:) PILATE: Redest du nicht mit mir? Weissest du nicht, dass ich Macht habe, dich zu kreuzigen, und Macht habe, dich loszugeben? (Dost Thou not speak with me? Knowest Thou not that I have the power to crucify Thee and the power to release Thee?) EVANGELIST: Jesus antwortete: (Jesus answered:) JESUS: Du hättest keine Macht über mich, wenn sie dir nicht wäre von oben herab gegeben. Darum, der mich dir überantwortet hat, der hat's gröss're Sünde. (Thou wouldst have no power over Me, if it had not been given down to thee from above. Therefore, he that delivered Me to thee hath the greater sin.) EVANGELIST: Von dem an trachtete Pilatus, wie er ihn losliesse. (From then on, Pilate sought how he might release Him.)

40. *Chorale.* The words for this chorale verse were written by an unknown author or by C. F. Postel of Hamburg in his passion of 1704. The melody was composed by J. H. Schein (1586–1630) for his hymn, "Mach's mit mir Gott, nach deiner Güt'" (Do with Me, God, according to Thy Goodness). Durch dein Gefängnis, Gottes Sohn, / ist uns die Freiheit kommen. / Dein Kerker ist der Gnadenthron, / die Freistatt aller Frommen. / Denn gingst du nicht die Knechtschaft ein. / Müsst' uns're Knechtschaft ewig sein. (Through Thy captivity, O Son of God, /

Freedom has come to us. / Thy prison is the throne of mercy, / The place of freedom for all pious people. / For if Thou didst not go into bondage, / Our bondage must have been eternal.)

41. *Recitative.* EVANGELIST: Die Juden aber schrieen und sprachen: (But the Jews cried out, saying:)

42. *Chorus — turba motif, sung in canon.* Lässest du diesen los, so bist du des Kaisers Freund nicht, denn wer sich zum Könige machet, der ist wider den Kaiser. (If you let this Man go free, then you are not Caesar's friend, for whoever makes himself a king, that man is against Caesar.)

43. *Recitative.* EVANGELIST: Da Pilatus das Wort hörete, führete er Jesum heraus, und setzte sich auf den Richtstuhl, an der Stätte, die da heisst Hochpflaster, auf Ebräisch aber Gabbatha. Es war aber der Rüsttag in Ostern, um die sechste Stunde, und er spricht zu den Juden: (When Pilate heard this saying, he led Jesus out, and sat down in the judgment seat in a place called the Pavement, but in Hebrew, Gabbatha. It was the preparation day in Passover, about the sixth hour, and he said to the Jews:) PILATE: Sehet, das ist euer König! (Behold, that is your King!) EVANGELIST: Sie schrieen aber: (But they cried out:)

44. *Chorus: turba motif, sung in canon: one oboe d'amore.* Weg, weg mit dem: kreuzige ihn! (Away, away with Him! Crucify Him!)

45. *Recitative.* EVANGELIST: Spricht Pilatus zu ihnen: Soll ich euren König kreuzigen? (Pilate says to them: Am I to crucify your King?) EVANGELIST: Die Hohenpriester antworteten: (The high priests answered:)

46. CHORUS — TURBA, IN UNISON, WITH ONE OBOE D'AMORE. Wir haben keinen König denn den Kaiser. (We have no king except Caesar.)

47. *Recitative.* EVANGELIST: Da überantwortete er ihn, dass er gekreuziget würde. Sie nahmen aber Jesum und führeten ihn hin. Und er trug sein Kreuz und ging hinaus zur Stätte, die da heisset Schädelstätt', welche heisset auf Ebräisch Golgotha. (Then he delivered Him to be crucified. They took Jesus and led Him away. And He carried His Cross and went to the place, called Place of the Skull, which is named in Hebrew Golgotha.)

48. *Aria — Bass and Chorus: strings, bassoon and continuo — free texts.* The bass voice may be that of one of the disciples, the chorus the voices of the others or of the crowd of spectators. Together they produce a very impressive dialogue within the aria — the chorus asking the question "Wohin?" (Where?) and the bass replying. The da capo structure of the aria, with a step motif in its rhythm to illustrate the imagery of movement in the text, which begins with the word *Eilt* (Hurry), really brings this picture of the road to Calvary to life. Only the genius of Bach could infuse such memorable and moving music into this scene! Eilt, ihr angefocht'nen Seelen, / Geht aus euren Marterhöhlen. / Eilt [Chor — Wohin?] nach Golgotha! / Nehmet an des Glaubens Flügel. / Eilt [Chor — Wohin?] zum Kreuzes Hügel. / Eure Wohlfahrt blüht allda. (Hurry, you troubled souls, / Go out of your torture chambers. / Hurry [Chorus — Where?] to Golgotha! / Put on the wings of faith. / Hurry [Chorus — Where?] to the hill of the Cross. / Your wellbeing blossoms there.)

49. *Recitative.* EVANGELIST: Allda kreuzigten sie ihn, und mit ihm zween andere zu beiden Seiten, Jesum aber mitten inne. Pilatus aber schrieb eine Überschrift, und setzte sie auf das Kreuz, und war geschrieben: Jesus von Nazareth, der Juden König! Diese Überschrift lasen viel Juden, denn die Stätte war nahe bei der Stadt, da Jesus gekreuziget ist. Und es war geschrieben auf ebräische, griechische und lateinische Sprache. Da sprachen die Hohenpriester der Juden zu Pilato: (And there they crucified Him, and with Him two others, one on either side, but Jesus in the middle. Pilate wrote a superscription and put in on the Cross, and the writing was: Jesus of Nazareth, the King of the Jews! Many Jews read this title, for the place where Jesus was crucified was near the city. It was written in Hebrew, Greek and Latin. Then the chief priests of the Jews said to Pilate:)

50. *Chorus — turba motif, in canon.* Schreibe nicht: der Juden König, sondern dass er gesaget habe: Ich bin der Juden König! (Do not write: the King of the Jews, but that He said: I am the King of the Jews!)

51. Recitative. EVANGELIST: Pilatus antwortet: (Pilate answered:) PILATE: was ich geschrieben habe, das habe ich geschrieben. (What I have written, that I have written.)

52. *Chorale — tutti, in unison by the choir.* This is verse 3 of "Valet will ich dir geben" (I will give thee farewell) by Valerius Herberger (1562–1627) on the same melody by Melchior Teschner (1584–1635). This tune is well known today in the hymn, "All Glory, Laud and Honor." In meines Herzens Grunde, / dein Nam' und Kreuz allein / Funkelt all' Zeit und Stunde, / drauf kann ich fröhlich sein. / Erschein' mir in dem Bilde / Zu Trost in meiner Not, / Wie du, Herr Christ, so milde, / Dich hast geblut't zu Tod. (In the depths of my heart, / Thy Name and Cross alone / Sparkles at all times and hours, / For that I can be happy. / Appear to me in that image / For comfort in my distress, / How Thou, Lord Christ, so gentle, / Hast bled Thyself to death.)

53. *Recitative.* EVANGELIST: Die Kriegsknechte aber, da sie Jesum gekreuziget hatten, nahmen seine Kleider und machten vier Teile, einem jeglichen Kriegsknechte sein Teil, dazu auch den Rock. Der Rock aber war ungenähet, von oben an gewürket durch und durch. Da sprachen sie untereinander: (The soldiers, when they had crucified Jesus, took His garments and made four parts, one to each soldier, and also His robe. But the robe was seamless, woven from the top throughout. Therefore they said among themselves:)

54. *Chorus — turba, sung in canon: One oboe d'amore.* Lasset uns den nicht zerteilen, sondern darum losen, wes er sein soll. (Let us not tear it up, but cast lots for it, whose it should be.)

55. *Recitative.* EVANGELIST: Auf dass erfüllet würde die Schrift, die da saget: Sie haben meine Kleider unter sich geteilet, und haben über meinen Rock das Los geworfen. Solches taten die Kriegesknechte. Es stunden aber bei dem Kreuze Jesu seine Mutter und seiner Mutter Schwester, Maria, Cleophas Weib, und Maria Magdalene. Da nun Jesus seine Mutter sahe und den Jünger dabei stehen, den er lieb hatte, spricht er zu seiner Mutter: (So that the Scripture might be fulfilled, which saith: They have divided My clothing among themselves, and cast lots over My robe. Such did the soldiers. There stood near Jesus's Cross His Mother and His Mother's sister, Mary, the wife of Cleophas, and Mary Magdalene. Now when Jesus saw his Mother and the disciple whom He loved standing by, He said to His Mother:) JESUS: Weib! siehe, das ist dein Sohn! (Woman! Behold, that is thy Son.) EVANGELIST: Darnach spricht er zu dem Jünger: (Then He said to the disciple:) JESUS: Siehe, das ist deine Mutter! (Behold, that is thy Mother!)

56. *Chorale.* This number is verse

20 of Paul Stockmann's hymn, "Jesu Leiden, Pein und Tod" (Jesus's Suffering, Pain and Death), (cf. number 20). Er nahm alles wohl in Acht / in her letzten Stunde. / Seine Mutter noch bedacht' / setzt ihr ein'n Vormunde. / O Mensch, mache Richtigkeit, / Gott und Menschen liebe. / Stirb darauf ohn' alles Leid, / und dich nicht betrübe. (He took everything into consideration / In His last hour. / He still thought about His Mother, / Set for Her a guardian. / O man, do what is right, / Love God and man. / Then die without any grief, / and do not be sad.)

57. *Recitative.* EVANGELIST: Und von Stund' an nahm sie der Jünger zu sich. Darnach, als Jesus wusste, dass schon alles vollbracht war, dass die Schrift erfüllet würde, spricht er: (And from that hour the disciple took Her into his care. After this, when Jesus knew that everything was already done, so that the Scriptures would be fulfilled, He said:) JESUS: Mich dürstet! (I am thirsty!) EVANGELIST: Da stund ein Gefässe voll Essigs. Sie fülleten aber einen Schwamm mit Essig und legten ihn um einen Isoppen und hielten es ihm dar zum Munde. Da nun Jesus den Essig genommen hatte, sprach er: (There stood a vessel full of vinegar. They filled a sponge with vinegar and put it around hyssop and held it to his mouth. Now when Jesus had taken the vinegar, He said:) JESUS: Es ist vollbracht! (It is finished!)

58. *Aria — Alto — free text: a viola da gamba, a bassoon, strings and continuo.* As noted for number 11 in this work, the alto seems to represent Mary Magdalene. The viola da gamba imparts a grief motif to the first two lines she sings, giving dramatic pathos at this crucial moment. The instrumental prelude and the viola da gamba ritornelli before and after the second line support this impression.

The sudden switch to a joy motif in the third and fourth lines, with vivace playing of all the instruments, is highly dramatic in contrast, before returning to the hushed tone at the end of the fourth line, "es ist vollbracht!" Es ist vollbracht! O Trost für die gekränkten Seelen; / Die Trauernacht lässt mich die letzte Stunde zählen. / Der Held aus Juda siegt mit Macht, / Und schliesst den Kampf; es ist vollbracht! (It is finished! O consolation for afflicted souls. / The night of mourning lets me count that last hour. / The Hero of Judah conquers with His strength / And ends the struggle; it is finished!)

59. *Recitative.* EVANGELIST. Und neigte das Haupt und verschied. (And bowed His head and gave up the ghost.)

60. *Aria — Bass, with Chorus — free text: strings and continuo.* The bass soloist would probably act as a disciple for this unusual number. The text is verse 34 of Paul Stockmann's hymn (cf. number 20) for the chorus, which sings simultaneously with the bass. The soloist in his free text asks how Jesus's suffering and death can help him; the chorus does not answer him, but instead adds their own chorale comments to his declamation. BASS: Mein teurer Heiland, lass dich fragen, / Da du nunmehr an's Kreuz geschlagen, / Und selbst gesaget: es ist vollbracht! / Bin ich vom Sterben frei gemacht? / Kann ich durch deine Pein und Sterben / Das Himmelreich ererben? / Ist aller Welt Erlösung da? / Du kannst vor Schmerzen zwar nichts sagen, / Doch neigest du das Haupt und sprichst / stillschweigend: Ja, ja! (My dear Savior, let me ask Thee, / Now that Thou art nailed to the Cross, / And hast Thyself said: It is finished! / Am I made free of dying? / Can I through Thy pain and dying / Inherit the Kingdom of Heaven? /

Is redemption of the whole world there? / Thou canst really say nothing with pain, / Yet Thou bowest Thy head and sayest: / in silence: Yes, yes!) CHORUS: Jesu, der du warest tot, / lebest nun ohn' Ende. / In der letzten Todesnot / nirgend mich hinwende, / als zu dir, der mich versühnt! / O mein trauter Herre! / Gib mir nur, was du verdient, / Mehr ich nicht begehre. (Jesus, Thou who wert dead, / now livest forever. / In my last pain of death / let me not turn anywhere, / than to Thee, who atonest for me! / O my beloved Lord! / Give me only what Thou hast won, / More I do not desire.)

61. *Recitative.* EVANGELIST. Und siehe da, der Vorhang im Tempel zerriss in zwei Stück, von oben bis unten aus. Und die Erde erbebete und die Felsen zerrissen, und die Gräber taten sich auf, und stunden auf viele Leiber der Heiligen! (And see there; the veil of the Temple was torn in two parts from the top to the bottom. And the earth quaked and the rocks were rent, and graves opened, and many bodies of saints arose.)

62. *Arioso — Tenor — free text: two flutes, two oboi da caccia (English horns), strings, continuo.* The regretful Peter might well be cast as the actor in this number, as he was presumed to be for numbers 19 and 32. There is a motif of movement, coming out of the words of the text, which Bach aptly illustrates both vocally and instrumentally. Mein Herz! indem die ganze Welt / Bei Jesu Leiden gleichfalls leidet, / Die Sonne sich in Trauer kleidet, / Der Vorhang reisst, der Fels zerfällt, / Die Erde bebt, die Gräber spalten, / Weil sie den Schöpfer sehn erkalten. / Was willst du deines Ortes tun? (My heart! While the whole world / Suffers likewise over Jesus's sufferings, / The sun conceals itself in mourning, / The

veil tears, the rock falls apart, / The earth trembles, graves split open, / Because they see the Creator turn cold. / What will you [my heart] do in your place?)

63. *Aria — Soprano — free text: one flute, two English horns, a bassoon, continuo.* The pathos, infused by the grief motif of this da capo aria, seems to indicate that the soloist is Mary, the Mother of Jesus. The da capo returns to her mourning, even though Bach has combined her sadness with another motif of beatific peace. Zerfliesse, mein Herze, in Fluten der Zähren, den Höchsten zu ehren. / Erzähle der Welt und dem Himmel die Not, dein Jesus ist tot! (Dissolve, my heart, in floods of tears, to honor the Highest. / Tell the world and heaven of your affliction; thy Jesus is dead!)

For its musical expression of emotion, this aria is the climax of this passion.

64. *Recitative.* EVANGELIST. Die Juden aber dieweil es der Rüsttag war, dass nicht die Leichname am Kreuze bleiben den Sabbat über (denn desselbigen Sabbatstag war sehr gross) baten sie Pilatum, dass ihre Beine gebrochen, und sie abgenommen würden. Da kamen die Kriegsknechte und brachen dem ersten die Beine, und dem andern, der mit ihm gekreuziget war. Als sie aber zu Jesu kamen, und sie sahen, dass er schon gestorben war, brachen sie ihm die Beine nicht, sondern der Kriegsknechte einer eröffnete seine Seite mit einem Speer, und alsobald ging Blut und Wasser heraus. Und der das gesehen hat, der hat es bezeuget, und sein Zeugnis ist wahr, und derselbige weiss, dass er die Wahrheit saget, auf dass ihr glaubet. Denn solches ist geschehen, auf dass die Schrift erfüllet würde: Ihr sollet ihm kein Bein zerbrechen, und abermal spricht eine andere Schrift: Sie werden sehen, in welchen sie gestochen haben. (The Jews, however, because it was the preparation, so that the bodies should not remain on the cross over the Sabbath [for the same Sabbath Day was very high] asked Pilate that their legs be broken and that they would be taken down. Then the soldiers came and broke the legs of the first and of the other one who was crucified with Him But when they came to Jesus, and saw that He was already dead, they did not break His legs, but one of the soldiers opened His side with a spear, and thereupon blood and water went out. And he who has seen that he has testified to it, and his testimony is true, and he knows that he tells the truth, so that you believe. For such happened, so that the Scripture would be fulfilled: Ye shalt not break any bone of His, and again another Scripture saith: They will see Him whom they pierced.)

65. *Chorale.* This is verse 8 of Calvisius's German version of the Latin hymn by Michael Weisse (cf. number 21), which begins, "Christus, der uns selig macht" (Christ, who makes us blessed). O hilf, Christe, Gottes Sohn, / durch dein bittres Leiden, / dass wir dir stets untertan, / all' Unglück meiden. / Deinen Tod und sein' Ursach' / fruchtbarlich bedenken. / Dafür, wie wohl arm und schwach, / dir Dankopfer schenken. (O help, Christ, God's Son, / Through Thy bitter suffering, / So that we may always be subject to Thee, / And avoid all misfortune. / Thy death and its cause / May we meditate fruitfully upon it. / For that, although we are poor and weak, / We may make thankofferings to Thee.)

66. *Recitative.* EVANGELIST. Darnach bat Pilatum Joseph von Arimathia, der ein Jünger Jesu war (doch heimlich, aus Furcht von den Juden), dass er möchte abnehmen

den Leichnam Jesu. Und Pilatus erlaubete es. Derwegen kam er und nahm den Leichnam Jesu herab. Es kam auch Nikodemus, der vormals in der Nacht zu Jesu kommen war, und brachte Myrrhen und Aloen untereinander, bei hundert Pfunden. Da nahmen sie den Leichnam Jesu, und bunden ihn in leinen Tücher mit Spezereien, wie die Juden pflegen zu begraben. Es war aber an der Stätte, da er gekreuziget ward, ein Garten, und im Garten ein neu Grab, in welches niemand je gelegen war. Daselbst hin legten sie Jesum, um des Rüsttags willen der Juden, dieweil das Grab nahe war. (After that, Joseph of Arimathea, who was a disciple of Jesus [but secretly out of fear of the Jews], asked Pilate whether he might take down the body of Jesus. And Pilate allowed that. Therefore he came and took down the body of Jesus. Nicodemus came also; he who had come earlier to Jesus by night, and brought a mixture of myrrh and aloes, about a hundred pound weight. Then they took the body of Jesus, bound it in linen cloth with spices, as the Jews are accustomed to bury. There was in the place where He was crucified a garden, and in the garden a new sepulchre into which no one had ever been laid. Therein they laid Jesus because of the Jews' preparation day and because the sepulchre was near.)

67. *Chorus — free text, with da capo of the whole text.* All instruments play (tutti), with unison singing by the choir as in all the chorales in this passion. With the opening chorus, it stands as one of the pillars between which the play was enacted. The final number (68) is a chorale with a prayer for its text which will serve as an epilogue to the drama.

This special chorus has an instrumental prelude and postlude on the same melody that accompanies the choir. The heart-rending melancholy of its grief motif in the first two lines changes, however, to a confident joy motif of faith and hope in the second two lines. It resembles a full da capo aria, but is sung by the whole chorus — in this way, it seems to be special. Ruht wohl, ruht wohl, ihr heiligen Gebeine, / die ich nun weiter nicht beweine. / Ruht wohl, ruht wohl und bringt auch mich zur Ruh'. / Das Grab, so euch bestimmet ist, / und ferner keine Not umschliesst, / Macht mir den Himmel auf und schliesst die Hölle zu. (Rest well, rest well, you sacred bones, / Over which I do not now weep any longer. / Rest well, rest well, and bring me also to rest. / The grave, that is intended for you / and contains no further agony, / Opens Heaven and closes Hell to me.)

68. *Chorale.* The text for this final hymn is verse 3 of "Herzlich lieb hab' ich dich, O Herr" (From my heart I love Thee, O Lord), a funeral hymn (1571) by Martin Schalling (1532–1608), set to music by Bernard Schmidt of the same period from an anonymous melody first published in 1577. Its prayer-like thought makes a suitable conclusion and it would be well known to the Lutheran congregation of Bach's time. Ach Herr, lass dein lieb' Engelein / am letzten End' die Seele mein / in Abrahams Schoss tragen! / Den Leib in sein'm Schlafkämmerlein / gar sanft ohn' ein'ge Qual und Pein, / ruhn bis am jüngsten Tage! / Alsdann vom Tod erwecke mich, / dass meine Augen sehen dich / in aller Freud, o Gottes Sohn, / mein Heiland und Gnadenthron! / Herr Jesu Christ, erhöre mich, / ich will dich preisen ewiglich! (Ah, Lord, let Thy dear little angel / Carry my soul at my end / Into Abraham's bosom! / Let my body in its little sleeping chamber / Rest quietly without any torment or pain until the Judgment

Day! / Then from death awaken me, / So that my eyes see Thee / In all joy, O Son of God, / My Savior and

Throne of mercy! / Lord Jesus Christ, hear me: / I will praise Thee eternally!)

# The St. Matthew Passion

## Leipzig 1727 or 1729; BWV 244

Picander was the librettist for this, the greatest and most lengthy of Bach's passion settings. Although its first performance in St. Thomas's Church has been thought to be April 15, 1729, it may have been performed April 11, 1727 (cf. Boyd, 142). The next presentation was in St. Thomas's on March 30, 1736, when Bach placed the chorale "O Mensch, bewein' dein' Sünde gross" (O man, bewail thy great sin), from the original beginning of the *St. John Passion* to the end of Part I of the *St. Matthew*. Bach made further revisions after 1740 for the version that we hear today.

Some comment on the chorale as a lyrical and as a dramatic element in Bach's passions should be made before examining Bach's masterpiece and the greatest achievement in this genre. Apparently Handel, Keiser, Telemann and Mattheson thought that the chorale was outdated, replaced by arias and choruses set in the new da capo operatic style, yet Bach alone among his contemporary composers still regarded the chorale as contributing to the unfolding of the drama, and therefore used these church hymns with his passions. In this he was following Lutheran tradition of the 17th century, although the increasing number of arias in this passion, as opposed to the previous two, show that he was not at all adverse to the new trend.

Bach's chorales, whether used in his vocal or for his organ compositions, were Protestant in their idea, being based on hymns sung in Lutheran churches during and after the Reformation. Sometimes Bach would set the text to be plainly sung (in the final movement of many of his cantatas), and often decorate the chorale text with his own musical inventions or embellishments (usually in the chorale fantasias forming the first movement of one of his chorale cantatas, so called because each contained one or more chorales).

The composer's innate religious feelings inspired him to compose fantasias on these chorales; such texts, like those of the choruses and arias that he set, motivated him to create suitable melodies for them. For Bach, the meaning of the words provides him with the necessary stimulation to express them musically.

For his libretti, Bach chose the works of such poets as Gerhardt, Neumeister and Picander, who seemed to write poetry with a sense of music in their lines. But when he tried himself to compose or edit poetry, he did not always succeed. Bach's musical settings for those texts that he carefully selected proved that as a musician he could be as appreciative of the poet's skill with words as he himself was with the melodies that they evoked for him.

The names and dates of the librettists and the composers of the melodies, and the musical form for each chorale of *The St. Matthew Passion* are as follows:

*Number* 1. Words—Nicolaus Decius

(d. 1541); Melody—Nicolaus Decius (1542 and 1545); Form—The Chorale (Soprano ripieno) is independent of the Double Chorus; there are two orchestras, each with two flutes, two oboes, strings, organ and continuo

*Number 3*. Words—Johann Heermann (1585–1647); Melody—Johann Crüger (1598–1662); Form—simple: flutes, oboes, strings, organ, continuo

*Number 16*. Words—Paul Gerhardt (1607–76); Melody—Heinrich Isaak (c.1440–c.1530); Form—simple: two oboes, strings, organ, continuo

*Number 21*. Words—Paul Gerhardt (1607–76); Melody—Hans Leo Hassler (1564–1612); Form—simple: two flutes, two oboes, strings, organ, continuo

*Number 23*. Words—Paul Gerhardt (as in 21 above); Melody—Hans Leo Hassler (as in 21 above); Form—simple: two oboes, strings, organ, continuo

*Number 25*. Words—Johann Heermann (as in 1 above); Melody—Johann Crüger (as in 1 above); Form—The Chorale (soprano, alto, tenor, bass) is sung with the strings, organ, continuo in three detached phrases, interrupting the Tenor Recitative which is accompanied by two flutes, two oboes da caccia, organ and continuo

*Number 31*. Words—Albrecht, Margrave of Brandenburg-Culmbach (1522–59); Melody—Anonymous (from a French chanson of 1529); Form—simple: two flutes, two oboes, strings, organ, continuo

*Number 35*. Words—Sebald Heyden (d. 1561); Melody—Matthäus Greitter (d. 1550 or 1552); Form—Chorale Fantasia: two flutes, two oboes d'amore, strings, organ, continuo

*Number 38*. Words—Adam Reissner (Reusner) (1496–1575); Melody—Seth Calvisius (1556–1615); Form—simple: two flutes, two oboes, strings, organ, continuo

*Number 44*. Words—Paul Gerhardt (cf. No. 16); Melody—Heinrich Isaak (cf. No. 16); Form—simple: two flutes, two oboes, strings, organ, continuo

*Number 48*. Words: Johann Rist (1607–67); Melody—Johann Schop (d. circa 1664); Form—simple: two flutes, two oboes, strings, organ, continuo

*Number 53*. Words—Paul Gerhardt (cf. No. 21); Melody—Hans Leo Hassler (cf. No. 21); Form—simple: two flutes, two oboes, strings, organ, continuo

*Number 55*. Words—Johann Heermann (cf. No. 3); Melody—Johann Crüger (cf. No. 3); Form—simple: two flutes, two oboes, strings, organ, continuo

*Number 63*. Words—Paul Gerhardt (cf. No. 21); Melody—Hans Leo Hassler (cf. No. 21); Form—simple: two flutes, two oboes, strings, organ, continuo

*Number 72*. Words—Paul Gerhardt (cf. No. 21); Melody—Hans Leo Hassler (cf. No. 21); Form—simple: two flutes, two oboes, strings, organ, continuo

Gradually during the 18th century, even the chorales, as well as the choruses and the arias, were sung by the choir or by soloists alone, rather than by the congregation which had always before joined in with the choir.

The Good Friday, April 15, 1729, performance of the *St. Matthew Passion* in St. Thomas's must have required the full afternoon; accordingly the vesper service would have to be curtailed or eliminated on that occasion.

Bach must have chosen the chorales himself and supervised the Biblical text for the recitatives in addition to the arias and the choruses composed by his librettist, Picander (cf. Spitta II, 537). He divided the story into two parts: the first, from St. Matthew, ch. 26 to verse 56, the second, verse 57 to the end of ch. 26 and all of ch. 27.

The idea for the gigantic scale of the *St. Matthew Passion* may have occurred to Bach from the double choir and the double orchestra writing of the Venetian composer Giovanni Gabrieli (1557–1612) who was followed in Germany by first Michael Praetorius (1571–1621), then Heinrich Schütz (1585–1672), and finally by Johann Christoph Bach (1642–1703) — Johann Sebastian's uncle. However, Johann Sebastian's conception surpasses them all.

Bach uses two 4-part choruses, with another soprano choir to sing the ripieno chorale of the first movement, and two orchestras, each having two flutes, two oboes, a bassoon, strings and an organ. Additional instruments are a viola da gamba, two recorders and three various oboes; thus the instrumental players must be numerous, even though some may play more than one instrument.

The soloists are soprano, alto, tenor, bass in *each* chorus, with an extra tenor (Evangelist) and an extra bass (Jesus) from Choir I. These soloists from each chorus sing the arias and act the roles of the minor characters. They also sing some of the recitatives.

Although the active character portrayal is focused on the recitatives, a vital part in this passion is played by the arias, choruses and chorales. The general opinion is that this passion is more reflective and emotional than the *St. John.* While both are dramatic, the increased number of arias (15 as opposed to 8) would lead to this judgment, but this is not to say

that the *St. Matthew* is less spectacular than the *St. John.*

The disposition of the choirs with their own orchestras was to the left and right sides of the choir loft in St. Thomas's Church. Usually, vocalists are accompanied by the instrumentalists of the orchestra assigned to their chorus. This will be indicated by 1 or 2 for the singers, and I or II for the orchestras.

## CAST

Evangelist — Tenor 1; Jesus — Bass 1, Joseph of Arimathea — Bass 1; Judas, Petrus (Peter), Pilatus (Pilate), Pontifex (High Priest) — Bass 1; Testis (Witnesses) — Alto 1, 2; Ancillae (Maids), Uxor Pilati (Pilate's Wife) — Soprano 1, 2; Die Tochter Zion (The Daughter of Zion) — Chorus 1 or Alto 1; Die Gläubigen (The Faithful) (or The Believers) — Chorus 2.

## PART I

1. *Choruses 1 and 2 — tutti on a free text, accompanied by flutes, oboes, strings and continuo of both I and II.* The interpolated chorale of ripieno sopranos is doubled by the organs of I and II; this chorale is verse 1 of a translation of "Agnus Dei, qui tollis peccata mundi" (Lamb of God, who removes the sin of the world) — "O Lamm Gottes unschuldig" (O Lamb of God, innocent) by Nikolaus Decius (d. 1541).

Bach conceives the dramatic idea of one Daughter of Zion summoning the other women of Jerusalem to grieve with her. He thus changes Picander's original setting of an aria with a chorus to full choruses representing combined tumult and grief motifs throughout.

DAUGHTER OF ZION — *Chorus 1* — Kommt, ihr Töchter, helft mir klagen ... Sehet! (Come, ye daughters, help me lament ... See!) FAITHFUL — *Chorus 2:* Wen? (Whom?) DAUGHTER OF ZION: ...den Bräutigam. Sehet ihn (...the Bridegroom. See him) FAITHFUL: Wie? (How?) DAUGHTER OF ZION: ...als wie ein Lamm. (...like a Lamb.) CHORALE: O Lamm Gottes unschuldig / Am Stamm des Kreuzes geschlachtet, (O guiltless Lamb of God / Slaughtered on the trunk of the Cross,) DAUGHTER OF ZION: Sehet! (See!) FAITHFUL: Was? (What?) DAUGHTER OF ZION: Sehet die Geduld. (See His patience.) CHORALE: All' Sünd hast du getragen / Sonst müssten wir verzagen. (All sin hast Thou borne, / Or else we must have despaired.) DAUGHTER OF ZION: Sehet ihn aus Lieb und Huld / Holz zum Kreuze selber tragen. (See Him, out of love and kindness, / Himself carrying wood for the Cross.) CHORALE: Erbarm dich unser, O Jesu! (Have mercy on us, O Jesus!)

The antiphonal effect of the two choirs produces an intensely dramatic dialogue, into which Bach adds the chorale verses, thus making a striking opening number: a combination of chorus, dialogue and chorale. Even in his cantatas to this date, he has not ventured so far.

2. *Recitative.* EVANGELIST: Da Jesus diese Rede vollendet hatte, sprach er zu seinen Jüngern: (When Jesus had finished this speech, He said to His disciples:) JESUS: Ihr wisset, dass nach zween Tagen Ostern wird, und des Menschen Sohn wird überantwortet werden, dass er gekreuziget werde. (Ye know that after two days will be the Passover, and the Son of man will be betrayed, so that He be crucified.)

Note Bach's melody on *gekreuziget* in the shape of a cross to illustrate the word "crucified."

3. *Chorale 1 and 2.* Unison singing by both choirs accompanied by their orchestras makes this first chorale number as effective a commentary as it was for the first chorale number (7) in the *St. John Passion.* Here it is the first verse of the hymn by Johann Heermann (1585–1647) with the melody by Johann Crüger (1598–1662). Herzliebster Jesu, was hast du verbrochen, / Dass man ein solch scharf Urteil hat gesprochen? / Was ist die Schuld? / In was für Missetaten bist du geraten? (Beloved Jesus, what crime has Thou committed, / That they have pronounced such a harsh judgment? / What is Thy guilt? / Into what kind of misdeeds has Thou come?)

4. *Recitative.* EVANGELIST: Da versammleten sich die Hohenpriester und Schriftgelehrten und die Ältesten im Volk in den Palast des Hohenpriesters, der da hiess Kaiphas. Und hielten Rat, wie sie Jesum mit Listen griffen und töteten. Sie sprachen aber: (Then the chief priests and the elders of the people assembled together in the palace of the high priest, who was called Caiaphas. And they consulted how they might seize Jesus by cunning and kill Him. But they said:)

5. *Choruses 1 and 2 — turba (tumult) motif, but short.* Ja, nicht auf das Fest, auf dass nicht ein Aufruhr werde im Volk. (Yes, not on the feast day, so that there may not be an uproar among the people.)

6. *Recitative.* Secco, but note the descriptive music Bach employs for *köstlichem Wasser* and the water motif for the clause *und goss es auf sein Haupt.* EVANGELIST: Da nun Jesus war zu Bethanien, im Hause Simonis, des Aussätzigen, trat zu ihm ein Weib, das hatte ein Glas mit köstlichem Wasser, und goss es auf sein Haupt, da er zu Tische sass. Da das seine

Jünger sahen, wurden sie unwillig und sprachen: (Now when Jesus was in Bethany, in the house of Simon the leper, a woman came to Him. She had a glass with precious liquid and poured it over His head, as He sat at the table. When the disciples saw that, they became unwilling and said:)

7. *Chorus 1; I—flutes, oboes, strings and organ continuo.* Wozu dient dieser Unrat? Dieses Wasser hätte mögen teuer verkauft, und den Armen gegeben werden. (Why this nonsense? This ointment might have been sold for much and given to the poor.)

8. *Recitative; I—strings and continuo.* EVANGELIST: Da das Jesus merkete, sprach er zu ihnen: (When Jesus noticed that, He said to them:) JESUS: Was bekümmert ihr das Weib? Sie hat ein gut Werk an mir getan. Ihr habt allezeit Armen bei euch, mich aber habt ihr nicht allezeit. Dass sie dies Wasser hat auf meinen Leib gegossen, hat sie getan, dass man mich begraben wird. Wahrlich, ich sage euch: Wo dies Evangelium geprediget wird in der ganzen Welt, da wird man auch sagen zu ihrem Gedächtnis, was sie getan hat. (Why does the woman worry you? She has done a good work for Me. You always have the poor with you, but you do not have Me with you always. That she has poured this ointment on my body, she did it so that I will be buried. Verily, I say to you: Where this gospel will be preached in the whole world, there they will also say in her memory what she has done.)

9. *Recitative—Alto 1; I—flutes and continuo.* The flutes play a grief motif during her declamation which comments on Jesus's words. She will enlarge upon this sadness in her following aria. She may be identified as one of the women summoned by the Daughter of Zion in the opening number, or as the Daughter of Zion herself, who is an alto. Du lieber Heiland du, / Wenn deine Jünger töricht streiten, / Dass dieses fromme Weib / Mit Salben deinen Leib / Zum Grabe will bereiten, / So lasse mir inzwischen zu, / Von meiner Augen Tränenflüssen / Ein Wasser auf dein Haupt zu giessen. (Thou, Thou dear Redeemer, / When Thy disciples foolishly quarrel / That this pious woman wishes / With ointment to prepare Thy body / For the grave, / Then let me meanwhile / By the floods of tears from my eyes / Pour water on Thy head.)

10. *Aria—Alto 1, free text, da capo; II—flutes and continuo.* The same woman as above bewails her sins in a combined grief and tear motif to the melody of a minuet, an unusual juxtaposition of theme and melody. Buss und Reu / Knirscht das Sündenherz entzwei, / Dass die Tropfen meiner Zähren / Angenehme Spezerei, / Treuer Jesu, dir gebären. (Penance and remorse / Grind the sinful heart apart, / So that the drops of my tears / May bring forth a pleasant anointing / To Thee, faithful Jesus.)

11. *Recitative; I—continuo.* EVANGELIST: Da ging hin der Zwölfen einer, mit Namen Judas Ischarioth, zu den Hohenpriestern und sprach: (Then one of the twelve, named Judas Iscariot, went away to the chief priests and said:) JUDAS—BASS 1: Was wollt ihr mir geben? Ich will ihn euch verraten. (What will you give me? I will betray Him to you.) EVANGELIST: Und sie boten ihm dreissig Silberlinge. Und von dem an suchte er Gelegenheit, dass er ihn verriete. (And they offered him thirty silver coins. And from then on he sought an opportuntiy to betray Him.)

12. *Aria—Soprano 2—free text, da capo; II—flutes, strings and continuo.*

Both the intonation of her voice and the falling melody of the flutes imbue this aria with a grief motif full of deeply felt sorrow. Repetitions and melismas on *blute* (bleed) and the treachery indicated in the text show that Bach is well aware of the poignant melancholy to be expressed in music from such an aria. The "actress" here is probably one of the Faithful from Chorus 2. Blute nur, du liebes Herz! / Ach, ein Kind, das du erzogen, / Das an deiner Brust gesogen, / Droht den Pfleger zu ermorden, / Denn es ist zur Schlange worden. (Just bleed, Thou dear heart! / Ah, a child that Thou hast reared, / That has sucked at Thy breast, / Threatens to murder its guardian, / For it has become a snake.)

13. *Recitative; I—continuo.* EVANGELIST: Aber am ersten Tage der süssen Brot traten die Jünger zu Jesu und sprachen zu ihm: (On the first day of the feast of the unleavened bread, the disciples came to Jesus and said to Him:)

14. *Chorus 1; I—one oboe, strings, continuo.* The direct reply of the disciples' chorus here and in the following recitative brings the Evangelist's words to life. Wo willst du, dass wir dir bereiten, das Osterlamm zu essen? (Where wilt Thou that we prepare for Thee to eat the Passover?)

15. *Recitative—Evangelist, Jesus and Chorus; I—strings and continuo.* EVANGELIST: Er sprach: (He spoke:) JESUS: Gehet hin in die Stadt zu einem, und sprecht zu ihm: Der Meister lässt dir sagen: Meine Zeit ist hie, ich will bei dir die Ostern halten mit meinen Jüngern. (Go into the city to someone and say to him: the Master saith: My time is nigh. I will keep the Passover at your house with My disciples.) EVANGELIST: Und die Jünger taten, wie ihnen Jesus befohlen

hatte, und bereiteten das Osterlamm. Und am Abend setzte er sich zu Tische mit den Zwölfen. Und da sie assen, sprach er: (And the disciples did as Jesus had ordered, and prepared the Passover. And in the evening He sat down at the table with the twelve. And as they ate, He said:) JESUS: Wahrlich ich sage euch: Einer unter euch wird mich verraten. (Verily I say unto you: One among you will betray Me.) EVANGELIST: Und sie wurden sehr betrübt, und huben an, ein jeglicher unter ihnen, und sagten zu ihm: (And they became very sad, and began, each one among them, to say to Him:) CHORUS 1: Herr, bin ich's? (Lord, is it I?)

16. *Chorale—1 and 2; I and II— oboes, strings, continuo.* This is verse 5 of the hymn by Paul Gerhardt, "O welt, sieh' hier dein Leben" (O World, see here thy Life), with its melody by Heinrich Isaak (b.c. 1440). Bach used this chorale also in the *St. John Passion,* number 15.

The dramatic effect here is that it shows the guilt complex of each disciple in supposing himself as the betrayer, and the same guilty feeling on the part of each member of the congregation whom the choruses represent. Ich bin's, ich sollte büssen, / An Händen und an Füssen / Gebunden in der Höll'! / Die Geisseln und die Banden, / Und was du ausgestanden, / Das hat verdienet meine Seel'. (It is I who should atone, / On hand and foot / Bound in hell! / The scourges and the fetters, / And what Thou hast endured / My soul has deserved that.)

17. *Recitative—Evangelist, Jesus, Judas; I—strings and continuo.* EVANGELIST: Er antwortete und sprach: (He answered and said:) JESUS: Der mit der Hand mit mir in die Schüssel tauchet, der wird mich verraten. Des Menschen Sohn gehet

zwar dahin, wie von ihm geschrieben stehet; doch wehe dem Menschen, durch welchen des Menschen Sohn verraten wird. Es wäre ihm besser, dass derselbige Mensch noch nie geboren wäre. (He who dips his hand with Me in the dish, he will betray Me. The Son of man surely goes away as it is written of Him, but woe to the man by whom the Son of man is betrayed. It would be better for him, if the same man had never been born.) EVANGELIST: Da antwortete Judas, der ihn verriet, und sprach: (Then Judas, who betrayed Him, answered saying:) JUDAS — BASS 1: Bin ich's, Rabbi? (Is it I, Master?) EVANGELIST: Er sprach zu ihm: (He said to him:) JESUS: Du sagtest's. (Thou hast said so.) EVANGELIST: Da sie aber assen, nahm Jesus das Brot, dankete und brach's, und gab's den Jüngern und sprach: (As they were eating, Jesus took the bread, gave thanks and brake it, and gave it to the disciples, saying:) JESUS: Nehmet, esset, das ist mein Leib. (Take, eat, that is My body.) EVANGELIST: Und er nahm den Kelch, und dankete, gab ihnen den, und sprach: (And He took the cup, gave thanks, and gave it to the disciples, saying:) JESUS: Trinket alle daraus, das ist mein Blut des neuen Testaments, welches vergossen wird für viele, zur Vergebung der Sünden. Ich sage euch: Ich werde von nun an nicht mehr von diesem Gewächs des Weinstocks trinken, bis an den Tag, da ich's neu trinken werde mit euch in meines Vaters Reich. (Drink ye all out of it. That is My blood of the new Testament which is shed for many for the forgiveness of sins. I say to you: I shall not drink from now on any more from this growth of the vine, until the day when I shall drink it anew with you in My Father's Kingdom.) This is a very long recitative, but there is plenty of dramatic action in it. The hypocrisy of Judas in asking Jesus if he will betray Him is well delineated, but the realism of the first Communion is certain to impress the audience as one of the highlights of this passion.

18. *Recitative — Soprano 1, free text; I — two oboes d'amore and continuo.* This is a very moving number on the institution of the first Communion. Note the wave motif suggested to Bach by the words *Tränen schwimmt*, which he continues throughout the rest of this recitative. Wiewohl mein Herz in Tränen schwimmt, / Dass Jesus von uns Abschied nimmt, / So macht mich doch sein Testament erfreut; / Sein Fleisch und Blut, o Kostbarkeit, / Vermacht er mir in meine Hände. / Wie er es auf der Welt mit denen Seinen / Nicht böse können meinen, / So liebt er sie bis an das Ende. (Although my heart swims in tears / Because Jesus takes leave of us, / Yet His Testament makes me glad. / His flesh and blood, o preciousness, / He bequeaths into my hands. / As He, in the world with His own / Could mean no evil, / So He loves them to the end.)

19. *Aria — Soprano 1, free text; I — two oboes d'amore and continuo.* This is a continuation of the faithful woman's recitative (18), but now bursting forth in fine lyrical expression, with a prayer motif repeated by the da capo. Ich will dir mein Herze schenken, / Senke dich, mein Heil, hinein, / Ich will mich in dir versenken, / Ist die gleich dir Welt zu klein, / Ei, so sollst du mir allein / Mehr als Welt und Himmel sein. (I will give Thee my heart; / Sink Thyself into it, my Salvation. / I will submerge myself in Thee. / If the world is too small for Thee, / O, then shalt Thou be for me alone / More than world and heaven.)

20. *Recitative; I — strings and continuo.* EVANGELIST: Und da sie den Lobgesang gesprochen hatten, gingen sie hinaus an den Ölberg. Da sprach Jesus zu ihnen: (And when They had sung the hymn, they went out to the Mount of Olives. Then Jesus said to them:) JESUS: In dieser Nacht werdet ihr euch alle ärgern an mir, denn es stehet geschrieben: Ich werde den Hirten schlagen, und die Schafe der Herde werden sich zerstreuen. Wann ich aber auferstehe, will ich vor euch hingehen in Galiläam. (In this night you will all be angry with Me, for it is written: I will smite the shepherd, and the sheep of the flock will be scattered. But when I arise again, I will go before you into Galilee.)

21. *Chorale — tutti 1 and 2; I and II.* The text is verse 5 of "O Haupt voll Blut und Wunden" (O Head full of blood and wounds) by Paul Gerhardt (1607–76), set to the melody "Herzlich tut mich verlangen" (I heartily long for) by Hans Leo Hassler (1564–1612).

This hymn has become symbolic of the *St. Matthew Passion,* although it occurs only five times out of the fifteen chorales used. Erkenne mich, mein Hüter, / Mein Hirte, nimm mich an! / Von dir, Quell aller Güter, / Ist mir viel Gut's getan. / Dein Mund hat mich gelabet / Mit Milch und süsser Kost, / Dein Geist hat mich begabet / Mit mancher Himmelslust. (Recognize me, my Protector, / My Shepherd, take me to Thee! / By Thee, Source of all good, / Much good has been done to me. / Thy mouth has refreshed me / With milk and sweet food; / Thy spirit has given me / Much heavenly pleasure.)

*Recitative; I — strings and continuo.* EVANGELIST: Petrus aber antwortete und sprach zu ihm: (Peter answered and said to Him:) PETER — BASS 1: Wenn sie auch alle sich an dir ärger-

ten, so will ich doch mich nimmermehr ärgern. (Even if they all should be angry at Thee, yet I will not be vexed.) EVANGELIST: Jesus sprach zu ihm: (Jesus said to him:) JESUS: Wahrlich, ich sage dir: In dieser Nacht, ehe der Hahn krähet, wirst du mich dreimal verleugnen. (Verily I say to thee: In this night, before the cock crows, thou shalt deny Me thrice.) EVANGELIST: Petrus sprach zu ihm: (Peter said to Him:) PETER — BASS 1: Und wenn ich mit dir sterben müsste, so will ich dich nicht verleugnen. (And if I had to die with Thee, yet I would not deny Thee.) EVANGELIST: Desgleichen sagten auch alle Jünger. (All the disciples also said likewise.)

23. *Chorale — tutti 1 and 2; I and II — oboes, strings, continuo.* This is verse 6 of the so-called "Passion Chorale" by Paul Gerhardt (cf. number 21), now reflecting on the vow that Peter has just made. Ich will bei dir stehen, / Verachte mich doch nicht! / Von dir will ich nicht gehen, / Wenn dir dein Herze bricht. / Wann dein Herz wird erblassen / Im letzten Todesstoss, / Alsdenn will ich dich fassen / In meinen Arm und Schoss. (I will stand here by Thee; / Do not despise me! / From Thee I will not go / Whenever Thy heart breaks. / When Thy heart grows pale / In the last pang of death, / Then I will clasp Thee / In my arms and lap.)

The two choirs express the sentiments of sympathy felt by each member of the congregation toward Jesus. Their sincere promise of loyalty to Jesus contrasts with the empty boast of Peter. Thus Bach brings the audience into indirect participation in the action of this drama.

24. *Recitative; I — strings and continuo.* EVANGELIST: Da kam Jesus mit ihnen zu einem Hofe, der hiess Gethsemane, und sprach zu seinen Jüngern: (Then Jesus came with them

to a courtyard called Gethsemane, and said to His disciples:) JESUS: Setzet euch hie, bis dass ich dorthin gehe und bete. (Sit here, until I go and pray yonder.) EVANGELIST: Und nahm zu sich Petrum und die zween Söhne Zebedai, und fing an zu trauern und zu zagen. Da sprach Jesus zu ihnen: (And He took with Him Peter and the two sons of Zebedee, and began to grieve and to hesitate. Then Jesus said to them:) JESUS: Meine Seele ist betrübt bis an den Tod; bleibet hie, und wachet mit mir. (My soul is sorrowful unto death. Stay here and watch with Me.)

*25. Recitative—Tenor 1, Chorus 2 with ripieno Soprano Chorus—free texts; I—two flutes or two recorders, two oboes da caccia and continuo, II—strings and continuo.* The chorale is verse 3 of "Herzliebster Jesu" (Beloved Jesus), (cf. number 3), which is sung in single lines by the ripieno sopranos after each pair of lines sung by the tenor. The tenor in this case may represent the Daughter of Zion, while the chorale interjections are uttered by the Faithful (the Believers). RECITATIVE—TENOR I: O Schmerz! Hier zittert das gequälte Herz! / Wie sinkt es hin, wie bleicht sein Angesicht! (O pain! Here trembles the tortured heart! / How it sinks; how His face pales!)

. . . . . . . . . . . . . . . . . . . . . . . . . . . . .

Der Richter führt ihn vor Gericht; / Da ist kein Trost, kein Helfer nicht. (The judge leads Him before the law court; / There is no comfort, no helper.)

. . . . . . . . . . . . . . . . . . . . . . . . . . . . .

Er leidet alle Höllenqualen; Er soll für fremden Raub bezahlen. (He suffers all the pains of hell; He must pay for the robbery of others.)

. . . . . . . . . . . . . . . . . . . . . . . . . . . . .

Ach! könnte meine Liebe dir, / Mein Heil, dein Zittern und dein Zagen / Vermindern oder helfen tragen, / Wie gerne blieb' ich hier! (Ah, could my love for Thee, / My Saviour, diminish or help Thee bear / Thy trembling and hesitation, / How gladly would I remain here!)

Chorale: (indicated by . . . . . . . . . above)

Was ist die Ursach' aller solcher Plagen? / Ach, meine Sünden haben dich geschlagen! / Ich, ach Herr Jesu, habe dies verschuldet, / was du erduldet! (What is the cause of all such woes? / Ah, my sins have stricken Thee! / Ah, Lord Jesus, it is I who have deserved this / That Thou hast suffered!)

*26. Aria—Tenor 1—free text—Chorus 2; I—1 oboe and continuo, II—two flutes, strings and continuo.* The dialogue method between the soloist and the chorus makes an interesting musical variation for this aria. There is a da capo of both parts and ritornelli before, after and in between for the instruments alone. ZION—TENOR I: Ich will bei meinem Jesu wachen, (I will watch beside my Jesus,) BELIEVERS—CHORUS 2: So schlafen unsre Sünden ein. (Then our sins go to sleep.) ZION—TENOR I: Meinen Tod büsset seiner Seelen Not. / Sein Trauren machet mich voll Freuden. (His soul's distress atones for my death. / His mourning makes me full of joy.) BELIEVERS—CHORUS 2: Drum muss uns sein verdienstlich Leiden / Recht bitter und doch süsse sein. (Therefore His deserving suffering must be / Really bitter and yet sweet for us.)

*27. Recitative; I—strings and continuo.* EVANGELIST: Und ging hin ein wenig, fiel nieder auf sein Angesicht, und betete und sprach: (And He went a little further away, fell down on His face, and prayed saying:) JESUS: Mein Vater, ist's möglich, so gehe dieser Kelch von mir; doch nicht wie ich will, sondern wie du willst. (My Father, if it is possible, let this cup go from Me; yet not as I will, but as Thou wilt.)

28. *Recitative—Bass 2—free text; II—strings and continuo.* It is difficult to assign a definite role for the bass in this number and in his following aria (number 29), since the disciples are absent from Jesus at this moment. One can only conjecture, therefore, that he is one of Jesus's followers, who is now later reflecting on the agony in Gethsemane. Der Heiland fällt vor seinem Vater nieder; dadurch erhebt er mich und alle von unserm Falle hinauf zu Gottes Gnade wieder. Er ist bereit, den Kelch des Todes Bitterkeit zu trinken, in welchen Sünden dieser Welt gegossen sind und hässlich stinken, weil es dem lieben Gott gefällt. (The Savior falls down before His Father, and thereby raises me and all men from our fall up again to God's grace. He is ready to drink the cup of death's bitterness into which the sins of this world are poured and stink horribly, because that pleases dear God.)

29. *Aria—Bass 2—free text; II—strings and continuo—da capo.* Gerne will ich mich bequemen / Kreuz und Becher anzunehmen, / Trink ich doch dem Heiland nach. / Denn sein Mund, / Der mit Milch und Honig fliesset, / Hat den Grund / Und des Leidens herbe Schmach / Durch den ersten Trunk versüsset. (Gladly will I accustom myself / To take Cross and Cup, / And I drink after my Savior. / For His mouth, / Which flows milk and honey, / Has made the reason / and the bitter shame of His suffering / Sweet through His first draught.)

There seems to be a certain mysterious restlessness in the melody of this aria which Bach may have intended to symbolize the Sacrament of Communion, or more probably, to

make the listener see how Christ's example should inspire him to face his own bitter cup of suffering on earth. A motif of obeisance or humility in the descending rhythm is replaced by a motif of confidence for the second part of the text, only to be changed back to the first motif in the da capo.

30. *Recitative—I strings, continuo.* EVANGELIST: Und er kam zu seinen Jüngern, und fand sie schlafend, und sprach zu ihnen: (And He came to His disciples and found them sleeping, and said to them:) JESUS: Könnet ihr denn nicht eine Stunde mit mir wachen? Wachet und betet, dass ihr nicht in Anfechtung fallet. Der Geist ist willig, aber das Fleisch ist schwach. (Could ye not watch with Me one hour? Watch and pray that ye fall not into temptation. The spirit is willing, but the flesh is weak.) EVANGELIST: Zum andern Mal ging er hin, betete und sprach: (He went away for the second time, prayed and said:) JESUS: Mein Vater, ist's nicht möglich, dass dieser Kelch von mir gehe, ich trinke ihn denn; so geschehe dein Wille. (My Father, if it is not possible that this cup go from Me, unless I drink it, then Thy will be done.)

31. *Chorale—tutti.* This chorale was composed by Albrecht, Margrave of Brandenburg-Culmbach (1522–57). Probably Bach inserted it at this point in Picander's libretto because it neatly fits the words of Jesus at the end of the preceding recitative (number 30). In fact, Bach had already composed a chorale cantata, BWV 111, on this same work in 1725, with the same opening verse. This cantata has been dated 1735–44 by Terry, but since Bach revised this passion after 1736, the date of the cantata is still earlier. Was mein Gott will, das g'scheh' allzeit, / Sein Will', der ist der beste. / Zu helfen den'n er ist bereit, / Die an ihn glauben feste. / Er hilft aus Not,

Der fromme Gott, / Und züchtiget mit Massen. / Wer Gott vertraut, / Fest auf ihn baut, / Den will er nicht verlassen. (What my God wills, that always happens, / His will, that is the best. / He is ready to help those / Who believe firmly in Him. / He helps [us] in need, / Our pious God, / And chastises moderately. / Whoever trusts God, / Builds firmly on Him, / Him will He not abandon.)

32. *Recitative; I—strings and continuo.* EVANGELIST: Und er kam und fand sie aber schlafend, und ihre Augen waren voll Schlaf's. Und er liess sie, und ging abermals hin und betete zum drittenmal, und redete dieselbigen Worte. Da kam er zu seinen Jüngern und sprach zu ihnen: (And He came and found them sleeping, and their eyes were full of sleep. And He left them, and went away again, and prayed for the third time, saying the same words. Then He came to His disciples and spoke to them:) JESUS: Ach! wollt ihr nun schlafen und ruhen? Siehe, die Stunde ist hie, dass des Menschen Sohn in der Sünder Hände überantwortet wird. Stehet auf, lasset uns gehen; siehe, er ist da, der mich verrät. (Ah! Do you now want to sleep and rest? Behold, the hour is here, when the Son of man is betrayed into sinners' hands. Stand up; let us go; behold, he is there who betrays Me.) EVANGELIST: Und als er noch redete, siehe, da kam Judas, der zwölfen einer, und mit ihm eine grosse Schar, mit Schwertern und mit Stangen, von den Hohenpriestern und Ältesten des Volks. Und der Verräter hatte ihnen ein Zeichen gegeben und gesagt: Welchen ich küssen werde, der ist's, den greifet. Und alsbald trat er zu Jesum und sprach: (And while He was still speaking, behold, there came Judas, one of the twelve, and with him a great crowd, with swords and staves, from the high

priests and elders of the people. And the betrayer had given them a sign, saying: Whom I shall kiss, He is the one, seize Him. And immediately he stepped up to Jesus, saying:) JUDAS—BASS 1: Gegrüsset sei'st du, Rabbi! (Greetings, Master!) EVANGELIST: Und küssete ihn. Jesus aber sprach zu ihm: (And kissed him. But Jesus said to him:) JESUS: Mein Freund, warum bist do kommen? (My friend, why dost thou come?) EVANGELIST: Da traten sie hinzu, und legten die Hände an Jesum, und griffen ihn. (Then they stepped up, laid hands on Jesus and seized Him.)

33. *Duet—Soprano 1, Alto 1, with Choruses 1 and 2—free text.* The dialogue is again featured in this duet between the Daughter of Zion (Soprano 1, Alto 1) and the Faithful (Believers) (Soprano Chorus 1), but ending in a double chorus. Note the tumult motif which Bach uses throughout to illustrate the violence in nature indicated by his text for the double chorus. Canon singing of Soprano and Alto representing the Daughter of Zion in themselves make this number really a double duet. DAUGHTER OF ZION: So ist mein Jesus nun gefangen. (So my Jesus is captured now.) FAITHFUL: Lasst ihn! haltet! bindet nicht! (Let Him go! stop! do not bind Him!) DAUGHTER OF ZION: Mond und Licht / Ist vor Schmerzen untergangen, / Weil mein Jesus ist gefangen. (Moon and light / Have disappeared from sorrow, / Because my Jesus is captured.) FAITHFUL: Lasst ihn! haltet! bindet nicht! (Release Him! halt! do not bind Him!) DAUGHTER OF ZION: Sie führen ihn, er ist gebunden. (They lead Him away; He is bound.) CHORUSES 1 AND 2: Sind Blitze, sind Donner in Wolken verschwunden? / Eröffne den feurigen Abgrund, o Hölle; / Zertrümmre, verderbe, verschlinge, zer-

schelle / Mit plötzlicher Wut / Den falschen Verräter, das mördrische Blut! (Have lightning and thunder vanished in clouds? / Open your fiery abyss, O hell; / Smash, ruin, engulf, shatter / With sudden rage / The false betrayer, the murderous blood!)

34. *Recitative; I—strings, continuo.* EVANGELIST: Und siehe, einer aus denen, die mit Jesu waren, reckete die Hand aus und schlug des Hohenpriesters Knecht und hieb ihm ein Ohr ab. Da sprach Jesus zu ihm: (And behold, one of those who were with Jesus stretched out his hand and struck a servant of the high priest, cutting off his ear. Then Jesus said to him:) JESUS: Stecke dein Schwert an seinen Ort; denn wer das Schwert nimmt, der soll durchs Schwert unkommen. Oder meinst du, dass ich nicht könnte meinen Vater bitten, dass er mir zuschickte mehr denn zwölf Legion Engel? Wie würde aber die Schrift erfüllet? Es muss also gehen. (Put thy sword in its place; for whoever takes the sword, he shall die by the sword. Or thinkest thou that I could not ask My Father to send Me more than twelve legions of angels? But how would the Scripture be fulfilled? So it must be.) EVANGELIST: Zu der Stund' sprach Jesus zu den Scharen: (At that hour Jesus said to the crowds:) JESUS: Ihr seid ausgegangen als zu einem Mörder, mit Schwerten und mit Stangen, mich zu fahen; bin ich doch täglich bei euch gesessen und habe gelehrt im Tempel, und ihr habt mich nicht gegriffen. Aber das ist alles geschehen, dass erfüllet würden die Schriften der Propheten. (You have gone out as against a murderer, with swords and staves to take Me. Yet I have sat daily with you, teaching in the Temple, and you did not seize Me. But all that was done, so that the Scriptures of the prophets would be fulfilled.)

EVANGELIST: Da verliessen ihn alle Jünger, und flohen. (Then all the disciples left Him and fled.)

35. *Chorale—tutti.* This is verse 1 of the hymn with the same title as its first line by Sebald Heyden (1525) on the melody of Matthäus Greitter (1525). This chorale was the original opening movement of Bach's *St. John Passion,* left unused until now. The grief motif in the voices as well as in the flutes and the oboes, though each are independent of the other, moves the listener to reflect on how he too has betrayed Christ. O Mensch, bewein' dein Sünde gross; / Darum Christus sein's Vaters Schoss / Äussert und kam auf Erden; / Von einer Jungfrau rein und zart / Für uns er hie geboren ward, / Er wollt' der Mittler werden; / Den'n Toten er das Leben gab, / Und legt' dabei all' Krankheit ab, / Bis sich die Zeit herdränge, / Dass er für uns geopfert würd', / Trüg' unser Sünden schwere Bürd' / Wohl an dem Kreuze lange. (O man, bewail thy great sin. / Therefore from His Father's bosom / Christ departed and came to earth. / Of a Virgin pure and tender / He was born for us here. / He wanted to become the Mediator. / To those dead He gave life, / And removed all sickness also. / Until the time arrived / That He would be sacrificed for us, / He would carry the heavy burden of our sins / Right along to the Cross.)

## PART II

36. *Aria—Alto 1, with Chorus 2—free texts; I—flute, oboe d'amore, strings, continuo; II strings and continuo.* The daughter of Zion (Alto 1) and the Faithful (Chorus 2) reappear here to converse in dialogue again, just as Bach had represented them both in numbers 1, 26, 33 and perhaps

the Daughter of Zion alone in numbers 9 and 10.

The Daughter of Zion is now in despair; the Faithful try to comfort her. The distracted terror motif in her voice contrasts with the motif of calm in the choir's replies, both in words and the music evoked therefrom. DAUGHTER OF ZION: Ach! nun ist mein Jesus hin! (Ah! Now is my Jesus gone!) FAITHFUL: Wo ist denn dein Freund hingegangen, O du schönste unter den Weibern? (Where has thy Friend gone, O thou fairest among women?) DAUGHTER OF ZION: Ist es möglich; kann ich schauen? (Is it possible? Can I look at it?) FAITHFUL: Wo hat sich dein Freund hingewandt? (Where has thy Friend strayed?) DAUGHTER OF ZION: Ach! mein Lamm in Tigerklauen! / Ach! Wo ist mein Jesus hin? (Ah! my Lamb in tiger's claws! / Ah! Where has my Jesus gone?) FAITHFUL: So wollen wir mit dir ihn suchen. (Then we want to seek Him with thee.) DAUGHTER OF ZION: Ach! was soll ich der Seele sagen, / Wenn sie mich wird ängstlich fragen? / Ach! wo ist mein Jesus hin? (Ah! what am I to say to my soul, / When it will ask me anxiously? / Ah! where has my Jesus gone?)

Note the coloratura on *Tigerklauen* (tiger's claws) with three stabs in the melody.

37. *Recitative; I — continuo.* EVANGE-LIST: Die aber Jesum gegriffen hatten, führeten ihn zu dem Hohenpriester Kaiphas, dahin die Schriftgelehrten und Ältesten sich versammelt hatten. Petrus aber folgete ihm nach von ferne, bis in den Palast des Hohenpriesters, und ging hinein und setzte sich bei den Knechten, auf dass er sähe, wo es hinaus wollte. Die Hohenpriester aber und Ältesten, und der ganze Rat, suchten falsches Zeugnis wider Jesum, auf dass sie ihn töteten; und funden keines. (Those who had seized Jesus led Him to the high priest Caiaphas, where the scribes and the elders had assembled. But Peter followed him from afar up to the high priest's palace, and went in to sit with the servants, so that he might see how it would come out. The chief priests and the elders with all the council sought false witness against Jesus, so that they might kill Him, but they found nothing.)

38. *Chorale — tutti.* This is verse 5 of the 1533 hymn by Adam Reissner (Reusner) (1496–1575) "In dich hab' ich gehoffet" (In Thee have I trusted), set to the melody (1581) of Seth Calvisius (1556–1615). Mir hat die Welt trüglich gericht't / Mit Lügen und mit falschem G'dicht, / Viel Netz und heimlich Stricken, / Herr, nimm mein wahr in dieser G'fahr, / B'hüt mich vor falschen Tücken. (The world has judged me deceitfully / With lies and false invention, / With many a net and secret snares. / Lord, look after me in this danger, / Shield me from false malice.)

39. *Recitative; I — continuo; II — continuo.* EVANGELIST: Und wiewohl viel falsche Zeugen herzutraten, funden sie doch keins. Zuletzt traten herzu zween falsche Zeugen, und sprachen: (And although many false witnesses stepped forth, yet they found nothing. Finally two false witnesses came forward, saying:) WITNESS 1, 2 (ALTO 2, TENOR 2): Er hat gesagt: Ich kann den Tempel Gottes abbrechen und in dreien Tagen denselbigen bauen. (He has said: I can break down God's Temple and build the same in three days.) EVANGELIST: Und der Hohenpriester stund auf und sprach zu ihm: (And the high priest stood up and spoke to Him:) HIGH PRIEST — BASS 1: Antwortest du nichts zu dem, was diese wider dich zeugen? (Answerest Thou nothing to that which these people testify against

Thee.) EVANGELIST: Aber Jesus schwieg stille. (But Jesus kept quiet.)

There is much dramatic development to the action in this number, even though only minor characters appear. Note tht the two false witnesses sing in canon to show that their story was thought up beforehand.

40. *Recitative — Tenor 2 — free text; II — oboes, viola da gamba and continuo*. Again we hear a grief motif in the melody, heightened by the viola da gamba playing pizzicato. For this number and in his following aria, the tenor might be expressing the thoughts of a spectator who has followed Peter into the palace, or those of a modern audience watching the play. Mein Jesus schweigt zu falschen Lügen stille, / Um uns damit zu zeigen, / Dass sein erbarmungsvoller Wille / Vor uns zum Leiden sei geneigt, / Und dass wir in der gleichen Pein / Ihm sollen ähnlich sein, / Und in Verfolgung stille schweigen. (My Jesus remains silent at false lying, / In order to show us thereby / That His merciful will / Is inclined to suffer for us, / And that we in the same agony / Should be like Him / And in persecution keep quiet.)

41. *Aria — Tenor 2 — free text; II — violoncello obbligato, continuo*. There is a pictorial quality painted by the obbligato cello in this da capo aria. An overall motif of calm includes a speaking motif with coloratura, which must have been suggested to Bach by the words *falsche Zungen* (false tongues) and *rächen* (avenge). Geduld, Geduld! / Wenn mich falsche Zungen stechen, / Leid' ich wider meine Schuld / Schimpf und Spott, / Ei! so mag der liebe Gott / Meines Herzens Unschuld rächen. (Patience, patience! / When false tongues sting me, / Against my guilt I suffer / Abuse and mockery. / Ah! then may dear God / Avenge the innocence of my heart.)

42. *Recitative*. EVANGELIST: Und der Hohenpriester antwortete und sprach zu ihm: (And the high priest answered and said to Him:) PONTIFEX (HIGH PRIEST) — BASS 1: Ich beschwöre dich bei dem lebendigen Gott, dass du uns sagest, ob du seiest Christus, der Sohn Gottes. (I entreat Thee by the living God to tell us, whether Thou be Christ, the Son of God.) EVANGELIST: Jesus sprach zu ihm: (Jesus said to him:) JESUS: Du sagtest's. Doch sage ich euch: Von nun an wird's geschehen, dass ihr sehen werdet des Menschen Sohn sitzen zur Rechten der Kraft, und kommen in den Wolken des Himmels. (Thou hast said so. Yet I tell you: From now on it will happen that you will see the Son of man sitting on the right of power, and coming in the clouds of heaven.) EVANGELIST: Da zerriss der Hohepriester seine Kleider, und sprach: (Then the high priest rent his clothes, saying:) PONTIFEX (HIGH PRIEST) — BASS 1: Er hat Gott gelästert. Was dürfen wir weiter Zeugnis? Siehe, jetzt habt ihr seine Gotteslästerung gehöret. Was denket euch? (He hath spoken blasphemy. Why do we need further testimony? Behold, now you have heard his blasphemy. What do you think?) EVANGELIST: Sie antworteten und sprachen: (They answered, saying:) CHORUSES 1 AND 2: Er ist des Todes schuldig! (He is guilty of death!)

Note the tonal picture that Bach paints for the arioso of Jesus: ". . . and coming in the clouds of heaven."

43. *Recitative*. EVANGELIST: Da speieten sie aus in sein Angesicht, und schlugen ihn mit Fäusten. Etliche aber schlugen ihn ins Angesicht, und sprachen: (Then they spat into His face, and struck Him with their fists. Some hit Him in the face, saying:) CHORUSES 1 AND 2: Weissage uns, Christe, wer ist's, der dich schlug?

(Prophesy for us, Christ, who it is who struck Thee?)

44. *Chorale — tutti.* This is verse 3 of "O Welt, sieh' hier dein Leben" (O World, see here thy Life) by Paul Gerhardt (cf. number 16), suitably chosen for this moment in Bach's drama. Wer hat dich so geschlagen, / Mein Heil, und dich mit Plagen / So übel zugericht. / Du bist ja nicht ein Sünder, / Wie wir und unsre Kinder; / Von Missetaten weisst du nicht. (Who has struck Thee so, / My Savior, and condemned Thee / So badly with torment? / Thou art certainly not a sinner, / As we and our children; / Thou dost not know of misdeeds.)

45. *Recitative.* As in the opening number (36) of Part II, here again the dramatic action comes to life with dialogue between Peter, the two Maids and the Chorus representing the crowd in the high priest's palace. The instrumental groups are: I — continuo; II — flutes, oboes, strings, continuo.

EVANGELIST: Petrus aber sass draussen im Palast; und es trat zu ihm eine Magd, und sprach: (Peter sat outside the others in the palace; and a maid stepped up to him, saying:) AN-CILLA 1 (MAID 1) — SOPRANO 1: Und du warest auch mit dem Jesu aus Galiläa. (And Thou wert also with Jesus of Galilee.) EVANGELIST: Er leugnete aber vor ihnen allen, und sprach: (But he lied before them all, saying:) PETER — BASS 1: Ich weiss nicht, was du sagest. (I do not know what thou sayest.) EVANGELIST: Als er aber zur Tür hinausging, sahe ihn eine andere, und sprach zu denen, die da waren: (When he went out by the door, another maid saw him, and said to them who were there:) ANCILLA 2 (MAID 2) — SOPRANO 2: Dieser war auch mit dem Jesu von Nazareth. (This man was also with Jesus of

Nazareth.) EVANGELIST: Und er leugnete abermal und schwur dazu: (And he lied again and also swore:) PETER — BASS 1: Ich kenne des Menschen nicht. (I do not know this Man.) EVANGELIST: Und über eine kleine Weile traten hinzu, die da stunden, und sprachen zu Petro: (And after a little while there came up those that stood by, and said to Peter:) CHORUS 2: Wahrlich, du bist auch einer von denen, denn deine Sprache verrät dich. (Truly, thou art also one of them, for thy speech betrayeth thee.)

46. *Recitative.* EVANGELIST: Da hub er an sich zu verfluchen und schwören. (Then he began to curse and swear.) PETER — BASS 1: Ich kenne des Menschen nicht. (I do not know the Man.) EVANGELIST: Und alsbald krähete der Hahn. Da dachte Petrus an die Worte Jesu, da er zu ihm sagte: ehe der Hahn krähen wird, wirst du mich dreimal verleugnen. Und ging heraus, und weinete bitterlich. (And immediately the cock crew. Then Peter thought about the words of Jesus, when He said to him: Before the cock crows, thou shalt deny Me thrice. And he went out and wept bitterly.)

As though to emphasize the emotions of Peter, Bach writes artistic runs on the words *weinete* (wept) and *bitterlich* (bitterly).

47. *Aria — Alto 1 — free text; I — solo violin, strings, continuo.* This da capo aria is one of the most beautiful that Bach ever composed. The lingering melancholy of the grief motif combined with a tear motif, plus the flowing harmony accompanied by pizzicato strings make a lasting impression on the listener.

The alto must here be acting in the role of Peter as he repents for his denial. Bach derives the emotion from the italicized words and from the instrumental ritornelli. *Erbarme dich / Mein Gott, um meiner Zähren willen; / Schaue hier, / Herz und Auge weint vor dir bitterlich. / Erbarme dich, / Mein Gott, um meiner Zähren* willen. (Have mercy / My God, for the sake of my *tears*; / *Look here!* / Heart and eye *weep* for Thee / *Bitterly. / Have mercy, My God,* for the sake of my *tears*.)

48. *Chorale — tutti.* This is verse 6 of the hymn "Werde munter, mein Gemüthe" (Be happy, my mind) by Johann Rist (1642), set to Johann Schop's melody (1642). The text expresses Peter's entreaty for forgiveness and at the same time the repentance of the audience. Bin ich gleich von dir gewichen, / Stell' ich mich doch wieder ein; / Hat uns doch dein Sohn verglichen / Durch sein' Angst und Todespein. / Ich verleugne nicht die Schuld, / Aber deine Gnad' und Huld / Ist viel grösser als die Sünde, / Die ich stets in mir befinde. (Even though I have strayed from Thee, / Yet I have come back again. / Thy Son has reconciled us / Through His agony and pain in death. / I do not deny my guilt, / But Thy grace and clemency / Is much greater than my sin, / Which always I find in myself.)

49. *Recitative — Evangelist, Judas, Double Chorus (tutti).* Bach and Picander give impetus to the drama in this recitative by adding Judas and a double chorus as actors. EVANGELIST: Des Morgens aber hielten alle Hohenpriester und die Ältesten des Volkes einen Rat über Jesum, dass sie ihn töteten. Und bunden ihn, führeten ihn hin, und überantworteten ihn dem Landpfleger Pontio Pilato. Da das sahe Judas, der ihn verraten hatte, dass er verdammt war zum Tode, gereuete es ihn, und brachte her wieder die dreissig Silberlinge den Hohenpriestern und Ältesten, und

sprach: (In the morning, all the high priests and elders of the people held council over Jesus to kill Him. They bound Him, led Him away, and delivered Him to Pontius Pilate, the governor. When Judas, who had betrayed Him, saw that He was condemned to death, he brought forth again the thirty pieces of silver to the chief priests and elders, saying:) JUDAS — BASS 1: Ich habe übel getan, dass ich unschuldig Blut verraten habe. (I have done evil to have betrayed innocent blood.) EVANGELIST: Sie sprachen: (They said:) CHORUSES 1 AND 2 — turba motif: Was gehet uns das an? Da siehe du zu. (How does that concern us? You see to that.)

50. *Recitative and Arioso (2 Priests); I — continuo; II — continuo for the Arioso.* EVANGELIST: Und er warf die Silberlinge in den Tempel, hub sich davon, ging hin, und erhängete sich selbst. Aber die Hohenpriester nahmen die Silberlinge, und sprachen: (And he threw the silver coins into the Temple, arose, went away and hanged himself. But the chief priests took the silver pieces, saying:) PONTIFEX 1, 2 (CHIEF PRIESTS 1, 2): Es taugt nicht, dass wir sie in den Gotteskasten legen, denn es ist Blutgeld. (It is no use putting them into God's treasury, for it is blood money.)

51. *Aria — Bass 2 — free text; II — solo violin, strings, continuo.* The actor for this da capo aria must be one of the disciples who has witnessed Judas's remorse, and who is now addressing the high priests. Note the step motif in the rhythm which seems to produce a march tempo, thus painting a tone picture of marching Jesus away. Gebt mir meinen Jesum wieder! / Seht das Geld, den Mörderlohn, / Wirft euch der verlorne Sohn / Zu den Füssen nieder. / Gebt

mir meinen Jesum wieder! (Give me back my Jesus! / See the money, the pay for murder, / Which the lost son throws / Down at your feet. / Give me back my Jesus!)

52. *Recitative; I—strings and continuo.* EVANGELIST: Sie hielten aber einen Rat, und kauften einen Töpfersacker darum, zum Begräbnis der Pilger. Daher ist derselbige Acker genennet der Blutacker, bis auf den heutigen Tag. Da ist erfüllet, das gesagt ist durch den Propheten Jeremias, da er spricht: Sie haben genommen dreissig Silberlinge, damit bezahlet ward der Verkaufte, welchen sie kauften von den Kindern Israel; und haben sie gegeben um einen Töpfersacker, als mir der Herr befohlen hat. Jesus aber stund vor dem Landpfleger, und der Landpfleger fragte ihn, und sprach: (They took counsel and bought a potter's field in which to bury pilgrims. Therefore that field is called the field of blood, even to this day. Then was fulfilled that which was spoken by Jeremiah the prophet, saying: They took the thirty pieces of silver, with which the sold One was paid for, whom they bought from the children of Israel, and gave them for a potter's field, as the Lord has commanded me [to say]. Jesus stood before the governor who asked Him, saying:) PILATE—BASS 1: Bist du der Jüden König? (Art Thou the King of the Jews?) EVANGELIST: Jesus aber sprach zu ihm: (But Jesus said to him:) JESUS Du sagtest's. (Thou hast said so.) EVANGELIST: Und da er verklagt ward von den Hohenpriestern und Ältesten, antwortete er nichts. Da sprach Pilatus zu ihm: (And when He was accused by the high priests and elders, He answered nothing. Then Pilate said to Him:) PILATUS (PILATE)—BASS 1: Hörest du nicht, wie hart sie dich verklagen? (Dost Thou not hear

how hard they accuse Thee?) EVANGELIST: Und er antwortete ihm nicht auf ein Wort, also, dass sich auch der Landpfleger sehr verwunderte. (And He answered him not a single word, so that the governor marvelled greatly.)

53. *Chorale—tutti.* Verse 1 of the hymn with the same title by Paul Gerhardt (1607–76) is sung to the melody by Hans Leo Hassler (1564–1612) (cf. numbers 21 and 23). This is the third time the "Passion Chorale" has been heard in this passion, and it will be followed by numbers 63 and 72. Here the role of the choirs appears to be that of passive commentators on the stoicism shown by Jesus before Pilate, while advocating that the listener too can put his trust in God for His guidance. Befiehl du deine Wege / Und was dein Herze kränkt / Der allertreusten Pflege / Des, der den Himmel lenkt, / Der Wolken, Luft und Winden / Gibt Wege, Lauf und Bahn, / Der wird auch Wege finden, / Da dein Fuss gehen kann. (Commend your ways / And what troubles your heart / To the trustiest cares / Of Him, who controls heaven. / He who gives clouds, air and winds / Their ways, course and path, / He will also find ways / Where your feet can go.)

54. *Recitative.* The drama continues with the Evangelist, Pilate, Pilate's wife and the tutti double chorus as the actors. EVANGELIST: Auf das Fest aber hatte der Landpfleger Gewohnheit, dem Volk einen Gefangenen loszulassen, welchen sie wollten. Er hatte aber zu der Zeit einen Gefangenen, einen sonderlichen vor andern, der hiess Barabbas. Und da sie versammelt waren, sprach Pilatus zu ihnen: (At that feast, the governor was accustomed to release to the people a prisoner, whomever they wanted. He had at that time a special

one before others, who was called Barabbas. When they had gathered, Pilate said to them:) PILATUS (PILATE) — BASS 1: Welchen wollet ihr, dass ich euch losgebe? Barabbam, oder Jesum, von dem gesaget wird, er sei Christus. (Whom do you want me to release to you? Barabbas or Jesus, of whom it is said that He is Christ?) EVANGELIST: Denn er wusste wohl, dass sie ihn aus Neid überantwortet hatten. Und da er auf dem Richtstuhl sass, schickete sein Weib zu ihm, und liess ihm sagen: (For he well knew that they had delivered Him out of envy. And when he was sitting on the judgment seat, his wife came to him, saying:) UXOR PILATI (PILATE'S WIFE) — SOPRANO 1: Habe du nichts zu schaffen mit diesem Gerechten; ich habe heute viel erlitten im Traum von seinetwegen. (Have nothing to do with this just Man. I have suffered much today in a dream on account of Him.) EVANGELIST: Aber die Hohenpriester und die Ältesten überredeten das Volk, dass sie um Barabbam bitten sollten, und Jesum umbrächten. Da antwortete nun der Landpfleger, und sprach zu ihnen: (But the chief priests and elders persuaded the people that they should ask for Barabbas and should kill Jesus. Now the governor answered and said to them:) PILATUS (PILATE) — BASS 1: Welcher wollt ihr unter diesen zweien, den ich euch soll losgeben? (Which one of these two do you want me to release to you?) EVANGELIST: Sie sprachen: (They said:) CHORUSES 1 AND 2: Barabbam! (Barabbas!) EVANGELIST: Pilatus sprach zu ihnen: (Pilate said to them:) PILATUS (PILATE) — BASS 1: Was soll ich denn machen mit Jesu, von dem gesagt wird, er sei Christus? (What am I then to do with Jesus, of whom it is said that He is Christ?) EVANGELIST: Sie sprachen alle: (They all said:) CHORUSES 1 AND 2 (forceful

turba motif): Lass ihn kreuzigen. (Let Him be crucified.)

55. *Chorale — tutti.* At the appropriate point in the drama, Bach inserts this verse 4 of Johann Heermann's "Herzliebster Jesu, was hast du verbrochen?" (Dearest heart Jesus, what crime hast Thou committed?) (cf. number 3). Wie wunderbar ist doch diese Strafe! / Der gute Hirte leidet für die Schafe; / Die Schuld bezahlt der Herre, der Gerechte, / Für seine Knechte! (How strange is this punishment! / The good Shepherd suffers for His sheep: / The Master, The Righteous One, pays the debt / For His servants!)

56. *Recitative; I — continuo.* EVANGELIST: Der Landpfleger sagte: (The governor said:) PILATUS (PILATE) — BASS 1: Was hat er denn Übels getan? (What evil hath He done then?)

57. *Recitative — Soprano 1 — free text; I — 2 oboi da caccia and continuo.* In answer to Pilate's question, the soprano delivers a short sermon in this and in her following aria on how Jesus has helped humanity. She might be acting as a woman in the crowd or as one of the followers of Jesus. Her replies confirm the doubt that Pilate feels that Jesus has ever done any wrong. Er hat uns allen wohlgetan; / Den Blinden gab er das Gesicht, / Die Lahmen macht er gehend; / Er sagt' uns seines Vaters Wort; / Er trieb die Teufel fort; / Betrübte hat er aufgericht't; / Er nahm die Sünder auf und an; / Sonst hat mein Jesus nichts getan. (He has done well for us all. / He gave sight to the blind; / He made the lame walk. / He told us His Father's word. / He drove devils away; / He has raised up the sorrowful; / He received and sheltered sinners; / Otherwise my Jesus has done nothing.)

58. *Aria — Soprano 1 — free text; I — one flute, two oboi da caccia.* No organ is used, so the flute and the

oboes da caccia provide the melody for the grief motif of this da capo aria. Yet a motif of ethereal peace predominates. Aus Liebe will mein Heiland sterben, / Von einer Sünde weiss er nichts, / Dass das ewige Verderben / Und die Strafe des Gerichts / Nicht auf meiner Seele bleibe. (Out of love my Savior is willing to die; / He knows nothing of any sin, / So that eternal ruin / And the punishment of the law / May not stay on my soul.)

59. *Recitative and Double Chorus 1, 2.* EVANGELIST: Sie schrieen aber noch mehr, und sprachen: (But they cried still more, saying:) CHORUSES I AND 2 (forceful turba motif, as in number 54): Lass ihn kreuzigen. (Let Him be crucified.) EVANGELIST: Da aber Pilatus sahe, dass er nichts schaffete, sondern dass ein viel grösser Getümmel ward, nahm er Wasser, und wusch die Hände vor dem Volk, und sprach: (When Pilate saw that he could do nothing, but that a much greater tumult was made, he took water, washing his hands before the people and saying:) PILATUS (PILATE)— BASS I: Ich bin unschuldig an dem Blut dieses Gerechten; sehet ihr zu. (I am innocent of the blood of this Righteous Man; you see to it.) EVANGELIST: Da antwortete das ganze Volk, und sprach: (Then all the people answered saying:) CHORUSES I AND 2: Sein Blut komme über uns und unsre Kinder. (turba motif) (Let His blood be upon us and our children.) EVANGELIST: Da gab er ihnen Barabbam los; aber Jesum liess er geisseln, und überantwortete ihn, dass er gekreuziget würde. (Then he released Barabbas to them, but he let Jesus be scourged and delivered Him to be crucified.)

60. *Recitative—Alto 2—free text; II—strings and continuo.* There is a motif of falling in the rhythm to represent the blows of the scourge, which Bach continues into her follow-ing aria. Erbarm es Gott! / Hier steht der Heiland angebunden. / O Geisselung, o Schläg', o Wunden! / Ihr Henker, haltet ein! / Erweichet euch der Seelen Schmerz, / Der Anblick Solchen Jammers nicht. / Ach ja, ihr habt ein Herz, / Das muss der Martersäule gleich, / Und noch viel härter sein. / Erbarmt euch, haltet ein! (Have mercy, God! / Here stands the Savior bound. / O scourging, o blows, o wounds! / Ye executioners, stop! / Does the pain in your souls not soften you, / The sight of such grief? / Ah yes, you have a heart, / That must be like the torture rack, / And still much harder. / Have mercy, stop!)

Since this Alto is from Chorus 2, the Believers, we can assume that she is one of the faithful band who followed Jesus during His ordeal.

61. *Aria—Alto 2—free text; II— strings, continuo.* Despite the sustained pathos evoked by the grief motif throughout this aria, the Siciliano rhythm lends an atmosphere of beauty to this sadness. Können Tränen meiner Wangen / Nichts erlangen, / Oh, so nehmt mein Herz hinein! / Aber lass es bei den Fluten, / Wenn die Wunden milde bluten, / Auch die Opferschale sein. (If the tears of my cheek / Can achieve nothing, / O, then take my heart! / But let it with the floods, / When the wounds gently bleed, / Also be the sacrificial cup.)

62. *Recitative—Evangelist and Double Chorus—tutti.* EVANGELIST: Da nahmen die Kriegsknechte des Landpflegers Jesum zu sich in das Richthaus, und sammelten über ihn die ganze Schar; und zogen ihn aus, und legeten ihm einen Purpurmantel an; und flochten eine Dornenkrone, und stezten sie auf sein Haupt, und ein Rohr in seine rechte Hand, und beugeten die Knie vor ihm, und spotteten ihn, und sprachen: (Then the

governor's soldiers took Jesus into the judgment hall, and gathered around Him the whole crowd. They stripped Him and put a scarlet robe on Him. They plaited a crown of thorns which they placed on His head and put a reed in His right hand. They bent their knees to Him, mocked Him and said:) CHORUSES I AND 2 — *turba motif*: Gegrüsset seist du, Jüdenkönig! (Hail, King of the Jews!) EVANGELIST: Und speieten ihn an, und nahmen das Rohr, und schlugen damit sein Haupt. (They spat upon Him, and took the reed, striking His head with it.)

63. *Chorale — tutti*. This is the fourth time the "Passion Chorale" tune has been heard in the play as its leitmotif, about two hundred years before Richard Wagner used the leitmotif to similar effect in his operas. Now the trial scene closes with verses 1 and 2 of the Paul Gerhardt hymn "O Sacred Head now wounded" in English hymnbook translations. (1) O Haupt voll Blut und Wunden, / Voll Schmerz und voller Hohn! / O Haupt zu Spott gebunden / Mit einer Dornenkron'! / O Haupt, sonst schön gezieret / Mit höchster Ehr' und Zier, / Jetzt aber hoch schimpfieret; / Gegrüsst seist du mir! (2) Du edles Angesichte, / Vor dem sonst schrickt und scheut / Das grosse Weltgewichte, / Wie bist du so bespeit! / Wie bist du so erbleichet, / Wer hat dein Augenlicht, / Dem sonst kein Licht nicht gleichet, / So schändlich zugericht't? (O Head full of blood and wounds, / Full of pain and full of scoffing! / O Head, wreathed in mockery / With a crown of thorns! / O Head, usually adorned beautifully / With highest honor and decoration / But now highly scolded, / Be Thou hailed by me! / Thou noble countenance / Before which are frightened and avoid / The great world powers, / How art Thou so spat upon! / How pallid Thou art. / Who has treated the light of Thine eyes, / To which no light equals, / So shamefully?)

64. *Recitative; I — continuo*. EVANGELIST: Und da sie ihn verspottet hatten, zogen sie ihm den Mantel aus, und zogen ihm seine Kleider an, und führeten ihn hin, dass sie ihn *kreuzigten*. Und indem sie hinausgingen, funden sie einen Menschen von Kyrene, mit Namen Simon; den zwungen sie, dass er sein Kreuz trug. (And after they had mocked Him, they took off His robe, putting His own clothes on Him, and led Him away to crucify Him. And while they went out, they found a man of Cyrene, Simon by name, whom they compelled to carry His Cross.) Notice the melisma treatment on the word *kreuzigten* (crucified).

65. *Recitative — Bass 1 — free text; I — 2 flutes, a viola da gamba, continuo*. The flutes describe a stumbling step motif to indicate Simon's stumbling movement along the road to Calvary. The actor here and in the following aria is Simon of Cyrene, but it seems that his words represent the feelings of all spectators of this drama, either in the crowd or in the present congregation. Ja, freilich will in uns das Fleisch und Blut / Zum Kreuz gezwungen sein; / Je mehr es unsrer Seele gut, / Je herber geht es ein. (Yes, of course our flesh and blood / Wishes to be compelled to the Cross. / The more it [the Cross] benefits our souls, / The harsher it penetrates.)

66. *Aria — Bass 1 — free text; I — a viola da gamba and continuo*. The viola da gamba gives this da capo number a peculiar grief motif throughout. It is like a prayer to the Lord, asking for His help to sustain us as we bear our own cross. This aria and the preceding recitative seem like miniature sermons on the imitation of Christ in

His suffering. Komm, süsses Kreuz, so will ich sagen, / Mein Jesu, gib es immer her! / Wird mir mein Leiden einst zu schwer, / So hilf du mir es selber tragen. (Come, sweet Cross, so will I say; / My Jesus, give it always to me! / Should my pain become too heavy, / Then help me to bear it myself.)

67. *Recitative — Evangelist and Double Chorus 1, 2 — tutti.* EVANGELIST: Und da sie an die Stätte kamen, mit Namen Golgatha, das ist verdeutschet, Schädelstätt', gaben sie ihm Essig zu trinken mit Gallen vermischet; und da er's schmeckete, wollte er nicht trinken. Da sie ihn aber gekreuziget hatten, teilten sie seine Kleider, und wurfen das Los darum; auf dass erfüllet würde, das gesagt ist durch den Propheten; sie haben meine Kleider unter sich geteilet, und über mein Gewand haben sie das Los geworfen. Und sie sassen allda und hüteten sein. Und oben zu seinem Haupte hefteten sie die Ursach' seines Todes beschrieben, nämlich: Dies ist Jesus, der Jüden König. Und da wurden zween Mörder mit ihm gekreuziget, einer zur Rechten, und einer zur Linken. Die aber vorübergingen, lästerten ihn, und schüttelten ihre Köpfe, und sprachen: (And when they came to the place called Golgotha, translated into German as the Place of the Skull, they gave Him vinegar to drink mixed with gall; and when He tasted it, He would not drink. When they had crucified Him, they divided His clothing and cast lots for it, so that there would be fulfilled what is said by the prophets: They have divided My garments among themselves, and have cast lots over My vesture. And they all sat there and guarded Him. And over His head they raised the reason for His death, namely: This is Jesus, the King of the Jews. And two murderers were crucified with Him there, one on the

right and one on the left. And they who passed by blasphemed against Him, shaking their heads and saying:) CHORUSES 1 AND 2 *(turba motif):* Der du den Tempel Gottes zerbrichst, und bauest ihn in dreien Tagen, hilf dir selber. Bist du Gottes Sohn, so steig herab vom Kreuz. (Thou who destroyest God's Temple and in three days buildest it, help Thyself. If Thou art God's Son, come down from the Cross.) EVANGELIST: Desgleichen auch die Hohenpriester spotteten sein, samt den Schriftgelehrten und Ältesten und sprachen: (Likewise the chief priests, together with the scribes and elders mocked Him saying:) CHORUSES 1 AND 2 *(turba motif):* Andern hat er geholfen, und kann sich selber nicht helfen. Ist er der König Israels, so steige er nun vom Kreuz, so wollen wir ihm glauben. Er hat Gott vertraut, der erlöse ihn nun, lüstet's ihn, denn er hat gesagt, Ich bin Gottes Sohn. (He has helped others, and cannot help Himself. If He is the King of Israel, let Him now come down from the Cross; then we will believe Him. He has trusted in God, let Him release Him now, if He wilt, for He has said: I am the Son of God.)

Although, like the other turba choruses with double choir in this work, both choruses are antiphonal, yet the second chorus ends in unison with the first (the only occasion in this passion) to show the unanimous hatred of the Jews toward Jesus.

68. *Recitative; I — continuo.* EVANGELIST: Desgleichen schmäheten ihn auch die Mörder, die mit ihm gekreuziget wurden. (In the same way the murderers, who were crucified with Him, slandered Him.)

69. *Recitative — Alto 1 — free text; I — 2 oboi da caccia, 2 celli (pizzicato), and continuo.* The orchestral tone color is really brought out by the oboi da caccia playing a grief motif,

while the violoncelli imitate the tolling of funeral bells in their pizzicato sound. This lament by the Daughter of Zion becomes extended by her following aria. Ach, Golgatha, unsel'ges Golgatha! / Der Herr der Herrlichkeit muss schimpflich hier verderben; / Der Segen und das Heil der Welt / Wird als ein Fluch ans Kreuz gestellt. / Der Schöpfer Himmels und der Erden / Soll Erd' und Luft entzogen werden; / Die Unschuld muss hier schuldig sterben; / Das gehet meiner Seele nah'; / Ach Golgatha, unsel'ges Golgatha! (Ah, Golgotha, unhappy Golgotha! / The Lord of Glory must miserably perish here; / The blessing and the salvation of the world / Is placed on the Cross as a curse. / The Creator of heaven and earth / Is to be taken away from the earth and the air; / Innocence must die here guilty; / That goes near to my soul. / Ah, Golgotha, unhappy Golgotha!)

70. *Aria—Alto 1, Chorus 2, free text; I—2 oboi da caccia and continuo; II—2 oboes, strings and continuo.* This is a two dimensional (i.e., dialogue) number, as were numbers 1, 25, 26, 33, 36, where the Daughter of Zion (Alto 2) conversed with the Believers (Chorus 2). Again, as in number 1, the soloist answers the Believers' question "Where?" In the melody, there is a motif of movement as the dying Redeemer stretches out His hand to draw all men to Him on His Cross. This rising motif of felicity comes as welcome relief from her previous number. DAUGHTER OF ZION: Sehet, Jesus hat die Hand, / Uns zu fassen ausgespannt; Kommt! (See Jesus has stretched out His hand / To clasp us. Come!) BELIEVERS: Wohin? (Where?) DAUGHTER OF ZION: In Jesu Armen / Sucht Erlösung, nehmt Erbarmen, Suchet! (In Jesus's arms / Seek redemption, find pity. Seek!) BELIEVERS: Wo?

(Where?) DAUGHTER OF ZION: In Jesu Armen. Lebet, sterbet, ruhet hier, / Ihr verlassnen Küchlein ihr. Bleibet! (In Jesus's arms. Live, die, rest here, / You forsaken chickens. Stay!) BELIEVERS: Wo? (Where?) DAUGHTER OF ZION: In Jesu Armen. (In Jesus's arms.)

71. *Recitative, Choruses 1 and 2; I—oboes, strings continuo.* EVANGELIST: Und von der sechsten Stunde an ward eine Finsternis über das ganze Land, bis zu der neunten Stunde. Und um die neunte Stunde schriee Jesus laut, und sprach: (And from the sixth hour on there was a darkness over the whole country until the ninth hour. And about the ninth hour Jesus cried aloud, saying:) JESUS: Eli, Eli, lama asabthani? EVANGELIST: Das ist: Mein Gott, mein Gott, warum hast du mich verlassen? Etliche aber, die da stunden, da sie das höreten, sprachen sie: (That is: My God, my God, why hast Thou forsaken Me? Some who stood there, when they heard that, said:) CHORUS 1: Der rufet dem Elias. (He calls to Elias.) EVANGELIST: Und bald lief einer unter ihnen, nahm einen Schwamm, und füllete ihn mit Essig, und steckete ihn auf ein Rohr, und tränkete ihn. Die andern aber sprachen: (And soon one of them ran, took a sponge, and filled it with vinegar, put it on a reed, and gave Him to drink. The others said:) CHORUS 2: Halt, lass sehen, ob Elias komme und ihm helfe? (Hold on, let us see whether Elias will come to help Him?) EVANGELIST: Aber Jesus schriee abermal laut, und verschied. (But Jesus cried out loudly again, and departed.)

72. *Chorale—tutti.* This is verse 9 of the so called "Passion Chorale" by Paul Gerhardt, now heard for the fifth and last time. Wenn ich einmal soll scheiden, / So scheide nicht von mir! / Wenn ich den Tod soll leiden, / So

tritt du dann herfür! / Wenn mir am allerbängsten / Wird um das Herze sein, / So reiss mich aus den Ängsten / Kraft deiner Angst und Pein! (When some time I must depart, / Then do not depart from me! / When I must suffer death, / Then Thou dost step beside me! / When my heart will be / Most anxious, / Then snatch me out of its terrors / By the power of Thy fear and pain!)

73. *Recitative and Double Chorus 1, 2 — tutti, but without flutes.* Bach depicts realistically in this number the earthquake and the rising of the saints, using a tremolo with a terror motif. EVANGELIST: Und siehe da, der Vorhang im Tempel zerriss in zwei Stück, von oben bis unten aus. Und die Erde erbebete, und die Felsen zerrissen, und die Gräber täten sich auf, und stunden auf viel Leiber der Heiligen, die da schliefen; und gingen aus den Gräbern nach seiner Auferstehung, und kamen in die heilige Stadt, und erschienen vielen. Aber der Hauptmann, und die bei ihm waren, und bewahreten Jesum, da sie sahen das Erdbeben und was da geschah, erschraken sie sehr und sprachen: (And behold, the veil of the Temple was torn in two from top to bottom. And the earth trembled and rocks shattered, graves opened and many bodies of saints who slept there arose and went out of their graves after His Resurrection, coming into the holy city to appear to many. But the centurion and those near him watching Jesus, when they saw the earthquake and what happened there, feared greatly, saying:)

CHORUSES 1 AND 2: There is a feeling of deep respect in the humility motif as the two choirs sing in unison: Wahrlich, dieser ist Gottes Sohn gewesen. (Truly, this was the Son of God.) EVANGELIST: Und es waren viel Weiber da, die von ferne zusahen, die

da waren nachgefolget aus Galiläa, und hatten ihm gedienete, unter welchen war Maria Magdalene, und Maria, die Mutter Jacobi und Joses, und die Mutter der Kinder Zebedai. (And there were many women there, looking on from afar and who had followed from Galilee and had served Him. Among them were Maria Magdalena, and Mary the mother of James and of Joses, and the mother of Zebedee's children.) Am Abend aber kam ein reicher Mann von Arimathia, der hiess Joseph, welcher auch ein Jünger Jesu war. Der ging zu Pilato, und bat ihn um den Leichnam Jesu. Da befahl Pilatus, man sollte ihm ihn geben. (In the evening a rich man from Arimathea, called Joseph, came; he was also a disciple of Jesus. He went to Pilate to ask for the body of Jesus. Then Pilate ordered that they should give it to him.)

74. *Recitative — Bass 1 — free text; 1 — strings and continuo.* In my opinion, the climax of the entire work comes in this recitative/arioso number with its following aria for the same bass voice. Joseph of Arimathea is the actor expressing his personal emotions as he attends to the burial of his Master. A motif of celestial peace permeates the whole number — a mystical aura unique in Bach's works which moves the listener by its text and entrances him by its sound.

Schweitzer (II, 217) thinks that "Bach expresses the tranquil peace of the falling twilight" in this arioso. It is certainly a miniature tone poem well suited to the descent from the Cross. Am Abend da es kühle war, / Ward Adams Fallen offenbar. / Am Abend drückete ihn der Heiland nieder; / Am Abend kam die Taube wieder, / Und trug ein Ölblatt in dem Munde. / O schöne Zeit! O Abendstunde! / Der Friedenschluss ist nun mit Gott gemacht; Denn Jesus hat sein Kreuz vollbracht. / Sein Leichnam kommt zur Rub. / Ach! liebe Seele, bitte du, / Geh, lasse dir den toten Jesum schenken, / O heilsames, o köstlich's Angedenken! (In the evening, when it was cool, / Adam's fall became evident. / In the evening the Savior casts him down; / In the evening the dove came again, / And carried an olive leaf in its bill. / O beautiful time! O evening hour! / Peace is now made with God, / For Jesus has completed His Cross. / His body comes to rest. / Ah, dear soul, ask, / Go, let the dead Jesus be given to thee. / O holy, precious memorial!)

75. *Aria—Bass 1—free text; I— strings, 2 oboi da caccia, continuo — da capo.* This aria is the other outstanding number in this passion. Its rhythm shows the suave melody of a Siciliano in 12/8 time, but it is the soloist's feeling for the emotions expressed in his text that makes the listener realize that he is listening to pure, spiritual music, as Joseph of Arimathea proclaims his lifelong devotion to Christ and his rejection of the world. The motif of calm in the first two lines (the da capo brings it back) is replaced by a motif of joy in the last four lines. The soloist's artistic runs on *begraben* (bury) and the effective orchestral ritornelli before, halfway, and at the end, make this aria a masterpiece. Mache dich, mein Herze, rein, / Ich will Jesum selbst *begraben.* / Denn er soll nunmehr in mir / Für und für / Seine süsse Ruhe haben. / Welt, geh aus, lass Jesum ein! (Make thyself clean, my heart, / I will bury Jesus myself. / For He shall henceforth in me / Forever and ever / Have His sweet rest. / World, go out, let Jesus in!)

76. *Recitative and Choruses 1, 2.* There seems to be a rolling melody to the Evangelist's narrative here, probably suggested to Bach by the words "wälzete einen grossen Stein vor die Tür des Grabes" (rolled a big stone before the door of the sepulchre). EVANGELIST: Und Joseph nahm den Leib, und wickelte ihn in ein rein Leinwand. Und legte ihn in sein eigen neu Grab, welches er hatte lassen in einen Fels hauen; und wälzete einen grossen Stein vor die Tür des Grabes, und ging davon. Es war aber allda Maria Magdalene und die andere Maria, die setzten sich gegen das Grab. (And Joseph took the body, wrapped it in a clean linen cloth, and laid it in his own new tomb, which he had hewn into a rock; and he rolled a big stone before the door of the sepulchre, and departed. There was Maria Magdalena and the other Mary sitting there against the sepulchre.) Des andern Tages, der da folget nach dem Rüsttage, kamen die Hohenpriester und Pharisäer sämtlich zu Pilato, und sprachen: (The next day, which followed the day of preparation, the chief priests and the Pharisees came together to Pilate, saying:) CHORUSES 1, 2 *(turba motif, sung in canon)*: Herr, wir haben gedacht, dass dieser Verführer sprach, da er noch lebete: Ich will nach dreien Tagen wieder auferstehen. Darum befiehl, dass man das Grab verwahre bis an den dritten Tag, auf das nicht seine Jünger kommen, und stehlen ihn, und sagen zu dem Volk: Er ist auferstanden von den Toten; und werde der letzte Betrug ärger, denn der erste. (Sir, we remembered that this seducer said, while He was still living: I will arise again after three days. Therefore order that the sepulchre be guarded until the third day, so that His disciples may not come, steal Him, and say to the people: He has risen from the dead; so the last deceit may be worse than the first.) EVANGELIST: Pilatus sprach zu ihnen: (Pilate said to them:) PILATUS (PILATE)—BASS 1: Da habt ihr die Hüter; gehet hin, und verwahret's,

wie ihr wisset. (You have watchmen there. Go away and guard it as you know how.) EVANGELIST: Sie gingen hin, und verwahreten das Grab mit Hütern, und versiegelten den Stein. (They went away, and guarded the sepulchre with watchmen, and sealed the stone.)

77. *Recitative — Soprano 1, Alto 1, Tenor 1, Bass 1 and Chorus 2 — free texts; I — strings and continuo; II — flutes, oboes, strings and continuo.* This number represents a very dramatic farewell to Jesus, each soloist acting the part of the Daughter of Zion, while Chorus 2 represents the antiphonal choir of mourners. The dialogue pattern which began the passion (number 1) is resumed here, but this time with a single voice, varying tenor, alto, soprano, bass, for the Daughter of Zion.

DAUGHTER OF ZION: Nun ist der Herr zur Ruh gebracht. (Now the Lord is brought to rest.) BELIEVERS: Mein Jesu, gute Nacht! (My Jesus, good night!) DAUGHTER OF ZION: Die Müh' ist aus, die unsre Sünden ihm gemacht. (The trouble is over, which our sins made for Him.) BELIEVERS: Mein Jesu, gute Nacht! (My Jesus, good night!) DAUGHTER OF ZION: O selige Gebeine / Seht, wie ich euch mit Buss und Reu beweine, / Dass euch mein Fall in solche Not gebracht. (O blessed limbs, / See how I weep for thee with penance and remorse, / That my fall brought thee into such distress.) BELIEVERS: Mein Jesu, gute Nacht! (My Jesus, good night!) DAUGHTER OF ZION: Habt lebenslang / Vor euer Leiden tausend Dank, / Dass ihr mein Seelenheil so wert geacht't. (Have, as long as life goes on, / For Thy suffering a thousand thanks, / That Thou has so highly prized the salvation of my soul.) BELIEVERS: Mein Jesu, gute Nacht! (My Jesus, good night!)

Terry (II, *The Passions,* 64) comments: "Picander, in writing the words, had in mind the funeral ceremony customary at Leipzig, where tributes to the departed were offered by relations and others. Here each voice in turn throws a blossom of remembrance into the tomb...."

78. *Double Chorus 1, 2 — tutti — free text, da capo.* Probably composed at Cöthen for the court there, the melody is a sarabande dance form, with the words *ruhe sanfte, sanfte ruh'* increasing from pianissimo to forte. The resulting motif of solemnity resembles a funeral march, thus involving the emotions of the audience with those of the choruses to bring the drama to a reverential close. Wir setzen uns mit Tränen nieder / Und rufen dir im Grabe zu: / Ruhe sanfte, sanfte ruh'! / Ruht, ihr ausgesognen Glieder! / Ruhe sanfte, sanfte ruh'! / Euer Grab und Leichenstein / Soll dem ängstlichen Gewissen / Ein bequemes Ruhekissen / Und der Seelen Ruhstatt sein. / Höchst vergnügt schlummern da die Augen ein. (We sit down with tears / And call to Thee in the tomb: / Rest softly, softly rest! / Rest, ye exhausted limbs, / Rest softly, softly rest! / Your grave and tombstone / Shall for the anxious conscience / Be a comfortable pillow / And the soul's resting place. / Highly delighted, our eyes slumber there.)

# The St. Mark Passion

## (Leipzig, March 23, 1731; BWV 247)

This is the fourth and last passion for which Bach composed music and which he conducted personally. There is no proof that Bach ever set a fifth passion after this one, nor that he set *Picander's Passion* of 1725 to music, although Picander may have intended him to do so.

Like the *St. Matthew Passion,* the *St. Mark* is divided into two parts — before and after the sermon (Vor der Predigt, nach der Predigt) — with heavy stress on the chorales and the Biblical narratives, which were the essence of Bach's passion compositions as we have seen before this one. Here Bach uses the literal Biblical translation of St. Mark's Gospel, chapters 14 and 15, complete.

Unfortunately, the score is no longer extant as it was until 1764, so that reconstruction of Bach's work, based on Picander's libretto, has taken over one hundred years to achieve, but still only in fragmentary musical form.

Wilhelm Rust, the editor of the Bachgesellschaft (B.G.) (Bach Society), first edition of Bach's works, was able to identify five movements of the *St. Mark Passion* with parts of the *Trauerode* (Mourning Ode) cantata (BWV 198), composed in 1727.

In 1940, Friedrich Smend discovered a relationship in two of its arias with arias from cantatas BWV 54 and BWV 7. More recently, Alfred Dürr has also established a close textual relationship of certain movements in the *St. Mark* with Bach's previous works.

This self-borrowing tendency was not unusual in Bach's time. It seems to have been over-emphasized in Bach's case, even leading to a study on it by Norman Carrell in his *Bach the Borrower* (Allen and Unwin: London, 1967).

Terry's *Bach, The Passions* (II, 1929–31) gives an outline of all the movements in Picander's libretto, while showing how Bach was involved in the composition from his own borrowings.*

Yet since the score is missing, there is no way of knowing how Bach set the music for the recitatives and their choruses which Terry indicated. To complete the text, these Biblical recitative numbers will be quoted in English, taken from St. Mark, Chapters 14, 15 of the King James version (1611). Comments on the music and the text will be made only on Bach's setting of choruses, chorales and arias because of their dramatic effect on what has been narrated in the immediately preceding Biblical recitative.

Terry notes that the movements of Picander's libretto are unnumbered, but he numbers them nevertheless as follows:

## PART I
### *Vor der Predigt*
### *(Before the Sermon)*

*1. Chorus.* There is a four part choir for this opening chorus, the chorales, and the concluding chorus. This choir includes Soprano, Alto, Tenor, and Bass sections, although the soloists are Soprano, Alto, and Tenor only for this reconstruction. The instrumentation for this number includes two flutes, two oboes d'amore, two violas da gamba, strings and continuo — the same as for its prototype, cantata BWV 198 (1).

We hear the same grief motif combined with a tear motif that marked the opening chorus of the *Trauerode* (BWV 198). Yet Picander has managed to fit his new text into the music that Bach had already composed, without any loss of religious feeling, even though this text seems inferior.

Geh, Jesu, geh zu deiner Pein! / Ich will so lange dich beweinen, / Bis mir dein Trost wird wieder scheinen,

---

*The Warsaw Chamber Opera under Joszef Bok performed a reconstructed version in 1983, using recitatives from Bach's St. Matthew and St. Luke passions.*

/ Da ich versöhnet werde sein. (Go, Jesus, go to Thy agony! / I will weep for Thee so long, / Until Thy consolation will appear to me again, / When I will be pardoned.)

2. *Recitatives and Choruses — St. Mark 14: 1–5.* (1) After two days was the feast of the passover, and of unleavened bread; and the chief priests and the scribes sought how they might take him by craft, and put him to death.

(2) But they said, Not on the feast day, lest there by an uproar in the people.

(3) And being in Bethany in the house of Simon, the leper, as he sat at meat, there came a woman having an alabaster box of ointment of spikenard very precious; and she brake the box, and poured it on his head.

(4) And there were some that had indignation within themselves, and said, Why was this waste of the ointment made?

(5) For it might have been sold for more than three hundred pence, and have been given to the poor. And they murmured against her.

3. *Chorale.* This is stanza 4 of Justus Jonas's hymn, "Wo Gott, der Herr, nicht bei uns hält" (If God the Lord does not hold with us) (1524), which Bach had used in a tenor chorale verse for chorale cantata BWV 178 in 1724, with the same title. Sie stellen uns wie Ketzern nach, / Nach unserm Blut sie trachten; / Noch rühmen sie sich Christen auch, / Die Gott allein gross achten. / Ach Gott, der teure Name dein / Muss ihrer Schalkheit Deckel sein, / Du wirst einmal aufwachen. (They make out that we are heretics, / And they seek our blood; / Yet they boast that they are also Christians, / Whom God alone greatly esteems. / Ah God, Thy dear Name / Must be the cover for their roguishness, / But Thou wilt awaken to it some time.)

How this chorale verse applies to the intrigues of the chief priests and the scribes is easy to see, but it is not so clear how it pertains to this woman's generosity to Jesus. Did Picander or Bach not perceive this when they chose this particular chorale verse?

4. *Recitatives — St. Mark 14: 6–11.* (6) And Jesus said, Let her alone; why trouble ye her? She hath wrought a good work on me.

(7) For ye have the poor with you always, and whensoever ye will ye may do them good; but me ye have not always.

(8) She hath done what she could; she is come aforehand to anoint my body to the burying.

(9) Verily I say unto you, Wheresoever this gospel shall be preached throughout the whole world, this also that she hath done shall be spoken of for a memorial of her.

(10) And Judas Iscariot, one of the twelve, went unto the chief priests, to betray him unto them.

(11) And when they heard it, they were glad, and promised to give him money. And he sought how he might conveniently betray him.

5. *Chorale.* This is stanza 5 of Adam Reissner's hymn (1533), "In dich hab' ich gehoffet, Herr" (In Thee have I hoped, Lord), also used in the *St. Matthew Passion* (number 38). Mir hat die Welt trüglich gericht't / Mit Lügen und mit falschem G'dicht, / Viel Netz und heimlich Stricken, / Herr, nimm mein wahr in dieser G'fahr, / B'hüt mich vor flaschen Tücken. (The world has judged me deceitfully / With lies and false invention, / With many a net and secret snares. / Lord, look after me in this danger, / Shield me from false malice.)

In this dramatic commentary, the Biblical verses of the previous recitative (number 4) are reflected more in the last two lines than in the first four—the reverse of the first chorale quoted (number 3).

6. *Recitatives and Chorus—St. Mark 14: 12–19.* (12) And the first day of unleavened bread, when they killed the passover, his disciples said unto him, Where wilt thou that we go and prepare that thou mayest eat the passover? (13) And he sendeth forth two of his disciples, and saith unto them, Go ye into the city, and there shall meet you a man bearing a pitcher of water; follow him. (14) And wheresoever he shall go in, say ye to the goodman of the house, The Master saith, Where is the guest-chamber, where I shall eat the passover with my disciples? (15) And he will show you a large upper room furnished and prepared; there make ready for us. (16) And his disciples went forth, and came into the city, and found as he had said unto them; and they made ready the passover. (17) And in the evening he cometh with the twelve. (18) And as they sat and did eat, Jesus said, Verily I say unto you, One of you which eateth with me shall betray me. (19) And they began to be sorrowful, and to say unto him one by one, Is it I? and another said, Is it I?

7. *Chorale.* We hear now stanza 4 of Paul Gerhardt's 1647 hymn, "O Welt, sieh' hier dein Leben" (O World, see here thy Life), which Bach had previously used in the *St. John Passion* (number 15). Ich, ich und meine Sünden, / die sich wie Körnlein finden / des Sandes an dem Meer, / die haben dir erreget / das Elend, das dich schläget, / und das bertrübte Marterheer. (I, I and my sins, / Which are found like little grains / Of sand at the sea-side, / They have caused Thee / The misery that strikes Thee / And the sad army of tortures.)

Once again, this chorale bears more on the last two recitatives (18 and 19) than on the first six (12–17) verses, which are unrelated to it. The feeling of guilt, common to all the disciples, is well expressed by the choir on behalf of each one of them as well as for each member of the congregation. Thus, by his use of chorales, however, Bach is trying to give dramatic life to affiliated recitatives, and at the same time to actively involve the audience in the scene.

8. *Recitatives—St. Mark 14: 20–25.* (20) And he answered and said unto them, It is one of the twelve, that dippeth with me in the dish. (21) The Son of man indeed goeth, as it is written of him; but woe to that man by whom the Son of man is betrayed! good were it for that man if he had never been born. (22) And as they did eat, Jesus took bread, and blessed, and brake it, and gave it to them, and said, Take, eat; this is my body. (23) And he took the cup, and when he had given thanks, he gave it to them; and they all drank of it. (24) And he said unto them, This is my blood of the new testament, which is shed for many. (25) Verily I say unto you, I will drink no more of the fruit of the vine, until that day that I drink it new in the kingdom of God.

9. *Aria—Alto—two violas da gamba, lute, violoncello, strings and continuo.* This is actually the alto aria (number 5) of the *Trauerode,* but the motif of solemnity does not mark the passing of Queen Christiane Eberhardine, as in the original aria, but rather the spiritual strength given to the singer by the Sacrament of Communion, which Jesus has just instituted in the foregoing recitative. She might be playing the part of one of the disciples, as Bach tries to instill a

touch of drama into this solemn moment, or again she might be voicing the feelings of any member of the congregation/audience.

Whoever this soloist may represent in her role, there is little doubt that, musically, this aria reflects the preceding recitative much better than the chorales have done up to this point. Mein Heiland, dich vergess' ich nicht. / Ich habe dich in mich verschlossen, / Und deinen Leib und Blut genossen, / Und meinen Trost auf dich gericht'. (My Savior, I do not forget Thee. / I have enclosed Thee in myself, / And have taken Thy body and blood, / And placed my consolation on Thee.)

Her artistic runs on *Heiland* (Savior) and *gericht'* (directed, placed), with the da capo make this number stand out, despite the self-borrowed music.

10. *Recitatives — St. Mark 14: 26–28.* (26) And when they had sung an hymn, they went out into the Mount of Olives.

(27) And Jesus saith unto them, All ye shall be offended because of me this night; for it is written, I will smite the shepherd, and the sheep shall be scattered.

(28) But after that I am risen, I will go before you into Galilee.

11. *Chorale.* This is stanza 13 of Johann Rist's "O Ewigkeit, du Donnerwort" (O Eternity, Thou Word of Thunder) (1642). Bach will compose two cantatas on this hymn, BWV 20 and BWV 60, in the following year, 1732. Wach auf, O Mensch, vom Sündenschlaf, / Ermuntre dich, verlornes Schaf / Und bessre bald dein Leben! / Wach auf, es ist doch hohe Zeit, / Es kommt heran die Ewigkeit, / Dir deinen Lohn zu geben: / Vielleicht ist heut' der letzte Tag; / Wer weiss noch, wie man sterben mag! (Wake up, O man, from your sleep of sin, / Take courage, lost sheep / And improve your life soon! / Wake up, it is certainly high time, / Eternity is coming along, / To give you your reward: / Perhaps today is the last day; / Who yet knows, how one may die!)

Once again, this is not a particularly apt choice for commenting on number 10 above, nor does the choir necessarily represent the disciples.

12. *Recitatives — St. Mark 14: 29–34.* (29) But Peter said unto him, Although all shall be offended, yet will I not.

(30) And Jesus saith unto him, Verily I say unto thee, That this day, even in this night, before the cock crows twice, thou shalt deny me thrice.

(31) But he spake the more vehemently, If I should die with thee, I will not deny thee in any wise. Likewise also said they all.

(32) And they came to a place which was named Gethsemane; and he said to his disciples, Sit ye here, while I shall pray.

(33) And he taketh with him Peter and James and John, and began to be more amazed, and to be very heavy;

(34) And saith unto them, My soul is exceeding sorrowful unto death; tarry ye here, and watch.

13. *Chorale.* This is stanza 1 of Andreas Kritzelmann's hymn (1627). The thought in this verse really suits the despondency of Jesus at being alone in Gethsemane as seen in the last two verses of number 12 above. The choir could very well be representing the thoughts of Peter, James and John, the disciples who are mentioned in number 12 (verse 33). Betrübtes Herz, sei wohlgemut, / tu' nicht so gar verzagen. / Es wird noch alles werden gut, / all dein Kreuz, Not und Klagen / wird sich in lauter Fröhlichkeit verwandeln / in gar kurzer Zeit, das wirst du wohl erfahren. (Afflicted heart, be of good spirits, / Do not despair so. / Every-

thing will still turn out well. / All your Cross, trouble and grief / Will be transformed into pure joy / In a very short time; that you will certainly discover.)

14. *Recitatives — St. Mark 14: 35–36.* (35) And he went forward a little, and fell on the ground, and prayed that, if it were possible, the hour might pass from him.

(36) And he said, Abba, Father, all things are possible unto thee; take away this cup from me; nevertheless not what I will, but what thou wilt.

15. *Chorale.* This is stanza 1 of Johann Hermann Schein's hymn "Mach's mit mir, Gott, nach deiner Güt'" (Do with me, God, according to Thy goodness) (1628). This number is closely connected with the previous recitatives (14), showing that Jesus submits to His Father's will and that we should do the same. Jesus's thoughts might be uttered by the choir on His behalf in this well chosen chorale. Mach's mit mir, Gott, nach deiner Güt', / Hilf mir in meinem Leiden. / Ruf' ich dich an, versag' mir's nicht. / Wenn sich mein Seel' soll scheiden, / So nimm sie, Herr, in deine Händ': / Ist alles gut, wenn gut das End'. (Do with me, God, according to Thy goodness, / Help me in my suffering. / I call to Thee, do not deny me. / When my soul is to depart, / Then take it, Lord, into Thy hands: / Everything is well, if the end is well.)

16. *Recitatives — St. Mark 14: 37–42.* (37) And he cometh, and findeth them sleeping, and saith unto Peter, Simon, sleepest thou? Couldest not thou watch one hour?

(38) Watch ye and pray, lest ye enter into temptation. The spirit truly is ready, but the flesh is weak.

(39) And again he went away, and prayed, and spake the same words.

(40) And when he returned, he found them asleep again (for their eyes were heavy), neither wist they what to answer him.

(41) And he cometh the third time, and saith unto them, Sleep on now, and take your rest; it is enough, the hour is come; behold, the Son of man is betrayed into the hands of sinners.

(42) Rise up, let us go; lo, he that betrayeth me is at hand.

17. *Aria — Soprano — da capo, with strings and continuo.* The soloist may be one of the disciples, as she brings this dramatic moment to life after the narrative of number 16. The transfer of the music from the soprano aria (number 3) of the *Trauerode* is smoothly and accurately done, even to the terror motif. Er kommt, er kommt, er ist vorhanden! / Mein Jesu, ach! er suchet dich, / Entfliehe doch und lasse mich, / Mein Heil, statt deiner in den Banden. (He [Judas] comes, he comes; he is here! / Ah, my Jesus, he is searching for Thee. / Flee then and let me, / My Savior, instead of Thee [be] in bonds.)

18. *Recitatives — St. Mark 14: 43–45.* (43) And immediately, while he yet spake, cometh Judas, one of the twelve, and with him a great multitude with swords and staves, from the chief priests and the scribes and the elders.

(44) And he that betrayed him had given them a token, saying, Whomsoever I shall kiss, that same is he; take him, and lead him away safely.

(45) And as soon as he was come, he goeth straightway to him, and saith, Master, master; and kissed him.

19. *Aria — Alto — da capo — two violins, two violas da gamba and continuo.* This solo alto aria is borrowed directly from the solo alto (number 1) of cantata BWV 54, "Widerstehe doch der Sünde" (Resist then Sin), which Bach must have composed well before 1731 and perhaps as early as 1714 in Weimar. Bach combines a fear motif with a step rhythm to denote that

we should abhor and march against hypocrisy whenever we see it in this "false world." Falsche Welt, dein schmeichelnd Küssen / Ist der Frommen-Seelen Gift. / Deine Zungen sind voll Stechen, / Und die Worte, die sie sprechen, / Sind zu Fallen angestift! (False world, your flattering kissing / Is the poison of pious souls. / Your tongues are full of barbs, / And the words which they speak / Are contrived for falling!)

The betrayal by Judas with his feigned kiss betokens the deceit in the world against which the alto warns in this little sermon. This aria is more thorough in is representation of the preceding recitative than any that we have heard thus far.

20. *Recitatives — St. Mark 14: 46–49.*
(46) And they laid their hands on him, and took him.

(47) And one of them that stood by drew a sword, and smote a servant of the high priest, and cut off his ear.

(48) And Jesus answered and said unto them, Are ye come out, as against a thief, with swords and with staves to take me?

(49) I was daily with you in the temple teaching, and ye took me not: but the scriptures must be fulfilled.

21. *Chorale.* This is stanza 8 of Paul Stockmann's "Jesu Leiden, Pein und Tod" (Jesus' Suffering, Pain and Death) (1633), previously used by Bach in the *St. John Passion,* numbers 20, 56, and 60. Bach and Picander must have strayed again from the thought contained in the previous Biblical recitative, since this chorale verse is more a prayer for divine help against evil than a reflection on the garden scene. There seems to be little, if any, dramatic action there. Jesu, ohne Missetat, im Garten vorhanden, / da man dich gebunden hat fest mit harten Banden. / Wenn uns will der böse Feind mit der Sünde binden, /

so lass uns, O Menschenfreund, dadurch Lösung finden. (Jesus, without wrong-doing, is present here in the garden / Where they have bound Thee firmly with harsh bonds. / If the wicked enemy wants to bind us with sin, / Then let us, O Friend of man, find release through it.)

22. *Recitative — St. Mark 14: 50–52.*
(50) And they all forsook him, and fled.

(51) And there followed him a certain young man, having a linen cloth cast about his naked body; and the young men laid hold on him:

(52) And he left the linen cloth, and fled from them naked.

23. *Chorale.* Stanza 6 of Paul Gerhardt's so-called "Passion Chorale," "O Haupt vol Blut und Wunden" (O Sacred Head now Wounded) (1656), is now sung exactly as it was in number 23 of the *St. Matthew Passion,* but not pertaining to Peter's vow of loyalty to Jesus. Here it is because the young man left his only linen garment for Jesus, whereas His other disciples merely fled, leaving Him nothing.

Obviously, the dramatic feeling has to do with the choir and the audience, as individually they assert their constant loyalty to Jesus. Ich will hier bei dir stehen, / Verachte mich doch nicht! / Von dir will ich nicht gehen, / Wenn dir dein Herze bricht. / Wann dein Herz wird erblassen / Im letzten Todesstoss, / Alsdenn will ich dich fassen / In meinen Arm und Schoss. (I will stand here by Thee, / Do not despise me! / From Thee I will not go / When Thy heart breaks. / When Thy heart grows pale / In the last pang of death, / Then I will clasp Thee / Into my arms and lap.)

## PART II
### Nach der Predigt
### (After the Sermon)

*24. Aria — Tenor — one flute, one oboe d'amore, two violas da gamba, lute, strings, continuo.* The introduction to the second part is identical with the tenor aria that began Part II of BWV 198, the *Trauerode* (number 8). Again the dance tempo still contains a motif of divine felicity, but the libretto seems at odds with this soothing rhythm. Perhaps Bach was unwilling to let this number pass into obscurity; therefore he decided to impose its music on such a sad text, so inferior to the original.

This is a rare case where Bach did not make the musical thought agree with his new libretto in his self-borrowing procedure. Terry's comment in this regard is very enlightening and worth quoting (*The Passions*, 75–76): "Clearly he [Bach] was anxious that the Passion for 1731 should make the smallest call upon him. The explanation is probably found in his circumstances at Leipzig, which were so unsatisfactory in the late autumn of 1730 that he was even ready to accept an appointment elsewhere. If he was composing the Passion required for 1731 at a moment when he was least disposed to make considerable effort towards its production, the character of Picander's libretto is explained." Mein Tröster ist nicht mehr bei mir, / Mein Jesu, soll ich dich verlieren, / Und zum Verderben sehen führen? / Das kommt der Seele schmerzlich für. / Der Unschuld, welche nichts verbrochen, / Dem Lamm, das ohne Missetat, / Wird in dem ungerechten Rat, / Ein Todes-Urteil zugesprochen. (My Comforter is no longer with me. / My Jesus, am I to lose Thee, / And see Thee led to Thy ruin? / That comes painfully to my soul. / Innocence, which has broken no law, / On the Lamb, that without sin, / A sentence of death is pronounced / In the unjust council.)

*25. Recitatives — St. Mark 14: 53–59.* (53) And they led Jesus away to the high priest; and with him were assembled all the chief priests and the elders and the scribes. (54) And Peter followed him afar off, even into the palace of the high priest; and he sat with the servants, and warmed himself at the fire. (55) And the chief priests and all the council sought for witness against Jesus to put him to death; and found none. (56) For many bare false witness against him, but their witness agreed not together. (57) And there arose certain, and bare false witness against him, saying, (58) We heard him say, I will destroy this temple that is made with hands, and within three days I will build another made without hands. (59) But neither so did their witness agree together.

*26. Chorale.* This chorale is stanza 2 of Justus Jonas's hymn, upon which Bach later composed his chorale cantata, BWV 178, "Wo Gott, der Herr, nicht bei uns hält" (Where God, the Lord, does not stand by us), about 1735. In this cantata, he interpolates the recitative lines into the chorale lines, but here just the chorale lines are sung, reflecting very well on the action recounted in the previous recitatives (25). The choir does not assume any role here, but is simply moralizing on the recitatives. Was Menschenkraft-und-witz anfäht, / Soll uns billig nicht schrecken; / Er sitzet an der höchsten Stätt, / Er wird ihr'n Rat aufdecken. / Wenn sie's aufs klügste greifen an, / So geht doch Gott ein ander Bahn: / Es steht in seinen Hände. (What mortal strength and wit creates / Shall certainly not frighten us; / He sits at the highest place. / He will disclose their council, / When they attack most knowingly. / Then God goes another way: / It rests in His hands.)

27. *Recitatives — St. Mark 14: 60–61.* (60) And the high priest stood up in the midst, and asked Jesus, saying, Answerest thou nothing? what is it which these witness against thee?

(61) But he held his peace, and answered nothing. Again the high priest asked him, and said unto him, Art thou the Christ, the Son of the Blessed?

28. *Chorale.* Stanza 1 of Paul Gerhardt's "Passion Chorale" (1656) is sung to Hans Leo Hassler's melody just as it was for number 53 of the *St. Matthew Passion.* This verse is well chosen to show how Jesus, and we too, should put confidence in God for His direction. Befiehl du deine Wege / Und was dein Herze kränkt / Der aller treusten Pflege / Des, der den Himmel lenkt, / Der Wolken, Luft und Winden / Gibt Wege, Lauf und Bahn, / Der wird auch Wege finden, / Da dein Fuss gehen kann. (Commend your ways / And what troubles your heart / To the trustiest cares / Of Him, who controls heaven. / He who gives clouds, air and winds / Their ways, course and path, / He will also find ways / Where your foot can go.)

29. *Recitatives and Chorus — St. Mark 14: 61–65.* (61) But he held his peace, and answered nothing. Again the high priest asked him, and said unto him, Art thou the Christ, the Son of the Blessed?

(62) And Jesus said, I am: and ye shall see the Son of man sitting on the right hand of power, and coming in the clouds of heaven.

(63) Then the high priest rent his clothes, and saith, What need we any further witnesses?

(64) Ye have heard the blasphemy: what think ye? And they all condemned him to be guilty of death.

(65) And some began to spit on him, and to cover his face, and to buffet him, and to say unto him, Prophesy: and the servants did strike him with the palms of their hands.

30. *Chorale.* This is stanza 2 of Paul Gerhardt's 1656 hymn, "O Haupt voll Blut und Wunden" (O Sacred Head now Wounded), which appeared as number 63 of the *St. Matthew Passion.* Although it does not cover the entire above recitative (29), it is well chosen for continuing the thought of verse 65. The choir deplores such treatment of the Lord; it does not represent any group of actors but simply comments in the manner of the classical Greek chorus (cf. number 28, likewise). Du edles Angesichte, / Vor dem sonst schrickt und scheut / Das grosse Weltgewichte, / Wie bist du so bespeit! / Wer hat dein Augenlicht, / Dem sonst kein Licht nicht gleichet, / So schändlich zugericht't? (Thou noble countenance, / Before which are frightened and avoid / The great world powers, / How Thou art so spat upon! / How pallid Thou art. / Who has treated the light of Thine eyes, / To which no light equals, / So shamefully?)

31. *Recitatives and Chorus — St. Mark 14: 66 to end.* (66) And as Peter was beneath in the palace, there cometh one of the maids of the high priest;

(67) And when she saw Peter warming himself, she looked upon him, and said, And thou also wast with Jesus of Nazareth.

(68) But he denied, saying, I know not, neither understand I what thou sayest. And he went out into the porch; and the cock crew.

(69) And a maid saw him again, and began to say to them that stood by, This is one of them.

(70) And he denied it again. And a little after, they that stood by said again to Peter, Surely thou art one of them; for thou art a Galilaean, and thy speech agreeth thereto.

(71) But he began to curse and to swear, saying, I know not of this man of whom ye speak.

(72) And the second time the cock crew. And Peter called to mind the word that Jesus said unto him, Before the cock crew twice, thou shalt deny me thrice. And when he thought thereon, he wept.

32. *Chorale*. This is stanza 1 of Johann Franck's 1649 hymn. It represents Peter's feelings of guilt and remorse after his denial, so we can imagine that the choir speaks for him now. As the congregation would know the words as a confessional/atonement hymn, its dramatic impact on them would be great at this moment. Herr, ich habe missgehandelt. / Ja, mich drückt der Sünden Last. / Ich bin nicht den Weg gewandelt, / Den du mir gezeiget hast; / Und jetzt wollt' ich gern aus Schrecken / Mich vor deinem Zorn verstecken. (Lord, I have done wrong. / Yes, the burden of sins oppresses me. / I have not taken the way / Which Thou hast showed me; / And now I wish out of fear / To hide myself before Thy anger.)

33. *Recitatives and Choruses — St. Mark 15: 1–14.* It would appear that the length of the recitatives increases with this number, so that the presumed Evangelist and "Choruses" would have much to do to hold the attention of the audience until the next chorale or aria would appear.

(1) And straightway in the morning the chief priests held a consultation with the elders and scribes and the whole council, and bound Jesus, and carried him away, and delivered him to Pilate.

(2) And Pilate asked him, Art thou the King of the Jews? And he answering said unto him, Thou sayest it.

(3) And the chief priests accused him of many things: but he answered nothing.

(4) And Pilate answered him again, saying, Answerest thou nothing? behold how many things they witness against thee.

(5) But Jesus yet answered nothing; so that Pilate marvelled.

(6) Now at that feast he released unto them one prisoner, whomsoever they desired.

(7) And there was one named Barabbas, which lay bound with them that had made insurrection with him, who had committed murder in the insurrection.

(8) And the multitude crying aloud began to desire him to do as he had ever done unto them.

(9) But Pilate answered them, saying, Will ye that I release unto you the King of the Jews?

(10) For he knew that the chief priests had delivered him for envy.

(11) But the chief priests moved the people, that he should rather release Barabbas unto them.

(12) And Pilate answered and said again unto them, What will ye then that I shall do unto him whom ye call the King of the Jews?

(13) And they cried out again, Crucify him.

(14) Then Pilate said unto them, Why, what evil hath he done? And they cried out the more exceedingly, Crucify him.

34. *Aria — Soprano*. Terry associates this aria with the final number (8) of Bach's secular cantata BWV 204, "Ich bin in mir vergnügt" (I am content in myself), also a soprano solo work composed about 1728. If Terry is correct, the emotion *Affekt* (effect) of the music would be as great in this transfer

as it was in the cantata. It was probably because the lines were metrically similar that Terry imputed Bach's self-borrowing, even though the new text conveys a grief motif opposite to the joy motif in the original. Angenehmes Mord-geschrei! / Jesus soll am Kreuze sterben, / Nur damit ich vom Verderben / Der verdammten Seelen frei, / Und damit mit Kreuz und Leiden / Sanfte zu ertragen sei. (Agreeable cry of murder! / Jesus is to die on the Cross, / Only so that I may be free / Of the ruin of damned souls, / And so that in cross and suffering / It may be easy to bear.)

35. *Recitatives and Choruses — St. Mark 14: 15–19.* (15) And so Pilate, willing to content the people, released Barabbas unto them, and delivered Jesus, when he had scourged him, to be crucified.

(16) And the soldiers led him away into the hall, called Praetorium; and they called together the whole band.

(17) And they clothed him with purple, and platted a crown of thorns, and put it about his head.

(18) And began to salute him, Hail, King of the Jews!

(19) And they smote him on the head with a reed, and did spit upon him, and bowing their knees worshipped him.

36. *Chorale.* This is stanza 4 of Ernst Christoph Homburg's 1659 hymn, "Jesu, meines Lebens Leben" (Jesus, Life of my life). This number comments very accurately on the action described in the preceding recitatives (35); it is also a prayer of thanks to Jesus for enduring such humiliation for us. Man hat dich sehr hart verhöhnet, / dich mit grossem Schimpf belegt, und mit Dornen gar gekrönet. / Was hat dich dazu bewegt? / Dass du möchtest mich ergötzen, / mir die Ehrenkron aufsetzen. / Tausend, tausend mal sei dir, /

liebster Jesu, Dank dafür. (They have mocked Thee very harshly, / Covered Thee with great blame, / And even crowned Thee with thorns. / What has brought Thee to that? / So that Thou mightest make me rejoice, / Put on me the crown of glory. / A thousand, thousand times be to Thee / Dearest Jesus, thanks for that.)

The dramatic significance of this chorale, like numbers 30 and 32 for example, would depend on the congregation's emotional involvement with the choir's singing.

37. *Recitative — St. Mark 15: 20–24.* (20) And when they had mocked him, they took off the purple from him, and led him out to crucify him.

(21) And they compel one Simon a Cyrenian, who passed by, coming out of the country, the father of Alexander and Rufus, to bear his cross.

(22) And they bring him unto the place Golgotha, which is, being interpreted, The place of a skull.

(23) And they gave him to drink wine mingled with myrrh; but he received it not.

(24) And when they had crucified him, they parted his garments, casting lots upon them, what every man should take.

38. *Chorale.* We now hear the choir singing stanza 4 of Luther's hymn "Ein feste Burg ist unser Gott" (A Mighty Fortress Is Our God) (1529), which Bach had also used for the last verse, number 8, of chorale cantata BWV 80. This cantata has the same title as the hymn and was composed in 1730 for the Reformation Festival, one year before this passion.

The remark after the text of number 36 applies here too. Yet once again, this chorale stanza is aptly chosen to support the thought of the preceding recitative, which also teaches us a lesson on tolerance toward our enemies.

Das Wort sie sollen lassen stahn / Und kein' Dank dazu haben. / Er ist bei uns wohl auf dem Plan / Mit seinem Geist und Gaben. / Nehmen sie uns den Leib, / Gut, Ehr, Kind und Weib, / Lass fahren dahin, / Sie haben's kein Gewinn; / Das Reich muss uns doch bleiben. (They [the enemies] must let the Word stand / And have no thanks for that. / He is right beside us on the battlefield / With His spirit and aid. / If they take our body, / Property, honor, child and wife, / Let them go. / They have no profit in it; / The Kingdom must stay with us still.)

39. *Recitatives and Choruses —
St. Mark 15: 25–34.* (25) And it was the third hour, and they crucified him.

(26) And the superscription of his accusation was written over, THE KING OF THE JEWS.

(27) And with him they crucify two thieves; the one on his right hand, and the other on his left.

(28) And the scripture was fulfilled, which saith, And he was numbered with the transgressors.

(29) And they that passed by railed on him, wagging their heads, and saying, Ah, thou that destroyest the temple, and buildest it in three days,

(30) Save thyself, and come down from the cross.

(31) Likewise also the chief priests mocking said among themselves with the scribes, He saved others; himself he cannot save.

(32) Let Christ the King of Israel descend now from the cross, that we may see and believe. And they that were crucified with him reviled him.

(33) And when the sixth hour was come, there was darkness over the whole land until the ninth hour.

(34) And at the ninth hour Jesus cried with a loud voice, saying, Eloi, Eloi, lama sabachthani? which is, be-

ing interpreted, My God, my God, why hast thou forsaken me?

40. *Chorale.* Terry states that the author of this chorale is either Andreas Kesler (or Kessler) who composed it in 1611 or someone anonymous. At any rate, the composer of the melody "O Gott, ich thu' dir's klagen" (O God, I do complain to Thee) (1609) is anonymous.

This is stanza 1 of the hymn, the first line of which answers Jesus's question to His Father as to why God has forsaken Him. The import of the verse is that God will protect His Son and all who believe in Him. The reactions of the choir (representing the audience) to Jesus's dramatic appeal to God at the end of number 39 are involved as they sing this hymn. Keinen hat Gott verlassen, / Der ihm vertraut allzeit; / Und ob ihn gleich viel hassen, / Geschieht ihm doch kein Leid. / Gott will die Seinen schützen, / Zuletzt erheben hoch; / Und geben, was ihn nützet / Hie zeitlich und auch dort. (Nobody has God left / Who always trusts him; / And although many hate him, / Yet no harm happens to him. / God will protect His own, / And one day raise them high; / And give what is useful to them / Here in this life and also there.)

41. *Recitatives and Choruses — St. Mark 15: 35–37.* (35) And some of them that stood by, when they heard it, said, Behold, he calleth Elias.

(36) And one ran and filled a sponge full of vinegar, and put it on a reed, and gave him to drink, saying, Let alone; let us see whether Elias will come to take him down.

(37) And Jesus cried with a loud voice, and gave up the ghost.

42. *Aria — Soprano — violin solo, strings, continuo — da capo.* In the reconstructed version, this aria appears to be the only original number that Bach composed for this work.

The haunting beauty of the melody, however, is heightened by the solo violin, so that the predominant grief motif throughout is unusually appealing to the listener. The soloist may be acting the part of one of the women standing before the Cross, as she sings of what she imagines Jesus to be saying to her while she watches Him. This aria is neatly tied into the narrative of number 41, but it does not resemble the bass solo (number 2) of BWV 7 in its melody as Smend thought it did in 1940. Welt und Himmel, nehmt zu Ohren, / Jesus schreiet überlaut. / Allen Sündern sagt er an, / Dass er nun genug getan, / Dass das Eden aufgebaut, / Welches wir zuvor verloren. (World and Heaven, pay heed; / Jesus cries out very loudly. / He says to all sinners / That He has done enough now, / That He has built up Eden / Which we lost before.)

43. *Recitatives — St. Mark 15: 38–45.* (38) And the veil of the temple was rent in twain from the top to the bottom.

(39) And when the centurion, which stood over against him, saw that he so cried out and gave up the ghost, he said, Truly this man was the Son of God.

(40) There were also women looking on afar off: among whom was Mary Magdalene, and Mary the mother of James the less and of Joses, and Salome;

(41) (Who also, when he was in Galilee, followed him, and ministered unto him;) and many other women which came up with him unto Jerusalem.

(42) And now when the even was come, because it was the preparation, that is, the day before the sabbath

(43) Joseph of Arimathaea, an honorable counselor, which also waited for the kingdom of God, came, and went boldly unto Pilate, and craved the body of Jesus.

(44) And Pilate marvelled if he were already dead: and calling unto him the centurion, he asked him whether he had been any while dead.

(45) And when he knew it of the centurion, he gave the body to Joseph.

44. *Chorale.* Stanza 8 of Johann Rist's "O Traurigkeit, O Herzeleid" (O Sadness, O Heart-pain) of 1641 provides the choral commentary on Joseph's action, just as if Joseph himself were uttering these words as he takes down Jesus's body. O, Jesu du, mein Hilf und Ruh! / Ich bitte dich mit Tränen, / Hilf dass ich mich bis ins Grab / Nach dir möge sehnen. (O Jesus, Thou my help and my repose! / I ask Thee with tears, / Help that until my grave / I may long for Thee.)

45. *Recitative — St. Mark 15: 46–47 (end).* (46) And he brought fine linen, and took him down, and wrapped him in the linen, and laid him in a sepulchre which was hewn out of a rock, and rolled a stone unto the door of the sepulchre.

(47) And Mary Magdalene and Mary the mother of Joses beheld where he was laid.

46. *Chorus.* For this final chorus with all instruments, Bach borrowed directly from the last chorus (number 10) of the *Trauerode* (BWV 198). The solemn rhythm befits this chorus as well as it did in the original — a funeral lament in both: one for the Queen, this for Jesus. Even Picander's poetry is closer in thought and in form to Gottsched's original verses than Picander was able to compose anywhere else in this libretto for Bach's *St. Mark Passion.* Bei deinem Grab und Leichenstein / Will ich mich stets, mein Jesu, weiden, / Und über dein verdienstlich Leiden / Von

Herzen froh und dankbar sein. / Schau, diese Grabschrift sollst du haben: / "Mein Leben kommt aus deinem Tod, / Hier hab' ich meine Sündennot / Und Jesum selbst in mich begraben." (At Thy grave and tombstone / I always want to live, my Jesus, / And over Thy meritorious suffering / Be happy and thankful from my heart. / See, this epitaph Thou shouldst have: / "My life comes from Thy death; / Here I have buried the troubles of my sins / And Jesus Himself within me.")

# III. The Masses

The Lutheran form of worship was closely affiliated with the Roman Catholic Mass, and although German was gradually replacing Latin in some Lutheran churches in Germany, much of the Roman Catholic ritual was still retained in the Protestant church services of Leipzig in the 18th century. Since the Reformation, hymns and responses were sung in Latin and in German during the procession and in the service; ceremonial robes for the clergy and the choir boys and the sound of a little bell at the consecration of the Lord's Supper were of Roman Catholic origin.

Yet there were many in Lutheran congregations of the 17th and 18th centuries who would have liked to change this resemblance through greater use of their own language (German) and less ostentation during the performance of a church service. In 1702, the Leipzig Town Council drew up a petition to the King-Elector, Augustus II, the Strong, who had recently converted to Roman Catholicism in order to gain the throne of Poland, requesting that hymns and texts in German be introduced in all the churches of Saxony! That this petition was not granted it not surprising.

Moreover, many in the Leipzig clergy and also their congregations wished to keep the Latin portions in their services, so the Lutheran *Missa brevis* (Short Mass) evolved. This modified mass consisted of only the

Kyrie and the Gloria movements; the other sections — the Credo, Sanctus, Benedictus, Osanna and Agnus Dei — could still be sung as separate numbers on special festivals, but were never performed in a connected full service at Leipzig.

For example, Bach wrote a *Sanctus in D Major* in six parts for Christmas 1724, which he later transferred into the *Mass in B Minor* as one of the movements he added after 1733. He  also composed another double choir *Sanctus in D* (BWV 238) for the previous Christmas 1723 as well as three more four part settings of the Sanctus, a *Christe eleison* (BWV 242) for a *Mass in C* by J. L. Krebs and a *Credo* (BWV 1083) for a *Mass in F* by Bassani, about 1740.

These works by Bach could have been performed singly during Leipzig church services on festival days. The time required for the regular morning church service would tend, however, to preclude performance of any one of the above works, in view of the fact that a complete Protestant church cantata (Hauptmusik) of 25 to 40 minutes duration as well as the other musical items were expected. Whether Bach could even fit one of his short masses into such a lengthy program is questionable (see the Introduction for details of the Leipzig morning service).

Spitta notes that "During the whole eighteenth century the tendency was towards the limitation or even elimi-

81

nation of the Latin portions of the liturgy. What the Town Council began in 1702 was still being carried on by Johann Adam Hiller in 1791, although by that time the existence of the Latin hymns or canticles had left no trace behind" (*Johann Sebastian Bach*, III, 27).

The reason why Bach began suddenly to compose masses and to turn away from passions must be sought in the lack of support he received from the Town Council for his training of the St. Thomas Church choir and for his writing and performance of his passions in Leipzig's two main churches, St. Thomas's and St. Nicholas's. He hoped to produce such works as would impress the Royal Court in Dresden, and since this court was Roman Catholic, what better way than to present them with masses, which would show his merit as one of their composers? Thus the Elector's favor would counteract the problems that he was facing as cantor in Leipzig.

Perhaps even Bach was hoping for some permanent appointment in Dresden where he had given organ recitals in the Sophienkirche and performances by his Collegium Musicum before the court in 1731. He was well-known throughout Saxony for his expertise in organ instruction and for his organ playing. His acquaintance and friendship with the court and opera composer Hasse began at the time of his visits to attend the Dresden opera with his eldest son, Friedemann, about 1730.

When the Elector of Saxony and Poland, Augustus II, died on February 1, 1733, the resulting five months of mourning left Bach free from composing cantatas or directing music in Leipzig, so that he had time to set the first two sections, the Kyrie and the Gloria of his *Mass in B Minor* (BWV 232). The remaining parts of the mass

were not completed until well after 1736 when Bach finally received the title of Court Composer which he had sought July 27, 1733, from the new Elector, Augustus III, on sending him the opening parts of his *B Minor Mass*. There is no record of any performance in Dresden of this Missa, in part or in its eventual completed version. Yet as Friedemann had become organist in the Sophienkirche in 1733, it is possible that its Kyrie and Gloria could have been performed there.

Both Schweitzer and Terry perceived in Bach the Biblical scholar and also the musician who could capture the significance of the words before him, whether in German or in Latin, and give them a tonal quality to make them live in sound. These motifs have been pointed out in the cantatas and in the passions; they give the work its drama which was never very far from Bach's thinking and which one can expect to find in the masses and to a lesser degree even in the motets.

Since these latter two religious genres are based on a fixed liturgy, little has been done in the past by musicologists to identify the characters or the dramatis personae in each movement, about whom Bach must have thought as he set the music for their choruses or arias in these works. With the cantatas and the passions this identification was much easier than it will be with the masses and the motets, where Bach's borrowing from his cantatas for certain numbers in the masses might help in this task.

The order in which the masses were composed are chronologically: BWV 232 *Mass in B Minor* (1724–c. 1749); BWV 233 *Mass in F* (?1735–1740 — It is assumed that these four short Lutheran masses were all composed about the same time); BWV 234 *Mass in A*; BWV 235 *Mass in G Minor*; BWV 236 *Mass in G*.

Bach's borrowing from his cantatas for movements in his masses has been censured by musicologists of our century, but it must be understood that he was only following the common practice of the 18th century (c.f. Handel's self-borrowings). What is surprising is that the recast "borrowed" movements often surpass the originals in spite of whole passages that are copied without apparent change, except for slight additions or altered harmony in the new mass versions.

In musical format, Bach's masses have both solo and choral movements. These latter seem to function as the orchestral tutti in a large sacred concerto, setting off the more personal solo numbers. The choral sections are often fugal in form, building up to a tremendous climax, while the vocal solos are accompanied by an instrumental solo obbligato equally featured with the vocal line.

As in Bach's other vocal works with arias and choruses, he often expresses by melisma (elaboration of a sound-syllable in the vocal line) such emotions as joy or grief as they occur in the text he sets.

It is known that Bach intended his *Mass in B Minor* to be performed in Dresden and probably expected the later additions to be performed there also. Opinion is divided on whether he intended the short masses for Dresden or Leipzig. If they were performed in Dresden, there is no record of it, but they were no doubt included as part of the Leipzig church services controlled by Bach. It is thought that they may have been commissioned by Bach's Bohemian patron, Franz Anton Count von Sporck, for use in his own chapel, because Bach had impressed him with a copy of the *Sanctus* which was later included in the *B Minor Mass.*

Whenever Bach's masses are mentioned, it is only the *Mass in B Minor* that immediately comes to mind, because that is the only mass that he completed in full with all its movements after he had composed its Kyrie and its Gloria in 1733. Like Handel's *Messiah,* to which it has been compared as the summit of Bach's religious composition, Bach's *Mass in B Minor* has stood the test of time. That both of these masterpieces should find fame in the concert hall rather than in church performances is not surprising because of their excessive length.

It is difficult to say why Bach persisted in working at the *B Minor Mass* even after he had completed the four Lutheran or short masses. Why did he not try to complete these four masses also, instead of abandoning this main form of sacred composition to which he had devoted so much effort? For with this one finished mass, his sacred vocal writing ceases, except for a few cantatas.

Probably Bach's intention in gradually adding movements to finish his first mass in its catholic sense was not to entertain the listener, as it does today, but to lead him to appreciate the origins of the Christian belief through a dramatic musical presentation of the basic rite of the Roman Catholic worshipper, the mass. His aim, no doubt, was to bring Lutherans and Roman Catholics to a better understanding of each other by this one common work, containing elements of both Christian denominations, i.e. Latin words combined with his own Lutheran melodies. Also, as court composer after 1736, Bach would want to continue to compose short masses to please his Sovereign, Augustus III, who, as a Roman Catholic, would favor these masses more than any other genre for performance in his Court.

Yet there must have been some

reason why he became indifferent to mass settings. A plausible explanation might be that all his masses became suspect when he submitted them to Dresden, because the Roman Catholic court and its clergy could not accept or perform a mass set by a Lutheran, despite Bach's sincere attempt to reconcile Catholic with Protestant doctrine. But this reason for ignoring his initial Kyrie and Gloria of the *B Minor Mass* was never given to him before or after his being named court composer in 1736.

After this date, Bach continued to work on the remainder of the *B minor Mass,* which, Spitta claims, was completed by 1738 at the latest (III, 39), but at the same time or soon after, he composed his four short masses (1737–38).

Both the *F Major* and the *A Major* masses could have been written for performance, first in Leipzig's Lutheran churches, and then later offered to the Dresden Court Chapel, but the *G Major* and *G Minor* masses, being composed entirely of Bach's borrowed movements from his cantatas, would have little chance of being performed in any Roman Catholic church in Dresden. Nevertheless, Bach must have tried. Spitta supports this theory by stating: "It is at once evident that Bach cannot have written the G major and the G minor masses for his churches at Leipzig. . . . These masses must have been intended for some other place, and Dresden at once occurs to mind. If we may assign the G minor mass to about the same period as the other, Bach may have intended to make his mark as Court composer by thus enriching it, and, at the same time, on account of his immediate difficulties at Leipzig, to keep himself in mind at Court. The work, which was evidently written in haste, indicates lack of time and of the humour for original production" (III, 31–32).

It was probably not "lack of time" that induced Bach to write these two short masses in G in such a hurry, but rather a wish to quickly signal his gratitude to Augustus III for finally condescending to his request to be named court composer. Knowing that any of his masses would never be performed in Dresden, just as the first two parts of his *B minor* had been ignored there, why not keep them as short masses for the Lutheran churches of Leipzig, where the full ordinary of the Roman Mass could not be presented? And apparently, this is what happened.

What is most surprising in all the mass settings by Bach is that the composer had to rely on the melodies that he had set in his cantatas for the majority of the movements, instead of original composition. Bach was well versed in church Latin; therefore, why would he force German verse into a Latin text? For this is exactly what Bach did in borrowing whole movements from his own cantatas from which neither the meaning of the German libretto nor its metrical adaptability into Latin agreed. It is a wonder that he could make the melody concur with the Latin words as often as he did! Whenever the borrowed melody seems to fit the Latin text, it is more because of Bach's arrangement of his music than his making the two meanings coincide.

Such wholesale adaptations of cantata melodies into Latin verse would naturally lead us to think that either Bach was in a hurry to finish that particular work, or that he had lost interest in the mass genre even while he was composing! The truth probably lies in both of these reasons, for why would he select only one cantata for four of the six numbers in the *Mass in G Minor*?

As has been pointed out, however,

Bach invariably changes his adaptation in some slight way, especially in the arias, so that the new number is often an improvement on the original. This revision would seem to refute the theory that Bach was indifferent or in haste in his self-borrowing.

The dramatic aspect of Bach's masses would depend on the emotional effect conveyed by the words and the music in the corresponding cantata movement, except where this chorus represented a choir of angels. Here there would be no problem in making this transfer. That Bach was rarely able to make the borrowed melody as dramatic in its new Latin text as it was in the original cantata is to be expected.

On the other hand, some of these mass "arias" have a tendency to be operatic in their da capo form and are therefore truly dramatic in form. For example, the da capo Bass aria (number 3) of the *Mass in F Major* (BWV 233), or the Soprano aria (number 4) of the *Mass in A Major* (BWV 234), and certainly the soloist movements interpolated in the Gloria chorus (number 2) of this latter mass prove that Bach's dramatic gift had also a touch of opera to be seen in them. In fact, it is as difficult to separate what is drama from what is opera in Bach's vocal work as to distinguish the difference between the chorales and the congregational hymns upon which he relied so much. Each is related to the other, although Bach never admitted his debt to opera in adopting its format for his own sacred composing. But then neither did the composers who were his contemporaries in setting sacred libretti: Graun, Handel, Hasse, and Telemann.

Forkel notes in his work, *J. S. Bach* (48), that Bach's attitude towards opera is reflected in his saying to his eldest son, Friedemann, that they should go to Dresden to hear the beautiful little songs, by which he meant the opera. However, if he was thinking of the operas of his friend, Hasse, he would not intend to disparage them, but rather to be entertained and learn from them all he could as it pertained to his own art.

Yet there is nothing of the levity of opera in Bach's religious works. Whether a number was borrowed from his previous sacred or secular compositions, the effect of its music is always deeply moving and serious.

The *Mass in B Minor* (BWV 232) is the only complete mass that Bach ever composed. It stands as a monument to Bach's highest achievement in vocal music setting. None of his other works  can be compared with it, because of the length of time he spent to complete it, and especially because of his accomplishment in amalgamating his music with its personal, Protestant feeling into the Roman Catholic Ordinary.

The popularity of this one mass in the concert hall today proves that Bach did succeed in leaving to posterity a work which has become one of the world's masterpieces since its first complete performance at Leipzig in 1859. Some have even considered this score as a textbook example of how to construct a mass in music.

It was not only because this long mass could not be performed in the time allotted within any church service that it had to wait over one hundred years for its renaissance, but also that the use of Latin was becoming more and more restricted in Lutheran churches as the eighteenth century progressed. Since the Kyrie and the Gloria of any of Bach's masses were never performed in the Roman Catholic churches of Dresden, because of his Lutheran overtones in music, he would not expect that his finished *Mass in B Minor* could be performed there during his lifetime.

The *Mass in B Minor* was Bach's last major vocal work, but it is the one that has achieved lasting recognition for several generations and will likely continue to do so in the future. If this were the only work that Bach had composed, it alone should have brought him fame for his attempt to harmonize Protestants with Roman Catholics in a work that is common to both denominations.

Even though the dramatic aspect in his masses is less apparent to the audience than it is in his passions, Bach can nevertheless motivate each movement in music, so that an appropriate audiovisual scene is conjured up to fit the Latin text.

Archibald T. Davison sees a parallel between Bach and the authors of Greek tragedy when he remarks: "It is Bach's music which transfigures the story, and it is the music that welds together all the dramatic components into an overpowering tragedy. Without writing a single opera, his Passions and the *B Minor Mass* more nearly satisfy the age-long requirements of the drama than do the out-and-out dramatic works of his contemporaries. While they were writing operas on classical subjects, requiring all the operatic panoply to be even superficially convincing, he was writing his Passions without asking any of the exteriors of dramatic presentation and was approaching much more closely than they to dramatic truth" (*Bach and Handel — The Consummation of the Baroque in Music,* 61–62).

# The Mass in B Minor

### (Leipzig 1733–c. 1749; BWV 232)

This mass was Bach's greatest effort to bring the Protestant and the Roman Catholic factions together by composing one lengthy but magnificent work based on the Latin text for the High Mass. Some of its choruses (Credo and Confiteor) evoke a Roman atmosphere, while the Protestant aspect of Bach's church cantatas emerges chiefly in the intimate feeling of the arias and in most choruses.

In its form, the Ordinarium of the Mass is divided into five sections, each about the length of a church cantata: the Kyrie has three numbers, the Gloria eight, the Credo nine, the Sanctus (with the Benedictus) three, and the Agnus Dei two. This style was in accord with the Neapolitan opera mass which was in vogue under Hasse in Dresden.

But Bach's manner of composing was unlike that of the Italian church composers. His personality and his style had been influenced mostly by German Protestant music. Bach's Lutheran upbringing impelled him to follow the Biblical meaning rather than the Latin liturgical text. Consequently to each division Bach ascribes a definite mood or feeling which predominates over the musical drama enacted therein: Kyrie — Confession; Gloria — Worship; Credo — Faith; Sanctus — Adoration; Agnus Dei — Thanksgiving. The soloists are Soprano 1, Soprano 2, Alto, Tenor, Bass 1, Bass 2 with a five part chorus (unusual for Bach), and a full orchestra: trumpets, tympani, strings, woodwinds and organ continuo.

*Kyrie (Nos. 1–3).* This opening

movement has only three numbers, two words per number, but Bach treats each number as a separate unit with its own emotional overtone. From these six words he develops 270 bars of music which require about half an hour to perform.

1. *Kyrie eleison — Tutti, Chorus (five part): B minor.* Kyrie eleison (Lord, have mercy upon us.)

Bach used Luther's *German Mass* of 1525 for the first part of this opening chorus, which is unique in comparison with any other beginning for a mass setting. No orchestral overture prepares for this opening invocation, dramatically pictured by Bach as a vast multitude, pleading with God to have mercy upon them for their sins. A lengthy orchestral ritornello then follows. The chorus represents the voices of all nations, as they make confession in a change of tempo to Largo ed un poco piano — a grief (sob) motif in a fugue which resembles a concerto movement on a vast scale with 126 bars in slow time, both of which Bach was adept at creating. The tenors appear first, then the altos and the sopranos, and this swelling throng reaches a vocal climax when the basses enter, eight bars from the end.

Spitta (III, 54) states that this first Kyrie is symbolic of mankind craving redemption from sin — the keynote of the whole work. He thinks that this universal plea for mercy is at first epic and then dramatic in the change to various voices with their grief motif.

2. *Christe eleison — Sopranos 1 and 2 — Duet: D major.* Christe eleison (Christ, have mercy upon us.)

This is the first of three duets in this work; there are six arias and 17 choruses, making a total of 26 numbers. No recitatives are used, since they and the chorales were not allowed in Catholic church music.

There is a motif of serenity in this second clause which imparts a feeling of confidence that Christ, our Mediator, will heed our prayer to Him as it is being sung by the vocalists.

The sopranos follow each other in flawless imitation which enhances the artistic beauty of the music in this number. Such a quiet prayer-like tone might identify the sopranos as women sinners beseeching Jesus for forgiveness, or as two angels pleading with Him to forgive sinning mankind. In either case, this is a highly dramatic number with pictorial qualities as in the two Kyrie movements.

3. *Kyrie eleison — Tutti, Chorus (four part): F♯ minor.* Kyrie eleison (Lord, have mercy upon us.)

This repetition of the Kyrie is again a fugue, but in different style, building itself around a single note in a tortuous way. It continues the lamenting tone of the first Kyrie with its grief motif but has only four voice parts instead of five and is less than half the length of number 1.

The theme is again their repentance as sinners, expressed in the same direct appeal to God which created the drama in number 1, but this time in a more subdued and contrite tone indicating their atonement.

Usually, the sequence of the numbers in this work will be divided into alternate solo and choral movements. So in this first division, we have heard a solo duet (2), between two choruses (1 and 3), these latter serving the same function as the orchestral tutti in a concerto, i.e. to set off the more personal feeling in the solo arias and duets. This opening division, with its theme of confession, could thus be considered as a sacred concerto in itself. Such personal emphasis in both words and music gives this dramatic opening division a definitely Protestant tone.

*Gloria (Nos. 4–11).*

4. *Chorus — Tutti: D Major.* Gloria in excelsis Deo. / Et in terra pax / hominibus bonae voluntatis. (Glory to God in the highest. / And in earth peace / to men of good will.)

As worship is the central theme of this second main division of the mass, Bach begins this opening section with an exuberant joy motif expressive of the homage to God that should be shown by the multitude of nations in Part I. Here we hear a chorus of angels singing a Christmas hymn in two parts — the jubilant first line, followed by a more tranquil peace motif to illustrate the words "Et in terra pax hominibus bonae voluntatis." This angelic chorus will also conclude the last number (11) in the Gloria division with a similar blaze of vocal and orchestral color including trumpet.

This movement is in swinging 3/8 time which Bach liked to use in choral settings; he will use it again twice more in this mass — for the "pleni sunt coeli" part of the Sanctus and for the Osanna, both in D major. It is worth noting that Bach will use four 3/8 choruses in the *Christmas Oratorio* of the following year (1734–35).

Bach borrowed the setting for this first movement of the Gloria verbatim for his Christmas cantata BWV 191, "Gloria in excelsis Deo," performed about 1740, for Soprano/Tenor soli, a five part Chorus, three trumpets, timpani, two flutes, two oboes, strings and continuo. Likewise he borrowed the other two movements of this cantata: the second number, a duet for soprano/tenor soli,* from the seventh, Domine Deus in the mass, while the final chorus originates in the final chorus Cum Sancto Spiritu (number 11) of the mass. Bach managed to fit his music for this text to the

new Latin words of the cantata: Sicut erat in principio et nunc et semper in saecula saeculorum. Amen. (As it was in the beginning, is now and ever shall be, world without end. Amen.)

5. *Aria — Soprano 2, violin solo: A major.* Laudamus te; / benedicimus te; / adoramus te; / glorificamus te. (We praise Thee; / we bless Thee; / we worship Thee; / we glorify Thee.)

The joy motif is continued in the playing of the solo violin, which with its light sparkle to set off the soprano voice as she sings these four lines, makes such an allegro-aria unique among Bach's solos for soprano.

She could be identified as one of the angels from the preceding chorus for, since she sings in the first person plural, it seems that her aria is sung on behalf of the entire chorus of angels in number 4. The feelings of the worshippers (the congregation) might be included in her expression of thanks to God for the Nativity. The da capo for this number reinforces the joy motif she has expressed.

6. *Chorus — Tutti, with trumpet obbligato: D major.* Gratias agimus tibi / propter magnam gloriam tuam. (We give thanks to Thee / on account of Thy great glory.)

This borrowed number is taken from the opening chorus of Bach's Ratswahl (Election of the Town Council) cantata BWV 29, composed for the Leipzig church service following the civic ceremony on August 27, 1731. Bach chose this movement because it fits the Latin text without the need to alter very much the melody that he had already composed for the German words: "Wir danken dir, Gott, wir danken dir, / und verkündigen deine Wunder." (We thank Thee, God, we thank Thee, / and proclaim Thy wonders.)

---

*Gloria Patri, et Filio, / et Spiritu Sancto. (Glory to the Father and to the Son, / and to the Holy Ghost.)

This choir would again consist of the angels, repeating the thoughts of the congregation, as they sing in canon with a motif of solemnity of their thanks for God's great glory. The respectful restraint in a motif of calm, as they offer their thanks, becomes more animated upon the word *gloriam*, as though Bach wished to emphasize this word in an otherwise tranquil movement. The obbligato trumpet brings out this emphasis, just as it does in all his trumpet choruses.

7. *Duet — Soprano 1, Tenor: G major.* Domine Deus, Rex coelestis, / Deus Pater omnipotens. / Domine Fili unigenite / Jesu Christe altissime: / Domine Deus, Agnus Dei, / Filius Patris, (Lord God, heavenly King, / God the Father almighty. / O Lord, the only begotten Son, / Jesus Christ most high: / Lord God, Lamb of God, / Son of the Father,)

Although Bach must have known the Latin text for this movement, he writes *altissime* which is not in the Roman Catholic canon, nor was it in the Leipzig Prayer Book. However, Bach does not use the word again in any of his other four Lutheran short masses.

A flute combines with violins to play the ethereal melody for the two voices singing in canon, one voice (the soprano) addressing the Father and the other (the tenor) the Son. These soloists would represent angels as in the previous chorus. Bach separates the two voices so that *Deus* and *Fili* only are heard together. Not until the last 21 bars do they sing the same words in unison, to symbolically join the two Persons of the Godhead. This movement continues into number 8 with scarcely any pause.

8. *Chorus — Tutti: B minor.* Qui tollis peccata mundi, / miserere nobis; / Qui tollis peccata mundi, / suscipe deprecationem nostram.

(Thou who takest away the sins of the world, / have mercy upon us; / Thou who takest away the sins of the world, / receive our prayer.)

This movement, the third adapted chorus, was borrowed from the first chorus of cantata BWV 46, originally composed about 1725 to the text from Lamentations 1:12 — "Schauet doch und sehet, ob irgend ein Schmerz sei wie mein Schmerz, der mich troffen hat." (Just behold and see, whether any other sorrow is like my sorrow, which has stricken me.)

The instruments used are four strings and two flutes with a four voice chorus — ten parts in total. We hear the same grief motif as Bach used in the cantata, accompanied by the same tearful sobs of the flutes, but, by modifying the motif of sadness in the words "wie mein Schmerz," he could fit in its place the "miserere nobis" with its tone imploring pity.

The choir is here speaking for itself and for the whole congregation as it begs God's Son to receive their prayer. From a dramatic point of view, it seems that from this number on, the choruses and soloists may vary between human beings and angels as "actors" in this mass.

9. *Aria — Alto: B minor.* Qui sedes ad dextram Patris, / miserere nobis. (Thou who sittest at the right hand of the Father, / have mercy upon us.)

It may be assumed that the alto represents a woman in the congregation of worshippers. Her plaintive longing for mercy is expressed in a grief motif similar to number 8. Her lowly condition is contrasted with that of Christ: He has finished His earthly mission and now sits beside His Father, whereas she must continue to struggle and fight against sin in this world. But what emotion she pours into her song! Bach's sense of drama can be detected in this and the next aria for bass.

And when Bach is moved by an emotional situation in the text, he usually chooses an alto to express his feelings, as now and for the Agnus Dei (number 25) in this mass, as well as for the alto arias in his *Magnificat* and in the passions.

10. *Aria — Bass: D major.* Bach features two bassoons, two celli, the organ and an obbligato corno da caccia to produce a picture of royal splendor. Again, the bass plays the part of an "actor" expressing the thoughts (the text) of the audience. Quoniam tu solus sanctus, / Tu solus Dominus, / Tu solus altissimus, / Jesu Christe; (For Thou only art holy, / Thou only art the Lord, / Thou only art the highest, / Jesus Christ;)

This aria certainly praises Christ and is more melodious than Denis Arnold judged it in his book *Bach* (62): "Here a bass voice contests (accompanied is certainly the wrong word) two bassoons and a corno da caccia, together with a continuo team of, presumably, cello, bass and organ. Historically this weird sound can be explained as an example of the German liking for the 'wind choirs' which dates back to the early seventeenth century at least. Yet there was nothing like it in the eighteenth century and the listeners, if there were any, at Dresden would have been completely baffled; even today, with our tolerant ears to unusual combinations, it still sounds very strange."

It is certain that Bach considered this number more as an aria than an instrumental showpiece, for he has definitely separated the bass voice from the instruments so that each word of his text is clearly audible. The instrumental writing is also very impressive, especially in the ritornello at the end.

11. *Chorus — Tutti: D major.* Cum Sancto Spiritu / in gloria Dei Patris.

Amen. (With the Holy Spirit / in the glory of God the Father. Amen.)

The choir returns to sing this mighty fugue, thus concluding the Gloria division. Now the singers represent the angelic "actors," last heard in number 7. The tenors begin this fugue into which the other voices are added in canon; they conjure up a picture of Heaven as trumpets punctuate the choral phrases. Such a powerful conclusion is a fitting final act of worship for the Trinity which began the Gloria division and was included in all its movements. Their skillful singing of this text, punctuated by devout "Amen"s and concluding with unison singing of "Amen," makes this a momentous finale.

This number completes Bach's "musical offering" to the new Elector Augustus III in 1733. All the other movements in this mass were composed by Bach after this date.

*Credo (Nos. 12–20) Symbolum Nicaenum (Nicene Creed).*

12. *Chorus — a cappella, but with continuo: A Major.* Credo in unum Deum, (I believe in one God,)

Since this entire third division will stress faith as its main theme, Bach focuses on the confession of faith by each individual among the performers and in the audience. The Nicene Creed must be personal when recited aloud, and therefore the soloists or the choirs involved will dramatize each movement of the Credo, acting directly as themselves. Still, the drama is surely there in Bach's musical settings.

Word pictures of the life of Christ and of our belief in Him are evoked by musical contrasts (forte and piano) between each movement. Thus recitative would be completely unnecessary.

The first movement is in the early

Church style of Palestrina, studied by Bach and which he deliberately uses here in the mixolydian mode, imitating the priests' chanting of the 16th century. The a cappella setting used here and in the Confiteor (number 19) chorus confirms the feeling that this is archaic musical language of the Middle Ages when the Creed was established.

Schweitzer's opinion on the Credo should be quoted: "In no Mass has the difficulty of writing music for the *Credo* been so completely overcome as in this of Bach's. He has taken the utmost possible advantage of any dramatic ideas in the text; when emotion can be read into it he does so. . . . One of the most striking features of the *B Minor Mass* in general and the *Credo* in particular is Bach's excellent Latin declamation. His most daring coloratura are only the artistic intensification of the natural syllabic values and accents of the words" (*J. S. Bach,* II, 317–18).

Bach symbolizes the unshakable solidarity of the faith taught by the Church by using a hurried step motif in the pedal bass, perhaps to denote the millions who have hurried to support their faith in bygone years. While the basses declaim the Intonation (*Credo in unum Deum*), the second sopranos and the altos sing it in canon with the basses. The first sopranos sing in imitation, accompanied by the violins. In this fugal movement, Bach uses these two methods simultaneously to illustrate firmness and unity in the faith.

After a pause, the Intonation line is repeated before the next Chorus (number 13).

13. *Chorus — Tutti: D major.* Patrem omnipotentem, / factorem coeli et terrae, / visibilium omnium et invisibilium: (The Father Almighty, / Creator of heaven and earth, / And of all things visible and invisible:)

Borrowed from the opening chorus of cantata BWV 171, "Gott, wie dein Name, so ist auch dein Ruhm bis an der Welt Ende" (God, as Thy Name, so is Thy fame until the end of the world), Bach has chosen this chorus very well, because it presents a fugal picture of the majesty and omnipotence of God, just as it did at the beginning of the cantata in 1730. The full orchestra with angelic trumpets paints a scene of God enthroned in Heaven; this will be augmented even more in the subsequent Sanctus movement of this mass.

Bach does not deviate from the setting of the original German text to exploit musically the mystical ideas contained in the words *visibilium omnium et invisibilium*. He is content to let the original music speak for itself.

14. *Duet — Soprano 1, Alto: G major.* Et in unum Dominum Jesum Christum / Filium Dei unigenitum, / et ex Patre natum ante omnia saecula. / Deum de Deo, Lumen de Lumine, / Deum verum de Deo vero; / genitum, non factum; / consubstantialem Patri, / per quem omnia facta sunt. / Qui propter nos homines / et propter nostram salutem / descendit de coelis, (And in one Lord, Jesus Christ, the only begotten Son of God; / and born of the Father before all ages. / God of God, Light of Light, / true God of true God; / begotten, not made; / of the same substance as the Father, / by Whom all things were made. / Who, for us men / and for our salvation, / came down from Heaven,)

This rather long Duet is related to Duet number 7, which also expounded the relations of the First and Second Persons of the Trinity. The voices follow each other in canonical imitation as Bach illustrates his text by a march rhythm showing the Son proceeding from the Father by a step motif. Bach uses descending orchestral passages to imply how God's power passed into His Son when He became Man. Note especially the orchestral conclusion to end this movement.

15. *Chorus: B minor.* Et incarnatus est de Spiritu Sancto / ex Maria Virgine, / et homo factus est. (And was made incarnate by the Holy Spirit / of the Virgin Mary, / and was made Man.)

Beginning with this chorus and followed by the next two choruses (numbers 16 and 17), Bach dramatizes the earthly life of Christ as the text indicates in three musical pictures: Christmas Day, Good Friday, and Easter Day.

According to the last line in number 14, number 15 was originally included in number 14. But as Bach preferred to have the Mystery of the Incarnation as a separate movement, he reset this in a short movement of 49 bars, and inserted this new number into his score on a separate sheet. Its five vocal parts are accompanied only by the violins and the organ. Their melody evokes an image of the hovering Holy Spirit, symbolically denoted by a throbbing in the organ continuo.

After the twice repeated words *et incarnatus est de Spiritu Sancto ex Maria Virgine,* there occurs a mystical seven beat pause; then the hovering theme stops in the violins but reappears in the organ continuo and in the ascending tones of the sopranos and the altos on the words *et homo factus est.*

Thus Bach illustrates dramatically through sound the Mystery of the Nativity.

16. *Chorus: E minor.* Crucifixus etiam pro nobis / sub Pontio Pilato; / passus et sepultus est. (He was crucified also for us / under Pontius Pilate; / He suffered and was buried.)

This is the second major scene of Christ's life — the Good Friday sequence. In a grief motif repeated 13 times in a phrase of four bars, Bach sets this tragedy to a dance form — a stately Passecaglia — played over a recurring ground-bass (basso ostinato). This music was borrowed directly from the opening chorus to his cantata BWV 12, "Weinen, Klagen, Sorgen, Zagen" (Weeping, Complaining, Worrying, Fearing), of 1724. It is adapted very well to this particular scene, as each vocal part enters separately, their hushed tone reflecting their horror at beholding the tragic picture of the Crucifixion on the Cross.

In the last line, Bach marks the score piano for the sopranos and the basses, as they sing with deep pathos of Christ's burial, and he changes the key from E minor to its relative G major at the end. With just a chorus, Bach paints a scene of the Crucifixion unequaled in sacred music, the sound evoking the dramatic vision of the listeners.

17. *Chorus — Tutti: D major.* Et resurrexit tertia die, / secundum Scripturas; / et ascendit in coelum, / sedet ad dexteram Dei Patris. / Et iterum venturus est cum gloria / judicare vivos et mortuos, / cujus regni non erit finis. (And He arose again the third day, / according to the Scriptures; / and ascended into Heaven; He sitteth at the right hand of God the Father. / And He shall come again with glory / to judge the quick and the dead, / Whose kingdom shall have no end.)

With this third scene from Christ's life on earth, we come to the Resurrection on Easter Day. This movement has three divisions in itself: the Resurrection, the Ascension, and the Second Advent; each division is separated from the next by an orchestral ritornello, thus presenting the three distinct scenes as indicated by the Latin text.

This entire movement is one of Bach's masterpieces, and is certainly the high point in this work. The dazzling joy motif with its mysterious triple sounding notes in the trumpets throughout the movement and the vivacious fugue to accompany the last division, beginning "Et iterum venturus est," should move any listener deeply. Bach's musical arrangement of this text is astounding for its originality. In my opinion, this section of the Credo will never be surpassed in its setting by any other composer.

18. *Aria – Bass: A major.* Et in Spiritum Sanctum / Dominum et vivificantem, / qui ex Patre Filioque procedit; / qui cum Patre et Filio simul / adoratur et conglorificatur; / qui locutus est per prophetas. / Et unam sanctam catholicam et / apostolicam ecclesiam. (And [I believe] in the Holy Ghost, / the Lord and Giver of Life, / Who proceedeth from the Father and the Son; / Who, with the Father and the Son at the same time, / is worshipped and glorified; / Who spake by the prophets. / And [I believe] in one Holy Catholic and / Apostolic Church.)

This aria is in quiet contrast with the preceding chorus (17), and with the two following choruses (19, 20). It seems to resemble more a lecture on church dogma than a musical number, despite the soloist's melismas on *Dominum* and *vivificantem.* The Holy Spirit appears to be less prominent in the music than in chorus number 15. Still, Bach sounds a sincere note on his belief in a universal Christian Church in the last two lines sung by the bass "actor."

19. *Chorus – A cappella, but with organ continuo: F♯ minor.* Confiteor

unum baptisma / in remissionem peccatorum. (I acknowledge one Baptism / for the remission of sins,)

Like the Credo movement (number 12), this a cappella number seems to recall the singing of the early Roman Catholic Church, but Bach uses a fugue rather than the old plainsong Intonation for the Confiteor. He bases this fugue, however, on the old form with basses and altos, followed by tenors.

There is little doubt that Bach agreed with these lines of the liturgy, whether the baptism was Lutheran or Roman Catholic, since he intended this mass to be compatible with both denominations in all its parts.

20. *Chorus – Tutti: D major.* Et expecto resurrectionem mortuorum, / et vitam venturi saeculi. Amen. (And I look for the resurrection of the dead, / and the life of the world to come. Amen.)

This is the second of a series of four choruses (numbers 19 to 22 inclusive). Such an arrangement does not occur in any of Bach's cantatas, but in a mass, without recitatives, repetition of choruses for movements was probably Bach's only alternative, if arias were not suitable.

Two sopranos begin *Et expecto,* singing in an atmosphere faithful to the words they declaim, after the other voices have sung the same words in adagio.

Then the tempo changes to vivace ed allegro in a "Resurrection" motif of joy for all voices, trumpets and the full orchestra, seemingly to conjure up a scene of triumph for the risen dead at the conclusion of the Credo here. Worthy of note is the blaze of trumpets to punctuate the concluding Amen.

*Sanctus (21–24).*

21. *Chorus – Tutti: D major.* Sanctus, sanctus, sanctus, / Dominus Deus

Sabaoth! / Pleni sunt coeli et terra gloria eius. (Holy, holy, holy, / Lord God of Hosts! / Heaven and earth are full of His glory.)

Since Bach had composed this chorus in 1724 for a separate Christmas performance in Leipzig, it was ready to hand to be borrowed for this mass.

Bach set this chorus for six voices because he had read in Isaiah 3:2, where the seraphims had six wings, thus giving him the idea of six voices. These illustrate the drama of Isaiah 5:3: "And one cried unto another and said, Holy, holy, holy, is the Lord of Hosts; the whole earth is full of his glory." The antiphony of the angels is represented by the two sopranos and the first altos singing one part of the angelic choir, and the second altos, the tenors and the basses the other. There is a step motif combined with a motif of sublime peace in the bass part of this hymn of praise.

Then the second section of the angels' hymn, *pleni sunt coeli,* overflows in a joy motif to conclude the movement. Bach changed the Roman text to *ejus* from *tuae.* Why he made this change from the Nicene Creed with its more intimate form and which prevailed in Leipzig is not known.

Spitta (III, 61) remarks as follows on this last part of the Sanctus: "After this majestic *Sanctus* follows an animated setting of *Pleni sunt coeli,* which so far exceeds any similar movement in the mass in ecstatic jubilation that we cannot help feeling that till this moment Bach has only given us hymns of praise and joy of mortal Christians, but that here 'the morning stars are singing together and the sons of God shouting for joy.'" (Spitta quotes from Job 38:7.)

The full instrumentation, trumpets, tympani, woodwinds and strings seems to affirm this judgment which makes this moment the climax of the mass. It is quickly followed by the next chorus (22).

22. *Chorus — Tutti: D major.* Osanna in excelsis. (Hosanna in the highest.)

This is the only secular cantata number borrowed by Bach in this mass. It is the first chorus of cantata BWV 215, "Preise dein Glücke, gesegnetes Sachsen" (Praise thy luck, blessed Saxony), hurriedly composed in 1734 to honor Augustus III's visit to Leipzig to receive this city's homage. To this monarch, Bach had sent the Kyrie and the Gloria of this mass with his petition to be court composer, but had received no reply.

It is the only Double Chorus in the mass, and its melody fits the words of the Latin text without any difficulty. In fact, the joy motif conjures up a dramatic picture of the rejoicing crowds who followed Jesus as He entered Jerusalem, or the Saxon ruler's jubilant subjects as they listened to Bach's cantata performed in his honor. The passage in St. Mark (11: 10), from which the words of the Benedictus are taken, concludes with the phrase, "Osanna in excelsis." Bach's Lutheran upbringing caused him to follow the Bible rather than the Roman Canon.

23. *Aria — Tenor: B minor.* Benedictus qui venit / in nomine Domini. (Blessed is he that cometh / in the name of the Lord.) (St. Mark 11: 9)

Schweitzer (II, 323) thinks that this only aria for tenor in this mass comes from an unknown composition by Bach. If this is true, Bach's numbers for the Sanctus IV and Agnus Dei V divisions would all be borrowed from his previous works. Whatever its source, it is well suited for this aria because of its motif of beatific peace imparted by the voice with its obbligato flute accompaniment and ritornello. The listener can visualize a scenario of heavenly peace in the soothing melody. It seems as though the tenor is singing these lines on his own behalf, personifying himself as the messenger of God.

24. *Chorus — Tutti: D major.* Osanna in excelsis. (Hosanna in the highest.)

This is a repeat of number 22, probably intended to surround the peaceful Benedictus with the same lively number, according to the alternating highs and lows as the numbers follow each other in this mass.

*V. Agnus Dei (25–26)*

25. *Aria — Alto: G minor.* Agnus Dei qui tollis peccata mundi, / miserere nobis. (Lamb of God, that takest away the sin of the world, / have mercy upon us.)

This aria is really a dramatic monologue, just as it was in its original cantata BWV 11, "Lobet Gott in seinen Reichen" (Praise God in His Kingdom) — Bach's Ascension Oratorio composed about 1735. It is shortened by about one half, but still retains the grief motif for alto as it did in the cantata (number 4): "Ach, bleibe doch, mein liebstes Leben, / Ach, fliehe nicht so bald von mir!" (Ah, do stay, my dearest Life, / Ah, do not flee so soon from me!)

The theme of regret at the departure of Jesus in the cantata is changed to thanksgiving in accordance with this division of the mass; the alto shows this in her quiet tone of confidence in God's pardon for sinners.

26. *Chorus — Tutti: D major.* Dona nobis pacem. (Give us peace.)

Since Bach added movements to this mass after 1733, it seems that he was intent on borrowing from his own previously composed vocal works. Now he concludes this mass with a repetition of chorus 6, "Gratias agimus," because the original words of cantata BWV 29 in German indicated thanks to God. But he included their prayer for peace in the solemn hymn of thanksgiving repeated from the original music.

Yet this borrowing cannot be any different from what he was doing during the years 1735 to 1740, for he was then taking many movements from his cantatas to fit them into the texts of the four short masses upon which he was working.

Gurlitt sees in Bach's *Mass in B Minor* "a brilliant companion piece for Händel's coronation anthem for George II of England," and states that the Kyrie-Gloria first part was offered as a token of homage by the citizens of Leipzig to their new sovereign, Augustus III. Furthermore, he asserts that Bach composed the rest of this mass because he expected to be commissioned to provide a coronation mass for the crowning of the new Elector in Cracow as King of Poland. For this completion of the *B Minor Mass,* he would receive the title that he had requested: "Hof-Compositeur der Kurfürstlich Sächsischen Hof-Capelle" (Court Composer of the Electoral Saxon Court Orchestra) in Dresden. Bach had already received a title that he had asked for: "Kapellmeister von Haus aus" (Director of Music *in absentia*) in 1723 from the Electoral Court of Weissenfels (cf. Gurlitt — *Johann Sebastian Bach,* 120).

Schweitzer sums up the *Mass in B Minor* as being both Catholic and Protestant, saying that Bach tried to compose a really "Catholic" mass with its objective choruses, but in other movements we find the same subjective and intimately personal approach as in his cantatas, which he calls "the Protestant element in Bach's religion. The sublime and the intimate do not interpenetrate; they coexist side by side;

they are separable from each other like the objective and the subjective in Bach's piety...." (Schweitzer—*J. S. Bach*, II, 314).

# The Lutheran Masses
## (Leipzig 1737–39; BWV 233–BWV 236)

As noted in the Introduction to this book, the reformed liturgy of the regular morning service in the Lutheran Church retained the Kyrie and the Gloria, which were sung in Latin during Bach's time as cantor in Leipzig, but depending on whether the principal chorus (chorus primus) was present. If the second chorus (chorus secundus) was to sing, its members would sing the Kyrie and the Gloria in the German version along with the congregation. Thus a new "shortened" mass was evolved within the framework of the Lutheran liturgy, giving rise to the name "Short Mass."

Bach composed four of these abbreviated masses, all with the same format in six sections: number 1 is a choral Kyrie and numbers 2 to 6 compose the Gloria, consisting of three arias between two choruses.

Just as Bach borrowed heavily from his own previously composed vocal works for movements in his *Mass in B Minor*, so he will do so even more for his settings of these Lutheran masses, BWV 233–236.

Note that these short masses begin and end on the same key in both the Kyrie and the Gloria sections; only the keynotes of the intervening arias will vary. The following chart will show the movements, their keys, the vocal performers and the cantata from which Bach borrowed (? if unknown):

*BWV 233 Mass in F Major.* Number: 1. Kyrie—Chorus F (original?); 2. Gloria—Chorus F (?); Laudamus—Chorus F (?); Gratias—Chorus F (?); 3. Domine Deus—Bass aria C (?);

4. Qui tollis—Soprano aria g minor; Qui sedes—Soprano, ex BWV 102(3); Alto aria f minor; 5. Quoniam—Alto aria d minor, ex BWV 102 (5); Tenor aria g minor; 6. Cum sancto—Chorus F, ex BWV 40 (1) F.

*BWV 234 Mass in A Major (c. 1739).* Number 1. Kyrie—Chorus A (?); 2. Gloria—Chorus A, ex BWV 67 (6); Laudamus—Chorus A; Gratias—Chorus A; 3. Domine Deus—Bass aria f♯ minor (?); 4. Qui tollis—Soprano aria b minor; Qui sedes—Soprano aria exc BWV 179 (5); Soprano aria a minor; 5. Quoniam—Alto aria D, ex Alto aria D BWV 79 (2); 6. Cum sancto—Chorus A, ex BWV 136 (1) A.

*BWV 235 Mass in G Minor.* Number 1. Kyrie—Chorus g, ex BWV 102 (1) Chorus g; 2. Gloria—Chorus g; Laudamus—Chorus g, ex BWV 72 (1) Chorus a; 3. Gratias—Bass aria d; Domine Deus—Bass aria d, ex BWV 187 (4) Bass aria g; 4. Domine Fili—Alto aria B♭, ex BWV 187 (3) Alto aria B♭; 5. Qui tollis—Tenor aria E♭; Qui sedes—Tenor aria E♭; Quoniam—Tenor aria E♭, ex BWV 187 (5) Soprano aria E♭; 6. Cum sancto—Chorus g, ex BWV 187 (1) Chorus g.

*BWV 236 Mass in G Major (c.1739).* Number 1. Kyrie—Chorus G, ex BWV 179 (1) Chorus G; 2. Gloria—Chorus G; Laudamus—Chorus G, ex BWV 79 (1) Chorus G; 3. Gratias—Bass aria D; Domine Deus—Bass aria D, ex BWV 138 (5) Bass aria D; 4. Qui tollis—Duet Soprano/Alto a; Qui sedes—Duet Soprano/Alto a, ex BWV 79 (5) Soprano/Bass Duet b; 5. Quoniam—Tenor aria c minor, ex BWV 179

(3) Tenor aria c minor; 6. Cum sancto — Chorus 6, ex BWV 17 (1) Chorus A.

Why did Bach decide to write these Latin masses after having taken the Kyrie and the Gloria of his *Mass in B Minor* to Dresden in 1733 without its being performed and without receiving any acknowledgment to his petition to be named court composer by Augustus III? A possible answer might be that he did not receive this appointment until 1736 and did not compose these masses until the following year as a sort of thank-you present to the Saxon Electoral Court for this long-awaited favor. However, if Bach did compose them to thank the Elector for his change of heart towards him, there is no evidence of this, because Bach did not enclose a letter with them as he had done with the *Mass in B Minor* (at least no such letters have been found).

Spitta (III, 32) claims that these three masses, with the exception of the *Mass in F Major* which was intended for a Protestant service, must have been written for Dresden, and Schweitzer states that all four were sent to Court "as tokens of his assiduity" (II, 326).

Another proof that these Lutheran masses were intended to be performed in Dresden was Bach's omission of the non–Roman word "altissime" from their texts after he had been criticized for using it in the *Mass in B Minor,* it is thought.

There is also the theory that Bach was commissioned to write these short masses for his Bohemian patron, Governor Count Sporck, who had been impressed by the Sanctus included in the *B Minor Mass* in its later completion. Bach had sent him this movement in its separate parts so that Count Sporck could perform it in his private chapel.

However true these speculations may be, it is evident that Bach composed these short versions of the mass to impress his Roman Catholic sovereign Augustus III, even though his chances of having them performed in a Roman Catholic Church in Dresden were slim, for he was well known as a Lutheran cantor throughout Saxony. Moreover, Bach must have realized that he was not deceiving Roman Catholic listeners by applying his Lutheran cantata melodies to their Latin texts, even though he did it exceedingly well. Only in some movements of the short masses did he fail to do so, resulting in awkward declamation for the singers.

Again, since Bach was under no pressure to produce the short masses for performance, why would he want to plunder movements from his own cantatas instead of composing original melodies? For example, masses BWV 235 (G minor) and BWV 236 (G major) are completely made up from movements of his previously composed cantatas. Was he beginning to realize that composing original melodies for a mass was not worth the adverse criticism that he would receive from both Lutherans and Roman Catholics for his efforts on their behalf? And since he had recently received his title as court composer, what more could he expect from Dresden? So the easiest way to merit this title was to borrow from his own previous cantatas to produce an offering of masses for Dresden in token of his thanks. Yet the thoroughly Protestant spirit of these masses would condemn them for Catholic Church services in the capital.

Regarding the dramatic aspect of the short masses, it will be necessary for the listener to refer to the cantata from which their movements were borrowed in order to discern how the vocalists (soloists or chorus) acted their roles in the original version and how Bach treated their parts in the masses. Usually they will be singing their parts as themselves (soloist or chorus) but this should not lessen the dramatic significance of Bach's musical setting, modified to conform with the new Latin text. Such dramatic numbers will be indicated as they occur in the detailed survey of each mass.

## MASS IN F MAJOR
### (c. 1737–1739; BWV 233)

Spitta dates the A major and the G major masses as about 1737, saying that no chronology can be given (III, 30), but he then proceeds to discuss the G major and the G minor masses first because they derive their movements entirely from Bach's cantatas and therefore must have been composed first.

Schweitzer asserts that the G major and the A major masses were composed about 1739 as were also the G minor and the F major (II, 326, note 1).

Actually, the order of composition is less important than the musical merit of each mass setting, so the four masses may be dated 1737 to 1739. They will be taken, therefore, according to their BWV sequence.

1. *Kyrie — Chorus, four part Soprano, Alto, Tenor, Bass, F major: Full orchestra with two horns, two oboes, bassoon, strings, continuo.* Kyrie eleison / Christe eleison / Kyrie eleison (Lord, have mercy / Christ, have mercy / Lord, have mercy)

This opening number with its triple invocations appears to be an original composition, displaying Bach's ability to insert a Protestant chorale into the Kyrie of the traditional Litany. Bach divides the chorus into three fugal sections, soprano, alto, tenor, who sing in unison with the strings (violins and violas). The basses sing along with the trombones (Fagotti), and declaim the three clauses in plain-song. While this is going on, the third group, horns and oboes, play the melody of the German *Agnus Dei — Christe, du Lamm Gottes* (Christ, Thou Lamb of God) three times in unison (once during the singing of each clause).

Christe, du Lamm Gottes, / Der du trägst die Sünd' der Welt, / Erbarm dich unser. (Christ, Thou Lamb of God, / Thou Who bearest the sin of the world, / Pity us.)

The cantus firmus is in the bass singing the three clauses of the Gregorian Litany and a second cantus firmus occurs in the Lutheran chorale played by the horns and the oboes.

This outstanding and most unusual opening setting places this short mass far above the other three, although Bach must have known that it would not be accepted for performance in any Catholic Church because he had included a Protestant chorale in it. Yet it seems that Bach's aim in these masses was to fuse his own Protestant theology into the Catholic liturgy via his music, whether based directly on the Latin text or, more often, applied to the Latin from his settings of German texts. Usually, he managed to accommodate the borrowed melody very well in the new Latin verses, but there are some awkward movements.

The drama, which the listener may perceive in this monumental opening chorus, appears to result from the threefold petition of the words of these clauses and also from the hymn tunes as they are sung or played. The "actors" may be either the choristers themselves, or they may represent the members of the congregation as they implore God for mercy.

2. *Gloria — Chorus, four part Soprano, Alto, Tenor, Bass, F major: Full orchestra with two horns, two*

*oboes, bassoon, strings, continuo.* Spitta claims that the Gloria of this mass was intended as a Christmas piece for chorus and formed a complete unit with the preceding Kyrie which was for the first Sunday in Advent (cf. III, 36).

The source of this number is unknown. The 6/8 dance rhythm might indicate that it comes from a lost secular cantata by Bach, perhaps a congratulatory cantata for Prince Leopold or an instrumental concerto of the Cöthen period.

Since this number can be deemed to be a separate Christmas presentation, the audience would have no difficulty in identifying the chorus as an angelic choir singing in canon: Gloria in excelsis Deo, / et in terra pax hominibus bonae voluntatis. / Laudamus te, benedicimus te, adoramus te, glorificamus te. / Gratias agimus tibi propter / magnam gloriam tuam. (Glory to God on high, / and on earth peace to men of good will. / We praise Thee, we bless Thee, we worship Thee, we glorify Thee. / We give thanks for / Thy great glory.)

This Latin text is well illustrated by the joy-motif throughout the movement. The same Protestant feeling as in the Kyrie seems to pervade the choir's declamation. With the brilliant horn playing, Bach has written a most impressive number, despite an abbreviated da capo.

3. *Domine Deus—Aria, Bass, C major: strings, continuo.* Arnold Schering, in the *Bach Jahrbuch* (1921, 93), states that this aria was adapted from an aria in a lost secular cantata, BWV Anhang 18, entited by its first line: "Froher Tag, verlangte Stunden" (Happy Day, Longed-for Hours), performed by Bach on June 5, 1732, which he wrote on a libretto by Johann Heinrich Winckler (1703–70) to celebrate the reopening of the newly reconstructed St. Thomas School before the assembled Town Council and the dignitaries of Leipzig. Bach's manuscript is extant in the Town Historical Museum of Leipzig, but the music has been lost.

It must have been difficult metrically for Bach to fit the music he set for this cantata aria into the Latin of this movement, even omitting the da capo of the original. That he could do so is a tribute to his skill in language as well as in music.

The cantata aria is octosyllabic in six lines while the mass aria varies in both respects: Geist und Herze sind begierig, / Den verdienten Dank zu weihen. / Doch vermögen sie den Willen / Auch im Werke zu erfüllen? / Nein, ach! nein, ihr ganz Bestreben / Kann sich weiter nicht erheben. (Heart and soul are desirous / To offer deserved thanks. / But do they have the power to fulfill their will in their work? No, ah, no, their whole effort / Cannot be raised further. [da capo])

Domine Deus, Rex coelestis, / Deus Pater omnipotens. / Domine Fili unigenite, / Jesu Christe, / Domine Deus, Agnus Dei, Filius Patris. (Lord God, King of heaven, / God the almighty Father. / Lord, the only begotten Son, / Jesus Christ, / Lord God, Lamb of God, Son of the Father.)

Interesting variations of tone in the vocal bass repeats of the Latin lines, with runs or melismas on *omnipotens* and *unigenite* would lead any listener to think that this was an original number. The prayer motif, supported by instrumental ritornelli, produce a really dramatic effect as though the bass were speaking directly to God and to His Son.

4. *Qui tollis* and *Qui sedes: Aria, Soprano, G minor: solo oboe, continuo.* Transposed from the Alto solo Aria in F minor in cantata BWV 102 (number 3) of 1731: "Herr, deine

Augen sehen nach dem Glauben" (Lord, Thine Eyes Look Towards Faith).

Qui tollis peccata mundi, / miserere nobis. / Qui tollis peccata mundi, / suscipe deprecationem nostram. / Qui sedes ad dexteram Patris, / miserere nobis. (Who takest away the sin of the world, / have mercy upon us. / Who takest away the sin of the world, / receive our prayer. / Who sittest at the right of the Father, / have mercy upon us.)

The tear motif is retained from the original aria, even though much of the melody has been altered. Instead of sounding a lament for a stubborn soul, this is a continuation of the previous bass aria as she prays directly to Christ for His mercy on her sins. Thus Bach ties the drama of this aria into that of the preceding bass aria and he will continue to do so with the following aria for alto (number 5).

The text for the original alto aria in BWV 102 (number 3) should be compared with the Latin text set to the same melody: Weh der Seele, die den Schaden / Nicht mehr kennt / Und die Straf' auf sich zu laden, / Störrig rennt. / Ja von ihres Gottes Gnaden / Selbst sich trennt. (Woe to the soul, which / No more knows the harm / And stubbornly runs / To load punishment on itself. / Yes, it separates itself / From the mercy of its God.)

Perhaps the word *Gnaden* (mercy) reminded Bach of the word *miserere*, repeated in the Latin text, when he selected this particular aria for this place in the mass.

5. *Quoniam* — Aria, Alto, D minor: *violin solo, continuo.* Taken from the same cantata, BWV 102 (number 5), and transposed from tenor with a solo flute in G minor, this aria retains the melody but changes the vocal line in the transposition. The alto continues

the invocation to Christ, the central theme of all three arias in this mass, while the solo violin lends a celestial motif to her song. Actually, the Latin text is preferable to the gloom and doom of the original German libretto: Erschrecke doch, / Du allzu sichre Seele! / Denk, was dich würdig zähle / Der Sünden Joch. / Die Gotteslangmut geht auf einem Fuss von Blei, / Damit der Zorn hernach dir desto schwerer sei. (Be afraid then, / Thou all too sure soul! / Think of what the yoke of your sins / Would reckon thee worthy. / God's patience goes on a foot of lead, / So that His anger afterwards may be all the harsher for thee.)

Comparing the thought of this stanza with the Latin words of the liturgy, we see that there is no connection: Quoniam tu solus Sanctus, / tu solus Dominus, / tu solus Altissimus, / Jesu Christe. (For Thou alone art holy; / Thou alone art the Lord; / Thou alone art the Most High, / Jesus Christ.

The solo violin ritornelli weave an aura of heavenly peace throughout this beautiful movement.

6. *Cum sancto Spiritu* — *Chorus, four part Soprano, Alto, Tenor, Bass, F major: two horns, two oboes, a bassoon, strings, continuo.* Borrowed from cantata BWV 40 (number 1) in F major with the same instrumentation, this movement adheres to the original chorus, but reduces the instrumental ritornello and changes the fugue in the melody. There appears to be a step motif in the rhythm, suggesting the movement of the Holy Spirit. Also we hear a motif of peace instead of the tumult motif in BWV 40 (number 1), of 1723: Cum sancto Spiritu / in gloria Dei Patris. / Amen. (With the Holy Spirit / in the glory of God, the Father. Amen.)

Recognition of the Holy Spirit by the choir maintains the drama expressed by each number in this mass in the form of a monologue sung by soloists or choir.

To the conclusion of a mass Bach has transferred the same powerful drama that the listener can visualize on hearing the opening chorus of BWV 40: Dazu ist erschienen der Sohn Gottes, / dass er die Werke des Teufels zerstöre. (To this end has appeared the Son of God, / that He may destroy the works of the Devil.)—1 John 3:8

## MASS IN A MAJOR
### (c. 1737–39; BWV 234)

1. *Kyrie — Chorus, Soprano, Alto, Tenor, Bass (four part), A major: two flutes, strings, continuo.* It is thought that this is the only one of Bach's short masses to have been performed in Leipzig. The original score for the Kyrie does not exist, but the copy may be from a lost cantata of Bach's Weimar years.

This opening movement has its three parts neatly divided unlike that of the masses in G major and in G minor. The listener can easily imagine himself to be participating in the fervent supplications expressed by the choir in Kyrie eleison (Lord, have mercy). The pastoral tone of the second part Christe eleison (Christ, have mercy) is even more dramatic with its exquisitely plaintive appeal of the flutes added to the masterly canon singing of the choir.

Spitta observes of this movement (III, 33): "There is no piece by Bach in which depth of purpose and sweetness of sound have more closely joined hands." Yet Bach did not originally compose such a wonderful melody for this text!

The third part Kyrie eleison (Lord, have mercy) is also in canon; it concludes the plea for mercy and redemp-

tion with the same melody and a dramatic effect as in the first Kyrie. But its crescendo, however, implies a feeling that Bach is trying to paint a universal appeal to God in his musical setting. Then, in great contrast, a quiet repetition of the Kyrie eleison text brings the movement to an end.

2. *Gloria — Chorus, four part Soprano, Alto, Tenor, Bass, A major: 2 flutes, strings, continuo.* This number has its origin in movement 6 of Bach's cantata BWV 67 (c. 1725), which was an aria for bass with the chorus, a flute, two oboes d'amore, strings and continuo. In this revision, instead of the bass, who represented Jesus in the cantata and who repeatedly sang "Friede sei mit euch" (Peace be with you), Bach has this sung now by three different soloists in turn, while substituting the Latin text for the German words but ending in four part unison.

The remarkable drama of the dialogue between the bass in the role of Jesus and the choir playing the part of the disciples in the cantata is not as clearly defined in this Latin libretto because the alternation between soloists and the choir prevents any similar identification of characters.

Schweitzer is hard on Bach for the way he has treated this movement borrowed from his earlier cantata:

> Memory of the earlier work makes him reproduce, in the instrumental accompaniment to the new movement, the contrast between the unrest of the world in which the disciples live in alarm, and the peace that the risen Lord brings to them. But in this new arrangement he does not trouble in the least about the significance of the music. He fits the instrumental accompaniment to a brisk chorus, and has the *Gloria in excelsis* sung to the "tumult" motif. In a number of

these adaptations he does not even trouble to declaim the words in accordance with their sense. [*J.S. Bach*, II, 327]

However true this opinion may be, the listener can nevertheless appreciate Bach's ability as a dramatist in the way that he composed for this Latin text. It is hard to believe that Bach deliberately ignored any text he set! The "tumult" motif of the chorus and the solo interpolations are not so out of place from a dramatic point of view: CHORUS (in canon): Gloria in excelsis Deo (Glory to God on high,) SOPRANO: et in terra pax hominibus bonae voluntatis. (and on earth peace to men of good will.) CHORUS (in canon): Laudamus te, benedicimuste, (we praise Thee, we bless Thee,) TENOR: adoramus te, (we adore Thee,) CHORUS (in canon): glorificamus te, (we glorify Thee,) BASS: adoramus te, (we adore Thee,) CHORUS (in canon): glorificamus te. (we glorify Thee.) SATB (with theme of the soli) (in canon but ending in unison): Gratias agimus tibi propter magnam gloriam tuam. (We give thanks to Thee for Thy great glory.)

3. *Domine Deus* — Bass solo, *f♯ minor: violin solo, continuo.* This number originates in another lost cantata. The prayer motif is very artistically exploited by the soloist, whose voice is enhanced by the solo violin to produce a fervent appeal to the Father and to the Son. He adds to the dramatic effect of his aria by singing each of its three sections separately according to Bach's setting. The instrumental ritornello at the end of each line produces a pleasant refrain. Domine Deus, Rex coelestis, / Deus Pater omnipotens. / Domine Fili unigenite, / Jesu Christe, / Domine Deus, agnus Dei, Filius Patris. (Lord God, heavenly King, / God the

almighty Father. / Only begotten Son of God, / Jesus Christ, / Lord God, Lamb of God, Son of the Father.)

4. *Qui tollis* — *Aria, Soprano, B minor: two flutes, violins, violas, continuo (in unison):* Like its model borrowed from cantata BWV 179 (number 5), this aria is also for soprano, but with two flutes and strings instead of the original two oboes in A minor for this aria in the 1724 cantata, BWV 179 "Siehe zu, dass deine Gottesfurcht nicht Heuchelei sei" (See to it, that thy fear of God is not hyprocrisy). The transposed new score raises the instruments an octave higher and this higher tone accentuates her voice in a motif of heavenly peace, symbolic of the innocence of Christ. She is praying to Christ for intercession just as the bass did in his previous aria and as the alto will do in her aria following this (number 5). All three arias are highly dramatic monologues.

Qui tollis peccata mundi, / miserere nobis. / Quo tollis peccata mundi, / suscipe deprecationem nostram. / Qui sedes ad dexteram Patris, / miserere nobis. (Who takest away the sins of the world, / have mercy upon us. / Who takest away the sins of the world, / receive our prayer. / Who sittest at the right of the Father, / have mercy upon us.)

Since this melody was, I feel, the best in the cantata, perhaps Bach decided to perpetuate it in this Latin version which is a great improvement in music and text over the original with its too graphically detailed description of the sins confessed (cantata BWV 179, number 5): Liebster Gott, erbarme dich, / Lass mir Trost und Gnad' erscheinen! / Meine Sünden kränken mich / Als ein Eiter in Gebeinen. / Hilf mir, Jesu, Gottes Lamm, / Ich versink' im tiefen Schlamm! (Dearest God, have pity; / Let consolation and mercy appear to me! / My sins afflict me / As a pus in my bones. / Help me, Jesus, God's lamb, / I am sinking in deep slime!) The plea for mercy is the same, but what a difference in the two texts!

5. *Quoniam tu solus — Aria, Alto, D Major: violins and violas in unison, continuo*. This number has the instruments lowered an octave from the original obbligato setting for the alto aria, also in D Major, taken from cantata BWV 79 (number 2) entitled "Gott der Herr ist Sonn' und Schild" (God, the Lord, is Sun and Shield) (1735). The obbligato solo oboe in the original was replaced by a solo transverse flute in later performances.

The text of this mass aria is much shorter than that of the cantata aria (thus entailing more repeats of the lines) and the thought is likewise much curtailed from the detailed idea of God protecting us from our enemies to the abstract or general praising the sanctity of Christ. The alto does add a definite dramatic touch by directly addressing Christ in her fine da capo aria, however. Quoniam tu solus Sanctus, / tu solus Dominus, / tu solus Altissimus, / Jesu Christe. (For Thou alone art holy, / Thou alone art the Lord, / Thou alone art the Most High, / Jesus Christ.)

Compare this with the original aria text: Gott ist unsre Sonn' und Schild! / Darum rühmet dessen Güte / Unser dankbares Gemüte, / Die er für sein Häuflein hegt. / Denn er will uns ferner schützen, / Ob die Feinde Pfeile schnitzen / Und ein Lästerhund gleich billt. (God is our Sun and Shield!) / Therefore His goodness / Our thankful mind praises, / Which he cherishes for His little flock. / For He will protect us further, / Whether our enemies carve arrows / And even if a blasphemous dog barks!)

6. *Cum sancto Spiritu — Chorus, four part Soprano, Alto, Tenor, Bass,*

*A major: two flutes, strings, continuo*. Except for the omission of the opening and the closing ritornelli of the original chorus, and also the substitution of flutes for horn, oboe, and oboe d'amore, this chorus follows its model, the opening chorus of cantata BWV 136 (number 1) in A Major: "Erforsche mich, Gott, und erfahre mein Herz," / prüfe mich und erfahre, wie ich's meine. (Search me, God, and learn of my heart, / test me and learn how I mean it.)

This cantata chorus may have been borrowed by Bach about 1725 when he composed this work from another cantata which has since been lost, because the libretto does not agree too well with the melody — a dance rhythm of a gavotte which would indicate a secular cantata. Cum sancto Spiritu / in gloria Dei Patris. / Amen. (With the holy Spirit / in the glory of God the Father. / Amen.)

Note the triple repetition of "Amen" at the end; perhaps to emphasize the importance of the third Person of the Trinity, who is the subject of this final movement.

## MASS IN G MINOR
### (c. 1737–39; BWV 235)

With BWV 236, the *Mass in G Major*, this work was also completely borrowed for all its final movements from Bach's previously composed cantatas. This G minor setting definitely reveals Bach's indifference in fitting the adapted melody to the Latin litany. The Kyrie is laboriously fashioned from the opening chorus of BWV 102, "Herr, deine Augen sehen nach dem Glauben," (Lord, Thine Eyes Look Toward Belief) (1726), while the Gloria from the first chorus of BWV 72, "Alles nur nach Gottes Willen" (Everything According to God's Will) (1726) seems to have nothing to do with its adapted text, nor does the final chorus from BWV 187 (number 1), "Es wartet alles auf dich" (Everything Waits for Thee), also dated 1726.

Exact imitation in the arias, however, is not as apparent, because Bach could transform them so well to fit the Latin that they appear to be virtually new pieces he has composed (e.g. the Domine Fili movement). Therefore the most eloquent and seemingly original music comes in the solo numbers.

For the *G Minor Mass,* Bach took four of its six numbers from cantata BWV 187, which might imply that he was in a hurry to finish this work, but his amendments to these numbers disprove this theory. If he thought that the number was suitable for adaptation, he would use it, even though his efforts were not always successful.

Yet why would Bach choose four successive numbers from only one of his cantatas? When he arranged the four masses, he had at hand the scores of more than two hundred cantatas that he had already composed.

In his book, *Bach: The Magnificat, Lutheran Masses and Motets* (28, 30), Terry affirms that the ten adaptations that Bach used in the Lutheran masses "owed their preference less to an arduous exploration of his resources, than to the fact that they happened conveniently to present themselves at the moment that he required assistance."

1. *Kyrie — Chorus, Soprano, Alto, Tenor, Bass: G minor: two oboes, strings, continuo.* Kyrie eleison. / Christe eleison. / Kyrie eleison. (Lord, have mercy.) / Christ, have mercy. / Lord, have mercy.)

Patterned on cantata BWV 102, 1726 or 1731–32, the opening chorus adheres to its model without change with the same instrumentation as the original, but the music does not fit the

Latin text now. A comparison of the cantata chorus text with the above will show how difficult it was to force the music into its new mold: Herr, deine Augen sehen nach dem Glauben! / Du schlägest sie, aber sie fühlen's nicht; / du plagest sie, aber sie bessern sich nicht. / Sie haben ein härter Angesicht denn ein Fels / und wollen sich nicht bekehren. (Lord, Thine eyes look towards faith! / Thou smitest them, but they do not feel it; / Thou tormentest them, but they do not improve. / They have a face harder than rock / and do not want to be converted.)

The chorus sings the words of the prophet Jeremiah 5:3 as he laments over the sins of the world quoted in this stanza. It is impossible to say why Bach would choose this text for the Latin verses, since there is no idea of divine mercy but rather the contrary. Furthermore, the music does not suit the Latin text either. Perhaps by running the three short verses together without any pause between them as they were declaimed to accommodate the original Biblical verse in German, Bach confused his listeners.

Still, the drama that Bach was striving to obtain is evident in this chorus just as it was in the corresponding chorus of the cantata.

2. *Gloria in excelsis Deo — Chorus, Soprano, Alto, Tenor, Bass, G minor: two oboes, strings, continuo.* Even though he did transpose this chorus from A minor, the key of the opening chorus of cantata BWV 72 (number 1), 1726, and omitting the ritornello, Bach has been criticized for too close borrowing from his own works. Spitta's comment (III, 31) on this movement is evidence that:

> In the G minor mass Bach has not even regarded that necessary contrast between the *Kyrie* and the

*Gloria* which, being based on the nature of the words, had already become typical. The *Gloria* does not stand out in radiant contrast of Christmas glory after the passionate and agitated *Kyrie*, but, on the contrary, continues the same strain of sad and unfulfilled longing.

It is indeed unusual for Bach to place two choruses in succession with the same motif of solemnity as in this instance. Also, since the text always suggested to Bach the melody he should use, it is evident that the theme of submission to God's will in the cantata is incompatible with that of praising God in the mass chorus. Why did Bach not perceive this difference in meaning and therefore choose a different setting?

A comparison of the two texts will illustrate their disparity. BWV 72 (1): Alles nur nach Gottes Willen / So bei Lust also Traurigkeit, / So bei gut als böser Zeit, / Gottes Wille soll mich stillen / Bei Gewölk und Sonnenschein. / Alles nur nach Gottes Willen! / Dies soll meine Losung sein. (Everything according to God's will / So in pleasure as in sadness, / So in good as in bad times, / God's will should calm me / In clouds and in sunshine. / Everything according to God's will! / This shall be my solution.)

It is a wonder that Bach should try to fit the meter of this stanza to BWV 235 (2): Gloria in excelsis Deo, / et in terra pax hominibus bonae voluntatis. / Laudamus te, benedicimus te, / adoramus te, glorificamus te. (Glory to God on high, / and peace on earth to men of good will. / We praise Thee, we bless Thee, / we worship Thee, we glorify Thee.)

3. *Gratias agimus tibi* — Aria, Bass, *D minor: unison violins, continuo.* This is the first in the pattern of three

arias in succession which occur in each of the four Lutheran masses. Bach transposed this aria from the bass G minor aria (number 4) in cantata BWV 187, "Es wartet alles auf dich," (Everything waits for Thee), (1726 or 1732), with the same instrumentation. The original aria is modified into an apparently new aria and the two following arias are also altered. These, with the final chorus, are likewise taken from BWV 187. Bach must have regarded this cantata highly, since he borrowed so much from it for this mass.

The libretto for this number in Latin does accord with the meaning of the German text in the cantata, but this does not happen in the two following arias. Again, there are more words in the cantata text than can be accommodated in the mass text — therefore the usual procedure of repeating the Latin lines in whole or in part: Gratias agimus tibi propter / magnam gloriam tuam. / Domine Deus, Rex coelestis, / Deus Pater omnipotens. (We give Thee thanks for / Thy great glory. / Lord God, heavenly King, / God the Father almighty.)

Reliance on God's providence and the thanks that we owe Him for that and for His omnipotence appear also in the drama enacted in the cantata aria, where the bass takes the part of Jesus: "Darum sollt ihr nicht sorgen noch sagen: 'Was werden wir essen, was werden wir trinken, womit werden wir uns kleiden?' Nach solchem allen trachten die Heiden. Denn euer himmlischer Vater weiss, dass ihr dies alles bedürfet." ("Therefore you ought not to worry or say: 'What shall we eat; what shall we drink; with what shall we clothe ourselves?' After all such things the heathen strive. For your heavenly Father knows that you need all these things.") (Matthew 6:31, 32).

4. *Domine Fili unigenite — Aria — Alto, Bb major: oboe, strings, continuo.* This aria moves even further from the original, which was also in Bb major with the same instruments, to become almost a new composition. This time the number of lines in the Latin text accords more closely with the number in the cantata aria (number 3), although the thought is once again completely different.

Du Herr, du krönst allein das Jahr mit deinem Gut. / Es träufet Fett und Segen / Auf deines Fusses Wegen, / Und deine Gnade ist's, die allen Gutes tut. (Thou Lord, Thou alone crownest the year with Thy goodness. / Fatness and blessing drip / On the paths of Thy foot, / And it is Thy mercy that does all that is good.)

Domine Fili unigenite, / Jesu Christe, / Domine Deus, agnus Dei, / Filius Patris. (Lord Jesus Christ, / Only begotten Son, / Lord God, Lamb of God, / Son of the Father.)

There seems to be no connection between the Lord's bounty towards man and these lines which simply mention Christ as the Son of God. The German text and its music are much more appealing.

5. *Qui tollis — Aria, Tenor, Eb major: solo oboe, continuo.* This second aria, like the original for soprano also in Eb major, adheres closely to its model, cantata BWV 187 (number 5). Apart from transposing for the change of voice, this aria would tend to prove that Bach did not always modify the arias which he borrowed from his own works. Although the number of lines in both arias is about the same, the thought of the liturgy does not correspond to that expressed in the cantata aria, even though Bach has matched the melody to the Latin words: Qui tollis peccata mundi / miserere nobis. / Qui tollis peccata mundi, / suscipe deprecationem nostram. / Qui sedes

ad dexteram Patris, / miserere nobis. / Quoniam tu solus Sanctus, / tu solus Dominus, / tu solus Altissimus, / Jesu Christe. (Who takest away the sins of the world, / have mercy upon us. / Who takest away the sins of the world, / receive our prayer. / Who sittest at the right of the Father, / have mercy upon us. / For Thou alone art holy, / Thou alone art the Lord, / Thou alóne art the Most High, / Jesus Christ.)

But this petition for clemency to Christ does not coincide with the idea of God providing for all His creatures in the cantata aria libretto: Gott versorget alles Leben, / Was hienieden Odem hegt. / Sollt er mir allein nicht geben, / Was er allen zugesagt? / Weicht, ihr Sorgen, seine Treue / Ist auch meiner eingedenk / Und wird ob mir täglich neue / Durch manch Vater-Liebsgeschenk. (God provides for all living things / That have breath down here. / Should He not give to me alone / What He allots to all? / Depart, ye cares, His faithfulness / Thinks also about me / And becomes for me daily new / Through His many Fatherly presents of Love.)

Since Bach was well-versed in Latin, it seems possible that he would not notice both libretti when he transferred the music representing the original German text. Was it oversight, indifference or disappointment at the reception that these short masses were getting in Dresden?

6. *Cum sancto Spiritu — Chorus, four part Soprano, Alto, Tenor, Bass, G minor: two oboes, strings, continuo.* Based on BWV 187 (number 1), also in G minor with the same voices and instruments, this final chorus omits the ritornello of the cantata movement but expands the two-clause statement to fit the three sections of the mass text: Es wartet alles auf dich, / dass du ihnen Speise gibest zu seiner

Zeit. (All things wait for Thee, / so that Thou mayest give food to them in its time.

This is only one half of the text, but Bach would not fit any more into the mold of the Latin text: Cum sancto spiritu: / in gloria Dei Patris. / Amen. (With the Holy Spirit / in the glory of God the Father. / Amen.)

This *Mass in G Minor* is, in my opinion, the weakest of Bach's four Lutheran masses. Most critics have judged it so because of Bach's failure to make his music suit the Latin text, but perhaps, in this case, it was because he relied on only one cantata, BWV 187, for the musical setting for four of its six numbers.

Schweitzer (III, 326, 327) condemns this mass, stating that Bach's "adaptations are perfunctory and occasionally quite nonsensical. . . . In a number of these adaptations he does not even trouble to declaim the words in accordance with their sense . . . for example, Bach adds the text of the *Gloria* to the gloomy music of the first chorus of the cantata *Alles nur nach Gottes Willen* (No. 72)."

This judgment seems partially true in regard to this mass, as has been pointed out, but this work does have some merit in the drama contained in its movements, even though it gives the impression of hasty borrowing from only one cantata to complete it.

Terry's opinion on this matter could be the most considerate for Bach: "If, like the others, the G minor was written for Dresden use, we can have little doubt that it shared the neglect which befell the B minor. The fact explains Bach's indifference in regard to the Masses, and indifference rather than haste explains their obvious blemishes. Still, they bear the stamp of his genius in every movement, and only our knowledge of their origin permits us to know that they are but the re-flections of a greater glory" (*The Magnificat, Lutheran Masses and Motets*, 33).

## MASS IN G MAJOR
(c. 1737–39; BWV 236)

1. *Kyrie — Chorus, four part Soprano, Alto, Tenor, Bass, G major: two oboes, strings, continuo.* Kyrie eleison. / Christe eleison. / Kyrie eleison. (Lord, have mercy. / Christ, have mercy. / Lord, have mercy.)

The chorus in G major of the first movement of cantata BWV 179 of 1724 did not have the two oboes, but it is otherwise unchanged in this adaptation. The fugal setting sounds better in the original than here. Again, as in the opening chorus of the *G Minor Mass*, this results probably from Bach's setting; he runs the three clauses of the Kyrie together with the same melody but without any pause or separation between them. Perhaps the short text in the cantata chorus with its single statement explains why Bach made this adaptation similar: "Siehe zu, dass deine Gottesfurcht nicht Heuchelei sei, und diene Gott nicht mit falschem Herzen!" (See to it, that thy fear of God is not hypocrisy, and do not serve God with a false heart!)

2. *Gloria — Chorus, four part Soprano, Alto, Tenor, Bass, G major: two oboes, strings, continuo.* Compared to its original model, the opening chorus of cantata BWV 79 (number 1), this chorus is much more subdued because of its motifs of tranquility and restrained joy contrasting with the motif of radiant, uninhibited joy in the cantata. The probable reason for this is that the first performance of the cantata in 1725 included two horns and timpani in its orchestra, which Bach transcribed by vocalizing their parts for the sopranos

and the altos for this chorus. The general feeling of rejoicing that is felt at the Reformation Festival, which the cantata celebrates, is lost in this transposition. Even the words are difficult to reconcile, when the two versions are compared:

Gloria in excelsis Deo, / et in terra pax hominibus bonae voluntatis. / Laudamus te, benedicimus te, / adoramus te, glorificamus te. (Glory to God on high, / and on earth peace to men of good will. / We praise Thee, we bless Thee, / we worship Thee, we glorify Thee.)

BWV 79 (number 1): Gott der Herr ist Sonn' und Schild. / Der Herr gibt Gnade und Ehre, / er wird kein Gutes mangeln lassen den Frommen. (God, the Lord, is sun and shield. / The Lord gives mercy and honor; / He will not let any good thing be lacking to the pious.) (Psalm 84: 11)

The incompatibility of these two texts might have been caused by Bach's carelessness or indifference, but when he went to the trouble of changing the orchestration, how can it be thought that he would not notice the discrepancy?

3. *Gratias agimus tibi* — Aria, Bass, *D major: strings, continuo.* The bass aris in D major in cantata BWV 138, "Warum betrübst du dich, mein Herz?" (Why Art Thou Sad, My Heart?) (1723?), with the same instruments, is the model from which this aria is borrowed. It conforms very closely, although the bass vocal line may even have been improved by Bach's artistic revision — da capo repeats of the first two lines like a refrain after each of the following pairs, melismas and runs on *gratias, Pater, unigenite,* and especially *gloriam,* and very striking orchestral ritornelli at the beginning, between sections, and at the end. Gratias agimus tibi propter / magnam

gloriam tuam. / Domine Deus, Rex coelestis, / Deus Pater omnipotens. / Domine Fili unigenite, / Jesu Christe, (We give Thee thanks for / Thy great glory. / Lord God, heavenly king, / God the almighty Father. / The only begotten Son of God, / Jesus Christ.)

Yet, once again, the thought expressed by this liturgy has no connection with the original text, even though Bach has made the original melody fit: Auf Gott steht meine Zuversicht; / Mein Glaube lässt ihn walten. / Nun kann mich keine Sorge nagen, / Nun kann mich auch kein Armut plagen. / Auch mitten in dem grössten Leide / Bleibt er mein Vater, meine Freude; / Er will mich wunderlich erhalten. (On God stands my confidence; / My faith lets Him rule. / Now no care can gnaw me, / Now, too, no poverty can torment me. / Even in the midst of the greatest pain / He remains my Father, my joy; / He will sustain me wonderfully.)

4. *Domine Deus, agnus Dei* — *Duet, Soprano, Alto, A minor: unison violins, continuo.* Transposed from a duet for soprano and bass in cantata BWV 79 (number 5) in B minor, and the same instruments, this duet is particularly attractive for its imitative sequences and graceful interweaving of the voices. Bach changed the instrumental ritornello toward the end of the movement, but his modifications to the original have improved the duet even more.

There is still the problem of the difference in the textual meaning between the two versions, but one may suppose in this case that Bach was more engrossed with the musical setting than the significance of the words — especially since he must have realized that any Dresden listener probably would not recognize the melody of the duet, performed some years before in Leipzig, but never before in Dresden. Moreover, Bach was extremely bold to clothe a Roman Catholic Latin verse in the melody that he had written for a Lutheran cantata to celebrate the Reformation Festival! Domine Deus, agnus Dei, Filius Patris, / Qui tollis peccata mundi, / miserere nobis. / Qui tollis peccata mundi, / suscipe deprecationem nostram. / Qui sedes ad dexteram Patris, / miserere nobis. (Lord God, Lamb of God, Son of the Father, / Who takest away the sins of the world, / have mercy upon us. / Who takest away the sins of the world, / receive our prayer. / Who sittest at the right of the Father, / have mercy upon us.)

This plea for mercy does not correspond to the prayer to God for His protection that we hear in the cantata aria: Gott, ach Gott, verlass die Deinen / Nimmermehr! / Lass dein Wort uns helle scheinen; / Obgleich sehr / Wider uns die Feinde toben, / So soll unser Mund dich loben. (God, ah God, leave Thy people / Nevermore! / Let Thy Word shine brightly on us; / Although sorely / Our enemies rage against us, / So shall our mouth praise Thee.)

In this cantata duet, there is a "tumult" motif implied in the two intertwining voices that is lost in the mass duet. However, the drama of the two singers addressing God is equally realistic in both versions.

5. *Quoniam — Aria, Tenor, E Minor: solo oboe, continuo.* Having its melody derived from cantata BWV 179 (number 3), also a tenor aria but with two oboes, strings and continuo, this number has changed the turbulent rhythm to a more peaceful adagio motif, thus giving proof that Bach was usually very thoughtful when he transcribed music from his cantatas to fit his other works. Yet he was very remiss in making the German libretto

agree in meaning with the Latin into which he was trying to fit the melody. Quoniam tu solus Sanctus, / tu solus Dominus, / tu solus Altissimus, / Jesu Christe. (For Thou alone art holy, / Thou alone art the Lord, / Thou alone art the Highest, / Jesus Christ.)

BWV 179 Siehe zu, dass deine Gottesfurcht nicht Heuchelei sei (See to it, that thy fear of God is not hypocrisy) (1724).

3. *Aria, Tenor, E minor.* Falscher Heuchler Ebenbild / Können Sodomsäpfel heissen, / Die mit Unflat angefüllt / Und von aussen herrlich gleissen. / Heuchler, die von aussen schön, / Können nicht vor Gott bestehn. (False hypocrites' likeness / Can be called Sodom's apples, / Which are filled with filth / And from outside glisten splendidly. / Hypocrites, who appear fine from without, / Cannot stand up before God.)

6. *Cum sancto Spiritu — Chorus, four part Soprano, Alto, Tenor, Bass, G major: two oboes, strings, continuo.* This final chorus in the form of a fugue was transposed from the opening chorus of cantata BWV 17 (number 1) of 1726 in A major with the same instrumentation. Bach changed the movement by placing a new introductory melody for the instruments before the chorus begins to sing, and by inserting short interjections of the second line, *in gloria Dei Patris,* before each of the part entries into the fugue. Its joy motif is the same as in the cantata chorus, but it does not relate directly to the words of the cantata from which it was borrowed: Cum sancto Spiritu / in gloria Dei Patris. / Amen. (With the Holy Spirit, / in the glory of God the Father. Amen.)

Here the Holy Spirit is being praised, whereas the Psalmist mentions thanks and praise to God through his teaching: BWV 17: "Wer Dank opfert" (1726) — Wer Dank opfert, der preiset mich, und das ist der Weg, dass ich ihm zeige das Heil Gottes. (Who offers thanks praises me, and that is the way that I may show him the salvation of God. (Psalms 50:23)

# IV. The Motets

The motets of Bach continued to be sung in St. Thomas's Church in Leipzig after his death, and it was there that Mozart heard one of them during his visit in 1789. Later, Mendelssohn discovered them also and was inspired to study and perform Bach's longer choral works. It is to Mendelssohn that credit is given to the rediscovery of Bach in the early nineteenth century, and the "Back to Bach" movement continues to the present time.

Motets had been written for the Roman Catholic liturgy in Latin, at first in plainchant, but becoming polyphonic at the end of the sixteenth century with the compositions of Giovanni Gabrieli, whose motets were sung in St. Mark's Cathedral in Venice. When Giovanni and his uncle Andrea (also a polychoral composer) performed their music in the churches of southern Germany, German composers began to study the Venetian style and imitate it in their own works. Heinrich Schütz, the greatest composer of seventeenth century Germany, even traveled twice to Venice so that he could study under Giovanni Gabrieli and later under Monteverdi. His collection of motets entitled *Geistliche Chormusik* (Spiritual Choral Music) (1648) testifies to his expertise in setting polychoral vocal and instrumental motets combining both in a Biblical libretto.

Polychoral style consisted of groups of singers and or instrumentalists in separate choirs; the vocal parts were sung in Latin or in German. Boys were included with other male vocalists in the German church choirs since women were not permitted to sing in performing roles in the church.

Samuel Scheidt, Johann Hermann Schein and Heinrich Schütz (the three S's), with Michael and Hieronymus Praetorius were the leading German composers of the seventeenth century and Bach's predecessors in the art of motet composing both in Latin and in German. Their motets depended heavily on instrumental accompaniment to the vocal forces employed, but in the eighteenth century the vocal choral parts began to outweigh the number of instruments used in a motet setting, so that the result would seem to be a cappella singing, although the German motet (including Bach's) was usually accompanied by an organ or strings, even though it was called a cappella. For special ceremonies, more instruments could be added (cf. BWV 118, 231).

There is some doubt that motets sung during a funeral procession would be accompanied by instruments. It is more likely that instruments were used only within the church or at the home of the deceased. Bach mentions the "motet Thaler" (motet dollar) that his choristers might earn by singing at funerals. Not that Bach always used his own motets for burial services; only for important persons with whom he was acquainted in Leipzig did he compose funeral motets. As for the Latin motets which began the Lutheran service in Leipzig, he had little interest in them, leaving their conducting to a prefect because he wished to concentrate his attention on the cantata that he had composed for the Hauptmusik (chief music).

When he wished to find a motet for use in the service, Bach could always look to one composed by one of his relatives, Johann Bach (1604–73), Johann Christoph Bach (1642–1703), or to Johann Ludwig Bach (1677–1731). We know that Johann Sebastian knew their works because he copied 11 church cantatas of the latter and was even credited with composing one of his cantatas, BWV 15, from the copy that he had made, presumably. There was also the rich repertory of motets from seventeenth century German composers from which he could borrow. All this can be assumed because he left so few motets of his own (7 or 8).

Parry (*Johann Sebastian Bach,* 284–85) goes more deeply into the actual performance of one of Bach's funeral motets:

In this respect a clue is said to be afforded by the existence at the St. Thomas School of a set of band parts to double the voices, from which it is inferred that the choir went to the house from which the funeral procession was to start, and sang the motet in the open air, and that the voice parts were doubled by the instruments to give them support. But besides these instrumental parts there is also a figured bass part for the organ, and as the organ was certainly not carried round the town with the funeral procession, the inference founded on the existence of band parts seems somewhat weakened. But again, on the other hand, the existence of an organ part is not absolutely conclusive proof that Bach contemplated performance in church... On the whole, the character of the work is unfavourable to the theory that the motet was sung in procession, and the existence of instrumental parts suggests to the open mind that such adjuncts were called in to give the motet exceptional effect, and one distinguishable from ordinary motets at ordinary services in view of the exceptional nature of the occasion.

From these remarks, one may conclude that the vocal parts were far more important than the instrumental for Bach's performance of his motets and that many of the instruments, including the organ, would not be used in "open air" processions. Only if the motet was performed within a church or in a home, and then for special effect for a commemoration would instruments support the voices.

But Spitta (II, 280) did not take this point of view: "The Thomasschule scholars, who never practised without the support of a string-bass, took with them, whenever they had to sing out of doors beyond their usual circuit of streets, a Regal belonging to the school."

The motet was important in the eighteenth century Lutheran church service because it was the first choral number to be sung after the organ prelude at the beginning of both the morning and the vesper services, the latter being also known as the motet service. In Bach's time, the choir sang this opening motet in Latin. That Bach was not greatly interested in this number is shown by his placing the less accomplished of his singers as a separate choir to sing it. But if the motet was afterwards sung in German as the Hauptmusik (main music) just before the sermon, he would use his best singers to perform it. It was unlikely that these main music motets would be his own compositions, since he wrote motets only to commemorate special occasions or for memorial services.

It has been pointed out that the cantata as a genre was derived from the motet; many of Bach's cantatas contain motet choral and instrumental movements which could stand alone as separate works. In fact, Bach often called his cantatas "motets"— for example, BWV 71 "Gott ist mein König" (God is my King). The motet in its original form was older than the cantata which evolved under the influence of Italian and French instrumental music.

Whittaker, in his *Fugitive Notes on Certain Cantatas and the Motets of J.S. Bach* (190), writes:

The "Principal Music" of the service was the cantata, which came immediately before the sermon, and the motet was but a kind of preliminary which, in the long three hours' service of the period, was not the Cantor's business. He looked upon it as a secondary matter. Bach was always a defender of his "rights," and fought with grim determination and often with bitter acrimony when there was any likelihood of his dignity, or the dignity of his office being trampled on. He lavished all the wealth of his genius on the portions of the service which were his particular care, and left the others to those whose duty it was to attend to them. Hence, he seldom, if ever, provided Latin motets for the opening of divine worship. As it is well known that three of the six motets we possess were written for special occasions, for funeral ceremonies, it is only reasonable to argue that the remainder were for

extraordinary functions, and not for the services, although it is probable that sometimes he performed them in place of the usual cantata.

The importance of instruments for Bach's production of opera-style sacred works is reflected by his writing on some of his scores not "cantata" but "concerto." Perhaps a reason for this could be that Bach always considered the human voice as an instrument when he composed.

Motets were based on chorale tunes fitted to a religious hymn-text. These chorales were well known to Lutheran congregations; they originally sang along with the choir in the form of the motet. Gradually, however, these congregations stopped singing in order to listen to the more artistic choral singing. This happened when the listening congregation was no longer able to even recognize the chorale tune because it was divided among several voices and instrumentalists. The motet thus became a cantata. Both genres were dramatic stage presentations without audience participation in Bach's treatment of them.

All of Bach's motets, except BWV 230, are chorale motets, so called because the words and the melody of a congregational hymn are included in all or part of the work. Apparently, since no evidence has come to light, Bach never composed a motet in Latin, although Spitta (II, 599) thinks that he did compose some which have been lost. Six motets in German, BWV 225 to BWV 230, were authentic settings by Bach. BWV 118, "O Jesu Christ, meins Lebens Licht" (O Jesus Christ, Light of My Life), might be added as a seventh, because Bach designated it as a "Motetto a quatre voci" (motet with four voices) on his autograph score and it is usually numbered among the Bach cantatas.

There are, however, two additional motets, BWV 231 and BWV Anhang 159, which were attributed to Bach, but the latter has now been shown to have been set by Johann Christoph Bach (1642–1703), and the former, BWV 231, was published by Breitkopf and Härtel as Bach's Motet Number 8. Although Terry doubted that Bach composed it (cf. *Bach: The Magnificat, Lutheran Masses and Motets*, 38), modern research has tended to think it was genuine, so this motet should be examined as well.

The themes of Bach's motets are either happy or sad—jubilation for those which celebrate some festive event (BWV 225, 230, 231), and mourning for funerals (BWV 226, 227, 228, 229, 118). These latter reveal Bach as a devout Christian for whom death is only a step for us to reach God. His faith is shown in his choice of chorale texts and libretti and the way he interprets them by his musical themes. Through his music, the listener can readily understand Bach's attitude towards both living and dying.

As with the composition of his cantatas and his passions, Bach turns to the words of the motet text to derive his musical themes; these give form and also dramatic significance to the work that he is composing. Dramatic "monologues" will be a regular feature for the choral singing of a motet by one or more choirs.

Five of Bach's motets, BWV 226, 227, 228, 229 and 118, were composed for the funeral ceremonies of Leipzig dignitaries. These would be sung in the church at a Sunday afternoon Gedächtnisfeier (commemorative service) after the Leichenpredigt (funeral sermon). In this case, the normal Vesperpredigt (afternoon or evening sermon) would be replaced by the following order of service: 1. Hymn (without organ); 2. Sermon (preached from a black-draped pulpit); 3. Trauermusik (mourning music)—a motet or a cantata, e.g. BWV 198 *Trauerode* (Ode of Mourning), conducted by the Cantor; 4. Collect; 5. Blessing.

This service would be in addition to or as a later memorial service after the main ceremony. That is not to say that Bach's motets in German could never be sung as the Hauptmusik (chief musical piece) during the morning or evening regular services, but Bach really intended them for funerals or special events. Spitta even states that BWV 227, "Jesu, meine Freude" (Jesus, My Joy), "was not intended as an introduction to the service, but as a substitute for the concerted music between the reading of the Gospel and the sermon" (II, 602).

The two motets of rejoicing, BWV 225 and BWV 230, would probably be sung in a morning service on a Feast Day, when their motifs of joy would be in keeping with the mood of jubilation.

Each of Bach's motets will be examined in the BWV sequence number, with BWV 118 last because of its cantata affiliation and its later date. The reason for this is that the date of some motets is unknown.

# Singet dem Herrn (Sing to the Lord)
## (1726–27; BWV 225)

Bach inscribed the score for this work "Motetto" for 2 four-part choirs with an instrumental accompaniment of two violas da gamba, a double bass viol and organ. The musical setting is based on Psalm 149: 1-3), the third stanza of Johann Graumann's hymn "Nun lob mein Seel" (Now praise my Soul), and Psalm 150: 2, 6).

The date of composition and the purpose of this motet have raised some speculation. Terry thinks that "despite its jubilant opening and closing sections, the words of the middle movement of "Singet dem Herrn" leave no doubt as to the ceremony for which it was composed (*The Music of Bach: An Introduction*, 86). Terry thought that Bach composed this motet in 1733 for the funeral of Georg Friedrich Menzel, a Leipzig goldsmith, or for the memorial service of a child of a prominent Leipzig citizen. On the other hand, Konrad Ameln, who edited it for the Neue Bach Ausgabe, stated that it was written for the birthday of Augustus the Strong in 1727, the same year in which this ruler recovered from a a serious illness. Its intensive joy motifs in the opening and the closing choruses have led some to believe that it is simply a work to celebrate the New Year; it could even have been composed as late as 1746 for the New Year's service to offer thanks for the peace treaty between Prussia and Austria which had just been concluded. Certainly its text would support the idea of trust in God and praise for Him rather than having a grieving meaning.

The first section takes the form of a toccata and fugue, symbolic of the exuberant joy expressed by the text. The second section is a decorated chorale with a second chorale sung simultaneously — the whole forming a prayer of entreaty. The last section has the same concertante effect as the first section: praise of God ending in a lively fugue with the two choirs singing in unison, beginning with the words "Alles, was Odem hat, lobe den Herrn" (Every-thing that has breath, praise the Lord).

This was the motet which impressed Mozart so much that he studied its parts and all the other Bach motets while he was visiting the Thomas-schule in 1789.

For all his motets, Bach gives his eight part choruses an antiphonal form, ending with a four part movement, as in this case. All are chorale motets (except BWV 230, "Lobet den Herrn") into which the words and the melody of a congregational hymn are included. Bach treats the opening and the closing choruses of this motet, BWV 225, as fantasias.

1. *Chorus — 2 four-part choirs.* Singet dem Herrn ein neues Lied! / Die Gemeine der Heiligen sollen ihn loben. / Israel freue sich des, der ihn gemacht hat. / Die Kinder Zion sei'n frölich über ihrem Könige. / Sie sollen loben seinen Namen im Reigen, / mit Pauken und Harfen sollen sie ihm spielen. (Sing unto the Lord a new song! / The congregation of saints shall praise Him. / Let Israel rejoice over Him who made it. / Let the children of Zion be joyful over their King. / They shall praise Him in the dance; / with timbrels and harps they shall play for Him.) (Psalm 149: 1-3)

The polychoral effect of this opening number is astounding. Beginning with a quietly dancing melody in the first two lines, the tempo then accelerates into a turba motif, representing the rejoicing of the crowds in song and dance as the words of the Psalm must have suggested to Bach. He really brings this text to vivid life by his word painting which results in one vast joy motif!

Terry is lavish in his praise for this number: "The first movement is a stupendous creation; only the Sanctus of the *B Minor Mass* can stand beside it, and both spread before us the same vision of angelic minstrels in burning row filling the vault of heaven with tireless adoration. Without preparation and abruptly the surge of praise engulfs us. From Coro II comes the insistent summons 'Singet, singet, singet' reiterated again and again, spurring the unflagging polyphony as each clause of the anthem is taken up by the heavenly singers. The fervour rises. 'Rejoice, O Israel' is thundered on every hand, til . . . Coro I bursts into a lively and jubilant fugue 'Die Kinder Zion sei'n fröhlich über ihrem Könige' which is then taken up by Coro II, swelling to a climax of jubilation" (*Bach: The Magnificat, Lutheran Masses and Motets*, 41–42).

Right from the beginning of this opening number, the drama of Bach's portrayal of two groups of people praising God in song comes realistically to life through their shouts of "Singet." This crowd scenario will be repeated in the following movements; whether they represent a host of earthly or heavenly singers, the impact of the music on our imagination should have the same dramatic effect.

2. *Chorus I (Aria) and Chorus II (Chorale)*. This unusual number has two different chorales which are sung concurrently in fantasia form by the two four part choirs. Each line of the second chorale (Chorus II) is separated from the next by interjections of the chorale aria lines sung by Chorus I. The lines of the first chorale by an unknown poet are superimposed onto the second chorale which sings the third stanza of the hymn by Johann Graumann, "Nun lob', mein Seel', den Herren" (Now praise, my Soul, the Lord) (1530), to the melody by Johann Kugelmann of about 1540. They sing the last part of Graumann's chorale as a massive four part fugue.

The import of these lines has changed from praise of God to imploring His mercy on our human frailty—this thought in the text of Graumann's chorale gives a funeral implication to the stanza and leads one to think that this motet may also be a funeral composition. It seems that this is Terry's opinion, although he is not sure for whom this motet was written: "Moreover, the words of the middle section clearly indicate a funerary purpose. Probably the Motet was commissioned for the 'Gedächtnisfeier' (memorial service) of a child of prominent citizens, whose death would less invite philosophic reflexions on human morality than the thought of the heavenly 'congregation' into which the young life entered, whose song of rejoicing the Psalmist invited and Bach provides" (*Bach: The Magnificat, Lutheran Masses and Motets*, 38).

*Chorus I (Aria):* Gott, nimm dich ferner unser an! / Denn ohne dich ist nichts getan / mit allen unsern Sachen. / Drum sei du unser Schirm und Licht, / und trügt uns unsre Hoffnung nicht, / so wirst du's ferner machen. / Wohl dem, der sich nur steif und fest / auf dich und deine Huld verlässt! (God, continue to take care of us! / For without Thee nothing is done / with all our affairs. / Therefore be our shield and light / and do not disappoint us in our hope, / so wilt Thou continue to do. / Blessed is he, who strictly and firmly / relies on Thee and Thy favor.) (Unknown poet)

*Chorus II (Chorale).* Wie sich ein Vater erbarmet / über seine jungen Kinderlein, / so tut der Herr uns allen, / so wir ihn kindlich fürchten rein. / Er kennt das arm gemächte. / Gott weiss, wir sind nur Staub, / gleich wie das Gras vom Rechen, / ein Blum' und fallend Laub! / Der Wind nur drüber wehet, / so ist es nicht mehr da! / Also der Mensch vergehet, / sein End', das ist ihm nah. (Just as a father pities / his own young children, / so does the Lord all of us, / if, like children, we truly fear Him. / He knows the poor creature. / God knows that we are only dust, / just as grass from the rake, / a flower and falling leaf! / The wind only blows over it, / then it is no longer there! / Thus man passes away; / his end, that is near him.) (Johann Graumann, 1530)

This chorale text that Graumann wrote might remind the listener of the text for the second chorus in *Ein deutsches Requiem* (A German Requiem) by Johannes Brahms. Perhaps Graumann was aware of the same Biblical verse, I Peter 1:24, when he wrote the libretto for this chorale?

3. *Chorus—2 four-part choirs.* The same exuberant joy motif heard in the opening chorus returns now with even more festive singing, as the antiphonal effect of the two choirs, tossing their jubilation back and forth between them, proves. This combines finally into two bars of eight part harmony before the fugue, which concludes for the singing of the last two

lines. The sopranos add the finishing touch to the work with "Halleluja"— their uninhibited joy would make the listener doubt that this motet was ever intended for a funeral commemoration.

Lobet den Herrn in seinen Taten, / lobet ihn in seiner grossen Herrlichkeit. / Alles, was Odem hat, lobe den Herrn. / Halleluja! (Praise the Lord for His deeds; / Praise Him for His great glory. / Let everything that has breath praise the Lord. / Alleluja!) (Psalm 150:2, 6)

The dramatic contrast obtained by placing the chorale verses between the Biblical text quotations is very effective, even though the difference in their motifs (joy/sorrow/joy) might confuse the listener. Yet I feel that Bach intended this chorale second movement to reflect on our trust in God and on human mortality even as we express joy in His praise.

Perhaps Bach wished to remind Friedrich Augustus I of the gratitude he owed to God for his recovery from illness or to express the thanks to God that was also appropriate for a New Year's church service. Could this, then, be a funeral motet?

# Der Geist hilft unsrer Schwachheit auf (The Spirit Helps Our Weakness)
## (1729; BWV 226)

This is the only one of his motets, apart from BWV 118, that Bach provided with a full orchestral accompaniment: two oboes da caccia, a bassoon, strings and basso continuo (organ). It was usually the custom in Leipzig that funeral motets should have no instrumental accompaniment (except for the organ), but Bach made an exception to this case, the first of

the four BWV listings (226 to 229 inclusive) for his funeral motets.

Spitta (II, 607) is more explicit than modern performers (cf. above) on the instrumentation: for the first choir, two violins, a viola and a cello, and for the second, two oboes, a bassoon and the organ for which Bach wrote a figured bass part, only to be used in church performances. Apparently, this funeral service was held in St. Paul's, the University Church of Leipzig, where an orchestra and the organ was allowed for burial services.

Bach composed this eight voice (two choir) motet for the Gedächtnispredigt (memorial sermon) at the funeral service, October 20, 1729, for Johann Heinrich Ernesti, rector of the Thomas School and Professor of Poetry at the University of Leipzig, whose death occurred October 16, 1729. Bach's rapport with him had been most friendly, unlike his dealings with his successor, Johann August Ernesti, who was not related. Yet Bach does not display his own personal affection for the deceased Rector in this motet, but confines himself to translating the Biblical texts that he had chosen into music. He does this by dividing the libretto into three parts: two Biblical quotes and then a final chorale verse. The central theme of the motet is to show how the Holy Ghost influences our lives, according to God's will. Bach has chosen two verses from Paul's Epistle to the Romans 8:26, 27, and the third stanza of a chorale by Martin Luther to illustrate this in words and in music.

1. *Double Chorus.* This first movement is built from three contrasting moods: (a) a joy motif, sung antiphonally by the two choirs in 3/8 time with a rapid toccata-like effect, then (b) a grief motif symbolic of human indecision, and finally (c) a unison expression of sadness, representing the Spirit's sighing ( = Seufzen) by the syncopated, broken rhythm of Bach's word painting in sound.

(a) Der Geist hilft unsrer Schwachheit auf. (The Spirit helps our weakness.) (b) Denn wir wissen nicht, was wir beten sollen, wie sich's gebühret; (For we do not know for what we should pray, as it ought to be;) (c) sondern der Geist selbst vertritt uns

aufs beste mit unaussprechlichem Seufzen. (but the Spirit Himself represents us best with inexpressible sighing.) (Romans 8:26)

The second section (b) seems to tone down the joy motif in section (a) which showed the Spirit's intervention on our behalf. Our dependence on divine help to aid us when we pray is now mentioned as a sign of our human weakness. But the Holy Spirit will represent us best with stifled groans (which Bach illustrates by a grief motif at this point) (c).

2. *Double Chorus.* This second double chorus continues with the next verse of Paul's Epistle to the Romans 8:27. It has two fugal themes which illustrate the two parts of the text. Bach brings them together in a double fugue at the end of the movement:

Der aben die Herzen forschet, der weiss, was des Geistes Sinn sei, denn er vertritt die Heiligen nach dem, das Gott gefället. (And He who searchest hearts, He knows what is the mind of the Spirit, for He maketh intercession for the saints according to the will of God.)

3. *Chorale.* Bach probably chose this third stanza of Martin Luther's 1524 chorale, "Komm, heiliger Geist" (Come, Holy Spirit), because it makes a fitting conclusion to the words of St. Paul in the two preceding numbers. Sung by only one of the four part choirs, it entreats the Holy Spirit to give us confidence and tolerance of our afflictions, so that we may be strengthened to serve God in our lives and to come to Him after we die. This chorale verse is a suitable ending for a funeral motet in that it shows the dramatic role of the Holy Spirit in leading us to God. Du heilige Brunst, süsser Trost, / nun hilf uns fröhlich und getrost / in dein'm Deinst beständig bleiben, / die Trübsal uns nicht abtreiben! / O Herr, durch dein

Kraft uns bereit / und stärk des Fleisches Blödigkeit, / dass wir hier ritterlich ringen, / durch Tod und Leben zu dir dringen. / Halleluja, halleluja! (Thou holy fire, sweet comfort, / now help us joyfully and comforted / to remain constant in Thy service. / do not let sadness drive us away from Thee! / O Lord, prepare us through Thy power / and strengthen the weakness of the flesh, / so that we may here strive nobly / to reach Thee through life and death. / Halleluja, halleluja!)

This motet is interesting because it reveals Bach's ability as a librettist. Although these three movements were not written personally by him, Bach is able to arrange them, from his reading of the Bible and from his own collection of chorales, into an impressive sermon on the Holy Spirit.

# Jesu, meine Freude
# (Jesus, My Joy)
## (1723; BWV 227)

This is the oldest of Bach's extant motets, composed soon after he had taken up his duties in Leipzig. It is the longest of his motets, and the one that is most often performed in concert today. The reason for this is the consummate artistry with which Bach has arranged his libretto and composed music to bring it to dramatic life.

It is the only motet for a five part (SSATB) choir, without the antiphonal effects of the double choir, but alternating its 11 movements between a chorale and a chorus. Like most of Bach's motets, it would be lightly accompanied by the organ, celli and double-bass for the continuo, but modern performances seem to increase the instrumentation to include violins, without impeding the vocal sound. The beginning and the closing lines are identical, being centered around the fugue in the sixth movement "Ihr aber seid nicht fleischlich" (But ye are not of the flesh). As he will do for BWV 226 in 1729, which like this motet was a funeral work, Bach takes the Biblical quotations for his choruses from St. Paul's Epistle to the

Romans and chooses Johann Franck's hymn, "Jesu, meine Freude," complete in all its six stanzas for the chorale parts.

Spitta thinks it probable that Bach wrote this motet which has much in common with a cantata by Buxtehude, based on the same chorale, because he had been inspired on hearing it (years before in Lübeck, perhaps?) (cf. I, 307–10).

The chorale sections are harmonizations of Johann Crüger's melody (1653) for Johann Franck's chorale (1650). St. Paul's Epistle to the Romans 8:1, 2, 9, 10, 11, provides Bach with the choruses, which form a ritornello after each of the six stanzas of Franck's hymn. Bach varied the number of vocalists for each movement between three and five, all taken from the one five-voice choir. Eight of the 11 movements are in E minor. Malcolm Boyd provides a diagram in his book (*Bach*, 139) showing the symmetrical design of this motet, how the movements are interrelated, their key and the soloists who perform them:

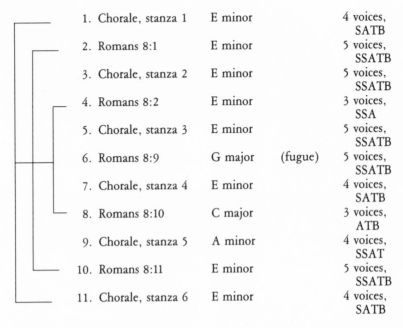

| | | | | |
|---|---|---|---|---|
| 1. | Chorale, stanza 1 | E minor | | 4 voices, SATB |
| 2. | Romans 8:1 | E minor | | 5 voices, SSATB |
| 3. | Chorale, stanza 2 | E minor | | 5 voices, SSATB |
| 4. | Romans 8:2 | E minor | | 3 voices, SSA |
| 5. | Chorale, stanza 3 | E minor | | 5 voices, SSATB |
| 6. | Romans 8:9 | G major | (fugue) | 5 voices, SSATB |
| 7. | Chorale, stanza 4 | E minor | | 4 voices, SATB |
| 8. | Romans 8:10 | C major | | 3 voices, ATB |
| 9. | Chorale, stanza 5 | A minor | | 4 voices, SSAT |
| 10. | Romans 8:11 | E minor | | 5 voices, SSATB |
| 11. | Chorale, stanza 6 | E minor | | 4 voices, SATB |

This motet was composed for the commemoration service for Johanna Maria Kees, wife of the postmaster general of Leipzig, held on July 18, 1723. The sermon, preached by Superintendent Deyling at St. Nicholas Church, was taken from Romans 8:11, which the chorus sings for the Biblical libretto parts from the same chapter. Bach has succeeded in fusing these with Franck's chorale verses in order to preach his own personal sermon in music on the fundamental tenets of his own faith—his joy in Christ.

1. *Chorale (4 part—SATB)*. A chorale verse begins and ends this motet, so that it resembles a chorale cantata, except that the chorale is not embellished in its first presentation as Bach usually does in his cantatas. Jesu, meine Freude / meines Herzens Weide, / Jesu meine Zier. / Ach wie lang, ach lange / ist dem Herzen bange / und verlangt nach dir. / Gottes Lamm, mein Bräutigam, / ausser dir soll mir auf Erden / nichts sonst

Liebers werden. (Jesus, my joy / my heart's pasture, / Jesus, my adornment. / O how long, o long / is my heart anxious / and longs for Thee. / God's Lamb, my bridegroom, / besides Thee for me on earth / nothing else becomes preferable.)

This first movement is a simple four part setting which emphasizes the singers' longing for Jesus in a dramatic form of prayer to Him—it is like a monologue, but sung in unison by the choir, to represent the prayer of each individual in the congregation.

2. *Chorus (5 part—SSATB)*. In this first free chorus on the Biblical text, Bach has the five voices repeat the key word *nichts* (nothing) three times to emphasize the Gospel lesson in this verse. Obviously, this word determines how he will set the remainder. This he does with a melody that is difficult to forget, because there seems to be a supernatural tone of awe, a motif of profound reverence before

divinity, which is reinforced by the fine singing in canon in the last half. Es ist nun *nichts* Verdammliches an denen, die in Christo Jesu sind, die nicht nach dem Fleische wandeln, sondern nach dem Geist. (Now there is *nothing* condemnatory in them, who are in Jesus Christ, who walk not after the flesh, but after the Spirit.) (Romans 8:1)

3. *Chorale (5 part—SSATB).* This is stanza 2 of the chorale and it has a more elaborate melody than stanza 1. A prayer motif is combined with a joy motif in this number as the choir sings in unison of its confidence in Jesus to protect each of us from evil. Bach has dramatically interpreted the contrast between the goodness of Jesus and the evil of Satan by motifs of calm and motifs of terror, respectively, derived from the text that he is setting. Every third line has this motif of calm, contrasting with the words denoting terror (in italics). Unter deinen Schirmen / bin ich vor den *Stürmen* / aller Feinde frei. / Lass den Satan *wittern,* / lass den Feind *erbittern,* / mir steht Jesus bei. / Ob es jetzt gleich *kracht* und *blitzt,* / ob gleich *Sünd* und *Hölle* schrecken, / Jesus will mich decken. (Beneath Thy protection / I am free from the *storming* / of all enemies. / Let Satan *rage,* / let our enemy *provoke,* / Jesus is standing by me. / Although it now *thunders* and *flashes,* although *sin* and *hell* terrify, Jesus will protect me.

4. *Chorus (3 part—SSA).* Bach set this second chorus for a trio in order to heighten the drama in the next chorale number (5). This trio is didactic, almost a miniature sermon, stressing the redemption from sin and death that Christ has given us. Denn das Gesetz des Geistes, der da labendig machet in Christo Jesu, hat mich frei gemacht von dem Gesetz der Sünde und des Todes. (For the law of

the Spirit, which then makes living in Jesus Christ, has made me free from the law of sin and death.) (Romans 8:2)

The hushed tone of this trio gives the impression of a motif of beatific peace, which has been brought to each one of us by Christ's self-sacrifice.

5. *Chorale (5 part—SSATB).* This is stanza 3 of Franck's hymn. Bach illustrates in sound each expressive word (in italics) in order to create a pictorial music-drama depicting unrest in Satan's kingdom. This notion of indignation over Christ's salvation of mankind fits very well into the thought expressed in the preceding number (4).

Terry thinks that "The movement exhibits dramatic intensity perhaps without parallel in Bach's music...." (*The Magnificat, Lutheran Masses and Motets,* 39) *Trotz* dem alten *Drachen,* / *Trotz* des *Todes Rachen,* / *Trotz* der *Furcht dazu*! / *Tobe, Welt,* und *springe*; / *ich steh hier* und *singe* / *in gar sicherer Ruh*! / *Gottes Macht* hält mich in acht; / *Erd* und *Abgrund* muss *verstummen,* / ob sie noch so *brummen.* (*Despite* the old *dragon,* / *despite* the *jaws* of *death,* / *despite* the *fear* of *that*! / *Rage, world,* and *fall apart*; / *I remain here* and *sing* / *in quite safe peace*! *God's power* holds my attention; *Earth* and *abyss* must *be silent,* even though they still *rumble.*)

The quiet tone that Bach uses to illustrate the verbs *verstummen* (be silent) and *brummen* (to rumble) provides a striking contrast with the turmoil of the first four lines. This change begins halfway through the stanza when I (*ich*) show my confidence in God's protection—a real dramatic turn that Bach illustrates by a motif of peace or calm. Bach's decrescendo in the tempo of the last line is meant to portray the discontented contortions of "the old dragon" in hell, mentioned in the first line.

6. *Chorus (5 part—*SSATB*)*. This is the centerpiece of the motet which Bach sets as a fugue. The text of the fugue is the first sentence. The second sentence has a new melody in broad and impressive style, first given by the soprano and then taken up by the bass.

It is not surprising that Bach chose this Scriptural verse as the climax for this funeral motet; it focuses on the importance of the Holy Spirit in our lives. Especially the emphasis that Bach places on the words "der ist nicht sein" (he is not His) makes the Apostle's words come alive. The grief motif that Bach uses for the second sentence seems to reflect his own regrets for those who do not have the Spirit of Christ.

Ihr aber seid nicht fleischlich, sondern geistlich, so anders Gottes Geist in euch wohnet. Wer aber Christi Geist nicht hat, der ist nicht sein. (But ye are not of flesh but of spirit, if so be that God's Spirit dwell in you. But who does not have the Spirit of Christ, he is not His.) (Romans 8:9)

7. *Chorale (4 part—*SATB*)*. This setting of the fourth stanza of the hymn divides its parts so that the soprano sings the canto, supported by the alto, tenor and bass in canon. Once again, the poetic text seems to supplement the thought of the preceding chorus (number 6), i.e. the temporal treasures of the world opposed to the spiritual wealth in Christ. The smoothly flowing melody of the last two lines, denoting a motif of calm, contrasts with the jerky effect of the piling up of nouns (in italics) in the preceding line. This is a most dramatic number in both its text and its music.

Weg mit allen Schätzen, / due bist mein Ergötzen, / Jesus, meine Lust. / Weg, ihr eitlen Ehren, / ich mag euch nicht hören, / bleibt mir unbewusst. / *Elend, Not, Kreuz, Schmach* und *Tod,* / soll mich, ob ich viel muss leiden, / nicht von Jesu scheiden. (Away with all treasures; / Thou art my delight, / Jesus, my joy. / Away, ye vain glories, / I cannot hear you, / stay unknown to me. / *Misery, need,* the *Cross, shame,* and *death,* / however much I must suffer, / shall not part me from Jesus.)

8. *Chorus (3 part—*ATB*)*. This trio is the balancing counterpart of number 4; it amplifies the thought that the Spirit lives beyond sin and death. Bach stresses the words *Geist* (spirit) and *Leben* (life) to show this. In 12/8 time, the three voices share the flowing melody, taking up each other's phrases but maintaining the rhythm. A florid double fugue comes with the last clause to dramatize its meaning.

So aber Christus in euch ist, so ist der Leib zwar tot um der Sünde willen; der Geist aber ist das Leben um der Gerechtigkeit willen. (But if Christ is in you, so is the body truly dead because of sin; but the Spirit is life because of righteousness.) (Romans 8:10)

The andante tempo of this movement suggests a step motif which indicates the coming of the Holy Spirit into our bodies, now dead to sin. This pensive mood leads now into the reflective chorale of the following movement.

9. *Chorale (4 part—*SSAT*)*. Here the fifth stanza of the chorale has the canto in the alto voices, supported by the other voices. They sing a slumber song for the dead body as it departs, either literally or figuratively, from this world of sin. Bach sets this verse of the hymn to a grief motif befitting the

funeral service for which he composed this motet. Gute Nacht, o Wesen, / das die Welt erlesen, / mir gefällst du nicht. / Gute Nacht, ihr Sünden, / bleibet weit dahinten, / kommt nicht mehr ans Licht. / Gute Nacht, du Stolz und Pracht. / Dir sei ganz, du Lasterleben, / gute Nacht gegeben. (Good night, O being, / that has chosen the world; / you do not please me. / Good night, you sins, / stay far behind, / come no more into the light. / Good night, thou pride and splendor. / To thee completely, life of wickedness, / may good night be given.)

Bach had already used this same chorale stanza as the final number of his cantata BWV 64.

Tovey comments on this ninth movement of the motet in his *Essays in Musical Analysis,* however, in an unusual way, that I feel should be quoted, because it shows Bach's own style of vocal composition from a modern conductor's point of view:

> The ninth movement, the fifth verse of the chorale, is one of Bach's great choral variations; not, this time, in the free declamatory style that so effectually disguises the structure of the third verse, but in a stupendously complete and clear form which only Bach has achieved, though his examples of it are so numerous that they are believed to be normal specimens of academic music. (The first chorus of the *Matthew Passion* is one.) The essence of this form is that, while one voice or part sings the chorale phrase by phrase, with pauses so long between each as to stretch the whole out to the length of a long movement, the other parts execute a complete design which may or may not have some connexion with the melody of the chorale, but which in any case would remain a perfectly

solid whole if the chorale were taken away. ... I have tried the experiment of playing this ninth movement through, leaving out the chorale-melody except for a few unemphasized notes to complete the mere harmony. The effect is not noticeably less solid and natural than that of the foregoing trio, No. 8. ... As the absence of a soprano in the eighth movement left the ensemble with a tone of sweet gravity, here the absence of a bass leaves it poetically aloof from the world. [*Essays in Musical Analysis,* V, Vocal Music, 81]

Leaving out the chorale-melody would not, in my opinion, enhance the overall feeling of awe and respect for death that Bach wished to show in this chorale text.

10. *Chorus — 5 part — SSATB).* Bach selected this verse from Paul's Epistle to the Romans 8:11, which he sets as a compressed version of the second movement — like a ritornello. The text points out the immortality of the soul which has the theme of Superintendent Deyling's Gedächtnispredigt (memorial sermon) for Frau Kees on the same Bible text. The miracle of the resurrection which was performed by and on Jesus will be repeated in everyone who is dead to sin, thanks to the Holy Spirit.

Dr. Salomon Deyling had made these memorial services customary in St. Nicholas's Church since 1722 when the first was held by him in memory of a high-ranking official. Motets BWV 226, 227, 228 and 229 were performed at such services.

So nun der Geist des, der Jesum von den Toten auferweckt hat, in euch wohnet, so wird auch derselbige, der Christum von den Toten auferwecket hat, eure sterblichen Leiber lebendig machen, um des willen, dass sein Geist in euch wohnet. (But if the

Spirit of Him that raised up Jesus from the dead dwell in you, so shall also the same One who awakened Christ from the dead quicken your mortal bodies for the sake of His spirit that dwelleth in you.) (Romans 8:11)

11. *Chorale (4 part — *SATB*)*. Repeating the unison singing of the first plain chorale (number 1), this concluding number of Franck's poem brings the symmetry of the text to completion in the last line by the repetition of the first line of number 1, "Jesu, meine Freude."

Weicht, ihr Trauergeister, / denn mein Freudenmeister, / Jesus, tritt herein. / Denen, die Gott lieben, / muss auch ihr Betrüben / lauter Zucker sein. / Duld' ich schon hier Spott und Hohn, / dennoch bleibst du auch im Leide, / Jesu, meine Freude. (Depart, ye ghosts of sadness, / for my Master of happiness, / Jesus, enters. / For those, who love God, / even their sorrow must be / nothing but sugar. / If I endure here mockery and derision, / still even in my suffering Thou remainest, / Jesus, my joy.) (Johann Franck, 1650)

For his motets, just as in the cantatas and the passions, Bach's source of inspiration lies in the words of the text that he is setting. From this libretto, which he himself has chosen from the Bible and his collection of chorales, including Erhard Bodenschatz's *Florilegium Portense,* an anthology compiled in 1603 through 1621 and used in the Leipzig motet repertory, Bach derives the musical motifs that he uses to illustrate the meaning of each word or group of words in each motet. So in BWV 227, "Jesu, meine Freude," the words have influenced the form that the music has taken, and this will be the case for the remainder of Bach's motets.

# Fürchte dich nicht (Fear Not)
## (1726; BWV 228)

This funeral motet was probably performed at the Gedächtnisfeier (memorial service) for Frau Winkler, wife of Stadthauptmann (captain of the town militia) Winkler, in St. Nicholas's Church on February 6, 1726. Unlike the other eight part motets, it consists of only one movement including the chorale; this chorale is woven into the second Biblical text sung by the main chorus.

The sermon was again preached by Superintendent Deyling on two passages this time: the first from Isaiah 41:10 and the second from Isaiah 43:1 — the certainty of God's promises of help and of human redemption. The chorale is taken from the eleventh and twelfth stanzas of Paul Gerhardt's hymn, "Warum soll ich mich denn grämen?" (Why should I then grieve?) (1653), sung by the sopranos alone to the melody by Johann Ebeling (1666).

Each of the two sections of this motet for two choirs is introduced by the same words from Isaiah, "Fürchte dich nicht" (Fear not), so that the motet has really only one movement, also ending in unison with the same words.

The words of the prophet and those in Gerhardt's hymn combine to form a dramatic dialogue between God and man. Each assures the other that they belong together, as their final unison line shows: "Fürchte dich nicht; du bist mein." (Fear not; thou art mine.)

1. *Chorus (8 part)*. This first chorus has the two choirs answering each

other in short phrases, resulting in a restless and broken melody. Fürchte dich nicht, ich bin bei dir; weiche nicht, denn ich bin dein Gott; ich stärke dich, ich helfe dir auch; ich erhalte dich durch die rechte Hand meiner Gerechtigkeit. (Fear not, for I am with thee; do not waver, for I am thy God; I strengthen thee, I help thee too; I uphold thee through the right hand of my righteousness.) (Isaiah 41:10)

This message of God's assurance is announced by both choirs as they dramatically repeat His words through the voice of His prophet Isaiah. These commands come from the basses of both choirs as they sing in unison; they give the impression that God is supporting the mourners in their grief. As both choirs sing the words "for I am with thee," their words denote a motif of confidence rather than one of lamentation which one might expect in a funeral motet; this motif continues up to the words "weiche nicht, denn ich bin dein Gott" (do not waver, for I am thy God). Then Bach emphasizes the three verbs of his text: *stärke* (strengthen), *helfe* (help) and *erhalte* (uphold), each by different musical tones to illustrate their meaning.

2. *Chorus with Chorale (Soprano).* The sopranos of both choruses sing interpolated verses from two stanzas (11 and 12) of Paul Gerhardt's hymn, while the basses are more noticeable in the chorus. It seems likely that Bach chose these stanzas from Gerhardt's chorale because the words "du bist mein" (thou art mine) appear in both the chorale and the chorus (Isaiah 43:1). The unison singing by both

choirs of the words common to both texts at the end: "Fürchte dich nicht, du bist mein" (Fear not; thou art mine) shows real imagination and originality on Bach's part when he devised this libretto.

Chorus (3 part): Fürchte dich nicht, denn ich habe dich erlöset, ich habe dich bei deinem Namen gerufen, du bist mein. (Fear not, for I have redeemed thee; I have called thee by thy name; thou art mine.) (Isaiah 43:1)

A fugue on the tune "Warum soll ich mich denn grämen" (Why should I then grieve) is added into the chorus by the chorale and returns 33 times, symbolic of the age of Christ at His Crucifixion.

Chorale (Sopranos): Herr, mein Hirt, Brunn aller Freuden! / Du bist mein, / ich bin dein, / niemand kann uns scheiden. / Ich bin dein, weil du dein Leben / und dein Blut, / mir zu gut, / in den Tod gegeben. (Lord, my Shepherd, source of all joys! / Thou art mine, / I am Thine, / nobody can part us. / I am Thine, because Thou has given Thy life / and Thy blood / for my benefit, / and embraced death.)

Du bist mein, weil ich dich fasse / und dich nicht, / o mein Licht, / aus dem Herzen lasse! / Lass mich, lass mich hingelangen, / wo du mich / und ich dich / lieblich werd' umfangen. (Thou art mine, because I hold Thee / and will not leave Thee, / o my Light, / out of my heart! / Let me, let me reach the place, / where Thou wilt embrace me / and I Thee / in love.) (Paul Gerhardt, 1653)

Fürchte dich nicht, du bist mein. (Fear not, thou art mine.)

# Komm, Jesu, komm
## (Come, Jesus, Come)
### (1723 to 1734, or 1730; BWV 229)

This funeral motet for an eight voice double choir was performed at the memorial service for Maria Elisabeth Schelle on March 26, 1730, although Bach could have composed it before or after this date. Terry says that the occasion of its first performance and for whom Bach wrote it are unknown.

It is unusual because it is made up of two stanzas of a congregational hymn by Paul Thymich, published in 1697 but without a melody. So Bach composed a melody for the closing movement which he marks "Aria." Similarly, for the first stanza, Bach composes a theme for each of the six sections of the text, derived from the words.

This motet is highly dramatic in the believer's direct appeal to Jesus to come to him. Its prayer motif comes out in both stanzas, while the first has additional musical motifs in each line.

1. *Chorale (double choir).* This first stanza is set as a continuous movement with six sections:

Section 1 (line 1)—the united invocation of the two choirs which sing antiphonally their call upon Jesus, until Bach concludes with a motif of exhaustion: Komm, Jesu, komm, mein Leib ist müde, (Come, Jesus, come, by body is tired;)

Section 2 (line 2)—an antiphonic movement in the vocal parts, leaping up and then falling down, continues the motif of exhaustion above: die Kraft verschwindt je mehr und mehr, (my strength disappears more and more.)

Sections 3 and 4 (lines 3 and 4)—

Bach's illustration of his text in these lines is most apparent in the motif of longing in the canon singing of *sehne* (long for) and the peculiar step motif of *saure Weg* (harsh road), the tone soothing for the first and jarring for the second: ich sehne mich nach deinem Frieden; / der saure Weg wird mir zu schwer! (I long for Thy peace; / the harsh road becomes too hard for me!)

Section 5 (line 5)—in a more lively 4/4 tempo, both choirs repeat their call upon the Lord that He should come to them: Komm, komm, ich will mich dir ergeben, (Come, come, I will give myself up to Thee;)

Sections 6 and 7—a sweeping panorama of sound, representing space or eternity, sung in canon with a fervent motif of praise for Jesus in the stressed nouns: *Weg* (way), *Wahrheit* (truth) and *Leben* (life). du bist der rechte *Weg*, / die *Wahrheit* und das *Leben*. (Thou art the right way, / the truth and the life.)

2. *Aria (Chorale).* This is stanza 11 of Thymich's hymn, which Bach set to his own melody, based on the theme that he set for the opening chorale. It expresses Bach's own sincerity of belief so well that he had little difficulty in fitting his melody to the text of the poem. The listener can understand Bach's personal attitude towards death in this verse of the poem—death is the means of being with Christ. Both the words and the music are fitting for a memorial service. It is like a miniature Requiem, dramatically sung by the choirs for the deceased.

Drum schliess ich mich in deine Hände / und sage, Welt, zu guter

Nacht! / Eilt gleich mein Lebenslauf zu Ende / ist doch der Geist wohl angebracht. / Er soll bei seinem Schöpfer schweben, / weil Jesus ist und bleibt / der wahre Weg zum Leben. (Therefore I enclose myself in

Thy hands / and say, world, good night to you! / Though the course of my life hurries to its end, / yet the spirit is quite ready. / It shall hover by its Creator, / because Jesus is and remains / the true way to life.)

# Lobet den Herrn, alle Heiden
# (Praise the Lord, All Nations)
## (1723?; BWV 230)

This short motet differs from the others in having only one four part chorus and no chorale. It is not mourning music and is the only motet to have a figured bass-line. Therefore it must have been accompanied by the organ and at least one of the bass strings. Further evidence that it had instrumental accompaniment comes from the possibility that it was the opening movement for SATB of a lost cantata that Bach had composed.

A joy motif pervades the whole chorus in a straightforward hymn of praise to God, according to the text of Psalm 117.

It may be of interest to note that Georg Philipp Telemann composed a motet on this same Psalm, which was published in Nürnberg in 1744, with a much more lavish instrumentation: three trumpets, timpani, strings and basso continuo, but using only a soprano and an alto with a choir of

just three parts. This later (?) motet by Telemann is a stupendous tonal painting, which might make the listener wonder whether he was trying to surpass Bach in his setting of this Psalm. No doubt he was aware of Bach's earlier (?) work.

Bach follows his text closely, dividing the text into three sections — an animated fugue with a joy motif for the first two lines, a motif of calm for the next two lines, and a return to the joy motif in the final Alleluja.

Chorus (4 part): Lobet den Herrn, alle Heiden, / und preiset ihn, alle Völker! / Denn seine Gnade und Wahrheit / waltet über uns in Ewigkeit. / Alleluja! (Praise the Lord, all nations, / and praise Him, all people. / For His mercy and truth / rule over us eternally. / Halleluja!)

All three sections are sung in canon by the four parts (SATB), only uniting at the end of the Alleluja.

# Sei Lob und Preis mit Ehren
# (Be Laud and Praise with Honor)
## (    ?; BWV 231)

This is another four part motet for SATB, consisting of only verse five of the chorale, "Nun lob, mein Seel, den Herren" (Now Praise, My Soul, the Lord), by Johann Graumann (Gra-

mann or Poliander), 1487–1541. Bach used verses from this chorale in some of his cantatas — BWV 17, 28, 29, 51, and 167 — and in the chorale (number 2) of motet BWV 225.

The date of composition is unknown, but this music for Graumann's text has been attributed to Bach and was included in the Breitkopf und Härtel edition of the works of Johann Sebastian Bach.

Possibly this motet was the opening movement of one of Bach's lost cantatas (cf. the preceding motet, BWV 230), because of its lavish instrumentation which includes a cornet, two oboes, three trombones, an oboe da caccia (taille), a bassoon, two violins, a viola, a violoncello, a bass violin and the usual organ. Like BWV 230, it is a work of praise, including a joy motif in its prayer, but this time there is only one continuous chorus of four parts, which is sung in canon throughout.

Sei Lob und Preis mit Ehren / Gott Vater, Sohn und heiligem Geist! /

Der woll in uns vermehren, / was er aus Gnaden uns verheisst. / Dass wir ihm fest vertrauen, / gänzlich verlassen auf ihn, / von Herzen auf ihn bauen, / dass uns'r Herz, Mut und Sinn / ihm festiglich anhangen; / drauf singen wir zur Stund: / Amen. Wir werd'ns erlangen, / glaub'n wir aus Herzens Grund. (Be laud and praise with honor / to God the Father, to the Son and Holy Ghost! / He will increase in us / what He has promised us from His mercy. / That we firmly trust in Him, / completely depend upon Him, / building from our hearts upon Him, / so that our heart, courage and mind / cling firmly to Him; / to this we sing at this moment: / Amen. We shall attain this, / if we believe from the bottom of our hearts.) (Johann Graumann, 1549)

# O Jesu Christ, mein's Lebens Licht
# (O Jesus Christ, Light of My Life)
### (1736–1737; BWV 118)

Although this chorale motet was listed as a cantata by Bach in the original Bachgesellschaft (B.G.) edition, and also by Wolfgang Schmieder in his 1950 Bach-Werke-Verzeichnis (BWV) Catalogue of Bach's works, its single stanza format points to it being a motet or the first movement of a funeral cantata from which the other movements have been lost. Bach composed it between the above dates, but its most notable performance occurred at the funeral service for Count Friedrich von Flemming on October 11, 1740.

The text is stanza one of Martin Behm's chorale, sung by only one 4 part choir accompanied by an instrumental group (a band) consisting of two litui (bass cornets), one regular

cornet, two bassoons, three trombones, two oboes da caccia (taille) and the organ, but without strings. This suggests that the motet was sung in the open air either at or en route to the cemetery, and if so, the organ could not have been used for the basso continuo.

Such heavy ornamentation, combined with the singing in canon of all voices produces a motif of deep solemnity to that found in some of the works of Scheidt, Schein and Schütz in the seventeenth century. Yet this work by Bach is unique in the class of funeral motets because of the austere beauty of Bach's dramatic word painting in sound.

O Jesu Christ, mein's Lebens Licht, / mein Hort, mein Trost, mein Zuversicht! / Auf Erden bin ich nur ein Gast, / und drückt mich sehr der Sünden Last. (O Jesus Christ, Light of my life, / My refuge, my comfort, my assurance! / On earth I am only a guest, / and the burden of my sins much oppresses me.) (Martin Behm, 1557–1622)

The manner in which this verse is sung and the innate emotion expressed make this short but dramatic invocation and prayer for help to Christ one of Bach's supreme musical achievements.

# V. Motet Movements Found in Bach Cantatas (Arranged Chronologically)

Bach may have composed other motets both in Mühlhausen and in Weimar, because his early cantatas, dating from these years, often contain a chorale movement in motet style and a great many of his Leipzig cantatas have a chorale fantasia at the beginning and the same chorale, plainly sung, at the end.

Spitta points out some of the motet movements in Bach's cantatas (II, 598, 599) which show how important they were for Bach's vocal and instrumental combinations. Bach even calls his first two extant Mühlhausen cantatas, BWV 131 and BWV 71, motets, perhaps because of their arias combined with a chorale.

The first separate choral movement in motet style occurs in his Weimar cantata BWV 21, "Ich hatte viel Bekümmernis" (I Had Much Worry) (1714), in its ninth movement (a chorus and chorale) "Sei nun wieder zufrieden meine Seele" (Be Now Again Satisfied My Soul). Cantata BWV 182, "Himmelskönig, sei willkommen" (King of Heaven, Be Welcome) (1715), has a chorale fantasia (number 7) in motet style.

For the Leipzig period, the only cantatas mentioned by Spitta which contain distinct motet movements are: BWV 4 (number 5), 28 (number 2), 38 (number 1), 2 (number 1), 64 (number 1), 108 (number 4). Yet Spitta in his index (III, 412), also states under the heading *Motetts,* "For the separate motetts the reader is referred to the list of sacred cantatas, in which they will be found under their first lines"; but these he discusses more as chorales than motets, it seems. He writes also that "the motet of Bach takes its rise from his cantatas.... Even the motet has been absorbed into the Bach cantata, and it was afterwards not so much born fresh from it as set free from its trammels. It reappeared, not as an independent form of art, but as an offshoot of the Bach cantata" (II, 597).

It will be noted that in most of these Leipzig cantatas the motet movement is usually the first and takes the form of a chorus combined with a chorale verse. There is little doubt that Bach used the motet in this chorus/chorale format because he had been acquainted with it long before he composed his first cantata. Therefore, he would naturally incorporate motet movements in his cantatas, but still keep motets apart from cantatas when he wished to use them for special occasions, such as for thanksgivings or funerals. Such motet insertions certainly enhanced the vocal and the instrumental effect of the number, both emotionally and dramatically for the congregation then or for a modern audience now.

I feel that a motet type chorus occurs when one choir produces an antiphonal effect with another group of voices or instruments, which sing or play the chorale at the same time or after each line sung by the main choir. This main choir may sing in unison, but usually it is divided into parts which sing in imitation of each other or in canon. Thus Bach adds additional contrast between soprano, alto, tenor and bass choristers; it is his own personal polyphonic style which he

has developed from the earlier motet form.

Since these motet movements in the cantatas may be traced beyond those that Spitta has indicated above, I have continued the list that begins with Spitta, and have added my own comments to each movement that I have quoted and translated. The movements are arranged chronologically according to C.S. Terry's dating (movement numbers are indicated in parentheses). The cantata texts and summaries may be found in my book, *The Cantatas of J.S. Bach*, McFarland (1989).

# Aus der Tiefe rufe ich, Herr, zu dir
# (Out of the Depths I Cry, Lord, to Thee)
## (1707; BWV 131)

(3) *Aria—Bass, with Chorale—Soprano.* ARIA B.: So du willst, Herr, Sünder zurechnen, / Herr, wer wird bestehen? / Denn bei dir ist die Vergebung, dass man dich fürchte. (As Thou wilt, Lord, count up sins, / Lord, who will stand? / For with Thee is forgiveness, so that Thou may be feared.)

CHORALE S.: The sopranos sing the second verse of Bartholomäus Ringwald's chorale, "Herr Jesu Christ, du höchstes Gut" (Lord Jesus Christ, Thou Greatest Good) (1588), as cantus firmus superimposed over the pass: Erbarm dich mein in solcher Last, / Nimm sie aus meinem Herzen, / Dieweil du sie gebüsset hast / Am Holz mit Todesschmerzen, / Auf dass ich nicht mit grossem Weh / In meinen Sünden untergeh, / Noch ewiglich verzage. (Pity me with such a burden; / Take it out of my heart, / Because Thou has atoned for it / On the wood of the Cross with death pains, / So

that I with great misery / Should not perish in my sins, / Nor despair forever.)

(5) *Aria—Tenor, with Chorale—Alto.* The same procedure is used again for the motet effect, this time with a tenor and alto chorus singing the fifth verse of Ringwald's chorale simultaneously: ARIA T.: Meine Seele wartet auf den Herren von einer Morgenwache bis zu der der andern. (My soul waiteth on the Lord from one morning to the next.)

CHORALE A.: Und weil ich denn in meinem Sinn, / Wie ich zuvor geklaget, / Auch ein betrübter Sünder bin, / Den sein Gewissen naget, / Und wollte gern im Blute dein / Von Sünden abgewaschen sein / Wie David und Manasse. (And then because I am in my mind, / As I have complained before, / A sad sinner too, / Whom his conscience gnaws, / And I would gladly in Thy Blood / Be washed from sins / As David and Mannasseh.)

# Gott ist mein König (God Is My King)
## (1708; BWV 71)

(2) *Aria — Tenor, and Chorale — Sopranos.* For this number, the tenor aria is based on 2 Samuel 19:35, 37, and the chorale is stanza six of Johann Heermann's "O Gott, du frommer Gott" (O God, Thou Pious God) (1630) as the superimposed cantus firmus.

ARIA T.: Ich bin nun achtzig Jahr, warum soll dein Knecht sich mehr beschweren? Ich will umkehren, dass ich sterbe in meiner Stadt, bei meines Vaters und meiner Mutter Grab. (I am now 80 years old; why should Thy servant be burdened more? I want to return so that I may die in my city, beside my father's and my mother's grave.)

CHORALE S.: Soll ich auf dieser Welt / Mein Leben höher bringen, / Durch manchen sauren Tritt / Hindurch ins Alter dringen, / So gib Geduld, für Sünd / Und Schanden mich bewahr, / Auf dass ich tragen mag / Mit Ehren graues Haar. (Should I in this world / Further my life / Through many a rough step / To come through into old age? / Then give me patience; from sin / And harm keep me, / So that I may wear / With honor my grey hair.)

# Ich hatte viel Bekümmernis (I Had Much Worry)
## (1714; BWV 21)

(9) *Chorus and Chorale.* Bach divides the SATB sections into fugal parts for the chorus, which is sung in canon at the same time as the chorale is sung, first by a tenor soloist and then by a soprano soloist. It is difficult, however, for the listener to clearly discern the words of the chorale stanzas, as these are overpowered by the main chorus. This may be because constant repetition by the main chorus of "Sei nun wieder zufrieden, mein Seele" (Be again now satisfied, my soul) does not detract from the general impression when combined with the words of the chorale, and then the chorale melody, familiar to Bach's congregation, governs the whole movement.

For the chorus, three solo voices, SAB with continuo enter first; then the alto, tenor and bass choral parts with an oboe, a bassoon, four trombones, strings and continuo. The two chorale stanzas have only the organ for accompaniment.

This contrast creates a spectacular motet, which for its thought and its musical expression is the best that Bach composed in any of his cantatas.

CHORUS: Sei nun wieder, zufrieden, meine Seele, denn der Herr tut dir Gut's. (Be again satisfied now, my soul, for the Lord does good things for thee.) (Psalm 116:7) CHORALE: Was helfen uns die schweren Sorgen, / Was hilft uns unser Weh und Ach? / Was hilft es, dass wir alle Morgen / Beseufzen unser Ungemach? / Wir machen unser Kreuz und Leid / Nur grösser durch die Traurigkeit. / Denk nicht in deiner Drangsalhitze, / Dass du von Gott verlassen seist, / Und dass Gott im Schosse sitze, / Der sich mit stetem Glücke speist. / Die folgend Zeit verändert viel / Und setzet jeglichem sein Ziel. (How do heavy cares help us? / How do our woes and sighs help us? / How does it help that every morning / We bemoan our misfortune? / We make our suffering and sorrow / Only greater by our sadness. / Think not in your oppressive heat / That you have been abandoned by God, / And that God resides in the breast / Of him who feeds on constant good-luck. / The time to come changes much / And sets his limit on everyone.)—stanzas 2 and 5 of the chorale by Georg Neumark, "Wer nur den lieben Gott lässt walten" (Who only lets dear God rule) (1657)

# Nun komm, der Heiden Heiland I
# (Now Come, Savior of the Heathen)
### (1714; BWV 61)

(1) *Chorus (Overture).* Bach set this 1524 hymn by Martin Luther as a magnificent fugue with part entries by the choir, beginning with the sopranos and the altos, then followed by the tenors and the basses. This movement is in the slow-fast-slow pattern of a French overture with an instrumental ritornello just before the last line sung. Part singing of the first line is followed by unison for the second, then a sweeping fugue in canon (fast) for the third line, before returning to the adagio tempo with unison singing of the beginning. All the features of a motet are apparent in the alternation between the voices and the orchestra.

Nun komm, der Heiden Heiland, / Der Jungfrauen Kind erkannt, / Des sich wundert alle Welt; / Gott solch Geburt ihm bestellt. (Now come, Savior of the heathen, / Recognized Child of the Virgin. / At whom the whole world wonders / That God has ordained such a birth for Him.)

# Himmelskönig, sei willkommen
# (King of Heaven, Be Welcome)
### (1715; BWV 182)

(7) *Chorale fantasia*—SATB. Bach will use this same verse again, which is the thirty-third or second to the last of Paul Stockmann's Passion hymn "Jesu Leiden, Pein und Tod" (Jesus's Suffering, Pain and Death) (1633), for the concluding chorale of BWV 159 (1728–29), plainly sung in unison there. Here for part writing for SATB, sung in canon and as a fugue, is exceptionally dramatic and emotional. The instrumental combination of recorder, strings and continuo plays a joy motif for this fantasia.

Jesu, deine Passion / Ist mir lauter Freude, / Deine Wunden, Kron und Hohn / Meines Herzens Weide; / Meine Seel' auf Rosen geht, / Wenn ich dran gedenke, / In dem Himmel eine Stätt / Uns deswegen schenke. (Jesus, Thy Passion / Is for me pure joy. / Thy wounds, crown and scorn / Are the pasture of my heart. / My soul walks on roses / When I think of it. / Give us therefore a place / In heaven.)

# Sehet, welch eine Liebe hat uns der Vater erzeiget (See What Love the Father Has Shown Us)

## (1723; BWV 64)

(1) *Chorus.* The libretto for this number is the First Epistle of John 3:1 which Bach treats as a motet in fugal style with the orchestra doubling the vocal parts in a joy motif. Sehet, welch eine Liebe hat uns der Vater erzeiget, dass wir Gottes Kinder heissen. (See what love the Father has shown us, so that we are called God's children.)

This is a marvelous opening movement, drawing the listener's attention with its arresting summons. In fact, this whole cantata is supercharged with personal emotion in its arias, recitatives and chorales. It is Bach's sacred drama at its best.

# Christ lag in Todesbanden (Christ Lay in the Bonds of Death)

## (1724; BWV 4)

(5) *Chorale fantasia — Altos, with Trio — Sopranos, Tenors, Basses.* This is a four part full chorus fantasia in the style of a Pachelbel motet as was the chorale fantasia for cantata BWV 182. The libretto is a seven stanza poem "Christ ist erstanden" (Christ is risen) by Martin Luther which was set to music by Johann Walther in 1524. Bach added a sinfonia for strings at the beginning as a tone-painting to evoke Christ's burial and resurrection. The four parts of the choir follow each other in imitation for each line right up to the last word, "Halleluja." The canto is with the alto voices, while the other parts make the trio.

Es war ein wunderlicher Krieg, / Da Tod und Leben rungen, / Das Leben behielt den Sieg, / Es hat den Tod verschlungen. / Die Schrift hat verkündigt das, / Wie ein Tod den andern frass, / Ein Spott aus dem Tod ist worden. / Halleluja! (It was a strange war, / Where death and life struggled. / Life held the victory; / It has swallowed up death. / The Scripture has told that, / How one death devoured the other. / Death has become a joke. / Halleluja!)

# Lobe den Herrn, meine Seele I (Praise the Lord, My Soul)

## (1724; BWV 69)

(1) *Chorus.* As if to prove that motet movements in his cantatas might often have as heavy an instrument as earlier Italian and German

motets of the sixteenth or seventeenth centuries, Bach's composition for this number would offer ample evidence. The SATB chorus is seconded by a lavish orchestra: three trumpets, timpani, three oboes, a bassoon, two violins, a viola and continuo. The altos and tenors begin the first half of the Biblical quotation, Psalm 103:2, followed by the sopranos and the basses and which is then repeated by all singers in unison. The movement concludes with a double fugue which is combined into one fugue at the end. The instrumental ritornelli give the impression of contrast between voices and instruments, thus creating a dramatic effect. The da capo emphasizes the full beauty of this music. "Lobe den Herrn, meine Seele, und vergiss nicht, was er die Gutes getan hat!" (Praise the Lord, my soul, and do not forget what good things He has done for thee!)

# Gottlob! nun geht das Jahr zu Ende
# (Thank God! Now the Year Draws to Its End)
## (1725–27; BWV 28)

(2) *Chorus.* This chorale fantasia is a tremendous achievement of 174 bars, based on the first stanza of Johann Graumann's hymn (1530) which, as has been noted in the separate motets, BWV 225 and 231, must have been one of Bach's favorites.

Nun lob', mein Seel', den Herren, / Was in mir ist, den Namen sein! / Sein Wohltat tut er mehren, / Vergiss es nicht, o Herze mein! / Hat dir dein Sünd' vergeben / Und heilt dein Schwachheit gross, / Errett' dein armes Leben, / Nimmt dich in seinen Schoss, / Mit reichem Trost beschüttet, / Verjüngt, dem Adler gleich. / Der König schafft Recht, behütet, / Die leid'n in seinem Reich. (Now praise, my soul, the Lord, / What is in me, His Name! / He doth increase His benefit, / Do not forget it, O my heart! / He hath forgiven thee thy sin / And heals thy weakness. / He saves thy poor life, / Takes thee into His bosom, / Endows thee with rich comfort, / Rejuvenates, like the eagle. / The King does right, cares for those / Who suffer in His kingdom.)

# Es ist euch gut, dass ich hingehe
# (It is Good for You, That I Go Away)
## (1725 or 1735; BWV 108)

(4) *Chorus.* This is more a motet than a chorus, since it has three separate fugues for the four part choir, each part singing in canon. The voices are doubled in a joy motif by the oboes and the strings. It is a very powerful number, seeming as though Bach wished to prove the strength of the Holy Spirit by this dramatic setting: "Wenn aber jener, der Geist der Wahrheit kommen wird, der wird euch in alle Wahrheit leiten. Denn er wird nicht von ihm selber reden, sondern was er hören wird, das wird er reden, und was zukünftig ist, wird er verkündigen." (When that One, how-

ever, the Spirit of Truth will come, He will lead you into the Truth. For He will not speak for Himself, but what

He will hear, that will He speak, and what is to come will He proclaim.) (St. John 16:13)

# Du sollst Gott, deinen Herren, lieben
# (Thou Shouldst Love the Lord, Thy God)
### (1725; BWV 77)

(1) *Chorus with Chorale.* The text for the chorus is St. Luke 10:27, accompanied by the trumpet and the continuo which play the melody for Luther's chorale, "Dies sind die heil'gen zehn Gebot" (These Are the Holy Ten Commandments). Each section of the SATB follows the preceding in imitation to create a sermon, sung in motet style, for the words of Christ's reply to the lawyer who tempted him: "Du sollst Gott, deinen Herren, lieben von ganzem Herzen, von ganzer

Seele, von allen Kräften und von ganzem Gemüte und deinen Nächsten als dich selbst." (Thou shouldst love God, thy Lord, from thy whole heart, from thy whole soul, with all thy might and all thy mind, and thy neighbor as thyself.)

Bach's setting for this number with its chorale tune, which was well known to the congregation, would certainly draw attention to the dramatic sermon that its text contained: love of God and of our fellow man.

# Singet dem Herrn ein neues Lied
# (Sing to the lord a New Song)
### (1725; BWV 190)

(1) *Chorus and Chorale.* Like BWV 69, this stunning opening number has the same four part choir and festive orchestra. The chorus has for its text Psalm 149:1 and Psalm 150:4, 6, which are sung fugally. Lines from Luther's German *Te Deum* (1529) are taken for the chorale, sung alternately with the lines of the chorus and in unison with the chorus for the final "Alleluja."

This number is really a complete motet in itself because of its contrasting antiphonal choral singing and its superb instrumental playing. It is an outstanding religious scene which Bach represents in sound.

Chorus: "Singet dem Herrn ein neues Lied! / Die Gemeine der Heiligen soll ihn loben! / Lobet ihn mit Pauken und Reigen, / lobet ihn mit Saiten und Pfeifen! (Sing to the Lord a new song! / The congregation of the saints shall praise Him! / Praise Him with drums and dance, / praise Him with strings and pipes!

Chorale: Herr Gott, dich loben wir! (Lord God, we praise Thee!) Chorus: "Alles, was Odem hat, lobe den Herrn!" (Everything that has breath, praise the Lord!) Chorale: Herr Gott, wir danken dir! (Lord god, we thank Thee!) *Chorus and Chorale:* Alleluja! (Halleluja!)

# Nimm was dein ist, und gehe hin
## (Take What Is Thine, and Go Away)
### (1725; BWV 144)

(1) *Chorus.* Upon these seven words for a text, Bach builds a fine fugue in motet style for a four part choir. The drama in this chorus is rhetorical but nevertheless very realistic, as though the master is actually speaking to the laborers in the parable (St. Matthew 20:14): "Nimm, was dein ist, und gehe hin." (Take what is thine and go away.)

This is a very moving introduction to a cantata which, though short, has two fine arias for alto and for soprano to illustrate the text just quoted: that one should be content in life with the lot that God has given him.

# Bringet dem Herrn Ehre seines Namens
## (Bring to the Lord the Honor of His Name)
### (1725; BWV 148)

(1) *Chorus.* Bach called this movement a concerto since he thought that the choir represented the concertino, while the orchestra (trumpet, oboes, strings and organ continuo) would be the ripieno. But he could have said that it was a motet because of its two antiphonal groups (choir and orchestra), which produce this dramatic summons to prayer based on Psalms 29:2 and 96:8. Such drama may be visualized from the melody as the choir urges the congregation to keep the Sabbath holy. "Bringet dem Herrn Ehre seines Namens, betet an den Herrn im heiligen Schmuck." (Bring to the Lord the honor of His Name; pray to the Lord in holy attire.)

Note that Bach changes the unison singing into a fugue for the second clause — a very effective way to denote praying as stated in the text.

# Wer nur den lieben Gott lässt walten
## (Who Only Lets Dear God Govern)
### (1728; BWV 93)

(1) *Chorus — Chorale fantasia.* This number takes the form of a fugue, the oboes and strings playing the melody as an introduction and as ritornelli after each line sung by the choir. The voices are divided into two parts, SA and TB, which sing each line either in canon or in unison and finally tutti. With only light instrumentation (two oboes, two violins, a viola and continuo) Bach has apparently emphasized the vocal sections in order to create a complete musical drama in motet form out of this chorus.

Wer nur den lieben Gott lässt walten / Und hoffet auf ihn allezeit, / Den wird er wunderlich erhalten / In allem Kreuz und Traurigkeit. / Wer Gott, dem Allerhöchsten, traut, / Der hat auf keinen Sand gebaut.

(Who only lets dear God govern / And hopes in Him at all times, / Him will He wonderfully uphold / In all suffering and sadness. / Who trusts God, the All-Highest, / He has not built on sand.) (Georg Neumark, 1657)

# Ein feste Burg ist unser Gott
# (A Mighty Fortress is Our God)
## (1730; BWV 80)

(1) *Chorus — Chorale fantasia.* Bach's festival orchestra — three trumpets, timpani, two oboes, two violins, a viola, a cello, a violone (double bass) and organ — performs for this opening chorus in fugal motet style. Each line of the stanza is sung in canon by the SATB sections of the choir. Martin Luther's chorale with this title is used here as for three other numbers in this cantata.

Ein feste Burg ist unser Gott, / Ein gute Wehr und Waffen; / Er hilft uns frei aus aller Not, / Die uns itzt hat betroffen. / Der alte böse Feind / Mit Ernst er's jetzt meint, / Gross Macht und viel List / Sein grausam Rüstung ist, / Auf Erd ist nicht seinesgleichen. (A mighty fortress is our God, / A good defense and weapon; / He helps to free us from all distress, / Which has now befallen us. / The old evil enemy / Now means it seriously. / Great power and much cunning / Are his cruel armament; / On earth is not his equal.)

# Es ist nichts Gesundes an meinem Leibe
# (There Is Nothing Healthy in My Body)
## (c. 1731; BWV 25)

(1) *Chorus with Chorale.* The four part chorus is divided into two parts: tenors, altos and sopranos, basses. Together, they sing in canon the third verse of Psalm 38, accompanied by the wind instruments playing Hassler's melody to the hymn "Ach Herr, mich armen Sünder" (Ah Lord, Me Poor Sinner). Bach brings the Biblical text dramatically to life with a motif of regretful sadness; the singers represent one of the lepers who acknowledges that his infirmity is caused by his sin, as he calls upon God: "Es ist nichts Gesundes an meinem Leibe vor deinem Dräuen, und ist kein Friede in meinen Gebeinen vor meiner Sünde." (There is nothing healthy in my body before Thy threatening, and there is no peace in my bones because of my sin.)

Bach treats this movement in polyphonic style, just as though it were a single, separate motet, contrasting voices and instruments — a cornet, three trombones, three recorders, two oboes, two violins, a viola and continuo.

# Erfreut euch, ihr Herzen
# (Rejoice, Ye Hearts)
## (1731; BWV 66)

(1) *Chorus and Duet.* All features of a Bach motet appear in this opening number: orchestral prelude, ritornelli and postlude, division of the choir into chorus and a duet for alto and bass as the antiphone in a slower tempo, and imitative singing in the two parts.

Chorus: Erfreut euch, ihr Herzen, / Entweichet, ihr Schmerzen, / Es lebet der Heiland und herrschet in euch! (Rejoice, ye hearts, / Vanish, ye pains, / The Savior lives and rules in you!)

Duet: Ihr könnet verjagen / Das Trauern, das Fürchten, das ängstliche Zagen, / Der Heiland erquicket sein geistliches Reich. (You can chase away / The mourning, the fear, the anxious hesitation, / The Savior revives His spiritual Realm.)

# Der Herr ist mein getreuer Hirt
# (The Lord Is My Faithful Shepherd)
## (1731; BWV 112)

(1) *Chorus.* By dividing the four part choir into two sections, high and low voices, sopranos and basses, Bach's setting for this chorus appears to be a motet, as the two groups follow each other in canon. The instrumental ritornelli after each line sung add to the pastoral melody featuring two horns. The joy motif in this chorus is in keeping with the trust in God expressed in this cantata based on the 23rd Psalm.

Der Herr ist mein getreuer Hirt, / Hält mich in seiner Hüte. / Darum mir gar nichts mangeln wird / Irgend an einem Güte. / Er weidet mich ohn' Unterlass, / Darauf wächst das wohlschmeckend Gras / Seines heilsamen Wortes. (The Lord is my faithful Shepherd, / Who holds me in His care. / Therefore nothing at all will I lack / Of any kind of good thing. / He gives me pasture incessantly / Where grows the well-tasting grass / Of His holy word.)

# Es ist das Heil uns kommen her
# (Salvation Has Come to Us)
## (1731; BWV 9)

(1) *Chorus — Chorale fantasia.* The four part choir sings in canon each line of this first stanza of the hymn by Paul Speratus, followed by the usual instrumental ritornelli, thus giving the motet effect. There is drama in Bach's setting of the Lutheran thought that faith is more important than good works. It is really a short sermon in music.

Es ist das Heil uns kommen her / Von Gnad' und lauter Güte. / Die

Werke, die helfen nimmermehr, / Sie mögen nicht behüten. / Der Glaub' sieht Jesum Christum an, / Der hat g'nug für uns getan, / Er ist der Mittler worden. (Salvation has come here to us / From grace and pure goodness.

/ Works, they never help, / They cannot protect. / Faith looks towards Jesus Christ; / He has done enough for all of us. / He has become our Mediator.)

# Herr, deine Augen sehen nach dem Glauben
# (Lord, Thine Eyes Look Towards Faith)
## (1731; BWV 102)

(1) *Chorus.* This text (Jeremiah 5:3) is set in a mighty fugue for the four part chorus, which Bach borrowed later for the Kyrie movement of his *Short Mass in G Minor.* Bach's innate sense for the dramatic brings this quotation to life, just as though the choir were representing the prophet's words to God. The choir sings the German text in exceptionally clear imitation for each part, even with the parts overlapping in their performance. By itself, this da capo chorus could stand as an independent motet.

Perhaps that is why Bach reused it for his *Short Mass in G Minor.*

"Herr, deine Augen sehen nach dem Glauben! Du schlägest sie, aber sie fühlen's nicht; du plagest sie, aber sie bessern sich nicht. Sie haben ein härter Angesicht denn ein Fels und wollen sich nicht bekehren." (Lord, Thine eyes look towards belief! Thou smitest them, but they do not feel it; Thou tormentest them, but they do not improve. They have a harder face than a rock and do not want to return (to faith).

# Man singet mit Freuden vom Sieg
# (They Sing with Joy of the Victory)
## (1731; BWV 149)

(1) *Chorus.* This da capo chorus introduces a Michaelmas cantata, of which the text for this number is taken from Psalm 118:15, 16, and the melody is borrowed from the last chorus of Bach's earlier secular cantata, BWV 208. A sumptuous orchestra, including trumpets and timpani, accompanies the four part choir. The first sentence is sung in canon and then Bach changes the rhythm to conform with the words of the text — praise for God's aid against the forces of evil.

The orchestral ritornelli after each

clause sung shows that Bach is aware of the antiphonal effect of a motet that this number seems to resemble.

"Man singet mit Freuden vom Sieg in den Hütten der Gerechten. Die Rechte des Herrn behält den Sieg; die Rechte des Herrn ist erhöhet; die Rechte des Herrn behält den Sieg." (They sing with joy at the victory in the dwellings of the righteous. The right hand of the Lord holds the victory; the right hand of the Lord is exalted; the right hand of the Lord holds the victory.)

# Lobe den Herren, den mächtigen König der Ehren (Praise the Lord, the Mighty King of Glory)

## (1732; BWV 137)

(1) *Chorus — Chorale fantasia.* Based on Joachim Neander's chorale with this title, this four part chorus is supported by three trumpets and timpani, decorating the end of each line as the four voices sing it in canon. Other supporting instruments include three oboes, two violins, a viola and continuo which, with the trumpets and drums, play a ritornello after each line has been sung. A motet effect is thus created in the antiphonal alternation of instruments and voices.

Lobe den Herren, den mächtigen König der Ehren, / Meine geliebte Seele, das ist mein Begehren. / Kommet zu Hauf, / Psalter und Harfen, wacht auf! / Lasset die Musicam hören. (Praise the Lord, the mighty King of Glory, / My beloved soul, that is my wish. / Come in multitudes, / Psaltery and harps, wake up! / Let the song of praise be heard.)

# Nun danket alle Gott (Now All Thank God)

## (c. 1732; BWV 192)

(1) *Chorus — Chorale fantasia.* This is the first stanza of a three stanza hymn by Martin Rinckart and Bach expands it into a chorale fantasia. Canon singing by the divided four part choir gives the listener the impression that he is hearing a motet sung by two choruses. Instrumental ritornelli after each sentence in the stanza add to the antiphonal sound. Right from the bright overture, Bach's setting is especially beautiful, even with only two transverse flutes, two oboes, strings and continuo for his orchestra.

Nun danket alle Gott / Mit Herzen, Mund und Händen, / Der grosse Dinge tut / An uns und allen Enden. / Der uns von Mutterleib / Und Kindesbeinen an / Unzählig viel zugut / Und noch jetzund getan. (Now all thank God / With heart, mouth and hands, / Who does great things / For us and all our ends. / Who for us from our mother's womb / And from infancy on / Has done much that is uncounted for our good / And has still done now.)

The emotional drama that this stanza contains and which Bach brings out in his musical composition for it would need no explanation to Lutheran congregations, well acquainted with this hymn in its plain form.

# Ich ruf' zu dir, Herr Jesu Christ
# (I Call to Thee, Lord Jesus Christ)
## (1732; BWV 177)

(1) *Chorus — Chorale fantasia.* The five stanzas of the hymn (c. 1531) by Johann Agricola are used for the libretto of this cantata. Each stanza is a dramatic prayer to God for help — three arias in succession, one for each of alto, soprano and tenor, are placed between the opening chorus and the final chorale. Each of these numbers, however, is a dramatic monologue, whether it is sung by a soloist or by a choir. But only this opening chorus is in motet style. The orchestra features a concertante violin to decorate the tune, two oboes, two violins, an obbligato bassoon, a viola and the organ in the continuo.

The cantus firmus is sung by the lower voices this time, while the higher voices repeat each line in imitation and are then followed by an orchestral ritornello.

Ich ruf' zu dir, Herr Jesu Christ, / Ich bitt', erhör' mein Klagen, / Verleih mir Gnad zu dieser Frist, / Lass mich doch nicht verzagen; / Den rechten Glauben, Herr, ich mein, / Den wollest du mir geben, / Dir zu leben, / Meinem Nächsten nütz zu sein, / Dein Wort zu halten eben. (I call to Thee, Lord Jesus Christ, I beg Thee, listen to my complaint. / Grant me grace at this time. / Let me not despair. / The right belief, Lord, I mean, / Which Thou wilt give to me, / To live for Thee, / To be useful to my neighbor, / To keep Thy word exactly.)

# Es wartet alles auf dich
# (All Things Wait for Thee)
## (1732; BWV 187)

(1) *Chorus.* This opening chorus has the cantus firmus in the higher voices while the lower voices repeat each line in imitation before joining with the first group to sing the line together in unison. Instrumental interludes by two oboes, two violins, a viola and continuo occur after each clause sung as well as at the beginning and the end. The same dramatic opening chorus as for BWV 177 is apparent in this motet beginning number. The second sentence becomes a fugue for all four parts of the chorus, thus giving the impression of a motet movement. Comparison of this chorus with the opening movement of Bach's *Short Mass in G Minor* will show his borrowing from this cantata. The text is taken from Psalm 104:27, 28.

"Es wartet alles auf dich, dass du ihnen Speise gebest zu seiner Zeit. / Wenn du ihnen gibest, so sammeln sie; / wenn due deine Hand auftust, so werden sie mit Gute gesättigt." (All things wait for Thee, that Thou mayest give to them food in its time. / When Thou givest to them, then they gather up; / when Thou openest Thy hand, then they are satisfied with Thy goodness.)

# Was Gott tut, das ist wohlgetan I
# (What God Does, That Is Done Well)
### (c. 1732; BWV 98)

(1) *Chorus — Chorus fantasia.* This is the first of three chorale cantatas (BWV 99 and BWV 100 are the others) that Bach composed on the hymn of this title by Samuel Rodigast. The beautiful melody, repeated by the instrumental ritornelli after the choir sings it, is begun by the sopranos for each line and then followed by the other parts. The antiphonal effect between choir and orchestra shows that Bach has applied his own motet style to his chorale fantasia opening numbers. The instruments include two oboes, a tenor oboe, two violins, a viola and continuo.

Was Gott tut, das ist wohlgetan, / Es bleibt gerecht sein Wille; / Wie er fängt meine Sachen an, / Will ich ihm halten stille. / Er ist mein Gott, / Der in der Not / Mich wohl weiss zu erhalten; / Drum lass ich ihn nur walten. (What God does, that is done well, / His will remains just; / However He manages my affairs, / I will hold quietly to Him. / He is my God, / Who in my trouble, / Well knows how to sustain me; / Therefore I let only Him rule me.)

# Gelobet sei der Herr
# (Praised Be the Lord)
### (1732; BWV 129)

(1) *Chorus — Chorale fantasia.* All five stanzas of the hymn (1665) by Johann Olearius are set in this cantata, one for each number. This first verse is a fantasia with the four part choir singing each line in canon and orchestral ritornelli placed between the lines. Three trumpets and timpani highlight this dramatic praise of God showed forth by the choir on behalf of everyone in the congregation. Such a brilliant number really brings Bach's development of the motet to perfection.

Gelobet sei der Herr, / Mein Gott, mein Licht, mein Leben, / Mein Schöpfer, der mir hat / Mein Leib und Seel' gegeben, / Mein Vater, der mich schützt / Von Mutterleibe an, / Der alle Augenblick / Viel Guts an mir getan. (Praised be the Lord, / My God, my Light, my Life, / My Creator, who has given to me / My body and my soul. / My Father, who protects me / From the womb on, / Who every moment / Has done much good for me.)

# Es ist dir gesagt, Mensch, was gut ist (It Has Been Told to Thee, Man, What Is Good)

## (1732–40; BWV 45)

(1) *Chorus*. Based on Micah 6:8, this didactic text is set to a lively joy motif, with the choir singing in imitation according to their parts. There is an instrumental overture, ritornelli and postlude alternating with the choral sections. It seems that the prophet himself comes to life in directly addressing the congregation, even though his words are sung by the choir and end in a fugue.

"Es ist dir gesagt, Mensch, was gut ist und was der Herr von dir fordert, nämlich Gottes Wort halten und Liebe üben und demütig sein vor deinem Gott." (It has been told to thee, man, what is good and what the Lord demands of thee, namely, to keep God's word and practice love and to be humble before thy God.)

# Ich elender Mensch, wer wird mich erlösen (I, Wretched Man, Who Will Deliver Me)

## (c. 1732; BWV 48)

(1) *Chorus with Chorale*. This is a fully developed motet movement in Bach's mature style. The text is Romans 7:24 with the chorale, "Herr Jesu Christ, ich schrei' zu dir" (Lord, Jesus Christ, I Cry to Thee) (1620), by an unknown poet, played by the trumpet and two oboes after the opening overture for strings alone.

The sopranos and the altos, followed by the tenors and the basses, sing the Biblical verse in canon, all lamenting with a suitable tear motif. The drama in this personal lament of the palsy-stricken man (St. Matthew 9:1–8) is very touching, even when it is sung by the choir.

"Ich elender Mensch, wer wird mich erlösen vom Leibe dieses Todes?" (I, wretched man, who will deliver me from the body of this death?)

# Was Gott tut, das ist wohlgetan II (What God Does, That Is Done Well)

## (c. 1733; BWV 99)

(1) *Chorus — Chorale fantasia*. The same hymn text as for BWV 98 is used with the same tune, but now with a horn, a flute, an oboe d'amore, strings and continuo.

The same remarks apply to this chorus as were made for the opening chorus of BWV 98 (see this number, p. 144, for the text).

# In allen meinen Taten (In All My Deeds)
## (1734; BWV 97)

(1) *Chorus — Chorale fantasia.* Set as a French overture for its first two sections, this chorus begins with an instrumental grave, followed by a vivace sung by the choir (begun by the sopranos and imitated fugally by the other parts of the four part choir). The chorale tune for this, as well as the final chorale at the end of the cantata, is Heinrich Isaak's "Innsbruck, ich muss dich lassen" (Innsbruck, I Must Leave Thee). With the orchestral prelude and the instrumental ritornelli (two oboes, two bassoons, strings and organ), this first verse of Paul Fleming's hymn resembles the first scene in a religious drama in which the chorus advises each one of us to accept God's will (cf. BWV 93 which has the same theme).

In allen meinen Taten / Lass ich den Höchsten raten, / Der alles kann und hat; / Er muss zu allen Dingen, / Soll's anders wohl gelingen / Selbst geben Rat und Tat. (In all my deeds / I let the Highest One advise me. / He who can do and has everything; / He must for all things, / If they are to succeed well / Himself give advice and action.)

# Unser Mund sei voll Lachens
# (May Our Mouth Be Full of Laughter)
## (1734–40; BWV 110)

(1) *Chorus — Chorale fantasia.* Among Bach's many great achievements, this opening chorus is in a class apart. Bach adapted the French overture opening movement of his *Orchestral Suite No. 4 in D Major,* (BWV 1069), the orchestra playing in the two outer sections (grave), while the choir sings in canon in the allegro middle section. The melody for this part fits the text of Psalm 126:2,3 perfectly. The choir depicts the joyous laughing of all Christendom for the birth of Jesus. After the part singing of the whole text, and its da capo, Bach adds a nice touch by having a bass soloist repeat the second sentence before the choir repeats both sentences.

Trumpets and timpani are perfectly suited to this work for Christmas Day. The antiphonal parts of the choir and the contrast to it of the soloist, plus the orchestral only sections produce a motet movement without peer in Bach's vocal work.

"Unser Mund sei voll Lachens, und unsre Zunge voll Rühmens. Denn der Herr hat Grosses an uns getan." (May our mouth be full of laughter, and our tongue full of praising. For the Lord hath done great things for us.)

# Wär' Gott nicht mit uns diese Zeit
# (If God Were Not With Us at This Time)
### (1735; BWV 14)

(1) *Chorus — Chorale fantasia*. This is the first stanza of Luther's translation of Psalm 124, sung in canon to a fugal melody by the four part choir as a motet.

Wär' Gott nicht mit uns diese Zeit, / So soll Israel sagen, / Wär' Gott nicht mit uns diese Zeit, / Wir hätten müssen verzagen, / Die so ein armes Häuflein sind, / Veracht' von so viel Menschenkind, / Die an uns setzen alle. (If God were not with us at this time, / Then Israel would say, / If God were not with us at this time, / We would have had to despair; / We who are such a poor little band, / Despised by so many children of man, / Who all set upon us.)

# Was frag' ich nach der Welt
# (What Do I Ask of the World)
### (1735; BWV 94)

(1) *Chorus — Chorale fantasia*. The transverse flute in this opening number deserves special mention, because it not only enhances the ritornelli, but also is featured, as the oboes, strings and organ accompany the choir. This movement is like a concerto for flute, but still sounds like a motet in the choral singing by parts — this is very dramatic in declaring its renunciation of the world.

Was frag' Ich nach der Welt / Und allen ihren Schätzen, / Wenn ich mich nur an dir, / Mein Jesu, kann ergötzen! / Dich hab' ich einzig mir / ur Wollust vorgestellt. / Du, du bist meine Ruh: / Was frag' ich nach der Welt! (What do I ask of the world / And all its treasures, / When I can delight, / My Jesus, only in Thee! / Only Thee have I imagined / To be my pleasure. / Thou, Thou art my rest: / What do I ask of the world!)

# Also hat Gott die Welt geliebet
# (God So Loved the World)
### (1735; BWV 68)

(5) *Chorus*. This final number is, surprisingly, the motet movement. The four part choir sings the text, St. John 3:18, in canon to a fugal melody. A dramatic picture in sound is thus created, quoting Christ's words to Nicodemus, as recorded by the Apostle John: "Wer an ihn glaubet, der wird nicht gerichtet, wer aber nicht glaubet, der ist schon gerichtet, denn er glaubet nicht an den Namen des eingebornen Sohnes Gottes." (Whoever believes in Him, he is not judged, but who does not believe, he is already judged, for he does not believe in the name of the only begotten Son of God.")

# Lobe den Herrn, meine Seele II
# (Praise the Lord, My Soul)
## (1735; BWV 143)

(7) *Chorus with Chorale.* This is the third stanza of Jakob Ebert's hymn, "Du Friedefürst, Herr Jesu Christ" (Thou Prince of Peace, Lord Jesus Christ), later to be set by Bach as a separate cantata (BWV 116) with this title, but here producing a stupendous motet to conclude this work as he did for BWV 68, above. The lower voices sing only the one word "Halleluja," while the sopranos sing the words of the chorale verse as an antiphone, with the whole being supported by an orchestral tutti.

Gedenk, Herr, jetzund an dein Amt, / Dass du ein Friedfürst bist, / Und hilf uns gnädig allesamt / Jetzt und zu dieser Frist; / Lass uns hinfort / Dein göttlich Wort / Im Fried noch länger hören. (Think, Lord, now on Thy ministry, / That Thou art a Prince of Peace, / And mercifully help all of us / Now and at this time; / Let us hear henceforth / Thy Godly Word / Still longer in peace.)

# Auf Christi Himmelfahrt allein
# (On Christ's Ascension into Heaven Alone)
## (1735; BWV 128)

(1) *Chorus—Chorale fantasia.* In my opinion, this motet-style chorus is one of the most impressive that Bach ever set in any of his cantatas. The four part choir is contrasted with its supporting antiphonal orchestra. The canto of the chorale melody is sung by the sopranos, and then followed by the other parts in imitation. A trumpet and two horns express the joy motif in the chorale tune in an astounding way with an overture, ritornelli, and conclusion—an independent concerto for voices and instruments, giving dramatic life to the chorale text. Bach's superlative setting from this text reveals his own religious thought—his happiness as he antici-

pates the life to come with Christ. This hymn is still in the Lutheran hymnal, also numbered 128—by coincidence?

Auf Christi Himmelfahrt allein / Ich meine Nachfahrt gründe / Und allen Zweifel, Angst und Pein / Hiermit stets überwinde; / Denn weil das Haupt im Himmel ist, / Wird seine Glieder Jesus Christ / Zu rechter Zeit nachholen. (On Christ's Ascension to heaven alone / I base my own following journey. / And all my doubt, worry and pain / With this I always overcome; / For as the Head is in heaven, / Jesus Christ will bring His members / After Him at the right time.) (Josua Wegelin, 1636)

# Christum wir sollen loben schon
# (Christ We Should Certainly Praise)
### (c. 1735–40; BWV 121)

(1) *Chorus — Chorale fantasia.* Martin Luther composed this Christmas hymn in 1524, and Bach turned it into a four part chorale fantasia. The voices of the choir follow each other as they sing each line in imitation, doubled by the instruments of the unusually large orchestra. These include a horn, an oboe d'amore, three trombones, two violins, a viola and organ continuo. This motet style chorus possesses a motif of solemnity conforming to its text.

Christum wir sollen loben schon, / Der reinen Magd Marien Sohn, / So weit die liebe Sonne leucht / Und an aller Welt Ende reicht. (Christ we should certainly praise, / The Son of the pure Maid Mary, / As far as the dear sun shines / And reaches to the end of the whole world.)

# Wer mich liebet, der wird
# mein Wort halten II (Whoever
# Loves Me Will Keep My Word)
### (1735; BWV 74)

(1) *Chorus.* Bach divides this four part choir into three separate groups: SA, TB, AT, to sing in canon the Biblical verse, St. John 14:23. This second version of a cantata based on this text has indications of its being a separate motet: canon singing, orchestral ritornelli after each clause sung, but using the same chorale tune as for the opening SB duet of BWV 59 (1716) with the same words of Jesus and the same dramatic effect. The orchestra has three trumpets, timpani, two oboes, an oboe da caccia, two violins, a viola and continuo.

"Wer mich liebet, / der wird mein Wort halten, / und mein Vater wird ihn lieben, / und wir werden zu ihm kommen und Wohnung bei ihm machen." (Whoever loves Me, / he will keep My Word, / and My Father will love him, / and we shall come to Him and dwell with Him.)

# Wo soll ich fliehen hin
# (Whither Shall I Flee)
### (1735; BWV 5)

(1) *Chorus — Chorale fantasia.* This is the first stanza of the hymn of this title by Johann Heermann (1630). The four part choir sings in canon as the orchestra (a slide trumpet, two oboes, two violins, a viola and continuo) play the chorale tune, with the ritornello instrumental pauses at the beginning, within, and at the end of the number. This results in a motet type chorus,

alternating vocal and instrumental groups.

Bach represents here, as the text indicates for his music, the wavering steps of a sinner searching for a refuge from his sins. This is really an independent drama in music, yet will still fit the thought to be detailed in the rest of the cantata.

Wo soll ich fliehen hin, / Weil ich beschweret bin / Mit viel und grossen Sünden? / Wo sollt' ich Rettung finden? / Wenn alle Welt herkäme, /

Mein Angst sie nicht wegnähme. (Whither shall I flee, / Because I am oppressed / With many great sins? / Where shall I find saving? / If the whole world should come here, / It would not take away my anxiety.)

The word "Angst" means anxiety (for fear of divine retribution for sins committed) and occurs frequently in the religious poetry of the sixteenth and seventeenth centuries in Germany.

# Was willst du dich betrüben
# (Why Wilt Thou Be Troubled)
## (1735; BWV 107)

(1) *Chorus—Chorale fantasia.* Based on Johann Heermann's hymn (1630) with this title, Bach's setting for four choral parts—first in imitation and then in unison—brings out the textual message of trust in God to deliver us from our distress. The beautiful melody, in which the flutes are featured, and the instrumental ritornelli give this dramatic monologue a personal touch, even though it is sung by the choir.

Was willst du dich betrüben, / O meine liebe Seel', / Ergib dich, den zu lieben, / Der heisst Immanuel. / Vertraue ihm allein; / Er wird gut alles machen / Und fördern deine Sachen, / Wie dir's wird selig sein. (Why wilt thou be troubled? / O my dear soul? / Give thyself up to love Him, / Who is called Immanuel. / Trust Him alone: / He will do everything well / And promote thy affairs, / As it will be blessed for thee.)

# Jesu, der du meine Seele
# (Jesus, Thou Who My Soul)
## (1735-44; BWV 78)

(1) *Chorus.* The sopranos carry the chorale melody, the other parts entering after them in imitation for each line. A horn and a flute double the melody and join the two oboes and strings for the ritornelli. In this chorus, the motet effect seems to come from the contrast in the vocal parts more than from the instrumental playing.

Jesu, der du meine Seele / Hast durch deinen bittern Tod / Aus des Teufels finstrer Höhle / Und der schweren Seelennot / Kräftiglich herausgerissen / Und mich solches lassen wissen / Durch dein angenehmes Wort; / Sei doch itzt, o Gott, mein Hort! (Jesus, Thou who my soul / Hast through Thy bitter death / Powerfully torn out of the devil's dark

cave / And from the deep distress of
my soul / And has let me know so /
Through Thy pleasing word, / Be

Thou now then, O God, my refuge!)
(Johann Rist, 1641)

# Was Gott tut, das ist Wohlgetan III
# (What God Does, That Is Done Well)
### (1735; BWV 100)

(1) *Chorus.* All remarks on the opening choruses of BWV 98 and BWV 99 pertain also to this movement, although Bach has enriched the or-chestra with two horns and timpani. The vocal parts, however, are sung in unison only. See BWV 98 for the text.

# Ach Gott, wie manches Herzeleid I
# (Ah God, How Much Heart Sorrow)
### (1735–44; BWV 3)

(1) *Chorus — Chorale fantasia.* This is the first stanza of the chorale (1587) by Martin Moller, which Bach sets to an adagio grief motif, begun by the basses and followed in imitation by the altos, tenors and sopranos. As a chorale fantasia, however, this motet attempt is not one of Bach's best.

Ach Gott, wie manches Herzeleid / Begegnet mir zu dieser Zeit! / Der schmale Weg ist trübsalvoll, / Den ich zum Himmel wandern muss. (Ah God, how much heart sorrow / Meets me at this time! / The narrow way is full of sadness, / On which I must travel to heaven.)

# Ihr werdet weinen und heulen
# (You Will Weep and Lament)
### (1735; BWV 103)

(1) *Chorus and Solo Basses.* The four part choir represents one section, the bass section entering afterwards in antiphony but preceded by a solo bass singer in the role of Christ. Thus the motet form is combined with a dramatic theme, which is concluded in a fugue by the full choir. Their libretto is taken from St. John 16:16–23.

The orchestra features a piccolo flute for this chorus, but has a trumpet, a transverse flute, two oboes d'amore, two violins, a viola and con-tinuo in the rest of the cantata.

"Ihr werdet weinen und heulen, aber die Welt wird sich freuen. Ihr aber werdet traurig sein. Doch eure Traurigkeit soll in Freude verkehret werden." (You will weep and lament, but the world will rejoice. You, how-ever, will be sad. Yet your sadness shall be changed into joy.)

# Wo Gott, der Herr, nicht bei uns hält
# (If God, the Lord, Does Not Hold with Us)
### (1735–40; BWV 178)

(1) *Chorus.* Stanza one of the hymn (1524) by Justus Jonas, based on Psalm 124, is the text for this chorale fantasia. It is a spectacular call to battle against the enemy—Satan's evildoers and false prophets.

The four part chorus sings in syncopated imitation by their parts for each line, with the rhythm suggesting a march in the melody and its ritornelli. Like all the other numbers in this cantata, this motet opening chorus is highly dramatic and adds a picture-like cameo of a march to battle. The marvel is that Bach could combine so much in one opening chorus!

Wo Gott, der Herr, nicht bei uns hält, / Wenn unsre Feinde toben, / Und er unsrer Sach' nicht zufällt / Im Himmel hoch dort oben, / Wo er Israels Schutz nicht ist / Und selber bricht der Feinde List, / So ist's mit uns verloren. (If God, the Lord, does not hold with us, / When our enemies rage, / And He does not agree with our cause / High up there in heaven. / When He is not Israel's protection / And Himself breaks the cunning of enemies, / Then it is lost with us.)

# Gott fähret auf mit Jauchzen
# (God Goes Up with Rejoicing)
### (1735; BWV 43)

(1) *Chorus — Chorale fantasia.* Bach set this cantata for Ascension Day; this opening fantasia is a resounding motif of joy after a short introductory adagio for oboes and strings. There are two fugues, one for each sentence, sung in canon by the four part choir and both accompanied by three trumpets and timpani. The basses begin, followed by the other parts but with no ritornelli. The text sung is Psalm 47:5, 6.

"Gott fähret auf mit Jauchzen, und der Herr mit heller Posaune. / Lobsinget, lobsinget Gott; lobsinget, lobsinget unserm Könige." (God goes up with rejoicing, and the Lord with a bright trumpet. / Sing praises, sing praises to God; sing praises, sing praises to our King.)

# Ich hab' in Gottes Herz und Sinn
# (I Have in God's Heart and Mind)
### (1735–44; BWV 92)

(1) *Chorus — Chorale fantasia.* This is stanza one of the chorale of this title (1647) by Paul Gerhardt. Bach's setting is unusual because he puts an orchestral ritornello at the beginning, after each line sung, and at the end. The orchestra is very simple: two oboes, two violins, a viola and continuo. The

sopranos begin the melody in each line and the other sections of the four part choir follow them in canon.

Ich hab' in Gottes Herz und Sinn / Mein Herz und Sinn ergeben. / Was böse scheint, ist mein Gewinn, / Der Tod selbst ist mein Leben. / Ich bin ein Sohn des, der den Thron / Des Himmels aufgezogen; / Ob er gleich schlägt und Kreuz auflegt, / Bleibt doch sein Herz gewogen. (I have into God's heart and mind / Surrendered my heart and mind. / What appears bad is my winning; / Death itself is my life. / I am a son of Him, who ascended / The throne of heaven; / Whether He now strikes and imposes suffering, / Yet His heart remains inclined toward me.)

# Was mein Gott will, das g'scheh allzeit (What My God Wills, That Happens Always)

## (1735–44; BWV 111)

(1) *Chorus — Chorale fantasia.* Submission to God's will and trust in Him is the theme for this cantata. Markgraf Albrecht von Brandenburg composed this hymn text in 1547. Like the other chorale fantasias that Bach set to begin a cantata, a four part choir sings in canon; orchestral ritornelli occur after each line sung and the same melody is played to introduce and conclude this number.

Was mein Gott will, das g'scheh allzeit, / Sein Will', der ist der beste; / Zu helfen den'n er ist bereit, / Die an ihn glauben feste. / Er hilft aus Not, der fromme Gott, / Und züchtiget mit Massen; / Wer Gott vertraut, fest auf ihn baut, / Den will er nicht verlassen. (What my God wills, that always happens; / His will, that is the best. / To help those He is ready, / Who firmly believe in Him. / He helps us out of trouble, our good Lord, / And chastises with moderation; / Who trusts God, firmly builds on Him, / Him will He not leave.)

# Meinen Jesum lass' ich nicht (My Jesus I Do Not Leave)

## (1735–44; BWV 124)

(1) *Chorus — Chorale fantasia.* Based on the 1658 hymn by Christian Keymann with this title, Bach treats this first stanza, a personal vow of fidelity to Christ, as a little motet in itself. The choir represents any one Christian believer as it sings this dramatic monologue. Part singing of the lines in canon recurs in this fantasia.

Meinen Jesum lass' ich nicht, / Weil er sich für mich gegeben, / So erfordert meine Pflicht, / Klettenweis' an ihm zu kleben. / Er ist meines Lebens Licht, / Meinen Jesum lass' ich nicht. (My Jesus I do not leave, / Because He has given Himself for me; / Thus my duty requires me / To cling to Him like a burr. / He is the Light of my life; I do not leave my Jesus.)

# Mit Fried' und Freud' ich fahr' dahin
## (With Peace and Joy I Travel There)
### (1735–44; BWV 125)

(1) *Chorus — Chorale fantasia.*
Luther's hymn with this opening line
from the *Nunc Dimittis* of Simeon,
St. Luke 2:22–32, is the text, which
Bach had used for chorales in two
other cantatas, BWV 95 (1732) and
BWV 106 (1707). The chorale tune has
a motif of peace suited to the solemnity of the text. The four part choir
sings this in canon, as the usual orchestral ritornello is played after each
line is sung.

Bach gives an exceptionally dramatic touch at the words "sanft und
stille" when he slows the tempo to end

in diminuendo, as these words indicated to him. He treats the last line of
the stanza similarly.

Mit Fried' und Freud' ich fahr'
dahin / In Gottes Willen; / Getrost
ist mir mein Herz und Sinn, / Sanft
und stille; / Wie Gott mir verheissen
hat, / Der Tod ist mein Schlaf
worden. (With peace and joy I travel
there / According to God's will. / My
heart and mind are comforted, /
Calmly and quietly; / As God has
promised me, / Death has become my
sleep.)

# Erhalt' uns, Herr, bei deinem Wort
## (Keep Us, Lord, in Thy Word)
### (1735–44; BWV 126)

(1) *Chorus — Chorale fantasia.*
Luther wrote this hymn at the time
that there was war with the Turks and
while he was struggling against the
power of the Papacy. Therefore, like
cantatas BWV 19 and BWV 79, this
opening chorus will have a martial
sound, as Bach dramatizes Luther's
text into a prayer to God for His help
in our political and religious problems. The usual four part choir sings

in canon, brilliantly supported by a
trumpet in the orchestra.

Erhalt' uns, Herr, bei deinem
Wort, / Und steur' des Papsts und
Türken Mord, / Die Jesum Christum,
deinen Sohn, / Stürzen wollen von
seinem Thron. (Keep us, Lord, in Thy
word, / And prevent the murder by
the Pope and the Turks, / Who, Jesus
Christ, Thy Son, / Wish to throw
down from His throne.)

# Herr Jesu Christ, wahr' Mensch und Gott
## (Lord Jesus Christ, True Man and God)
### (1735–44; BWV 127)

(1) *Chorus — Chorale fantasia.* Paul
Eber's hymn (1562) provides the
chorale for all numbers in this can-

tata. The opening chorus has all the
qualities of a beautiful motet: imitative repetition by the four vocal

parts, ritornelli of the melody to give antiphonal sound, and drama in the direct plea to Christ for mercy, as the words in the text indicate. It is a moving experience for any listener who can associate the words with the profound sentiment in Bach's musical setting.

Herr Jesu Christ, wahr' Mensch und Gott, / Der du littst Marter, Angst und Spott, / Für mich am Kreuz auch endlich starbst, / Und mir deins Vaters Huld erwarbst, / Ich bitt' durchs bittre Leiden dein: / Du wollst mir Sünder gnädig sein. (Lord Jesus Christ, true Man and God, / Thou who suffered martyrdom, anguish, scorn, / And for me on the Cross finally died / And for me gained Thy Father's favor, / I ask through Thy bitter suffering: / Thou wilt be merciful to me, a sinner.)

# Mache dich, mein Geist, bereit
# (Make Thyself, My Spirit, Ready)
### (1735–44; BWV 115)

(1) *Chorus—Chorale fantasia.* Set to Johann Freystein's hymn (1697), the charming musical accompaniment, with ritornelli complementing the four part choir in motet style, shows Bach's originality. Even while adhering to this usual format for an opening chorale fantasia, Bach surprises the listener with a modern dance tempo with flute trills to embellish it. The orchestra, playing tutti in this fantasia, includes a transverse flute, an oboe d'amore, two violins, a viola, a violoncello piccolo, a horn and continuo.

Mache dich, mein Geist, bereit, / Wache, fleh' und bete, / Dass dich nicht die böse Zeit / Unverhofft betrete, / Denn es ist / Satans List / Über viele Frommen / Zur Versuchung kommen. (Make thyself, my spirit, ready, / Watch, beseech and pray, / That the bad time does not / Unexpectedly come upon thee; / For it is / Satan's cunning / Coming over many pious people / For their temptation.)

# Jesu, nun sei gepreiset
# (Jesus, Now Be Praised)
### (1736; BWV 41)

(1) *Chorus—Chorale fantasia.* The most striking feature about this number is the instrumental ritornello after each line of the hymn (1593) by Johann Heermann, the first verse of which Bach sets to begin this New Year's Day cantata. Once again Bach utilizes the antiphonal alternation of vocal and instrumental groups, thereby reproducing the drama of the early motet. This movement is divided into three parts: the first eight lines are an allegro which the four part choir sings in unison; then the last six lines are sung adagio which turns into a fugue; the first section is a return to the allegro unison singing of the beginning but now repeating the last two lines.

Jesu, nun sei gepreiset / Zu diesem neuen Jahr / Für dein Gut, uns beweiset / In aller Not und Gefahr, / Dass wir haben erlebet / Die neu fröhliche Zeit, / Die voller Gnade schwebet / Und ewiger Seligkeit; / Dass wir in guter Stille / Das alte Jahr haben erfüllet. / Wir wollen uns dir ergeben / Itzund und immerdar. / Behüt' Leib, Seel' und Leben / Hinfort durch's ganze Jahr. (Jesus, now be praised / At this New Year / For Thy goodness, shown to us / In all trouble and danger; / That we have survived / Into the new happy time, / Which hovers full of grace / And eternal blessedness; / That we in good peace / Have fulfilled the old year. / We want to devote ourselves to Thee / Now and forever. / Conserve our body, soul and life / Henceforth through the whole year.)

# Bleib' bei uns, denn es will Abend werden (Abide with Us, for It Will Become Evening)

## (1736; BWV 6)

(1) *Chorus.* From this short verse from St. Luke 24:29, Bach develops an exceptionally realistic tone poem. Yet at the same time, the four part choir brings out the drama as each of the disciples entreats Jesus to stay with him. This canon singing makes this number an emotional motet in itself, with a double fugue as they all call upon Jesus to stay.

"Bleib' bei uns, denn es will Abend werden, und der Tag hat sich geneiget." (Abide with us, for it will become evening, and the day has bent to a close.)

# Nun komm, der Heiden Heiland II (Now Come, Savior of the Heathen)

## (c. 1736–40; BWV 62)

(1) *Chorus — Chorale fantasia.* With the same text by Luther that he had set for cantata BWV 61 in Weimar, Bach repeated his efforts in this second version of the work, beginning now with a chorale fantasia for the four part choir. The same theme continues through the whole stanza, with instrumental ritornelli after each line sung and at the end. After the orchestral introduction (oboes, strings and a horn), the sopranos sing the melody, followed by the other parts of the choir in canon. The appeal by the choir for the Lord to come makes a most dramatic impression in its motet style.

Nun komm, der Heiden Heiland, / Der Jungfrauen Kind erkannt, / Des sich wundert alle Welt; / Gott solch Geburt ihm bestellt. (Now come, Savior of the heathen, / Recognized Child of the Virgin, / At Whom the whole world wonders / That God has ordained such a birth for Him.)

# Gelobt seist du, Jesu Christ
# (Praised Be Thou, Jesus Christ)
### (1735–36; BWV 91)

(1) *Chorus.* Horns and timpani are added to the melody played by the oboes and strings, as the sopranos begin each line and are imitated by the other voices. Each line is followed by an instrumental ritornello. The regal splendor of this fantasia on Luther's hymn of this title is Bach's way of celebrating Christmas in motet form.

Gelobt seist du, Jesu Christ, / Dass du Mensch geboren bist / Von einer Jungfrau, das ist wahr, / Des freuet sich der Engel Schar. / Kyrie eleis! (Praised be Thou, Jesus Christ, / That Thou hast been born Man / Of a Virgin, that is true, / Where the hosts of angels rejoices. / Lord, have mercy.

# Wer Dank opfert, der preiset mich
# (Who Offers Thanks, He Praises Me)
### (1737; BWV 17)

(1) *Chorus.* The text for this number is Psalm 50:23, which Bach interprets by a step motif, suggested by the words *der Weg* (the way). There is an exuberant joy motif in both the melody and the four part singing of this motet-like chorus. The higher voices begin each section of the text and are followed by the other parts in imitation. Ritornelli of the beginning theme occur between these sections and at the end of the number. Bach borrowed this chorus for the Cum sancto Spiritu movement of his *Short Mass in G Major.*

"Wer dank Opfert, / der preiset mich, / und das ist der Weg, / dass ich ihm zeige das Heil Gottes." (Whoever offers thanks, / he praises Me, / and that is the way / that I show him the salvation of God.)

# Ich freue mich in dir (I Rejoice in Thee)
### (c. 1737; BWV 133)

(1) *Chorus — Chorale fantasia.* Singing most in unison, the four part choir, alternating with the instrumental ritornelli after each line sung, creates a motet of this first stanza of the Christmas hymn (1697) with this title by Kaspar Ziegler. The joy motif is magnificent both in the words and in the music.

Ich freue mich in dir / Und heisse dich willkommen, / Mein liebes Jesulein! / Du hast dir vorgenommen, / Mein Brüderlein zu sein. / Ach, wie ein süsser Ton! / Wie freundlich sieht er aus, / Der grosse Gottessohn! (I rejoice in Thee / And bid Thee welcome, / My dear little Jesus! / Thou hast undertaken / To be my Brother. / Ah, how sweet a sound! / How friendly He looks, The great son of God!)

# Freue dich, erlöste Schar
# (Rejoice, Redeemed Flock)
## (1738; BWV 30)

(1) *Chorus.* Based on the Gospel for St. John's Day (St. Luke 1:57–80) which tells of the birth of John and the song of praise of his father Zacharias, this opening chorus dramatizes the role of Zacharias as he praises God in his song. Bach divides the choir into two sections, both of which represent Zacharias.

Freue dich, erlöste Schar, / Freue dich in Sions Hütten. / Dein Gedeihen hat itzund / Einen rechten festen Grund, / Dich mit Wohl zu über-schütten. (Rejoice, redeemed flock, / Rejoice in Zion's dwellings. / Thy thriving has now / A really firm basis / For pouring well-being over thee.)

This chorus has fewer motet qualities than many of Bach's opening cantata movements, but it deserves to be included because of its drama which continues in all the following numbers. Yet is is complete in itself, as is its repetition in the final number of the cantata.

# Aus tiefer Not schrei ich zu dir
# (Out of Deep Distress I Cry to Thee)
## (c. 1740; BWV 38)

(1) *Chorus — Chorale fantasia.* Bach sets the melody for this chorus in the style of a Pachelbel motet. Without any instrumental prelude, the basses begin each pair of lines with a fugue into which the other voices join in turn, singing in canon. This first stanza of Luther's chorale with this title has a motif of solemnity, which Bach has derived appropriately from the text.

Aus tiefer Not schrei ich zu dir, / Herr Gott, erhör' mein Rufen; / Dein gnädig Ohr neig her zu mir / Und meiner Bitt sie öffne! / Denn so du willst das sehen an, / Was Sünd und Unrecht ist getan, / Wer kann, Herr, vor dir bleiben? (Out of deep distress I cry to Thee, / Lord God, hear my calling; / Thy gracious ears turn to me / And open them to my pleading! / For as Thou wilt perceive / What sin and wrong is done, / Who can, Lord, stay before Thee?) (Martin Luther, 1524, from Psalm 130)

Note that the last number (6) of this cantata has the fifth stanza of Luther's hymn simply sung by the four part choir (SATB) in unison to contrast with this opening fantasia (number 1) but with the same melody.

There is drama in both versions: the first is a personal prayer to God by the choir in a dramatic monologue, and the last chorale stanza is another personal song of praise, just as though the choir represents each individual in the congregation.

(6) *Chorale.* Ob bei uns ist der Sünden viel, / Bei Gott ist viel mehr Gnade; / Sein Hand zu helfen hat kein Ziel, / Wie gross auch sei der Schade. / Er ist allein der gute Hirt, / Der Israel erlösen wird / Aus seinen Sünden allen. (Whether there is much

sinning with us, / With God there is much more mercy; / His helping hand has no limit, / However great the harm may be. / He alone is the good Shepherd, / Who will redeem Israel / From all its sins.)

# Ach Gott, vom Himmel sieh darein
# (Ah God, from Heaven See into It)
### (c. 1740; BWV 2)

(1) *Chorus — Chorale fantasia.* Dating from about the same time as BWV 38, this cantata has the same format — a motet type opening chorus, and an unadorned rendering of the same chorale for the final number. These two stanzas are paraphrases of Psalm 12: 1, 6 (1524) by Martin Luther. The part singing is also the same — the basses begin the section, followed by the other parts in canon.

Ach Gott, vom Himmel sieh darein / Und lass dich's erbarmen! / Wie wenig sind der Heil'gen dein, / Verlassen sind wir Armen; / Dein Wort man nicht lässt haben wahr, / Der Glaub ist auch verloschen gar / Bei allen Menschenkindern. (Ah God, from heaven see into it / And let Thyself pity it! / How few are Thy saints, / Forsaken are we poor people; / Thy word is not taken as true. / Faith is also quite extinguished / Among all the children of man.)

(6) *Chorale.* Das wollst du Gott bewahren rein / Vor diesem arg'n Geschlechte; / Und lass uns dir befohlen sein, / Dass sich's in uns nicht flechte. / Der gottlos Hauf sich umher findt, / Wo solche lose Leute sind / In deinem Volk erhaben. (Thou wilt keep that pure / From the wicked race; / And let us be commended to Thee, / So that it may not fasten itself in us. / The godless band is found around us, / Where such loose people are / In Thy exalted folk.)

# Nimm von uns, Herr, du treuer Gott
# (Take from Us, Lord, Thou True God)
### (c. 1740; BWV 101)

(1) *Chorus — Chorale fantasia.* A motif of solemnity in the march rhythm of this motet movement makes a dramatic impression on the listener. Repeated orchestral ritornelli add to the mysterious beauty of the choir as it sings in canon. The text is based on Martin Moller's hymn (1584), with the chorale melody taken from the anonymous "Vater unser in Himmelreich" (Our Father in Heaven).

This must be one of Bach's most profound and emotional motet movements to begin a cantata, and it is certainly most original in his setting.

Nimm von uns, Herr, du treuer Gott, / Die schwere Straf' und grosse Not, / Die wir mit Sünden ohne Zahl / Verdienet haben allzumal. / Behüt' vor Krieg und teurer Zeit / Vor Seuchen, Feu'r und grossem Leid. (Take from us, Lord, Thou faithful God, / The heavy punishment and great distress, / Which we with countless sins / Have deserved so often. Protect from war and famine, From pestilence, fire and great sorrow.

# Wie schön leuchtet der Morgenstern
# (How Beautifully Gleams the Morning Star)
## (c. 1740; BWV 1)

(1) *Chorus — Chorale fantasia.* This chorale (1599) by Philipp Nicolai, which is Number 294 in the modern Lutheran hymnbook, gave Bach a beautiful opening text on the melody of which he could compose this wonderful fantasia.

The four part choir brings out all the reverence shown by the Wise Men for the Divine Infant, symbolized by the morning star in the text. Each line is sung by the four parts in canon, while the brilliant orchestra, consisting of two horns, two oboi da caccia, two concertante violins, two ripieno violins, a viola and continuo, plays the chorale tune as an overture, as ritornelli after each line sung and as a postlude.

Besides being an outstanding motet, this chorus is a tone poem which depicts a nocturnal scene, unique in the way that Bach paints it in sound.

Wie schön leuchtet der Morgenstern / Voll Gnad und Wahrheit von dem Herrn, / Die süsse Wurzel Jessel / Du Sohn Davids aus Jakobs Stamm, / Mein König und mein Bräutigam, / Hast mir mein Herz besessen, / Lieblich, / Freundlich, / Schön und herrlich, gross und ehrlich, reich von Gaben, / Hoch und sehr prächtig erhaben. (How beautifully gleams the Morning Star / Full of grace and truth from the Lord, / The sweet root of Jesse! / Thou Son of David from Jacob's line, / My King and my Bridegroom, / Thou hast possessed my heart, / Lovely, / Friendly, / Beautiful and glorious, great and honest, rich in gifts, / High and very splendidly exalted.)

# O ewiges Feuer, O Ursprung der Liebe
# (O Eternal Fire, O Source of Love)
## (1740–41; BWV 34)

(1) *Chorus.* For Whitsunday of either of the above years, Bach arranged this cantata from a wedding cantata that he had composed in 1726 (BWV 34a) which is incomplete in its music. This later work celebrates the descent of the Holy Spirit upon us. Bach's musical setting brings out the drama of the choir's appeal to the Holy Ghost to come into everyone's soul. The choir would again represent the congregation.

Bach's motet style is evident in the canon singing, the instrumental ritornelli between, and the da capo conclusion by the four parts and the orchstra.

O ewiges Feuer, o Ursprung der Liebe, / Entzünde die Herzen und weihe sie ein! / Lass himmlische Flammen durchdringen und wallen, / Wir wünschen, o Höchster, dein Tempel zu sein. / Ach lass dir die Seelen im Glauben gefallen! (O Eternal Fire, O Source of Love, / Kindle our hearts and consecrate them! / Let heavenly flames penetrate and undulate; / We wish, O Highest, to be Thy temple. / Ah, let our souls in faith please Thee!)

# Ach Herr, mich armen Sünder
# (Ah Lord, Me Poor Sinner)
### (c. 1740; BWV 135)

(1) *Chorus — Chorale fantasia.* This first stanza of a hymn (1597) based on Psalm 6 by Cyriakus Schneegass was set by Bach to the melody of H.L. Hassler's chorale "Herzlich tut mir verlangen" (With All My Heart I Long For). Each line of the hymn is preceded by an instrumental ritornello of a trombone, two oboes and strings. This effect, with each section of the four part choir singing every line in imitation, is usual for Bach's treatment of a chorale in the opening chorus — his own version of a motet movement in a cantata. This number is also, however, a beautiful tone poem in itself, with a very personal prayer motif dramatically sung by the choir.

Ach Herr, mich armen Sünder / Straf' mich nicht in deinem Zorn, / Dein' ernsten Grimm doch linder, / Sonst ist's mit mir verlor'n. / Ach Herr, wollst mir vergeben / Mein' Sünd' und gnädig sein, / Dass ich mag ewig leben, / Entflieh'n der Höllenpein. (Ah Lord, me poor sinner / Do not punish me in Thy anger; / Moderate Thy stern wrath, / Otherwise all is lost with me. / Ah Lord, Thou wilt forgive me / My sin and be merciful, / So that I may ever live / To escape the pain of hell.)

# Nun ist das Heil und die Kraft
# (Now Has the Salvation and the Strength)
### (c. 1740; BWV 50)

(1) *Chorus.* This double chorus with three trumpets, timpani, three oboes, strings and continuo for accompaniment was listed as a separate cantata by the Bachgesellschaft (B.G.), and Spitta stated that "It must certainly have formed the opening of a complete cantata for Michaelmas, and it may be assumed to have had an orchestral prelude" (*Johann Sebastian Bach,* III, 83).

On the same page, Spitta says that the rich orchestral accompaniment precluded its being a motet. But this argument does not hold because many of Bach's motet movements, separate works or included in the cantatas, were often accompanied by a festive orchestra.

It is therefore possible that this chorus, which is a double fugue, was Bach's last motet composition because of its late date. A further proof that it was a motet is shown by its eight part chorus, which is not found in any other sacred cantata by Bach.

The text is quoted from Revelation 12:10, the Epistle for St. Michael's Day, telling of the Archangel's fight with the dragon. A joy motif is combined with a motif of strength to represent the defeat of Satan.

"Nun ist das Heil und die Kraft und das Reich und die Macht unsers Gottes seines Christus worden, weil der verworfen ist, der sie (uns) verklagete Tag und Nacht vor Gott." (Now has the salvation and the strength and the kingdom and the might of our God becomes His Christ's, be-

cause he is cast out, who accused them [us] day and night before God.)

# Liebster Immanuel, Herzog der Frommen
# (Dearest Immanuel, Lord of the Righteous)
## (c. 1740; BWV 123)

(1) *Chorus — Chorale fantasia.* This is the only time that Bach writes a courante, a French dance tune, in any of his cantatas. The first stanza of the hymn (1679) by Ahasverus Fritsch is accompanied by unison flutes — to conjure up a vision of Christ in Heaven. The melody set by Bach is full of devout longing to be with Him, dramatized by the choir.

Liebster Immanuel, Herzog der Frommen, / Du, meiner Seele Heil, komm, komm nur bald! / Du hast mir, höchster Schatz, mein Herz genommen, / So ganz vor Liebe brennt und nach dir wallt. / Nichts kann auf Erden / Mir liebers werden, / Als wenn ich meinen Jesum stets behalt. (Dearest Immanuel, Lord of the righteous, / Thou, Savior of my soul, come, only come soon! / Thou, Highest Treasure, hast taken my heart from me, / Which burns so with love and flows toward Thee. / Nothing on earth can / Become dearer to me, / Than when I always hold my Jesus.)

By interpolating instrumental ritornelli after each line sung by the choir, Bach creates the antiphony effect of a motet, just as he had done in the opening chorus of BWV 41.

# Herr Christ, der ein'ge Gottessohn
# (Lord Christ, the Only Son of God)
## (c. 1740; BWV 96)

(1) *Chorus — Chorale fantasia.* Following his pattern of placing instrumental ritornelli after each line sung, this four part chorus is one of the most beautiful motet-chorales that Bach ever composed. Wonderful flourishes by the piccolo flute and piccolo violin at the instrumental intervals and within the melody add to the artistic charm.

The chorale is based on the hymn (1524) of Elisabeth Kreuziger.

Herr Christ, der ein'ge Gottessohn, / Vaters in Ewigkeit, / Aus seinem Herzen entsprossen, / Gleichwie geschrieben steht. / Er ist der Morgensterne, / Sein' Glanz strecket so ferne / Vor andern Sternen klar. (Lord Christ, the only Son of God, / Of the Father in eternity, / Sprung from His heart, / Just as it stands written. / He is the Morning Star; / He extends His gleaming so far / As to be clear before other stars.)

# Christ, unser Herr, zum Jordan kam
# (Christ, Our Lord, Came to the Jordan)
### (c. 1740; BWV 7)

(1) *Chorus — Chorale fantasia.* Like all the other opening choruses of about this time, Bach sets this as a chorale fantasia, in this case based on an arrangement of Luther's chorale with this title. The orchestral setting for two oboi d'amore, two violins, a viola and organ continuo has the usual ritornelli after each line sung in canon. A motif of solemnity is combined with a wave motif in the rhythm to illustrate the libretto.

Christ, unser Herr, zum Jordan kam / Nach seines Vaters Willen, / Von Sankt Johanns die Taufe nahm, / Sein Werk und Amt zu erfüllen; / Da wollt' er stiften uns ein Bad, / Zu waschen uns von Sünden, / Ersäufen auch den bittern Tod / Durch sein selbst Blut und Wunden; / Es galt ein neues Leben. (Christ, our Lord, came to the Jordan / According to His Father's will. / From Saint John He took baptism / To fulfill His work and ministry. There He wanted to establish a bath for us, / To wash us from our sins, / Also to drown bitter death / Through his own blood and wounds; / It was worth a new life.)

# Meine Seel' erhebt den Herren
# (My Soul Doth Magnify the Lord)
### (c. 1740; BWV 10)

(1) *Chorus.* Even at this late date in his cantata performances, it cannot be thought that Bach had forgotten the origins of his motets, because this opening chorus retains the original plainchant melody of the early motet. A trumpet, two oboes, two violins, a viola and continuo accompany this four part choir, singing each section of the text in imitation, and followed by the plainchant melody in the ritornelli. Again, Bach uses the same pattern of antiphony between choir and orchestra that all his later chorale cantatas have in their opening choruses or chorale fantasias.

"Meine Seel' erhebt den Herren, / und mein Geist freuet sich Gottes, meines Heilandes; / denn er hat seine elende Magd angesehen. / Siehe, von nun an werden mich selig preisen alle Kindeskind." (My soul doth magnify the Lord / and my spirit doth rejoice in God, my Savior; / for He hath regarded His wretched maiden. / Behold, from now on, all children's children will praise me as being blessed.) (Luke 1: 46–48)

# Allein zu dir, Herr Jesu Christ
# (Only in Thee, Lord Jesus Christ)
(c. 1740; BWV 33)

(1) *Chorus — Chorale fantasia.* This opening chorus shows the characteristics of a motet with its vocal presentation alternating with instrumental ritornelli, but it is also a very dramatic prayer to Christ, sung in canon by the choir. Once more the choir seems to represent any troubled individual.

The orchestra has two oboes, two violins, a viola, and organ continuo.

Allein zu dir, Herr Jesu christ / Mein' Hoffnung steht auf Erden; / Ich weiss, dass du mein Tröster bist, / Kein Trost mag mir sonsst werden. /

Von Anbeginn ist nichts erkor'n, / Auf Erden war kein Mensch gebor'n, / Der mir aus Nöten helfen kann. / Ich ruf' dich an, / Zu dem ich mein Vertrauen hab'. (Only in Thee, Lord Jesus Christ, / Stands my hope on earth. / I know that Thou art my Comforter, / There can be no comfort for me otherwise. / From the beginning nothing is ordained, / On earth no man was born, / Who can help me out of my troubles. / I call to Thee, / In Whom I have my trust.) (Konrad Hubert, 1540)

# Ach, lieben Christen, seid getrost
# (Ah, Dear Christians, Be Comforted)
(c. 1740; BWV 114)

(1) *Chorus — Chorale fantasia.* The orchestra is brightened up considerably by the horn, which is added to two oboes, a flute, two violins, a viola and continuo, for this opening chorus on the hymn text by Johannes Gigas. The orchestral prelude, repeated in the ritornelli, highlights the imitative singing by the four parts of the choir to a sprightly joy motif.

Ach, lieben Christen, seid getrost, / Wie tut ihr so verzagen! / Weil uns

der Herr heimsuchen tut, / Lasst uns von Herzen sagen: / Die Straf' wir wohl verdienet han, / Solchs muss bekennen jedermann, / Niemand darf sich ausschliessen. (Ah, dear Christians, be comforted; / How you do so despair! / Because the Lord punishes us, / Let us say from our hearts: / We have well deserved the punishment. / Such must everyone admit; / Nobody may exclude himself.)

# Herr Gott, dich loben alle wir
# (Lord God, We All Praise Thee)
(c. 1740; BWV 130)

(1) *Chorale.* This text is the first stanza of Paul Eber's hymn (c. 1561) for St. Michael's Day — this time only a complete chorale fantasia, without being designated "chorus." Never

theless, the brilliant orchestra with trumpets playing the ritornello between the lines sung, and the unison followed by the canon singing of the last line makes it no different from

Bach's usual opening motet choruses of this period.

Herr Gott, dich loben alle wir / Und sollen billig danken dir / Für dein Geschöpf der Engel schon, / Die um dich schweb'n um deinen Thron. (Lord God, we all praise Thee / And should rightly thank Thee / For Thy creation of angels, too, / Who hover around Thee round Thy throne.)

# Wohl dem, der sich auf seinen Gott (Well for Him, Who on His God)
## (c. 1740; BWV 139)

(1) *Chorus.* Bach sets a chorale fantasia for this first stanza of Johann Christoph Rube's hymn (1692). The melody, Mach's mit mir Gott, nach deiner Güt'" (Do with Me, God, According to Thy Goodness) (1628), by Johann Hermann Schein, is very beautiful. The sopranos begin each line, followed by other voices in imitation. The melody is played as a refrain, repeated after each line sung and at the end of the chorus. While less dramatic than some of Bach's other opening choruses, it is still impressive as an independent motet in itself.

Wohl dem, der sich auf seinen Gott / Recht kindlich kann verlassen; / Den mag gleich Sünde, Welt und Tod / Und alle Teufel hassen, / So bleibt er dennoch wohlvergnügt, / Wenn er nur Gott zum Freunde kriegt. (Well for him, who on his God / Can really child-like rely. / Him may even sin, world and death / And all devils hate. / Nevertheless, he remains well contented, / If only he obtains God for his Friend.)

# Schmücke dich, o liebe Seele (Adorn Thyself, O Dear Soul)
## (c. 1740; BWV 180)

(1) *Chorus — Chorale fantasia.* The text of this hymn (1653) by Johann Franck no doubt suggested to Bach the pastoral melody he used to set this first stanza. The drama of the choir's apostrophe to the soul to join itself to Christ symbolizes the Sacrament of Communion that the text mentions. The cantus firmus is carried by the sopranos, whom the other parts follow in imitation. In the melody of the ritornelli after each line sung, Bach combines motifs of peace and serenity which cannot fail to impress the listener with the quiet beauty that results. Voices alternating with the instrumental playing make this number a magnificent motet in itself.

Schmücke dich, o liebe Seele; / Lass die dunkle Sündenhöhle; / Komm ans helle Licht gegangen; / Fange herrlich an zu prangen; / Denn der Herr voll Heil und Gnaden / Lässt dich itzt zu Gaste laden. / Der der Himmel kann verwalten, / Will selbst Herberg in dir halten. (Adorn thyself, O dear soul. / Leave the dark cave of sin; / Come into the bright light; / Begin to sparkle splendidly. / For the Lord, full of salvation and mercy / Lets you now be invited as His guest. / He, Who can rule heaven, / Wishes Himself to take lodging in you.)

# Ach wie flüchtig, ach wie nichtig
# (Ah, How Fleeting, Ah, How Vain)
## (c. 1740; BWV 26)

(1) *Chorus — Chorale fantasia.* The impression that this is a motet results from the orchestral ritornelli in apposition to the part singing of the choir. This fantasia is based on the first verse of the hymn (1652) by Michael Franck. The four parts of the choir sing in unison at the beginning, but in imitation for the last three lines.

Ach wie flüchtig, ach wie nichtig / Ist der Menschen Leben! / Wie ein Nebel bald entstehet / Und auch wieder bald vergehet, / So ist unser Leben, sehet! (Ah, how fleeting, ah, how vain / Is the life of men! / As a mist soon arises / And again disappears, / So is our life, you see!)

# Das neugeborne Kindelein
# (The Newborn Little Child)
## (c. 1742; BWV 122)

(1) *Chorus — Chorale fantasia.* Based on the hymn (1597) by Cyriakus Schneegass with this title, this cantata for the Sunday after Christmas features joy throughout all its numbers. The joy motif is evident immediately in this opening melody, a fantasia which is Bach's usual method of embellishing the opening chorale stanza, and then having it sung plainly as the final number in the cantata. Again, the sopranas carry the cantus firmus, followed by the other parts in imitation for each line. The orchestra consists of three oboes, a bassoon, two violins, a viola and organ continuo; it accompanies the choir and plays the ritornello after each line sung. A great motet effect results.

Das neugeborn Kindelein / Das herzeliebe Jesulein / Bringt abermal ein neues Jahr / Der auserwählten Christenschar. (The newborn little Child, / Dearly loved little Jesus / Brings again a New Year / To the chosen Christian flock.)

# Du Friedefürst, Herr Jesu Christ
# (Thou Prince of Peace, Lord Jesus Christ)
## (1744; BWV 16)

(1) *Chorus — Chorale fantasia.* The first stanza of the chorale (1601) by Jakob Ebert forms the text for this chorus. The melody of the ritornello occurs at the beginning and after each line sung in imitation by the four part choir. There is personal drama in the choir's appeal to Christ to intercede for us; a peace motif is combined in the melody.

Du Friedefürst, Herr Jesu Christ, / Wahr Mensch und wahrer Gott, / Ein starker Nothelfer du bist / Im Leben und im Tod. / Drum wir allein / Im Namen dein / Zu deinem Vater schreien. (Thou Prince of Peace, Lord Jesus Christ, / True Man and True God, / Thou art a strong Helper in need / In life and in death. / Therefore we alone, / In Thy Name / Cry to Thy Father.)

# VI. The Sacred Songs

Bach's *Geistliche Lieder* (Spiritual Songs) were composed of arias drawn from Lutheran chorale texts, upon which melodies his own settings were based. These chorale melodies have been compiled in Halle by Johann Anastasius Freylinghausen in 1704, and this first edition was followed by a second part in 1714.

Bach must have been aware of these two "Spiritual Song Books" by Freylinghausen when he composed several chorale melodies as songs for the second notebook (*Notenbüchlein*) that he gave to his wife, Anna Magdalena, in 1725. Six of these chorale melodies would be added to the 69 hymns that Georg Christian Schemelli, the cantor at Zeitz, would publish in 1736 at Leipzig in his *Musical Song Book*. The preface to this work states that these 69 tunes were all either newly composed or partly improved in their thorough-bass by Sebastian Bach. Many of the sacred songs in Schemelli's collection were taken from Freylinghauen (e.g. BWV 45, 446, 461, 475, 506), but it is difficult to say how much Bach improved on them.

Thus the chorale gave rise to the sacred aria, set for home use or for private devotional services usually, but which could be transferred to church performance, if a choir were added for some or part of the verses. Sometimes the two scores were conjoined to form one song; this happened with BWV 405 and 495, and with BWV 320 and 461. Both of these

songs will be treated in the section on Schemelli.

Since most sacred arias were set for a solo voice, male or female (outside the church for this latter), they would be accompanied by a bass instrument, such as a cello or a gamba with harpsichord continuo. Such individualistic and refined art music, as it appeared in Schemelli's collection and contrasting with the largely pietistic strain in Freylinghausen, would induce Bach to compose similar arias himself.

The drama of such art songs, however, seems less apparent than if choruses were involved, but still the lyrical monologue, which is usually a prayer to God, can have a deep emotional effect on the listener.

The texts of the Schemelli hymns were written by various poets and set by different composers, although Bach was credited with setting all 75, each with its own BWV number! How many scores were really new Bach compositions is a question that is still being disputed today. Only BWV 478 "Komm, süsser Tod" (Come, Sweet Death) and BWV 452 "Dir, dir, Jehova will ich singen" (To Thee, to Thee, Jehova, I Will Sing) have been definitely attributed to Bach, because his name is printed on the former, and evidence that Bach composed the latter is noted in Anna Magdalena's *Notenbüchlein* (1725). This is the opinion of Alfred Dürr, but Wolfgang Schmieder thought that BWV 505 "Vergiss mein nicht, vergiss mein nicht" (Forget Me Not, Forget Me Not) was also an authentic Bach composition.

These three songs are included in Schemelli's *Gesangbuch* (Song Book) which contains the libretti and the melodies for 75 songs (B.G. xxxix). Schweitzer lists 24 which, presumably, had melodies set by Bach (*J.S. Bach*, II, 300—footnote 2). Some of these sacred songs appeared in Anna Magdalena's *Notenbüchlein* 11 years before Bach contributed to the Schemelli collection.

Therefore, these sacred songs from the *Notenbüchlein* should be examined before the 24 that Schweitzer mentioned in Schemelli, and where these are repeated in the later collection a note will be made.

# Sacred Songs and Arias from the 1722/25 Notebooks of Anna Magdalena Bach

## JESUS, MEINE ZUVERSICHT (JESUS, MY ASSURANCE) BWV 728

Bach had composed the melody for this 1653 hymn by Luise Henriette von Brandenburg in the 1722 *Notebook* of Anna Magdalena. Presumably she sang this herself as a solo soprano. In the 1725 *Notebook*, however, Bach embellishes the melody and adds a bass part—perhaps so that it could be performed by a choir in a social gathering in his home or in a church. This later version, BWV 365, is hymn number 566 in the Lutheran *Liederbuch* (Hymnal) and consists of ten verses, each expressing in a personal and dramatic manner our trust in Jesus in this life and in the life to come.

*Chorus (first verse):* Jesus, meine Zuversicht / Und mein Heiland ist im Leben; / Dieses weiss ich, soll ich nicht / Darum mich zufrieden geben, / Was die lange Todesnacht / Mir auch für Gedanken macht? (Jesus is my assurance / And my Savior in life; / This I know: should I not / Therefore be satisfied / With even what the long night of death / Gives me to think about?)

## DIR, DIR, JEHOVA WILL ICH SINGEN (TO THEE, TO THEE, JEHOVA I WILL SING) (BWV 452)

This 1697 hymn by Bartholomäus Crasselius also has more verses (8) than the three that Bach set. The soprano stanza was probably sung by Anna Magdalena after the tenor's rendition of the first stanza (at least it is so in my recording). The third stanza for a four part chorus could have been sung by the audience which may have gathered in Bach's home (cf. Spitta II, 147). If this hymn were used in a church service, the other verses could have been sung by the congregation. Apparently the Lutheran churchgoers of Bach's time knew which verses of any humn they were expected to sing and which they were only to listen to, when performed by the soloist(s) or the choir. Contrast between the soloists and the choir in this case gives a dramatic touch, which the listeners would certainly notice.

*Tenor (first verse):* Dir, dir, Jehova will ich singen; / denn wo ist doch ein solcher Gott wie du? / Dir will ich meine Lieder bringen, / ach, gib mir deines Geistes Kraft dazu, / dass ich es tu' im Namen Jesu Christ, / so wie es dir durch ihn gefällig ist. (To Thee, to Thee, Jehova, I will sing; / for where is then such a God as Thee? / To Thee I will bring my songs, / Ah, give me for that the strength of Thy Spirit, / that I may do it in the Name of Jesus Christ, / as it is pleasing to Thee through Him.)

*Soprano (second verse):* Zieh mich, o Vater, zu dem Sohne, / damit dein Sohn mich wieder zieh zu dir; / dein Geist in meinem Herzen wohne / und meine Sinne und Verstand regier, / dass ich den Freiden Gottes schmeck und fühl / und dir darob im Herzen sing und spiel. (Draw me, O Father, to Thy Son, / so that Thy Son draw me again to Thee; / may Thy Spirit dwell in my heart / and govern my senses and understanding, / so that I may enjoy and feel God's peace / and for that sing and play to Thee in my heart.)

*Chorus (third verse):* Verleih mir, Höchster, solche Gute, / so wird gewiss mein Singen recht getan: / so klingt es schön in meinem Liede, / und ich bet' dich im Geist und Wahrheit an: / so hebt dein Geist mein Herz zu dir empor, / dass ich dir Psalmen sing' im höhern Chor. (Grant me, O Highest, such a boon, / then will my singing be rightly done: / thus it sounds beautifully in my song, / and I ask Thee in my spirit and in truth: / then Thy Spirit raises my heart up to Thee, / that I may sing psalms to Thee in the higher chorus.)

## SCHAFFS MIT MIR, GOTT, NACH DEINEM WILLEN (DO WITH ME, GOD, ACCORDING TO THY WILL) (BWV 514)

In Anna Magdalena's *Notebook,* this hymn comes before the preceding

BWV 452. It is a personal prayer to God, dramatically expressed, signifying submission to His will and confidence in His protection.

*Soprano or Tenor:* Schaff's mit mir, Gott, nach deinem Willen, / es bleibt dir alles heimgestellt; / du wirst mein Wünschen so erfüllen, / wie's deiner Weisheit wohlgefällt. / Du bist mein Vater, du wirst mich versorgen, / darauf hoffe ich. (Do with me, God, according to Thy will, / everything remains left up to Thee; / Thou wilt so fulfill my wishing, / as it pleases Thy wisdom. / Thou art my Father; Thou wilt care for me, / for that I hope.)

Zu dir, mein Gott, steht mein Vertrauen, / du bist mein Gott, mein Heil, mein Schutz! / Auf dich will ich beständig bauen, / mit dir biet' ich dem Teufel Trutz. / Ist Gott für mich und bleibet mein, / wer mag mir dann zuwider sein! (In Thee, my God, stands my trust; / Thou art my God, my Salvation, my Protection! / On Thee will I constantly build; / With Thee I give defiance to the devil. / If God is for me and remains mine, / who may then be against me!) (Benjamin Schmolch, 1725)

## WIE WOHL IST MIR, O FREUND DER SEELEN (HOW WELL I FEEL, O FRIEND OF SOULS) (BWV 517)

This 1692 hymn by Wolfgang Christoph Dessler follows immediately after BWV 452, "Dir, dir Jehova will ich singen." It, too, has six verses, of which the first and the last were sung solo by a soprano or a tenor. Praise of Jesus as the Protector of the singer, who represents the feelings of any Christian towards his Master, continues the theme of BWV 514, above. This time the love of Christ is stressed.

*Soprano or Tenor (first verse):* Wie wohl ist mir, o Freund der Seelen, / Wenn ich in deiner Liebe ruh'! / Ich steige aus den Schwermuthshöhlen / Und eile deinen Armen zu; / Da muss die Nacht des Trauerns scheiden, / Wenn mit so angenehmen Freuden / Die Liebe strahlt aus deiner Brust, / Hier ist mein Himmel schon auf Erden; / Wer wollte nicht vergnüget werden, / Der in dir suchet Ruh und Lust! (How well I feel, O Friend of souls, / When I rest in Thy love! / I climb out of the caves of melancholy / And hasten to Thy arms; / There must the night of sorrow depart, / When with such pleasant joys / Love radiates out of Thy breast. / Here is my heaven on earth; / Who would not become delighted, / Who seeks in Thee rest and joy!)

*Sixth verse:* Wie ist mir dann, o Freund der Seelen, / so wohl, wenn ich mich lehn auf dich! / Mich kann die Welt, der Tod nicht quälen, / weil du mein Gott beseligst mich. / Lass solche Ruh in dem Gemüte / nach deiner unbeschränkten Güte / des Himmels süssen Vorschmack sein! / Weg, Welt, mit allen Schmeicheleien! / Nichts kann als Jesus mich erfreuen. / O reicher Trost; mein Freund ist mein! (How do I feel then, O Friend of souls, / so well, when I lean on Thee! / The world, death cannot torment me, / because Thou, my God, blessest me. / Let such rest of the mind, / according to Thy limitless goodness, / be the sweet foretaste of heaven! / Away, world, with all thy flattery! / Nothing else than Jesus can make me joyful. / O rich consolation; my Friend is mine!)

# WARUM BETRÜBST DU DICH (WHY ART THOU SAD) (BWV 516)

This hymn is marked as an aria on the score that Bach set. It is a dramatic soliloquy by the soloist to his or her own soul, asking why it does not accept God's will.

Warum betrübst du dich und beugest dich zur Erden, / mein sehr geplagter Geist, mein abgemattet Sinn? / Du sorgst, wie will es doch endlich mit dir werden / und fährest über Welt und über Himmel hin. / Wirst du dich nicht recht fest / in Gottes Willen gründen, / kannst du in Ewigkeit / nicht wahre Ruhe finden. (Why art thou sad and bowest to earth, / my much tormented spirit, my worn out mind? / Thou worriest how it will finally turn out for thee / and travellest away over world and heaven. / If thou dost not really firmly / base thyself in God's will, / thou canst not in eternity / find real rest.)

Drum, Jesu, will ich stets in dir zufrieden leben, / will stets begehren nur, was dir, mein Gott gefällt. / Und diesem Willen sei der meine stets ergeben; / denselben hab' ich mir zum festen Ziel gestellt. / Herr Jesu, wie du willst, / so will ich alles leiden; / es soll mich ewig nichts / von deiner Liebe scheiden. (Therefore, Jesus, I want to live always content in Thee; / I will only desire what pleases Thee my God. / And to Thy will may mine be always submissive; / I have set the same as my firm aim. / Lord Jesus, as Thou wilt / so will I suffer everything; / nothing shall ever separate me / from Thy love.) (? Johann Sebastian Bach, 1725)

## O EWIGKEIT, DU DONNERWORT (O ETERNITY, THOU WORD OF THUNDER) (BWV 513)

Of the six verses in this 1642 hymn by Johann Rist, Bach chose the first and the fourth as they appear in number 592 of the Lutheran *Liederbuch*. This chorale inspired Bach to compose a chorale cantata, BWV 20, on all its verses. This cantata had its first performance in 1725, about the same time as it appeared in a version for one soloist in Anna Magdalena's *Notebook*.

It is surprising that Bach should include such a melancholy work dealing with the Last Judgment in this gift to his wife. But there can be no doubt that she could sing this song artistically and in a very dramatic way, when she performed it before their family or friends.

*First verse:* O Ewigkeit, du Donnerwort, / O Schwert, das durch sie Seele bohrt, / O Anfang sonder Ende! / O Ewigkeit, Zeit ohne Zeit, / ich weiss vor grosser Traurigkeit nicht, / wo ich mich hinwende! / Mein ganz erschrock'nes Herz erbebt, / dass mir die Zung' am Gaumen klebt. (O eternity, thou word of thunder, / O sword, that pierces the soul, / O beginning without end! / O eternity, time without time, / I do not know because of great sadness, / where I should turn! / My totally terrified heart trembles, / so that my tongue sticks to my gums.)

*Fourth verse:* Ach Gott, wie bist du so gerecht, / wie strafst du den bösen Knecht / mit unerhörten Schmerzen! / Auf kurze Sünden dieser Welt / hast du so lange Pein bestellt! / Ach, nimm dies wohl zu Herzen, / und merke dies, o Menschenkind: / Kurz ist die Zeit, der Tod geschwind. (Ah God, how just Thou art; / how Thou dost punish Thy bad servant / with unheard of pains! / For small sins in this world / hast Thou ordained such long pain! / Ah, take this well to heart, / and notice this, o mortal child: / Short is time, death is quick.)

## GIB DICH ZUFRIEDEN UND SEI STILLE (REST CONTENT AND BE QUIET) (BWV 460)

There are three versions of this 1666 hymn by Paul Gerhardt in Schemelli's collection. Spitta (*J.S. Bach*, II, 149–150) says of this hymn: "It must have been a favourite with Bach, for it is to be found three times in succession, and with two quite new melodies in F major and E minor (or G minor). With regard to the last, Bach is stated to be the composer of it, and a special importance is very justly attached to this melody, for it is one of the most impressive sacred arias in existence, and any one who hears it under conditions worthy of it, in Bach's own four-part setting, will carry away an impression which he will not forget so long as he lives."

It is a long hymn of 13 verses, of which the first, third, and sixty have been performed by tenor or soprano soloists. I have never heard it sung by a four-part choir as Spitta recommended, but I am sure that it would justify his judgment. The hymn again advocates dramatically acceptance of God's will and trust in His providence and protection.

(1) Gib dich zufrieden und sei stille / in dem Gotte deines Lebens; / in ihm ruht aller Freuden Fülle, / ohn' ihn mühst du dich vergebens. / Er ist dein Quell und deine Sonne, / scheint täglich hell zu deiner Wonne.

Gib dich zufrieden, zufrieden. (Rest content and be quiet / in the God of thy life; / in Him reposes the fullness of all joy, / without Him, thou troublest thyself in vain. / He is thy source and thy sun, / Who shines daily brightly for thy bliss, / Rest content, rest content.)

(3) Wie dirs und andern oft ergehe, / ist ihm wahrlich nichts verborgen; / er sieht und kennet aus der Höhe / der betrübten Herzen Sorgen. / Er zählt den Lauf der heissen Tränen / und fasst zu Hauf all unser Sehnen. / Gib dich zufrieden. (As it often happens to thee and to others, / nothing is really hidden from Him. / He sees and knows from on high / the cares of sorrowful hearts. / He counts the course of hot tears / And totals up all our longing. / Rest content.)

(6) Lass dich dein Elend nicht bezwingen, / halt an Gott, so wirst du siegen! / Ob hoch die Fluten einhergingen, / dennoch wirst du nicht erliegen. / Gott ist nicht fern, steht in der Mitten, / hört bald und gern der Armen Bitten; / gib dich zufrieden. (Let not thy misery overcome thee; / hold to God, then thou wilt conquer! / Whether the floods rush along highly, / Nevertheless thou wilt not succumb. / God is not far; He stands in our midst. / He soon and gladly hears the pleas of the poor; rest content.)

## ICH HABE GENUG
## (I HAVE ENOUGH)
## (BWV 82)

This recitative and its following aria were taken from the cantata by Bach with this title, and were included as a solo soprano number in the 1725 *Notenbüchlein* (*Notebook*) of Anna Magdalena Bach. It is surprising to find it there, since the cantata was composed several years after 1725, but still Bach may have written it as chamber music for his family before the cantata version for soprano appeared about 1731. Originally, the cantata was for solo bass as it is now sung today.

This number is very dramatic in that it brings to life in song the words of the aged Simeon to the 12-year-old Jesus in the Temple (Luke 2:25–32), and expresses our own hope of being with Jesus after death.

*Recitative:* Ich habe genug! / Mein Trost ist nur allein, / dass Jesus mein / und ich sein eigen möchte sein. / Im Glauben halt' ich ihn, / da seh' ich auch mit Simeon / die Freude jenes Lebens schon. (I have enough! / My consolation is only / that Jesus is mine / And that I may be His own. / In my belief I hold Him, / since I already see also with Simeon / the joy of that life.)

Lasst uns mit diesem Manne ziehen. / Ach! möchte mich von meines Leibes Ketten / der Herr erretten! / Ach! wäre doch mein Abschied hier, / mit Freuden sagt' ich, Welt, zu dir: / Ich habe genug! (Let us go with this man! / Ah! might the Lord save me / from the chains of my body! / Ah! if my departure were here, / with joy I would say, world, to thee: / I have enough!)

*Aria:* Schlummert ein, ihr matten Augen, / fallet sanft und selig zu. / Welt, ich bleibe nicht mehr hier, / hab' ich doch kein Teil an dir, / das der Seelen könnte taugen. / Hier muss ich das Elend bauen, / aber dort, dort werd' ich schauen / süssen Frieden, stille Ruh. (Fall asleep, you weary eyes, / close softly and blessedly. / World, I am staying here no more; / I have no part in you / that can serve my soul. / Here I must build my misery, / but there, there will I look at / sweet peace, quiet rest.)

(librettist unknown)

# Sacred Songs and Arias from
# the 1736 Schemelli Collection of Hymns

For some time before Bach contributed to Schemelli's *Musikalisches Gesangbuch* (*Musical Song Book*), published in Leipzig in 1736, he had been himself gathering chorales of the sixteenth and seventeenth centuries. Some of these he had selected for the composition of his passions and cantatas (including some numbers of the *Christmas Oratorio*). Not that he was the only German composer of his time to use the chorale in his vocal compositions—his cousin Johann Ludwig Bach of Meiningen composed cantatas in which he had the choir sing a chorale at the end and some of which Johann Sebastian performed—but Johann Sebastian was the only composer of his time to stress the use of the chorale within as well as at the end of a cantata.

The title page of Schemelli's collection stated that it contained 954 spiritual songs and arias, but not that Bach had composed melodies for all of them. The preface to this work mentioned that Bach had composed "some melodies" and had revised the thorough-bass in many others, but failed to say which ones.

We have seen how extensively Bach used the chorale in Chapter V of this book—Motet Movements to Be Found in Bach Cantatas. It seems that the resultant chorale cantata (a church hymn at the beginning and paraphrases of it for the following stanzas) was peculiar to Bach's personal style for his cantata setting. However, Bach did not make extensive use of the chorale for his cantatas until he came to Weimar. There he used Johann Franck's texts, which contained chorale verses, especially for his clos-

ing movements. But it was when he came to Leipzig that Bach's insertion of the chorale into his cantatas becomes most apparent.

Günther Stiller in his *Johann Sebastian Bach and Liturgical Life in Leipzig* stresses Bach's relation to the church hymn in his cantatas as follows:

> Bach's interest in the church hymn becomes particularly clear at the beginning of the Leipzig term of office. Of the 44 cantatas of the first Leipzig cycle, 39 close with a simple setting of a church hymn, seven times cantatas with soloistic treatments of hymns turn up, 29 of a total of 30 chorale cantatas begin with a chorus on a passage from the Bible which in four instances is again combined with a hymn cantus firmus. ... In the later years, too, Bach once more turned to the hymn in a special way to produce chorale cantatas that made use of pure hymn texts, especially between 1732 and 1735. ... In the entire output of Bach cantatas there are only 11 completely preserved cantatas that have no relation to the hymn, namely, BWV 34, 35, 63, 82, 134, 150, 152, 170, 173, 181, 196 (and the two special cantatas BWV 191 and 198). [231]

Stiller points out also (248) that Bach tried to use traditional Lutheran hymns as much as possible and so used his own collections of hymns, in which he could find the stanzas he required for any libretto that he was setting.

It cannot be doubted that Bach's lifelong acquaintance with the evangelical hymn in the vernacular influenced his method of composing, so that he would incorporate the chorale into all his vocal and into many of his organ works.

Günther Stiller does not discuss the chorales set by Bach apart from those in his cantatas, but Jaroslav Pelikan in his *Bach Among the Theologians* (59) mentions that Bach did not set the melodies for all of the over 250 BWV numbers which the Bach scholars of the nineteenth century ascribed to his sacred songs, arias and chorales to the publishers as it was believed in the nineteenth century. He states that since Arnold Schering doubted this in the *Bachjahrbuch* (BJB) of 1924, "more recent research has made it necessary to be considerably more cautious about such ascriptions" (123).

The 954 chorales in Schemelli's 1736 collection were a mixture of pietist and orthodox Lutheran hymns, which were certainly not all set by Bach as previously thought.

Albert Schweitzer gives a more realistic picture of Bach's part in the Schemelli hymnary: "Of the sixty-nine melodies, twenty-four cannot be dated earlier than Bach. As the preface states that the melodies are 'partly composed and partly improved in the figured basses by Herr Johann Sebastian Bach of Leipzig, these

twenty-four are presumably his own.' ... They are sacred arias rather than chorale melodies" (*J.S. Bach,* II, 300).

The melodies for these 24 songs, which Schweitzer supposed to be set by Bach, would lead us to examine the texts of each of these hymns first. I have then added six others from Schemelli's text (B.G., xxxix) Bach Gesellschaft Vol 39, as I feel that Bach must have been involved with them and because I was impressed by an arrangement with chorus for five of them.

The personal tone of each hymn or aria as it is sung by a tenor or an alto is strikingly dramatic in its expression. One can readily understand how these sacred songs could be sung both for private family devotions, as they were originally intended, and for church services, especially when supplemented by a choir.

The following table will give these hymns in alphabetical order according to title, with translations and comments on each. I have given the second stanza also (and more if possible), since at least two stanzas of any hymn were usually sung by Lutheran congregations at this time. Moreover, the second verse tends to complete the thought of the first.

| BWV No. | B.G. (Bach-gesellschaft No. in Vol. 39 | Title of Chorale |
|---|---|---|
| 439 | 1. | Ach, dass nicht die letzte Stunde |
| 440 | 2. | Auf, auf, die rechte Zeit ist hier |
| 443 | 5. | Beschränkt, ihr Weisen dieser Welt |
| 449 | 11. | Dich bet' ich an, mein höchster Gott |
| 452 | 14. | Dir, dir, Jehovah, will ich singen (in Anna Magdalena's *Notebook* |
| 453 | 15. | Eins ist Not! ach Herr, dies Eine |
| 462 | 26. | Gott, wie gross ist deine Güte |
| 466 | 30. | Ich halte treulich still |
| 467 | 31. | Ich lass' dich nicht |
| 468 | 32. | Ich liebe Jesum alle Stund' |

The following six chorales should be added to Schweitzer's list of the 24 that Bach set for Schemelli's collection. Five of them have been recorded for alternating soloists and chorus, and the sixth, BWV 475 (39), could readily include a chorus to sing the "Halleluja!" at the end of each stanza.

These chorales bring out the dramatic effect that their choral parts produce, when sung either by the choir or by the congregation in conjunction with the soloists.

These words begin the first stanza of each of the above chorales and thus give the title. For a translation, see the listing on the following pages of this section.

## ACH, DASS NICHT DIE LETZTE STUNDE (BWV 439; B.G. 1)

The soloist reflects on his or her own death, considering it as the gateway through which heaven can be reached. A grief motif befits the melody of this funeral-like aria, but this is mixed with a confident joy motif as he looks for happiness in the life to come.

Ach, dass nicht die litzte Stunde / meines Lebens heute schlägt! / Mich verlangt von Herzens Grunde, / dass man mich zu Grabe trägt; / denn ich darf den Tod nicht scheuen, / ich bin längst mit ihm bekannt, / führt er

doch aus Wüsteneien / mich in das gelobte Land. (Ah, that the last hour / of my life does not strike today! / I long from the depths of my heart / that I may be carried to the grave; / for I may not shun death; / I have been acquainted with him for a long time; / he leads me out of the waste land / into the promised land.)
Gute Nacht ihr Eitelkeiten! / falsches Leben, gute Nacht! / Gute Nacht, ihr schnöden Zeiten, / denn mein Abschied ist gemacht! / Weil ich lebe, will ich sterben, / bis die Todesstunde schlägt, / da man mich als Gottes Erben / durch das Grab zum Himmel trägt. (Good-night, you vanities! / false life, good-night! / Good-night, you worthless times, / for my departure has been made! / Because I live, I wish to die / until the hour of death strikes, / when I am carried as God's heir / through the grave to heaven.) (Erdmann Neumeister, 1717)

## AUF, AUF, DIE RECHTE ZEIT IST HIER (BWV 440; B.G. 2)

This aria contrasts with the sadness apparent in the preceding hymn. Its joy motif exhorts listeners to turn their thoughts towards the Savior, and to forget the world from this moment.
Auf, auf, die rechte Zeit ist hier, / die Stunde wartet vor der Tür, / ihr Brüder, lasset uns erwachen, / vergesst die Welt und ihre Sachen. / Bezwingt den Schlaf und kommt in Eil, / denn unser Licht und Gnadenheil / der rechte Trost und Schutz der Seinen, / ist näher schon als wir es meinen. (Up, up, the right time is here; / the hour waits before your door; / brothers, let us wake up, / forget the world and its affairs. / Overcome your sleep and come in

haste, / for our LIght and Salvation, / the real Consolation and Protector of His own, / is already nearer than we think.) (Martin Opitz, 1628)
This is a very suitable hymn for an intimate family or social gathering. It would move the audience to think about Christ rather than about themselves.

## BESCHRÄNKT, IHR WEISEN DIESER WELT (BWV 443; B.G. 5)

The text for this aria was written by Christoph Wegleiter in 1690. It advises the listeners to make friends only with those who are equal to them in their fear of God. True friendship with God can only come through friendship with Christ, because He is the Mediator between His Father and mankind. This hymn also contrasts God's omnipotence with our vices and weaknesses from which Jesus has redeemed us.
Beschränkt, ihr Weisen dieser Welt, / die Freundschaft immer auf die Gleichen, / und leugnet, dass sich Gott gesellt / mit denen, die ihn nicht erreichen. / Ist Gott schon alles und ich nichts, / ich Schatten, er der Quell des Lichts, / er noch so stark, ich noch so blöde, / er noch so rein, ich noch so schnöde, / er noch so gross, ich noch so klein; / mein Freund ist mein, und ich bin sein. (Limit, you wise ones of this world, / Your friendship always with your likes, / and deny that God associates / with those who do not reach Him. / If God is everything and I am nothing, / I a shadow, He the Source of light, / He ever so strong, I ever so stupid, / He ever so pure, I ever so vile, / He ever so great, I ever so small; / my Friend is mine, and I am His.)
Gott, welcher seinen Sohn mir gab,

/ gewährt mir alles mit dem Sohne; /
nicht nur sein Kreuz, nicht nur sein
Grab, / auch seinen Thron, auch
seine Krone. / Ja, was er redet, hat
und tut, / sein Wort, sein Geist, sein
Fleisch und Blut, / was er gewonnen
und erstritten, / was er geleistet und
gelitten, / das räumet er mir alles ein;
/ mein Freund ist mein, und ich bin
sein. (God, who gave His Son for me,
/ grants me everything with His Son;
/ not only His cross, not only His
grave, / but also His throne and
crown. / Yes, what He says, has and
does, / His word, His spirit, His flesh
and blood, / what He has won and
obtained by strife, / what He has accomplished and suffered, / all that He
gives to me; / my Friend is mine, and
I am His.)

This chorale is very dramatic in its
declamation, which shows submission
to God and thanks to Him for sending
His Son to us.

## DICH BET' ICH AN,
## MEIN HÖCHSTER GOTT
## (BWV 449; B.G. 11)

This chorale is a personal prayer to
God, as this first line states, thanking
Him for the protection that He has
given the soloist since his youth. He
expresses further thanks for the
blessedness of heaven that God has
given him as a gift. May he be ready
to die when God calls him in death.
This is a dramatic monologue, expressed in the form of a prayer.

Dich bet' ich an, mein höchster
Gott, / der du mich hast regieret, /
und gnädiglich von Jugend auf
geführet / aus vieler Angst, Gefahr
und Not. / Gib, dass mein Sinn zum
rechten Ziel sich lenke / und ich
allzeit mein Ende wohl bedenke. (I
ask Thee, my God most high, / Thou
who hast governed me, / and merci-

fully led me up from my youth / out
of much worry, danger and need. /
Grant, that my mind turns to the
right / and that I always think about
my end.)

Lass mich erwarten, wohlbereit, /
wann du mich wirst abholen; / lass
mich allein dir bleiben stets befohlen
/ und denken an die Seligkeit, / die
du mir gibst aus Gnaden zum
Geschenke, / wenn ich mein End'
recht seliglich bedenke. (Let me
await, well prepared, / when Thou
wilt fetch me away; / let me always
stay commended to Thee alone / and
think about the bliss, / that Thou
givest to me as a gift of mercy, / when
I think really blessedly about my
end.) (Johann Gottfried Olearius,
1686)

## DIR, DIR, JEHOVAH,
## WILL ICH SINGEN
## (BWV 452; B.G. 14)

This hymn from Anna Magdalena's
*Notebook* may also be found in the
previous section. See the entry for
BWV 452 in the Sacred Songs and
Arias from the 1722/25 Notebooks of
Anna Magdalena Bach.

## EINS IST NOT!
## ACH HERR, DIES EINE
## (BWV 453; B.G. 15)

Once again it can be noticed that
this aria reflects Bach's philosophy on
life and the spiritual values that surpass our earthly existence. Bach must
have chosen this chorale text for his
own special setting, because its religious teaching is in accord with his
own belief. Such a dramatically personal prayer would seem to make it
more suitable for a presentation in the
home or in a private gathering than
for choral performance in a church.

Eins ist Not! Ach Herr, dies Eine / lehre mich erkennen doch! / Alles andre, wie's auch scheine, / ist ja nur ein schweres Joch, / darunter das Herze sich naget und plaget / und dennoch kein wahres Vergnügen erjaget. / Erlang' ich dies Eine, das Alles ersetzt, / so werd' ich mit Einem in Allem ergötzt. (One Thing is needed! O Lord, this one Thing / Teach me to know it! / Everything else, however it may appear, / is only a heavy yoke, / under which the heart grieves and torments / and still finds no true delight. / If I obtain this one Thing, that replaces all, / then I shall be delighted with one Thing in all.)

Seele, willst du dieses finden, / such's bei keiner Creatur. / Lass was irdisch ist dahinten, / schwing' dich über die Natur; / wo Gott und die Menschheit in Einem vereinet, / wo aller Vollkommenheit Fülle erscheinet, / da, da ist das beste, notwendigste Teil, / mein Ein' und mein Alles, mein seligstes Heil. (Soul, if thou wilt find this, / seek it not near any creature. / Leave behind thee what is earthy, / soar above nature; / where God and mankind unite in one, / where the fullness of all perfection appears, / there, there is the best, most necessary part / My One and my All, my most blessed Salvation.) (Johann Heinrich Schröder, 1695)

## GOTT, WIE GROSS IST DEINE GÜTE (BWV 462; B.G. 26)

A sincere tone of humility makes this hymn one of the most impressive that Bach set for the Schemelli collection. The melody reveals Bach's own confidence in God's influence on his life. A motif of solemnity throughout seems to emphasize the vocalist's appeal for faith, while he sings his thanks to God for the goodness He has shown towards him in the past. This prayer would certainly inspire Bach to set it in his own style.

Gott, wie gross ist deine Güte, / die mein Herz auf Erden schmeckt. / Ach, wie labt sich mein Gemüte, / wenn mich Not und Tod erschreckt. / Wenn mich etwas will betrüben, / wenn mich meine Sünde presst, / zeiget sie von deinem Lieben, / das sich nicht verzagen lässt, / drauf ich mich zufrieden stelle / und Trotz bieten kann der Hölle. (God, how great is Thy goodness, / which my heart enjoys on earth. / Ah, how my spirit is refreshed, / when need and death terrify me. / When something wants to make me sad, / when my sin oppresses me, / it [Thy goodness] shows by Thy love, / that does not allow itself to despair, / and on which I can be satisfied, / giving defiance to hell.)

Darum bitt' ich deine Güte, / deine Gnad' und ew'ge Treu, / o mein Vater, mich behüte, / dass ich nicht verlassen sei! / Stärke mich mit deinem Geiste, / wenn ich werde hingerafft, / und vor allem was das meiste, / gib mir stets des Glaubens Kraft. / Lass mich deine Liebe schmecken, / wenn du wirst mich auferwecken. (Therefore I ask for Thy goodness, / Thy mercy and everlasting faith; / o my Father, protect me, / so that I may not be abandoned! / Strengthen me with Thy Spirit / when I am swept away, / and especially, what is the most, / give me always strength in my belief. / Let me enjoy Thy love, / when Thou wilt awaken me.) (Georg Christian Schemelli, 1736)

## ICH HALTE TREULICH STILL (BWV 466; B.G. 30)

A motif of joy pervades both stanzas, which comes from the knowledge that God has ordained everyone's lot in life. For the soloist, he sings that it is enough to patiently endure whatever befalls him here on earth.

Ich halte treulich still und liebe meinen Gott, / Ob mich schon öftermals drückt Kummer, Angst und Not. / Ich bin mit Gott vergnügt und halt' geduldig aus; / Gott ist mein Schutz und Schirm um mich und um mein Haus. (I stay faithfully quiet and love my God, / Whether worry, anxiety and want often oppress me. / I am happy with God and patiently endure; / God is my protection and shield for me and for my house.)

Drum dank' ich meinem Gott und halte treulich still, / Es gehe in der Welt, wie es mein Gott nur will. / Ich lege kindlich mich in seine Vaterhand / Und bin mit ihm vergnügt in meinem Amt und Stand. (Therefore I thank my God and stay faithfully quiet. / It may go in the world as my God wishes. / I place myself child-like in His paternal hand / and am pleased with Him in my position and station in life.) (G.H. Till, 1736)

## ICH LASS' DICH NICHT (BWV 467; B.G. 31)

This hymn shows deep devotion to Jesus. The soloist interprets his or her constant faith, expressed by the text, by a personal prayer with a motif of solemnity.

Ich lass' dich nicht, du musst mein Jesus bleiben, / will herbe Not, Welt, Höll' und Tod mich aus dem Feld beständiger Treue treiben. / Nur her, ich halte mich, mein starker Held, an dich, / hör', was die Seele spricht, / Du musst mein Jesus bleiben. / Ich lass' dich nicht; ich lass' dich nicht! (I do not leave Thee; Thou must stay, my Jesus, / if harsh need, the world, hell and death wish to drive me from the field of constant faith / But here; I hold myself, my strong Hero, to Thee. / Hear what my soul says: / Thou must stay, my Jesus. / I do not leave Thee; I do not leave Thee!)

Ich lass' dich nicht, mein Gott, mein Herr, mein Leben! / Mich trennt das Grab von dir nicht ab, der du für mich dich in den Tod gegeben. / Du starbst aus Liebe mir, ich sag' in Liebe dir, / auch wenn mein Herz zerbricht: / Mein Gott, mein Herr, mein Leben! / Ich lass' dich nicht, ich lass' dich nicht! (I do not leave Thee, my God, my Lord, my Life! / The grave does not separate me from Thee, Thou, who for me, gave Thyself to death. / Thou didst die out of love for me; I say in love to Thee, / even if my heart breaks: / My God, my Lord, my Life! / I do not leave Thee; I do not leave Thee!) (Wolfgang Christoph Dessler, 1692)

## ICH LIEBE JESUM ALLE STUND' (BWV 468; B.G. 32)

Three verses of this hymn will be quoted here, to show that more than two verses were often sung by two singers in succession or by one or more vocalists plus a choir, especially for performances in a church. In this case, the last two lines of each stanza is repeated as a refrain. This seems to reinforce the assertion of both vocalists of their love for Jesus, and would reflect Bach's own attitude towards his Savior until his own death.

*Tenor:* Ich liebe Jesum alle Stund', / ach, wen sollt' ich sonst lieben? / Ich liebe ihn mit Herz und Mund, / der

Welt Gunst macht Betrüben. / Ich liebe Jesum in der Not, / ich liebe, ich liebe Jesum bis zum Tod. (I love Jesus every hour. / O whom should I love otherwise? / I love Him with my heart and mouth; / the approbation of the world makes [me] sad. / I love Jesus in my distress, / I love, I love Jesus unto death.)

*Soprano:* Mich scheidet nichts von Jesu Lieb', / kein Trübsal Angst und Schmerzen. / Ob Kreuzeslast mich drückt und trieb, / bleibt Jesus mir im Herzen. / Ich liebe Jesum in der Not, / ich liebe, ich liebe Jesum bis zum Tod. (Nothing separates me from the love of Jesus, / no sadness, anxiety or pain. / Whether the weight of torment oppresses and forces me, / Jesus remains in my heart. / I love Jesus in my distress, / I love, I love Jesus unto death.)

*Tenor:* Von Jesu Liebe lass' ich nicht; / ich hab' mich ihm versprochen. / Ich lieb', bis löscht mein Lebenslicht / und bis mein Herz gebrochen. / Ich liebe Jesum in der Not, / ich liebe, ich liebe Jesum bis zum Tod. (I do not leave the love of Jesus; / I have promised myself to Him. / I will love, until my life's light goes out / and until my heart has broken. / I love Jesus in my distress, / I love, I love Jesus unto death.) (Author ? — Text in Schemelli's *Song Book,* 1736)

## ICH STEH' AN DEINER KRIPPEN HIER
## (BWV 455; B.G. 33)

This Christmas hymn, by some touch of magic in its melody, joins the listeners' emotions with those of the soloist. Therefore, it is not surprising that this chorale might be sung as a congregational hymn within the church at a Christmas service, as it indeed appears in the Lutheran hym-

nary of the present time. Bach's setting for this piece in praise of the Infant Savior has an exceptionally beautiful joy motif, which paints an audiovisual picture of the scene as the worshippers, or the soloist, give thanks to the Savior as He lies in His crib. Bach had used the same first verse of this chorale for Part VI, number 59, of his *Christmas Oratorio.*

Ich steh' an deiner Krippen hier, / o Jesu, du mein Leben; / ich komme, bring' und schenke dir, / was du mir hast gegeben. / Nimm hin, es ist mein Geist und Sinn, / Herz, Seel' und Mut, nimm alles hin / und lass dir's wohlgefallen. (I stand here at Thy cradle, / o Jesus, my life; / I come, bring and give to Thee / what Thou hast given me. / Take it; it is my spirit and mind, / heart, soul and courage, take them all / and let them be well pleasing to Thee.)

Ich lag in tiefster Todesnacht; / du wurdest meine Sonne. / Die Sonne, die mir zugebracht / Licht, Leben, Freud' und Wonne. / O Sonne, die das helle Licht / des Glaubens in mir zugericht', / wie schön sind deine Strahlen! (I was lying in death's deepest night; / Thou didst become my Sun. / The Sun, which brought to me / light, life, joy and bliss. / O Sun, who turned the bright light / of faith in me, / How beautiful are Thy rays!) (Paul Gerhardt, 1653)

## JESU, JESU, DU BIST MEIN
## (BWV 470; B.G. 34)

This hymn has a refrain in the first and last lines of each stanza in the words, "Jesu, Jesu, du bist mein." Repetition of this line forms a motto which seems to consolidate the thought of the hymn — a prayer expressed by the soloist either at a home gathering or in church.

Jesu, Jesu, du bist mein, / weil ich muss auf Erden wallen. / Lass mich ganz dein eigen sein, / lass mein Leben dir gefallen. / Dir will ich mich ganz ergeben / und im Tode an dir kleben, / dir vertraue ich allein, / Jesu, Jesu, du bist mein! Jesu, Jesu, du bist mein, / lass mich dort einst zu dir kommen; / nimm mich in den Himmel ein, / dass ich habe mit den Frommen / Himmelsfreude, Lust und Wonne / und auch seh' die Gnadensonne, / dir vertraue ich allein, / Jesu, Jesu, du bist mein! (Jesus, Jesus, Thou art mine, / because I must wander about on earth. / Let me be completely Thine own, / let my life please Thee. / To Thee I want to give myself entirely / and in death stick to Thee; / in Thee alone I trust, / Jesus, Jesus, Thou art mine! Jesus, Jesus, Thou art mine; / let me come there to Thee some day; / take me into heaven, / so that I may have with the pious / the joy of heaven, pleasure and bliss / and also see the Sun of mercy, / in Thee alone I trust, / Jesus, Jesus, Thou art mine!) (Anonymous, 1687)

## JESU, DEINE LIEBESWUNDEN (BWV 471; B.G. 35)

This chorale probably pertains to Good Friday, according to the thought of the first stanza. A motif of grief is combined with one of solemnity to make this a short but very moving avowal of constant devotion to Jesus in a dramatic prayer to Him.

Jesu, deine Liebeswunden, / dein Angst und Todespein / haben mich so hoch verbunden, / dass ich kann beständig sein. / Geist und Seele, Leib und Leben, / Herz und Sinn sind alle dein. / Alles hab' ich der ergeben, / dein will ich beständig sein. (Jesus, Thy wounds of love, / Thy worry and pain of death / have bound me so

much to Thee / that I can be constant. / My spirit and soul, body and life, / heart and mind are all Thine. / Everything have I given to Thee, / I want to be constantly Thine.) (Author is "C.W.," 1736)

## KOMM, SÜSSER TOD, KOMM SEL'GE RUH' (BWV 478; B.G. 42)

An unknown author wrote the verses to this hymn, before Bach set the melody for it in 1724. Since that time, Bach's name has always been associated with both its words and its music, because the melody has a combined rhythm of solemnity and beatific peace which Bach invariably seems to use in setting such funeral themes. Furthermore, Bach had his named printed on this chorale, which might indicate that he was or would have wished to be the librettist as well as the composer.

His personal philosophy towards death is certainly expressed by this text. He personifies and apostrophizes death as being a "sweet" release from the world's strife and as the means by which he can be with Jesus and His angels after a "blessed rest." This outlook on life and death typifies Bach's religious thinking. As a sacred drama in abbreviated monologue form, it has become synonymous with Bach's music to modern audiences. Certainly this is the serious composer, but to be fair, one should not forget that Bach also knew the joys of heaven and earth as his other vocal work testifies.

Komm, süsser Tod, komm, sel'ge Ruh'! / Komm, führe mich in Friede, / Weil ich der Welt bin müde. / Ach komm! ich wart' auf dich, / Komm bald und führe mich. / Drück mir die Augen zu. / Komm, sel'ge Ruh'!

Komm, süsser Tod, komm, sel'ge Ruh'! / Ich will nun Jesum sehen / Und bei den Engeln stehen. / Es ist ja nun vollbracht. / Welt, darum gute Nacht. / Mein' Augen schliess' ich zu. / Komm, sel'ge Ruh'! (Come, sweet death, come, blessed rest! / Come, lead me to peace, / Because I am tired of the world. / Ah come! I am waiting for thee, / Come soon and guide me. / Close my eyes. / Come, blessed rest! Come, sweet death, come blessed rest! / I wish now to see Jesus / And stand with the angels. / It is now finished. / World, therefore good night. / I close my eyes. / Come, blessed rest!) (Author unknown, 1724 [Bach's name is printed on the hymn])

## KOMMT, SEELEN, DIESER TAG
### (BWV 479; B.G. 43)

The text of this hymn pertains to a Feast-Day in the church calendar. It is probably a Whitsunday hymn, referring to the descent of the Holy Ghost upon us, but it also exhorts each member of the congregation to praise God for giving His word and His spirit. Bach's setting of the melody in 6/8 time seems to paint a sound-picture of the lively moment of the Holy Spirit.

Kommt, Seelen, dieser Tag / muss heilig sein besungen; / sprecht Gottes Taten aus / mit neuerweckten Zungen; / heut' hat der werte Geist / viel Helden ausgerüst, / so betet, dass er auch / die Herzen hier begrüsst. Wen Gottes Geist beseelt, / wen Gottes Wort erreget, / wer Gottes Gnade fromm / in seinem Herzen heget, / der stimme mit uns ein, / und preise Gottes Treu'; / sie ist an diesem Fest / und alle Morgen neu. (Come, souls, this day / must be celebrated in song in a holy way; / speak out the deeds of God / with newly awakened tongues; / today the worthy Spirit / has fitted out many heroes in armor. / Then pray that He too / greets our hearts here. Whom God's Spirit inspires, / whom God's Word moves, / who reverently cherishes God's mercy / in his heart, / he may join in with us / and praise God's fidelity; / it is new on this festival / and every morning.) (Valentin Ernst Löscher, 1713)

## KOMMT WIEDER AUS DER FINSTERN GRUFT
### (BWV 480; B.G. 44)

Reference to the Resurrection in the first stanza and confidence in God to also raise us up after death indicate that this chorale was an Easter hymn. It is itself a brief sermon in music, giving thanks to God who has offered us victory over death in the life hereafter.

Kommt wieder aus der finstern Gruft / ihr Gott ergebnen Sinnen! / Schöpft neuen Mut und frische Luft, / blickt hin hach Zions Zinnen; / denn Jesus, der im Grabe lag, / hat als ein Held am dritten Tag / des Todes Reich besieget. (Come forth again from your dismal tomb / you God-given minds! / Take new courage and fresh air, / look away to Zion's pinnacles; / for Jesus, who lay in the grave, / has, as a hero on the third day, / conquered death's kingdom.)

Gott, unsrem Gott sei Lob und Dank, / der uns den Sieg gegeben; / der das, was hin zum Tode sank, / hat neu gebracht zum Leben! / Der Sieg ist unser: Jesus lebt, / der uns zur Herrlichkeit erhebt, / Gott sei dafür gelobet. (To God, our God, be praise and thanks, / He who has given us the victory; / He who, that which sank down in death, / has brought anew to life. / The victory is ours: Jesus lives; / He who raises us up to glory— /

praise be to God for that. (Valentin Ernst Löscher, 1713)

## LIEBSTER HERR JESU, WO BLEIBST DU SO LANGE? (BWV 484; B.G. 48)

Longing for the return of Jesus creates a grief motif in this chorale. Its seven stanzas, of which the following three are sung alternately by the soprano and the tenor soloists, all have a vocal refrain with an echo effect in their last two lines. This repetition emphasizes the theme of longing. Schweitzer describes this as an "expressive" chorale, by which he means that "the succession of words, phrases or ideas is duplicated in the music" (*J.S. Bach, II,* 68).

The text of the third stanza that is quoted below seems to recall the soprano/bass duet in cantata BWV 140, "Wachet auf, ruft uns die Stimme" (Wake up, the Voice Calls to Us), which Bach had composed in 1731. But in this chorale the dramatic dialogue has become a dramatic monologue.

*Soprano:* Liebster Herr Jesu, wo bleibst du so lange? / Komm doch, mir wird hier auf Erden so bange, / komm doch und nimm mich, wenn dir es gefällt, / von dieser argen, beschwerlichen Welt. / Komm doch, Herr Jesu, wo bleibst du so lange? / Komm doch, mir wird hier auf Erden so bange. (Dearest Lord Jesus, where stayest Thou so long? / Come then, I feel so anxious here on earth; / come then and take me, if it pleases Thee, / from this harsh, difficult world. / Come them, Lord Jesus, where dost Thou stay so long? / Come then, I feel so anxious here on earth.)

*Tenor:* Alles ist eitel, was unter der Sonne, / flüchtig die Freude, vergänglich die Wonne; / Herrlichkeit, Wol-

lüste, Reichtum und Kunst, / alles ist schattiger Nebel und Dunst. / Komm doch, Herr Jesu, wo bleibst du so lange? / Komm doch, mir wird hier auf Erden so bange. (Everything which is under the sun is vain; / fleeting is joy, passing is bliss; / glory, pleasures, wealth and art, / everything is shadowy fog and vapor. / Come then, Lord Jesus, where dost Thou stay so long? / Come then, I feel so anxious here on earth.)

*Soprano:* Allbereit schmück' ich dich, gläubige Seele, / fülle die brennende Lampe mit Öle, / auch um die Mitternacht fertig zu steh'n / und auf die ewige Hochzeit zu geh'n. / Komm doch, Herr Jesu, wo bleibst du so lange? / Komm doch, mir wird hier auf Erden so bange. (Already I, believing soul, adorn Thee; / I fill my burning lamp with oil, / even at midnight to stand ready / and to go to the eternal wedding. / Come then, Lord Jesus, where dost Thou stay so long? / Come then, I feel so anxious here on earth.) (Christoph Wesolowius, 1676)

## MEIN JESU, WAS FÜR SEELENWEH (BWV 487; B.G. 51)

This is another chorale for Good Friday, probably composed by Schemelli for his collection and set to music by Bach in 1736. The complete hymn consists of six stanzas of ten lines, each giving the soloist scope to express his emotions as he visualizes the scene.

In the first stanza, for example, the words of the text vividly depict Christ's agony in Gethsemane, while the following stanza is the singer's personal plea to Jesus to let him share the pain He bore, in order to be with Him and the righteous because of the pain that he has likewise suffered.

Bach sets these stanzas with a grief motif in keeping with the mourning tone of Good Friday.

Mein Jesu, was für Seelenweh / Befällt dich in Gethsemane, / Darein du bist gegangen. / Des Todes Angst, der Hölle Qual / Und alle Pein des Belial, / Die haben dich umfangen. / Du zagst, du klagst, / Zitterst, bebest und erhebest / Im Elende / Zu dem Himmel deine Hände. (My Jesus, what agony of the soul / Befalls Thee in Gethsemane, / Into which Thou hast gone. / The worry of death, the torment of hell / And all the pain of Belial, / They have surrounded Thee. / Thou dost hesitate and lament, / Tremble, shiver and raise up / In Thy distress / Thy hands to heaven.

Du treuster Immanuel, / Erretter meiner armen Seel' / Von allen Höllenplagen, / Lass doch die grosse Seelenangst, / In der du mit dem Tode rangst, / Im Herzen stets mich tragen. / Bis ich endlich / Aus dem Leiden in die Freuden / Möge kommen, / Wo du lebst mit allen Frommen. (Thou most faithful Immanuel, / Savior of my poor soul / From all the pains of hell, / Let me always bear in my heart / The great anguish of soul / In which Thou didst struggle with death. / Until I finally / May come / Out of suffering into the joys / In which Thou livest with all the righteous.) (Georg Christian Schemelli ?, 1736)

## MEINES LEBENS LETZTE ZEIT (BWV 488; B.G. 52)

This is a peculiar hymn, especially if sung at a domestic gathering, since it combines the grief motif of a funeral with a motif of confidence in God that He will give us eternal life after death. These musical settings

that Bach uses here for this text really illustrate the personal sadness in his life and his innate trust in God. Such a libretto would definitely appeal to him.

Meines Lebens letzte Zeit / ist nun mehro angekommen, / da der schnöden Eitelkeit / meine Seele wird entnommen. / Wer kann widerstreben, / dass uns Menschen Gott das Leben / auf ein zeitlich Wiedernehmen hat gegeben! (The last time of my life / has once more now come, / when from base vanity / my soul is removed. / Who can resist / that for us men God has given life / for a timely taking it back!

Nun wohlan denn, gute Nacht, / gute Nacht, ihr meine Lieben! / Meine Tage sind vollbracht, / die mein Gott hat vorgeschrieben. / Wer will widerstreben? / Hat doch Gott ein künftig Leben, / da ich gleich den Engeln werde sein gegeben! (Well then, good night, / good night, thou my loving! / My days are finished, / which God has prescribed for me. / Who will strive against that? / Yet God has given a life to come / in which I will be like the angels!) (Georg Christian Schemelli or anonymous, 1726 — original melody is anonymous, 1726)

## O FINSTRE NACHT, WANN WIRST DU DOCH VERGEHEN? (BWV 492; B.G. 57)

As in the previous hymn, BWV 488, this chorale's text has the same motif of longing for Christ and contrasts the light of His presence with the gloom created by the dismal night of sin in the world. Bach's setting for the melody has a similar grief motif to that which he composed for his other chorale settings on death and the afterlife with Jesus.

O finstre Nacht, wann wirst du doch vergehen, / wann bricht dein Lebenslicht herfür? / Wanne werd' ich doch von Sünden auferstehen, / und leben nur allein in dir? / Wann werd' ich in Gerechtigkeit / dein Antlitz sehen alle Zeit! / Wann werd' ich satt und froh mit Lachen, / o Herr, nach deinem Bild erwachen? (O gloomy night, when wilt thou pass; / when dost thy light of life break forth? / When shall I rise up from sin, / and just live in Thee alone? / When shall I in righteousness / always see Thy countenance? / When shall I awaken satisfied and happy with laughter, / o Lord, according to Thy image?)

O süsser Tod, o lang' gehofftes Ende! / Wann kommst du doch einmal heran, / dass ich den Lauf auf Erden einst vollende / und völlig überwinden kann? / Der Sünde Macht gar bald erliegt, / wenn sie durch Jesum wird besiegt; / wenn du, mein Licht, wirst ganz aufgehen, / so kann die Nacht nicht mehr bestehen. (O sweet death, o long hoped for end! / When art thou coming then, / so that I may finish my course on earth / and can fully overcome it? / The power of sin quite soon submits, / when it is conquered through Jesus; / when Thou, my Light, will really arise, / then night can remain no more.) (Georg Freidrich Breithaupt, 1704)

is a very suitable chorale for home performance as Schemelli intended for any chorale in his collection.

O liebe Seele, zieh' die Sinnen / von schnöder Welt und Wollust ab, / so ruft dein Schöpfer von der Zinnen / der hohen Himmelsburg herab. / Er zeigt die Wege und schöne Stege, / auf welchen du dich recht kannst laben / und alles haben / worinnen deine Seele findet Ruh'. (O dear soul, draw they senses away / from the vile world and lust; / so the Creator calls down from the pinnacles / of the high fortress of heaven. / He shows thee ways and beautiful paths, / on which thou canst really refresh thyself / and have everything / in which thy soul finds rest.)

Es gibt dir alles gute Lehren, / wenn due nur suchst wie's billig ist, / das Lob des Höchsten zu vermehren / und nicht mehr eit'len Sinnes bist. / Lass deine Augen nur Gutes saugen / aus jedem Blatt! Komm, lass dich lehren / von Halm und Ähren, / ob man nicht Ursach' oft zu preisen hat! (Everything gives thee good teaching, / if only thou seekest as it is reasonable / to spread the praise of the Highest / and art no more of a vain mind. / Let thy eyes extract only good / from every leaf! Come, let thyself be taught / by blade and ear of corn / whether one does not often have cause for praising!) (Georg Christian Schemelli, 1736)

## O LIEBE SEELE, ZIEH' DIE SINNEN (BWV 494; B.G. 59)

The connection between the soul and God's creation in nature makes this hymn an exceptional dramatic monologue. Bach's setting with a joy motif seems to reflect the lesson of God in nature as stated by the text. It

## SELIG WER AN JESUM DENKT (BWV 498; B.G. 64)

This chorale returns to the pattern of repeating the last two lines in each stanzas as a refrain. Bach sets these lines with a grief motif, thus making the hymn a lament, although the didactic tone of the text would probably indicate a joy motif for the thought expressed.

It seems as though the soloist has assumed the role of a preacher, who admonishes mankind to remember how God has favored us by sending His Son to bear our guilt.

Selig wer an Jesum denkt, / der für uns am Kreuz gestorben, / der das Leben uns geschenkt, / der uns seine Gnad' erworben. / Ach, ihr Menschen, denket d'ran, / ach gedenket, was Gott hat für euch getan! (Blessed is whoever thinks of Jesus, / who died for us on the cross, / who gave us the gift of life, / who won for us His mercy. / Ah, ye men, think about it; / ah, remember what God has done for you!)

O wie gross ist seine Huld! / O wie hat er uns begnadet, / dass sein liebster Sohn die Schuld / uns'rer Sünden auf sich ladet! / Ach, ihr Menschen, denket d'ran, / ach gedenket, was Gott hat für euch getan! (O how great is His kindness! / O how He has favored us, / in that His dearest Son loads upon Himself / the guilt of our sins! / Ah, ye men, think about it, / ah, remember what God has done for you!) (Text by "A.G.B.," 1736 — melody is anonymous, 1736)

## SO WÜNSCH' ICH MIR ZU GUTER LETZT (BWV 502; B.G. 68)

This hymn is in the form of a personal prayer for a peaceful death. A motif of solemnity befits the mood in which the soloist addresses death with a personification that reminds the listener of the chorale BWV 478, "Komm, süsser Tod," which has been previously treated in this section. Both chorales express a longing to be with Jesus after death, but this chorale differs by adding a pastoral touch in

the first stanza, which Bach's melody brings out in the last four lines: Jesus is the Friend mentioned as a Shepherd.

So wünsch' ich mir zu guter Letzt, / ein selig Stündlein, wohl zu sterben, / das mich für allem Leid ergötzt, / und krönet mich zum Himmelserben. / Komm, sanfter Tod, und zeige mir, / wo doch mein Freund in Ruhe weidet, / bis meine Seel' auch mit Begier / zu ihm aus dieser Welt abscheidet. (So I wish finally for myself / a blessed short hour to die well, / that delights me for all my sorrow, / and crowns me as an heir to heaven. / Come, gentle death, and show me / where my Friend gives pasture in peace, / until my soul too with eager desire / departs out of this world to Him.)

Sei gnädig mir, mein treuer Gott, / zu meinen letzten Lebensstunden! / Versüsse mir die Todesnot, / erbarme dich um Christi Wunden! / Mein letzter Wunsch soll dieser sein: / Herr Jesu, nimm in deine Hände / mein Leib und Seel'! So schlaf' ich ein / recht selig dann am Lebensende. (Be merciful to me, my faithful God, / in my last hours of life! / Sweeten the pain of death for me, / pity me for Christ's wounds! / My last wish shall be this: / Lord Jesus, take into Thy hands / my body and soul! Thus I may fall asleep / truly blessed then at the end of my life.) (Johann Rist, 1641 — melody is anonymous [Bach?], 1736)

## VERGISS MEIN NICHT (BWV 505; B.G. 71)

Bach marked this chorale "Aria — Adagio" on his score for it. It must have been one of his favorite prayers to God, as his autograph and the motif of solemnity that he set for its melody would signify. Such deep emotion cannot fail to impress the listener as much as any spoken dramatic scene.

Vergiss mein nicht, vergiss mein nicht, / mein allerliebster Gott. / Ach, höre doch mein Flehen; / ach, lass mir Gnad' geschehen, / wenn ich hab' Angst und Not. / Du meine Zuversicht, vergiss mein nicht, / vergiss mein nicht! (Forget me not; forget me not, / my dearest God. / Ah, hear my beseeching; / ah, let Thy mercy come upon me, / when I have worry and pain. / Thou, my assurance, forget me not, / forget me not!)

Vergiss mein nicht, vergiss mein nicht, / wenn einst der herbe Tod / mir nimmt mein zeitlich Leben; / du kannst ein bess'res geben. / Mein allerliebster Gott, / hör, wenn dein Kind doch spricht: / Vergiss mein nicht, vergiss mein nicht! (Forget me not; forget me not, / when some day harsh death / takes from me my temporal life; / Thou canst give a better one. / My dearest God, / hear, when Thy child speaks: / Forget me not; forget me not!) (Georg Christian Schemelli, 1736)

## GOTT LEBET NOCH
## (BWV 320 + 461; B.G. 25)

The singing of these stanzas from this chorale shows that it could be performed within a church by a choir and soloists with great dramatic impact. The central idea in the text — our confidence in God's protection and guidance — would appeal to all Christians, including Bach and his Leipzig congregations. Throughout his text, a joy motif expresses a general feeling of trust in God.

*Chorus:* Gott lebet noch! / Seele, was verzagst du doch? / Gott ist gut, der aus Erbarmen / alle Hilf auf Erden tut, / der mit Macht und starken Armen / machet alles wohl und gut. / Gott kann besser als wir denken / alle Not zum besten lenken. / Seele, so bedenke doch: / lebt doch unser Herr Gott noch! (God still lives! / Soul, why dost thou then despair? / God is good; He who out of pity / gives all help on earth; / He, who with might and strong arms / does everything well and good. / God can better than we think / direct all trouble for the best. / Soul, then bear in mind: / our Lord God still lives!)

*Soprano:* Gott lebet noch! / Seele, was verzagst du doch? / Sollt der schlummern oder schlafen, / der das Aug' hat zugericht', / der die Ohren hat erschaffen, / sollte dieser hören nicht? / Gott ist Gott, der hört und siehet, / wo den Frommen Weh geschiehet. / Seele, so bedenke doch: / lebt doch unser Herr Gott noch! (God still lives! / Soul, why dost thou then despair? / Should He slumber or sleep, / who has turned His eyes towards thee, / who has created ears, / should this One not hear? / God is God, who hears and sees / where woe occurs to the righteous. / Soul, then bear in mind: / our Lord God still lives!)

*Tenor:* Gott lebet noch! / Seele, was verzagst du doch? / Der den Erdenkreis verhüllet / mit den Wolken weit und breit, / der die ganze Welt erfüllet, / ist von uns nicht fern und weit. / Werr Gott liebt, dem will er senden / Hilf und Trost an allen Enden. / Seele, so bedenke doch: / lebt doch unser Herr Gott noch! (God still lives! / Soul, why dost thou then despair? / He, who covers the earth's orbit / far and wide with clouds, / who fills up the whole world, / is not far away from us. / Whoever loves God, to him will He send / help and comfort for everything. / Soul, then bear in mind: / our Lord God still lives!) (Johann

Friedrich Zihn, 1688 — anonymous melody, 1714)

## IHR GESTIRN',
## IHR HOHLEN LÜFTE
## (BWV 366 + 476; B.G. 40)

The Christmas message in this chorale deserves consideration by any listener, although it does not appear in the present Lutheran hymnary (*Liederbuch*). Bach's setting for this hymn combines a joy motif with a rhythm of solemnity, quite in keeping with the cameo-like scene depicted by the text.

By dividing these selected four stanzas (there are nine in the complete hymn) into two for the chorus and two for the soloists, the dramatic aspect of the scene is highlighted as it would sound to a congregation in Bach's time. In this case, the dialogue would seem to be between the shepherds (the chorus) and two individuals (the soloists) representing the listening congregation in the church.

The modern reconstruction on record has been done by Helmuth Rilling on the CBS Label D2 38972, giving the tenor two stanzas and the soprano soloist one.

*Chorus:* Ihr Gestirn', ihr hohlen Lüfte / und du lichtes Firmament, / tiefes Rund, ihr dunklen Klüfte, / die der Widerschall zertrennt, / jauchzet fröhlich, lass das Singen / jetzt bis durch die Wolken dringen. (You stars, you hollow airs / and you luminous firmament, / you deep sphere, you dark chasms, / which re-echo divides, / rejoice happily, let your singing / now penetrate right through the clouds.)

*Tenor:* Aber du, o Mensch, vor allen / hebe deine Stimme empor, / lass ein Freudenlied erschallen / dort mit jenem Engelchor, / der den Hirten auf der Weide / heut' verkündigt grosse Freude! (But thou, o man, especially / raise up thy voice, / let a song of joy resound / there with the choir of angels, / which to the shepherds in the pasture / today announces great joy!)

*Soprano:* Bethlehem, uns wundert alle, / wie es immer zu mag geh'n, / dass in deinem kleinen Stalle / kann der ganze Himmel steh'n. / Hat denn nun der Sterne Menge / Raum in einer solchen Enge? (Bethlehem, we all wonder, / how it may ever happen, / that in thy small stable / all heaven can stand. / Has the host of stars now / space in such narrowness?)

*Chorus:* Weil du denn die schlechten Hütten, / Jesu, nie verschmähet hast, / ei, so lass dich doch erbitten, / komm doch, komm, du edler Gast! / komm doch in mein Herz hinein, / lass es deine Krippen sein. (Because Thou, Jesus, hast / never despised our mean huts, / o, then let Thyself be requested: / come then, come, Thou noble Guest! / come into my heart, / let it be Thy cradle.) (Johann Franck, 1655 — original melody by Christoph Peter, 1655)

Note that Bach had previously used stanza nine to conclude his *Christmas Oratorio*, Part V. For the text of this stanza nine, see the following section, Chorales in the *Christmas Oratorio*.

## JESUS, UNSER
## TROST UND LEBEN
## (BWV 475; B.G. 39)

Each stanza of this Easter chorale ends up with a repeated "Halleluja" as though to ring out the happiness of this time of year. The association of nature in the joy motif in the second stanza is worthy of note and in keeping with the theme of the Resurrection. This hymn is a dramatic monologue, but which can be adapted to a choral piece, expressing personal human happiness at this time of awakening to new life, symbolized by the Lord's Resurrection.

Jesus, unser Trost und Leben, / welcher war dem Tod ergeben, / der hat herrlich und mit Macht / Sieg und Leben wiederbracht. / Er ist aus des Todes Banden / als ein Siegsfürst auferstanden. / Halleluja, Halleluja. (Jesus, our comfort and life, / who was delivered up to death, / has wonderfully and with power / brought again victory and life. / He has risen out of death's bonds / as a victorious Prince. / Halleluja, Halleluja.)

Alle Welt sich dess' erfreuet, / sich verjünget und erneuet, / alles, alles weit und breit / leget an ein Freuden-kleid; / ja, das Meer vor Freuden wallet, / Berg und Tal weithin er-schallet: Halleluja, Halleluja! (The whole world rejoices over that, / becomes young and renewed; / everything far and wide / puts on a garment of joy; / yes, the sea undulates with joy, / mountain and valley resound afar: Halleluja, Halleluja!) (Ernst Christoph Homburg [1605–81])

## LASSET UNS MIT JESU ZEIHEN (BWV 481; B.G. 45)

This remarkable hymn becomes intensely dramatic when it is performed in the three part arrangement given below, and including all four verses as they appear today in the Lutheran hymnbook. As an Easter chorale, the melody fits the text so well that, with its motif of solemnity, it would seem that Bach must have improved on the original tune to express this degree of emotion.

The text of this Easter chorale points out everything a Christian should seek: imitation of Christ while He was on earth, belief in Him, living a pure life, bearing our suffering as He bore His, and hoping to be with Him in paradise after our own death.

*Chorus:* Lasset uns mit Jesu ziehen, / seinem Vorbild folgen nach, / in der Welt der Welt entfliehen; / auf der Bahn, der er uns brach, / immerfort zum Himmel reisen, / irdisch noch, schon himmlisch sein, / glauben recht und leben rein, / in der Lieb den Glauben weisen. / Treuer Jesu, bleib' bei mir; / gehe vor, ich folge dir. (Let us go with Jesus, / following after His model, / in the world fleeing from the world; / on the path that He broke for us, / continuously travelling to heaven, / being still on earth but already in heaven, / believing rightly and living purely, / showing in love our belief. / Faithful Jesus, stay with me; / go ahead, I am following Thee.)

*Soprano:* Lasset uns mit Jesu leiden, / seinem Vorbild werden gleich. / Nach dem Leide folgen Freuden, / Armut hier macht dorten reich. / Tränensaat, die erntet Lachen; / Hoffnung tröste die Geduld. / Es kann leichtlich Gottes Huld / aus dem Regen Sonne machen. / Jesu, hier leid' ich mit dir, / dort teil' deine Freud' mit mir. (Let us suffer with Jesus, / becoming like His model. / After suffering joys follow; / poverty here makes [us] rich there. / Seed of tears, they harvest laughter; / patience comforts hope. / God's kindness can easily / make sun out of rain. / Jesus, here I suffer with Thee, / there share Thy joy with me.)

*Tenor:* Lasset uns mit Jesu sterben; / sein Tod uns von dem andern Tod / rettet uns vom Seelverderben, / von der ewiglichen Not. / Lasst uns töten, weil wir leben, / unser Fleisch, ihm sterben ab, / so wird er uns aus dem Grab / in das Himmelsleben heben. /

Jesu, sterb' ich, sterb' ich dir, / dass ich lebe für und für. (Let us die with Jesus; / His death saves us from the destruction / of our souls of the other death, / [and] from eternal pain. / Let us mortify our flesh, / because we live, to die for Him, / so that He will raise us out of the grave / into the life of Heaven. / Jesus, if I die, I die for Thee, / so that I may live forever.)

*Chorus:* Lasset uns mit Jesu leben; / weil er auferstanden ist, / muss das Grab uns wiedergeben. / Jesu, unser Haupt du bist; / wir sind deines Leibes Glieder, / wo du lebst, da leben wir; / ach, erkenn' uns für und für, / trauter Freund, für deine Brüder. / Jesu, dir ich lebe hier, / dorten ewig auch bei dir. (Let us live with Jesus; / because He has risen, / the grave must give Him back to us. / Jesus, Thou art our head; / we are the limbs of Thy body, / where Thou livest, there we live; / ah, recognize us forever, / beloved Friend, for Thy brethren. / Jesus, I live for Thee here, / [and] there, too, always with Thee.) (Sigmund von Birken, 1652 — melody by Johann Schop, 1641)

## O WIE SELIG SEID IHR DOCH, IHR FROMMEN (BWV 405 + 495; B.G. 60)

As in the case of BWV 481, all verses of this hymn should be quoted as they appear in the present Lutheran hymnary (No. 579). These six verses seem to prove that it was performed more within a church than for a private social gathering — so it is arranged for chorus and soloists in Helmuth Rilling's modern recording. Also its classification as a funeral chorale, with a grief motif in the melody, would point to this type of service within the church.

It would be difficult to find another hymn in German as dramatic, with alternating chorus and soloists, and as moving, in addressing the departed and Christ at the end.

1. *Chorus:* O wie selig seid ihr doch, ihr Frommen, / die ihr durch den Tod zu Gott gekommen! / Ihr seid entgangen / aller Not, die uns noch hält gefangen. (O how blessed are you, you righteous, / who have come to God through death! / You have departed / from all trouble, that still holds us captive.)

2. *Tenor:* Muss man hier doch wie im Kerker leben, / da nur Sorge, Furcht und Schrecken schweben; / was wir hier kennen, / ist nur Müh und Herzeleid zu nennen. (Must we still live here as in prison, / where only worry, fear and fright hover; / what we know here / is only to be called care and deep sorrow.)

3. *Soprano:* Ihr hingegen ruht in eurer Kammer, / sicher und befreit von allem Jammer; / kein Kreuz und Leiden / ist euch hinderlich in euren Freuden. (You, on the other hand, rest in your small room, / safe and freed from all misery; / no torment and suffering / is hindering you in your joy.)

4. *Tenor:* Christus wischet ab euch alle Tränen, / ihr habt schon, wonach wir uns erst sehnen; / euch wird gesungen, / was durch keines Ohr allhier gedrungen. (Christ wipes away all your tears, / you have already what we have longed for; / to you is sung / what has gone through no ears here.)

5. *Soprano:* Ach, we wollte denn nicht gerne sterben / und den Himmel für die Welt ererben? / Wer wollt' hier bleiben, / sich den Jammer länger lassen treiben? (Ah, who would not gladly wish to die / and inherit heaven for the world? / Who would stay here, / letting misery drive him any longer?)

6. *Chorus:* Komm, o Christe, komme

uns auszuspannen, / lös' uns auf und führ' uns bald von dannen. / Bei dir, o Sonne, / ist der frommen Seelen Freud' und Wonne. (Come, oh Christ, come to release us, / free us and lead us soon from here. / With Thee, oh Sun, / is the joy and bliss of righteous souls.) (Simon Dach, 1635 — melody by Johann Crüger, 1649)

## SEI GEGRÜSSET, JESU GÜTIG (BWV 499 + 410; B.G. 65)

This magnificent hymn for Good Friday consists of five six-line stanzas, but it is doubtful that they were all sung in any solo performance by a tenor or by a soprano. When sung by the congregation, the entire hymn probably was sung. Helmuth Rilling's recording takes four of the five stanzas, and arranges the last two lines in each to be sung by a chorus as a refrain, much as one would hear this chorale inside an eighteenth century Lutheran church.

Either when sung by a soloist or two soloists and a chorus, the words and their musical setting for this chorale surpass many of the other hymns in Schemelli's collection. This personal appeal to Christ in prayer has drama and an emotion that is unique; it would certain attract Bach's attention.

*Tenor:* Sei gegrüsset, Jesu gütig / über alle Mass sanftmütig! / Ach, wie bist du so zerschmissen / und dein ganzer Leib zerrissen! (Be greeted, kind Jesus, / tender-hearted beyond measure! / Ah, how art Thou beaten so / and Thy whole body torn up!)
*Chorus:* Lass mich deine Lieb' ererben / und darinnene selig sterben. (Let me inherit Thy love / and in that die blessed.)

\* \* \*

*Soprano:* O mein Jesu, Gott und mein Heil, / meines Herzens Trost und meine Teil, / beut' mir deine Hand und Seiten, / wenn ich werde sollen streiten. (O my Jesus, my God and my Salvation, / the comfort of my heart and my share, / offer me Thy hand and Thy side, / when I will have to fight.)
*Chorus:* Lass mich deine Lieb' ererben / und darinnen selig sterben. (Let me inherit Thy love / and in that die blessed.)

\* \* \*

*Tenor:* Schone, Jesu, meiner Sünde, / weil ich mich zu dir ja finde / mit betrübtem Geist und Herzen; / dein Blut lindert meine Schmerzen. (Spare [me], Jesus, for my sin, / because I have come to Thee / with a sad spirit and heart; / Thy blood alleviates my pain.)
*Chorus:* Lass mich deine Lieb' ererben / und darinnen selig sterben. (Let me inherit Thy love / and in that die blessed.)

\* \* \*

*Soprano:* O wie freundlich kannst du laben, / Jesu, alle, die dich haben; / die sich halten an dein Leiden, / können seliglich abscheiden. (O in how friendly a way Thou canst refresh, / Jesus, all those who hold to Thee; / those who endure with Thy suffering / can depart with Thy blessing.)
*Chorus:* Lass much deine lieb' ererben / und darinnen selig sterben. (Let me inherit Thy love / and in it die blessed.)

\* \* \*

(Christian Keymann, 1663 — melody by Gottfried Vopelius, 1682)

## UNS IST EIN KINDLEIN HEUT GEBORN (BWV 414)

To illustrate that the chorale texts and their tunes were changing in the seventeenth and in the eighteenth centuries in Germany, this Christmas chorale in the Schemelli collection must have been drawn to Bach's attention, as it has a BWV number given to it. The anonymous text, dated 1601 as number 40 in the present Lutheran *Liederbuch,* was originally written by Lucas Lossius in the previous century. Therefore, Bach must have known both these texts when he submitted his version to Schemelli. The Lossius version has the last two lines of each stanza repeated as a refrain, as follows:

*Chorus:*

1. Uns ist ein Kindelein heut geborn / von einer Jungfrau auserkorn. / Des freuen sich die Engelein; / sollen wir Menschen nicht fröhlich sein? / Lob, Preis und Dank sei Gott bereit' / für solche Gnad in Ewigkeit. (Unto us a little Child is born today, / chosen from one Maiden. / At that the little angels rejoice; / should we men not be happy? / Laud, praise and thanks be to God / eternally for such mercy.)

2. Er hat erlöset uns vom Tod / und wieder bracht zu Gnad bei Gott; / er heilt der gift'gen / Schlangen Biss, / den wir bekamen im Paradies. / Lob, Preis und Dank sei Gott bereit' / für solche Gnad in Ewigkeit. (He has redeemed us from death / and brought us again to God's mercy; / He heals the bite of the poisonous snakes, / which we received in Paradise. / Laud, praise and thanks be to God / eternally for such mercy.)

3. Drum preiset dieses Kindelein / mit allen heilgen Engelein, / das freundlich aus sein Windelein / uns lachet an im Krippelein. / Lob, Preis und Gnad sei Gott bereit' / für solche Gnad in Ewigkeit. (Therefore praise this little Child / with all little holy angels, / Who in a friendly way, from His swaddling, / laughs to us in His little crib. / Laud, praise and thanks be to God / eternally for such mercy.) (Lucas Lossius, 1508–82)

This chorale, sung in unison by the choir, is a most moving tribute to the Child.

# Chorales in the *Christmas Oratorio*
# (1734; BWV 24)

Bach's interest in the Lutheran chorales of his own and of the time since Luther is shown by their use in the chorale cantatas that he composed in Leipzig. He had made his own private collection of these chorales, which he could consult as he composed his organ or vocal works.

Terry, in his book *The Music of Bach: An Introduction* (68–69), mentions the four different types of chorale that bach set:

1. Extended Chorale — simple four-part settings, but each line of the melody separated from the next by instrumental interludes.

2. Unison Chorale — the hymn is sung by one or more voices with instrumental accompaniment.

3. Aria Chorale — the melody of the hymn is woven into the movement as a solo, duet or trio.

4. Recitative and Chorale — a "dialogue chorale" between two voices, one singing the hymn, while the other comments on it in free poetry.

Of the sixteen chorale movements in the *Christmas Oratorio,* the majority belong to the Unison Chorale type. For this work they would be classified as:

1. Extended — numbers 9, 23, 42, 64

2. Unison—numbers 5, 12, 17, 28, 33, 35, 46, 53, 59
3. Aria—numbers 38, 40
4. Recitative and Chorale—number 7

These chorale insertions into the total libretto show how important the church hymn was for Bach. Like the chorus in a classical Greek tragedy, each chorale is a comment in song on the dramatic action that has just taken place, but as Spitta observes: "The ground covered by the Gospel narrative of Christmas events is much narrower, and the incidents themselves are less tragical and vivid than those of the Passions; hence the lyric element becomes more important, and, as a whole, it decidedly tends to the style of the church cantata.... Even connected portions of the Gospel, treated as such by Bach himself, are not unfrequently interrupted by reflections in verse, which never occur in the Passions" (II, 581).

This is not to say, however, that this work is lacking in drama, but rather that the chorale interjections enhance the dramatic action by expressing the reaction of the congregation to what has taken place. Furthermore, these hymns, sung from Christmas Day to Epiphany, were familiar to the Lutheran population of Saxony, so Bach could be sure that they would make his *Christmas Oratorio* appealing.

The Christmas drama is unfolded in three sections: the first three parts narrate the birth of Christ, the fourth the naming of Jesus, and the fifth and sixth the visit of the three kings. Although each part or cantata is for a separate day, together they form a complete work as shown by the first chorale of Part I being repeated as a chorale fantasia at the end of Part VI. (The numeral represents the number of the chorale movement in the complete work.)

# PART I

5. *Unison Chorale.* This number is sung by the full four-part choir with instrumental accompaniment. Following the beautiful alto aria (number 4), which is addressed to Zion, personified as a bride, on how she should receive her bridegroom Christ at His birth, this first chorale stanza in the work conveys the emotion that every Christian should feel, as he too greets the newborn Child.

The melody for this number will be repeated in number 17 following, and again enlarged for the full orchestra in the final chorale, number 64. Bach had already used this melody for the "Passion Chorale" (numbers 21, 23, 53, 63, 72)—"O Haupt voll Blut und Wunden" (O Sacred Head Now Wounded) by Hans Leo Hassler in the *St. Matthew Passion.* Spitta sees in this "a premonition of Christ's death ... which falls across the bright festal tone like a dim shadow" (II, 579).

Wie soll ich dich empfangen, / Und wie begegn' ich dir? / O aller Welt Verlangen, / O meiner Seelen Zier! / O Jesu, Jesu, setze / Mir selbst die Fackel bei, / Damit, was dich ergötze, / Mir kund und wissend sei. (How should I receive Thee, / And how do I meet Thee? / O Thou longing of the whole world, / O Thou adornment of my soul! / O Jesus, Jesus, set / Thy torch beside me, / So that, whatever delights Thee, / Be made clear and known to me.) (Paul Gerhardt, 1653 [stanza one])

7. *Chorale and Recitative (Soprano, Bass):* This number is a combination of a hymn text, sung by the soprano, alternating with a recitative in free poetry that is sung by the bass in cantus firmus. This verse six of Martin Luther's 1524 hymn "Gelobet seist du, Jesu Christ" (Praised Be Thou, Jesus Christ" occurs after the Evangelist has

quoted St. Luke 2:7 — describing the scene of the birth of Christ. The soprano sings each line of the hymn, after which the bass comments on it. Both chorale and recitative add to the drama which affects the emotions of the congregation.

Bach had used this method before in setting some movements in his cantatas (e.g. BWV 27 of 1731 — the first movement: "Wer Weiss, Wie Nahe Mir Mein Ende" [Who Knows, How Near to Me My End]).

*Soprano.* Er ist auf Erden kommen arm. (He has come to earth poor.)

*Bass.* Wer kann die Liebe recht erhöhn, / Die unser Heiland vor uns hegt? (Who can really estimate the love / That our Savior has for us?)

*Soprano.* Dass er unser sich erbarm, (So that He pities us,)

*Bass.* Ja, wer vermag es einzusehen, / Wie ihn der Menschen Leid bewegt? (Yes, who may perceive / How men's sorrow moves Him?)

*Soprano.* Und in dem Himmel mache reich, (And that it may make us rich in heaven.)

*Bass.* Des Höchsten Sohn kömmt in die Welt, / Weil ihm ihr Heil so wohl gefällt, (The Son of the Highest comes into the world, / Because its salvation pleases Him so well,)

*Soprano.* Und seinen lieben Engeln gleich, (And likewise His dear angels,)

*Bass.* So will er selbst als Mensch geboren werden. (So He Himself wishes to be born as a Man.)

*Soprano.* Kyrieleis! (God, have mercy!)

9. *Extended Chorale.* This is the thirteenth stanza of Martin Luther's chorale "Vom Himmel hoch, da komm ich her" (From Heaven Above, I Come), with which the congregation would be well acquainted on every Christmas Day since its composition in 1535. The orchestral interlude after each line is sung by a four part choir

with spectacular effect to reinforce the prayer of this text; after the tribute to the Christ Child, expressed in the preceding bass aria (number 8), this verse continues the thought that the newborn Child can find a soft bed in our hearts rather than in the hard crib just mentioned. The transfer in this thought from the bass soloist to the choir, representing the congregation, makes the drama even more realistic.

Ach, mein herzliches Jesulein! / Mach' dir ein rein sanft Bettelein, / Zu ruh'n in meines Herzens Schrein, / Dass ich nimmer vergesse dein. (Ah, my heart-beloved little Jesus! / Make Thyself a pure soft little bed, / To rest in the shrine of my heart, / So that I may never forget Thee.)

## PART II

12. *Unison Chorale.* Following the pastorale sinfonia (number 10) and the Evangelist's recitative (number 11), this aptly chosen ninth stanza of Johann Rist's 1641 hymn, "Ermuntre dich, mein schwacher Geist" (Take Courage, My Weak Spirit), supports the scriptural passage (St. Luke 2:8–9) with a similar imagery in its text. This choral number resembles a classical Greek chorus as it comments on the dramatic action with a Christmas hymn, familiar to all the congregation.

Brich an, due schönes Morgenlicht, / Und lass den Himmel tagen! / Du Hirtenvolk, erschrecke nicht, / Weil dir die Engel sagen: / Dass dieses schwache Knäbelein / Soll unser Trost und Freude sein, / Dazu den Satan zwingen / Und letztlich Friede bringen. (Break forth, thou beautiful morning light, / And let the sky become day! / You shepherd folk, be not afraid, / Because the angels say to you: / That this weak little boy / Is to be our consolation and joy, / In that He will overcome Satan / And finally bring peace.)

17. *Unison Chorale*. Stanza eight of Paul Gerhardt's 1667 hymn, "Schaut, schaut, was für Wunder dar" (Look, Look, What a Wonder Is There), begins this verse with the same verb (*schaut*—look) and refers to the Evangelist's Biblical quotation just given (St. Luke 2:12)—that the shepherds will find the Child lying in a manger. The command to behold the scene is given to both the shepherds and the audience, thus bringing the latter immediately into the drama.

Schaut hin! dort liegt im finstern Stall, / Des Herrschaft gehet über all. / Da Speise vormals sucht ein Rind, / Da ruhet itzt der Jungfrau's Kind. (Look there! There lies in the gloomy stable / He whose glory goes over all. / There formerly a steer sought fodder, / There now rests the Virgin's Child.)

Bach uses the same melody for this verse as he had set for chorale nine, above.

23. *Extended Chorale*. Bach chose stanza two of Paul Gerhardt's chorale, "Wir singen dir, Immanuel" (We Sing to Thee, Immanuel) (1653), for the final number of Part II. Decorated with instrumental playing after each line sung, this number reflects in its joy motif the angelic jubilation of the chorus in number 21 (St. Luke 2:13–14).

Once again, the congregation is brought into the drama by the chorus representing it, as the well known melody, "Vom Himmel hoch" (From Heaven Above), is heard. This was the same melody as was heard in numbers nine and seventeen, above.

Wir singen dir in deinem Heer / Aus aller Kraft Lob, Preis und Ehr, / Dass du, o langgewünschter Gast, / Dich nunmehr eingestellet hast. (We sing to Thee in Thy host / With all our strength: laud, praise and honor, / That Thou, o long wished for Guest, / Hast now come among us.)

## PART II

28. *Unison Chorale*. As for Chorale number seven in this work, Martin Luther's melody for his hymn "Gelobet seist du, Jesu Christ" (Praised Be Thou, Jesus Christ) (1524) is used again here in the seventh stanza of the hymn. The two preceding numbers having mentioned the shepherds' resolve to go to Bethlehem to see the Infant and to learn of the benefits that He would bring to His people, this verse extends the feeling of thanksgiving beyond Israel to all Christendom for the same help and redemption that He will give.

Dies hat er alles uns getan, / Sein gross Lieb zu zeigen an; / Des freu sich alle Christenheit, / Und dank ihm des in Ewigkeit. / Kyrieleis! (All this He has done for us, / To show His great love. / For this may all Christendom rejoice, / And thank Him eternally for that. / Lord, have mercy!)

33. *Unison Chorale*. Here stanza 15 of the 1653 chorale by Paul Gerhardt, "Fröhlich soll mein Herze springen" (Happily Shall My Heart Leap), repeats the joy that Mary expresses in her aria (number 31) and recitative (number 32) at the birth of her Son. The choir could as well represent our own happiness as it sings the words of the text with a joy motif of voices and instruments.

Ich will dich mit Fleiss bewahren, / Ich will dir / Leben hier, / Dir will ich abfahren. / Mit dir will ich endlich schweben, / Voller Freud', / Ohne Zeit, / Dort im andern Leben. (I will diligently keep Thee. / I will for Thee / Live here; / To Thee will I depart. / With Thee finally soar, / Full of joy, / Without time, / There in the other life.)

35. *Unison Chorale*. Bach chose here a different chorale, stanza four of "Lasst Furcht und Pein" (Leave Fear and Pain (1653), by Christoph Runge,

to comment on the departure of the shepherds from Bethlehem. Via the choir, this verse once again brings the congregation into active participation in the drama.

Seid froh dieweil, / Dass euer Heil / Ist hie ein Gott und auch ein Mensch geboren. / Der, welcher ist / Derr Herr und Christ / In Davids Stadt, von vielen auserkoren. (Be glad the while, / That your Savior / Has here been born a God and also a Man. / He who is / The Lord and Christ, / In David's city, chosen from many.)

## PART IV

Spitta states that Part IV pertains the least of any part to the Christmas festival, because it contains no true Christmas hymn, but rather sections of chorales and one complete chorale stanza. Therefore this section "bears more strongly the stamp merely of a religious composition... and can only have derived its full significance for congregational use from its position in context with the rest of the work" (II, 585).

This judgment seems to be true, since all the chorale parts can be considered as being independent of the preceding Biblical recitative (number 37), the circumcision and the naming of Jesus (St. Luke 2:21). Yet the insertion of chorale verses into this recitative and into number 40 following shows how Bach could vary a recitative with a chorale interpolation, just as he had done in number 7 before.

38. *Aria Chorale: Recitative (Bass) and Duet (Soprano, Bass).* In this number the duet is embedded in the middle of a lengthy recitative, part of the first stanza of "Jesu, du mein liebstes Leben" (Jesus, Thou My Dearest Life) by Johann Rist, 1642, being sung by the soprano alternating with the bass.

*Bass:* Immanuel, o süsses Wort! / Mein Jesus heisst mein Hort, / Mein Jesus heisst mein Leben. / Mein Jesus hat sich mir ergeben, / Mein Jesus soll mir immerfort / Vor meinen Augen schweben. / Mein Jesus heisset mein Lust, / Mein Jesus labet Herz und Brust. (Immanuel, o sweet word! / My Jesus is my protector; / My Jesus is my life. / My Jesus has given Himself for me; / My Jesus shall forever more / Be present before my eyes. / My Jesus is my pleasure; / My Jesus refreshes my heart and breast.)

*Soprano:* Jesu, du mein liebstes Leben (Jesu, Thou my dearest life,)

*Bass:* Komm, ich will dich mit Lust umfassen. (Come, I will embrace Thee with joy.)

*Soprano:* Meiner Seelen Bräutigam, (Thou Bridegroom of my soul,)

*Bass:* Mein Herze soll dich nimmer lassen; (My heart shall never leave Thee;)

*Soprano:* Der du dich vor mich gegeben (Thou who gavest Thyself for me)

*Bass:* Ach! so nimm mich zu dir! (Ah! Then take me unto Thee!)

*Soprano:* An des bittern Kreuzes Stamm! (On the tree of the bitter Cross!)

In the above duet, Bach endows the bass part with a sense of deep pathos in each of his lines, but increasing in the last line of his arioso.

*Bass:* Auch in dem Sterben sollst du mir / Das Allerliebste sein; / In Not, Gefahr und Ungemach / Seh' ich dir sehnlichst nach. / Was jagte mir zuletzt der Tod für Grauen ein? / Mein Jesus! Wenn ich sterbe, / So weiss ich, dass ich nicht verderbe. / Dein Name steht in mir geschrieben, / Der hat des Todes Furcht vertrieben. (Even in dying shalt Thou / Be to me the dearest of all; / In need, danger and trouble / I look to Thee most yearningly. / Why did death terrify me until now? / My Jesus! When I die, / Then I know that I will not perish. / Thy Name stands written upon me; / It hath driven away the fear of death.)

40. *Aria Chorale: Recitative (Bass) and Chorale (Soprano)*. The same duet as in number 38 is continued here, with the bass and the soprano lines being sung independently of each other with even more dramatic effect. The chorale is the second part of Johann Rist's 1642 composition, begun in number 38.

*Bass:* Wohlan! dein Name soll allein (So be it! Thy Name shall alone)

*Soprano:* Jesu, meine Freud' und Wonne, / Mein Hoffnung, Schatz und Teil, (Jesus, my joy and bliss, / My hope, treasure and share,)

*Bass:* In meinem Herzen sein. (Be in my heart.)

*Soprano:* Mein Erlöser, Schutz und Heil, / Hirt und König, Licht und Sonne! (My Redeemer, Protector and Salvation, / Shepherd and King, Light and Sun!)

*Bass:* So will ich dich entzücket nennen, / Wenn Brust und Herz zu dir vor Liebe brennen. / Doch, Liebster, sage mir: (Therefore I will call Thy Name delightedly, / When my breast and heart burn with love for Thee. / Yet, dearest One, tell me:)

*Soprano:* Ach, wie soll ich würdiglich, / Mein Herr Jesu, preisen dich? (Ah, how am I worthily, / My Lord Jesus, to praise Thee?)

*Bass:* Wie rühm' ich dich, wie dank' ich dir? (How do I praise Thee; how do I thank Thee?)

Note how the bass repeats this last line several times in arioso until the soprano finishes her chorale. This resulted because at the beginning the bass had to repeat his first two lines to enable the soprano to overtake him. This would prove that Bach had devoted considerable thought to how he

should set a chorale into a recitative.

42. *Extended Chorale*. This is stanza 15 of a 1642 chorale by Johann Rist, "Hilf, Herr Jesu, lass gelingen" (Help, Lord Jesus, Let It Succeed).

Although Spitta had pointed out that this cantata had no Christmas connotations (cf. II, 585), he does say on the next page that "In the verse of the final chorale, Rist begins every line with the name in whose honour the day is held sacred." This would then indicate a personal prayer to Jesus in public or private worship on a day that was sacred for Him.

Therefore, Part IV of this work certainly fits into the scheme of six cantatas comprising the main feast days of Christmas, even though its narrative may be meager with only one recitative for the Evangelist. The joy motif in the instrumental ritornelli featuring the trumpet after each line sung by the choir would surely prove that Bach meant to glorify his Savior on this festive day. Intense drama is certainly built up with each line beginning with a call to Jesus—a group prayer in which the audience can identify itself.

Jesus richte mein Beginnen, / Jesus bleibe stets bei mir! / Jesus zäume mir die Sinnen, / Jesus sei nur mein Begier, / Jesus sei mir in Gedanken, / Jesu, lasse mich nicht wanken! (Jesus, direct my beginning; / Jesus, stay always with me! / Jesus, discipline my senses; / Jesus, be my only desire; / Jesus, be in my thoughts; / Jesus, let me not waver!)

This chorale is still in the present Lutheran *Liederbuch*, number 522 for New Years Day, but has been reduced to five stanzas.

## PART V

The two chorale numbers in this part of the *Christmas Oratorio* are of the unison type and comment effectively on the preceding action.

Both the opening chorus (number 48) and the trio (number 51) were "borrowed" from two of his unknown cantatas, but in my opinion, they are two of the most moving numbers in the entire work.

Concerning all parts of the *Christmas Oratorio,* Denis Arnold writes: "Whether taken from other sources or not, the music is magnificent, a great antidote to the picture of Bach the lover of death, and the musician of the Passions. Here he loves birth (there is a rare tenderness in a number of movements) and the Saving of the World by the word incarnate. What the *Christmas Oratorio* is not, is dramatic. Though the series of scenes which it paints tell a story, there is little sense of movement, no feeling of urgency" (*Bach*, 64).

I would agree with the first two sentences of the above, but strongly disagree with the last two. Even in this Part V alone, there is drama in the visit of the Wise Men (number 45)—the dialogue between the Wise Men (the Chorus) and Mary (the Alto Recitative)—and movement implied in Herod's reaction to the news of Christ's birth. Certainly this sort of drama and movement are different from what one would expect in opera, but the same "feeling of urgency" is definitely there in the emotions expressed (cf. numbers 48, 49, 50).

46. *Unison Chorale.* Georg Weissel (1590–1635) was the poet for this chorale, "Nun, liebe Seel', nun ist es Zeit" (Now, Dear Soul, Now It Is Time) of which this is the fifth stanza. Immediately following the dialogue between the Wise Men and Mary (number 45), this text could have been chosen to represent the words of divine adoration uttered by the Magi before the Divine Child. Again, Bach

may have intended it to involve the emotions of each person in the congregation as it is sung by the choir on his behalf.

Dein Glanz all Finsternis verzehrt, / Die trübe Nacht in Licht verkehrt. / Leit uns auf deinen Wegen, / Dass dein Gesicht / Und herrlichs Licht / Wir ewig schauen mögen. (Thy splendor consumes all darkness; / It turns sad night into light. / Lead us into Thy paths, / So that upon Thy face / And radiant light / We evermore may look.)

The following bass aria (number 47) would also tend to influence the individual worshipper's reaction to the scene.

53. *Unison Chorale.* This is stanza nine of Johann Franck's 1655 hymn "Ihr Gestirn, ihr hohlen Lüfte" (Ye Stars, Ye Empty Airs), which concludes Part V. This chorale must have been one of Bach's favorite Christmas hymns, because it appears here two years before it was included in Schemelli's collection.

The metaphor of the heart being the dwelling of Christ begins with the Trio (number 51) and continues in the Alto Recitative (number 52). This imagery is extended to this chorale stanza, as if to reinforce the thought that Christ must be in our hearts just as He was for Mary and for the Wise Men.

Zwar ist solche Herzensstube, / Wohl kein schöner Fürstensaal, / Sondern eine finstre Grube; / Doch, sobald dein Gnadenstrahl / In denselben nur wird blinken, / Wird es voller Sonnen dünken. (Certainly such a room for the heart / Is not a beautiful princely hall, / But a dismal cavity; / Yet, as soon as Thy ray of mercy / Only sparkles in the same, / It will appear to be full of suns.)

## PART VI

59. *Unison Chorale.* This is stanza one of Paul Gerhardt's Christmas hymn of this title (1653), which Bach has placed right after the Evangelist's Recitative (number 58), describing the offerings of the Wise Men: gold, frankincense and myrrh, to impress on each member of the congregation his own obligation to give to the Divine Infant. Bach uses the traditional melody by Johannes Magdeburg "Es ist gewisslich an der Zeit" (It Is Truly at This Time) (1565) for his setting here (number 582 in the modern Lutheran hymnbook), but gave his own melody in Schemelli's Song Book (number 45).

Ich steh' an deiner Krippen hier, / O Jesulein, mein Leben. / Ich komme, bring' und schenke dir, / Was du mir hast gegeben. / Nimm hin, es ist mein Geist und Sinn, / Herz, Seel' und Mut, nimm alles hin / Und lass dirs wohlgefallen! (I stand here beside Thy manger, / O little Jesus, my life. / I come, bring and present to Thee / What Thou hast given me. / Take it; it is my soul and mind, / Heart, spirit and courage; take everything / And let it please Thee well!)

64. *Extended Chorale.* Stanza four of "Ihr Christen auserkoren" (Ye Chosen Christians) (1648), by Georg Werner (1589–1643) is set to conclude this last part of the work. The penultimate number (63) is a recita-tive-quartet for the four soloists, which, though brief, turns the dramatic action from the threatened evil of Herod's persecution to the ultimate good of Christ's triumph.

Confidence that our belief in Jesus will protect us from the evils that beset us in this world is well expressed by each line of this verse followed by its own instrumental ritornelli. The melody for this chorale is the same as that which Bach had used for the first chorale (number 5) in the work; he thus achieves a symmetry in format — at least for the way that he inserts these two chorale stanzas to the same tune.

Nun seid ihr wohy gerochen / An eurer Feinde Schar, / Denn Christus hat zerbrochen / Was euch zuwider war. / Tod, Teufel, Sünd' und Hölle / Sind ganz und gar geschwächt; / Bei Gott hat seine Stelle / Das menschliche Geschlecht. (Now you are well avenged / On the host of your enemies, / For Christ has broken up / That which was against you. / Death, the Devil, sin and hell / Are completely weakened; / With God has its place / The human race.)

It is fitting that Bach should close this masterpiece with a chorale, since he was the champion of this type of religious composition, not only in this work but in all his vocal writing. And the dramatic value of the chorale to illustrate and comment on events is as apparent here as it was in Bach's passions.

# VII. The Importance of the Chorale in Bach's Style of Composing

From his first thought of composing for his Church, Bach was preoccupied with the hymns that had been sung by Protestant congregations since Luther's time. He expressed the tunes for these chorales not only in his vocal settings, but also in his instrumental works, especially his organ chorales. The chorale thus became the basis upon which Bach built much of his vocal work.

Terry summarizes the importance that Bach placed on the chorale:

> Of the Cantata, Passion, Oratorio, Motet, Organ Prelude, Fugue, and Variation, it (the chorale) controlled the form and supplied the material. Bach's art is inextricably associated with it. His earliest and his last work as a composer was based on it. All the Chorals in common use he harmonized with matchless skill. They are rarely absent from his Cantatas and Oratorios. They provide the core of his Passions, the most intimate part of his Motets. His Organ technique was developed on them, and they are the theme of the bulk of his music for that instrument. In brief, he associated them with all he did in the service of God, embellishing them like precious jewels in a holy shrine" [*Bach: The Historial Approach*, 30–31].

The essential part that the chorale plays in the development of drama in both the passions and the Church cantatas is most evident to the audience. The role of the chorale in the passions has been given in detail under the heading for that particular work; that in the cantatas may be generally indicated for many of them by saying that Bach begins with a chorale fantasia to introduce the cantata, and then concludes with a plainly sung version of the same (or another) hymn. Moreover, he inserts chorales frequently into the inner movements of cantatas, thus producing a dramatic effect similar to sections of the passions where chorales occur.

Basil Smallman points out how Bach's use of the chorale made him different from his contemporary composers:

> Bach is unique for his time in the use he makes of the chorale. His great contemporaries, Handel, Keiser, Telemann and Mattheson tended to regard the ancient hymns as an outmoded form of expression in church music, which had no place in the new, elegant, more theatrical style. But in the Passions and the later church cantatas and organ works, Bach repeatedly affirms the importance of the chorales as a vital source

of religious and musical inspiration and thereby retains a valuable link with the true Lutheran tradition [*The Background of Passion Music: J.S. Bach and His Predecessors*, 87].

There is no doubt that Bach was keenly aware of the value of the chorale for developing his sacred dramas, whether they were in a long form (the passions) or in a short form (the cantatas and the sacred songs). By inserting chorale tunes into his vocal works, Bach heightens the emotional tension of the unfolding drama.

This is the view of many musicologists on Bach's chorales. For example, Archibald T. Davison, referring to the *St. Matthew,* states:

> The chorales represent, to a great extent, the meditative element, and as such would appear to be an unwarranted interruption of dramatic progress; but upon examination they prove to be, both in text and music, most apposite links between the sections of the work. Bach used the music of the Passion chorale five times in the *St. Matthew*; similarly, the melody "Herzliebster Jesu" is introduced three times and "Welt, sieh'hier dein Leben" twice. Thus these chorales have actual dramatic virtue, as the

repeated ritornelli do in Monteverdi's *Orfeo,* reminding us of the tragic continuity of the story [*Bach and Handel: The Consummation of the Baroque in Music,* 53].

This appreciation of Bach's exploitation of the chorale for its dramatic effect might also be extended to include his sacred cantatas, motets and sacred songs, which he treated as miniature religious "stage" presentations in musical form. The dramatic aspect in the latter two categories has already been mentioned, so that now only those various chorales that Bach set for his sacred cantata movements remain to be amplified. Yet it is Bach's music that unites these hymns into the dramatic unity.

Under section III (The Masses) of this book, four types of chorale in the *Christmas Oratorio* with its six cantatas were indicated. Terry adds three more to make seven in his classification of the chorales in Bach's cantatas (cf. *Bach's Chorals, Part II, The Hymns and Hymn Melodies of the Cantatas and Motetts,* 35–44).

The next chapter will define each of these seven categories and show the movement in the cantata where they occur.

# VIII. Table of the Chorale Movements in the Bach Cantatas

*(indicated by the numbers in parentheses)*

1. *The Chorale Fantasia.* This number is usually, but not always, the opening movement in a cantata. In my opinion, most of these movements are really chorale motets; this I have tried to show in section V — Motet Movements Found in the Bach Cantatas. From his organ chorale preludes, Bach developed their tunes into concertos for voices and instruments, i.e. a chorale fantasia.

There are 78 movements in this form.

BWV number: 1 (1), 2 (1), 3 (1), 4 (2), 4 (5), 5 (1), 7 (1), 8 (1), 9 (1), 10 (1), 11 (11), 14 (1), 16 (1), 20 (1), 21 (9), 23 (4), 26 (1), 27 (1), 28 (2), 33 (1), 38 (1), 41 (1), 61 (1), 61 (6), 62 (1), 68 (5), 73 (1), 77 (1), 78 (1), 80 (1), 80 (5), 91 (1), 92 (1), 93 (1), 94 (1), 95 (1), 96 (1), 97 (1), 98 (1), 99 (1), 100 (1), 101 (1), 106 (3), 107 (1), 109 (5), 111 (1), 112 (1), 113, (1), 114 (1), 115 (1), 116 (1), 117 (1), 118, 121 (1), 122 (1), 123 (1), 124 (1), 125 (1), 126 (1), 127 (1), 128 (1), 129 (1), 130 (1), 133 (1), 135 (1), 137 (1), 138 (1), 138 (3), 138 (7), 139 (1), 140 (1), 143 (7), 177 (1), 178 (1), 180 (1), 182 (7), 192 (1), 192 (3).

2. *The Simple Chorale.* Most choral movements in the cantatas are in simple hymn form, just as they were in the passions. It should be noted that they are the unadorned version of the chorale fantasias listed above and are

regularly the last movement, whether the same or a different chorale than used in the opening.

There are 131 simple hymns in the cantatas.

BWV number: 2 (6), 3 (6), 4 (8), 5 (7), 6 (6), 7 (7), 8 (6), 9 (7), 10 (7), 11 (6), 13 (6), 14 (6), 16 (6), 17 (7), 18 (5), 20 (7), 20 (11), 25 (6), 26 (6), 27 (6), 28 (6), 30 (6), 32 (6), 33 (6), 36 (4), 36 (8), 37 (6), 38 (6), 39 (7), 40 (3), 40 (8), 42 (7), 43 (11), 44 (7), 45 (7), 47 (5), 48 (3), 48 (7), 55 (5), 56 (5), 57 (8), 60 (5), 62 (6), 64 (2), 64 (8), 65 (7), 66 (6), 67 (4), 67 (7), 70 (7), 72 (6), 73 (5), 74 (8), 77 (6), 78 (7), 80 (8), 81 (7), 83 (5), 84 (5), 85 (6), 86 (6), 87 (7), 88 (7), 89 (6), 90 (5), 92 (9), 93 (7), 94 (8), 96 (6), 99 (6), 102 (7), 103 (6), 108 (6), 110 (7), 111 (6), 113 (8), 114 (7), 115 (6), 116 (6), 117 (4), 117 (9), 119 (9), 120 (6), 121 (6), 122 (6), 123 (6), 124 (6), 125 (6), 126 (6), 127 (5), 132 (6), 133 (6), 135 (6), 139 (6), 140 (7), 144 (3), 144 (6), 145 (5), 146 (8), 148 (6), 151 (5), 153 (1), 153 (5), 153 (9), 154 (3), 154 (8), 155 (5), 156 (6), 157 (5), 158 (4), 159 (5), 161 (1), 162 (6), 163 (6), 164 (6), 165 (6), 166 (6), 168 (6), 169 (7), 176 (6), 177 (5), 178 (7), 179 (6), 180 (7), 183 (5), 184 (5), 187 (7), 188 (6), 194 (6), 197 (5), 197 (10).

3. *The Embellished Chorale.* These chorales are simply a decorated form

of the simple chorale. Whereas in the simple chorale, the orchestra only doubles the vocal parts, in this type the instruments play independently to ornament the tune.

There are 31 embellished chorales, of which most occur in the last movement.

BWV number: 1 (7), 12 (7), 19 (7), 29 (7), 31 (9), 52 (6), 59 (3), 64 (4), 65 (2), 69 (6), 70 (11), 79 (6), 91 (6), 95 (9), 97 (9), 101 (7), 104 (6), 112 (5), 128 (5), 130 (6), 136 (6), 137 (5), 149 (7), 161 (6), 172 (6), 174 (5), 175 (7), 185 (6), 190 (7), 194 (12), 195 (6).

For details on the instruments used for the above, see Terry (*Bach's Chorals*, II, 39, 40).

4. *The Extended Chorale.* There are 22 chorales of this type in the cantatas. An additional four were pointed out in the *Christmas Oratorio*: numbers 9, 23, 42 and 64. These feature orchestral interludes at the beginning, between each line sung in simple four part form, and at the end. They may therefore resemble chorale fantasias, especially those chorales indicated for BWV 100, 129, 147, 167 and 186 in the following list:

BWV number: 3 (2), 22 (5), 24 (6), 41 (6), 46 (6), 75 (7), 75 (14), 76 (7), 76 (14), 79 (3), 92 (7), 100 (6), 105 (6), 107 (7), 129 (5), 147 (6), 147 (10), 167 (5), 171 (6), 178 (5), 186 (6), 190 (1).

5. *The Unison Chorale.* In this class, one or more voices carry the melody, accompanied by instruments. There are 21 in this group (the voice is indicated after the movement number).

BWV number: 4 (4−T), 4 (6−B), 6 (3−S), 13 (3−A), 36 (6−T), 44 (4−T), 51 (4−S), 85 (3−S), 86 (3−S), 92 (4−A), 95 (5−S), 113 (2−A), 114 (4−S), 137 (2−A), 140 (4−T), 143 (2−S), 166 (3−S), 178

(4−T), 180 (3−S), 199 (6−S), 80 (5−SATB).

6. *The Aria Chorale.* This group of chorale setting contains a song for one or more voices which is combined with the chorale melody. There are three versions of this:

(1) Solo arias − these have only a part of the chorale melody (voices shown): BWV number: 93 (3−T), 93 (6−S), 101 (4−B).

(2) Duet arias − the chorale melody (cantus) is sung by both voices in canon: BWV number: 4 (7−ST), 36 (2−SA), 37 (3−SA) − or the cantus is in the first voice, while the other sings a different text: BWV number: 4 (3−SA), 71 (2−ST), 80 (2−SB), 131 (3−SB), 131 (5−AT), 156 (2−ST), 158 (2−SB), 159 (2−SA) − or in canon with the cantus in the instrumental accompaniment: BWV number: 93 (4−SA, with cantus in the strings), 137 (4−T, has cantus in the tromba), 101 (6−SA, using the chorale melody), 113 (7−SA, using the chorale melody).

(3) Trio arias − there is only one example of this Terzett form:

BWV 122 (4−SAT, the alto with the violins and the viola having the cantus).

7. *The Dialogue Chorale.* This type consists of a "conversation" in song between two or more different voices; one "speaks" (sings) the chorale cantus and the other, or others, the recitative. There are three classes of this type of chorale:

(1) conversation between two contrasting voices (the chorale cantus is in the first):

BWV number 49 (6−SB), 58 (1−SB), 58 (5−SB), 60 (1−AT), 106 (2− AB), 126 (3−AT, both sharing cantus).

(2) a larger number have only one voice for the conversation:

BWV number: 91 (2−S), 92 (2−B),

93 (2−B), 93 (5−T), 94 (3−T), 94 (5−B), 101 (3−S), 101 (5−T), 113 (4−B), 125 (3−B), 178 (2−A).

(3) the choir sings parts of the chorale, alternating with recitative sections sung by one or more of the SATB:

BWV: 3(2), 27 (1), 73 (1), 92 (7), 95 (1), 138 (1), 138 (1), 138 (3), 178 (2), 178 (5), 190 (2).

# Bibliography

Arnold, Denis. *Bach.* Oxford University Press, 1984.

Blume, Friedrich. *Two Centuries of Bach.* London, 1950 (German original, Kassel, 1947).

Boyd, Malcolm. *Bach.* London: J.M. Dent, 1983.

Carrell, Norman. *Bach, the Borrower.* Allen and Unwin: London, 1967.

Davison, Archibald T. *Bach and Handel: The Consummation of the Baroque.* Harvard, 1951.

Dickinson, A.E.F. *The Art of J.S. Bach.* London, 1936, 1950.

Forkel, Johann N. *Johann Sebastian Bach: His Life, Art, and Work.* Charles Terry, trans. New York: Vienna House, 1974.

Grew, Eva and Sydney. *Bach.* J.M. Dent: London, 1947, 1965)

Gurlitt, Willibald. *Johann Sebastian Bach, the Master and His Work.* St. Louis, Missouri: Concordia, 1957.

Mellers, Wilfrid. *Bach and the Dance of God.* London: Faber, 1980.

Neumann, Werner. *Bach and His World.* London: Thames and Hudson, 1961, 1964.

Parry, C. Hubert H. *Johann Sebastian Bach.* New York: Putnams, 1909.

Pelikan, Jaroslav. *Bach Among the Theologians.* Philadelphia: Fortress Press, 1986.

Schweitzer, Albert. *J.S. Bach.* E. Newman, trans. 2 vols. Black, 1955.

Smallman, Basil. *The Background of Passion Music: J.S. Bach and His Predecessors.* London, 1957; 2nd ed. 1970.

Spitta, Philipp. *Johann Sebastian Bach.* 3 vols. in 2, London, 1884-85; Dover, 1963.

Stamitz, Paul. *Bach's Passions.* London, 1979.

Stiller, Günther. *Johann Sebastian Bach and Liturgical Life in Leipzig.* St. Louis, Miss.: Concordia, 1984.

Terry, Charles Sanford. *Bach: The Historial Approach.* Oxford and London, 1930.

_____. *Bach: The Magnificat, Lutheran Masses and Motets.* Oxford and London, 1929.

_____. *Bach: The Passions.* 2 vols. Oxford University Press, 1926 (reprinted by Greenwood Press, 1970-77).

_____. *Bach's Chorals.* 3 vols. I. *The Hymns and Hymn Melodies of the "Passions" and Oratorios*; II. *The Hymns and Hymn Melodies of the Cantatas and Motetts*; III. *The Chorals of the Organ Works.* Cambridge University Press, 1915-21.

_____. *Bach's Mass in B Minor.* Oxford and London, 1924 (from Aberdeen Bach Society, 1915).

_____. *Bach's Orchestra.* Oxford and London, 1932.

_____. *The Four Part Chorals of J.S. Bach.* Oxford University Press, 1929, 1964.

_____. *The Music of Bach: An Introduction.* Dover, 1963 (Original—London, 1933).

Tovey, Donald Francis. *Essays in Musical Analysis,* vol. V: Vocal Music. Oxford University Press, 1937, 1968.

Whittaker, W. Gillies. *The Cantatas of Johann Sebastian Bach, Sacred and Secular.* 2 vols. Oxford University Press, 1959.

Young, Percy M. *The Bachs.* London: J.M. Dent, 1970.
Young, W. Murray. *The Cantatas of J.S. Bach.* Jefferson, N.C.: McFarland, 1989.


*In German*:

Neumann, Werner. *Johann Sebastian Bach: Sämtliche Kantaten Texte.* Leipzig:
    Breitkopf & Härtel, 1956.
Schering, Arnold. *Bach's Texbehandlung.* Leipzig: C.F. Kahnt, 1900.

# Index